The Haskell School of Music

This textbook explores the fundamentals of computer music and functional programming through the Haskell programming language. Functional programming is typically considered difficult to learn. This introduction in the context of creating music will allow students and professionals with a musical inclination to leverage their experience to help understand concepts that might be intimidating in more traditional computer science settings. Conversely, the book opens the door for programmers to interact with music by using a medium that is familiar to them.

Readers will learn how to use the Euterpea library for Haskell (www.euterpea.com) to represent and create their own music with code, without the need for other music software. The book explores common paradigms used in algorithmic music composition, such as stochastic generation, musical grammars, self-similarity, and real-time interactive systems. Other topics covered include the basics of signal-based systems in Haskell, sound synthesis, and virtual instrument design.

PAUL HUDAK was a professor of computer science at Yale University, Connecticut, from 1982 to 2015. He was best known for his contributions to the development of the Haskell programming language. A skilled saxophonist and jazz musician, Hudak had used a combination of his enthusiasm for music and computer science to create the Euterpea library for representing music in Haskell.

DONYA QUICK is Research Assistant Professor of Music and Computation at Stevens Institute of Technology, New Jersey. Her research explores the intersection of artificial intelligence and computational linguistics with music, and includes working on an automated composition system called Kulitta. In addition, she is also involved in the MUSICA project for interactive improvisation and composition by conversion, which is part of the DAPRA Communicating with Computers program.

The Haskell School of Music
From Signals to Symphonies

PAUL HUDAK

DONYA QUICK
Stevens Institute of Technology

CAMBRIDGE
UNIVERSITY PRESS

CAMBRIDGE
UNIVERSITY PRESS

University Printing House, Cambridge CB2 8BS, United Kingdom

One Liberty Plaza, 20th Floor, New York, NY 10006, USA

477 Williamstown Road, Port Melbourne, VIC 3207, Australia

314-321, 3rd Floor, Plot 3, Splendor Forum, Jasola District Centre, New Delhi - 110025, India

79 Anson Road, #06-04/06, Singapore 079906

Cambridge University Press is part of the University of Cambridge.

It furthers the University's mission by disseminating knowledge in the pursuit of
education, learning and research at the highest international levels of excellence.

www.cambridge.org
Information on this title: www.cambridge.org/9781108416757
DOI: 10.1017/9781108241861

First published 2018

A catalogue record for this publication is available from the British Library

Library of Congress Cataloging in Publication data
Names: Hudak, Paul, author. | Quick, Donya, author.
Title: The Haskell school of music : from signals to symphonies / Paul Hudak, Donya Quick.
Description: Cambridge, United Kingdom ; New York, NY :
Cambridge University Press, 2018. | Includes bibliographical references and index.
Identifiers: LCCN 2018016879 | ISBN 9781108416757 (hardback : alk. paper)
Subjects: LCSH: Haskell (Computer program language) | Computer music–Instruction
and study. | Functional programming (Computer science)
Classification: LCC ML74.4.H37 H84 2018 | DDC 781.3/45133–dc23
LC record available at https://lccn.loc.gov/2018016879

ISBN 978-1-108-41675-7 Hardback

Contents

Preface   *page* xi

Acknowledgments   xvi

1   **Computer Music, Euterpea, and Haskell**   1

1.1   The Note versus Signal Dichotomy   2

1.2   Basic Principles of Programming   3

1.3   Computation by Calculation   4

1.4   Expressions and Values   8

1.5   Types   9

1.6   Function Types and Type Signatures   11

1.7   Abstraction, Abstraction, Abstraction   12

1.8   Haskell Equality versus Musical Equality   21

1.9   Code Reuse and Modularity   22

1.10   [Advanced] Programming with Numbers   23

2   **Simple Music**   27

2.1   Preliminaries   27

2.2   Notes, Music, and Polymorphism   29

2.3   Convenient Auxiliary Functions   34

2.4   Absolute Pitches   39

3   **Polymorphic and Higher-Order Functions**   42

3.1   Polymorphic Types   42

3.2   Abstraction over Recursive Definitions   44

3.3   Append   47

3.4   Fold   49

3.5   [Advanced] A Final Example: Reverse   54

3.6   Currying   56

3.7   Errors   60

4   A Musical Interlude   63
4.1   Transcribing an Existing Score   63
4.2   Modules   65
4.3   Transcribing a More Complex Score   67
4.4   Simple Algorithmic Composition   72

5   Syntactic Magic   74
5.1   Sections   74
5.2   Anonymous Functions   75
5.3   List Comprehensions   77
5.4   Function Composition   80
5.5   Higher-Order Thinking   81
5.6   Infix Function Application   82

6   More Music   84
6.1   Delay and Repeat   84
6.2   Inversion and Retrograde   85
6.3   Computing Duration   87
6.4   Super-Retrograde   87
6.5   *cut* and *remove*   88
6.6   Removing Zeros   89
6.7   Truncating Parallel Composition   91
6.8   Trills   93
6.9   Grace Notes   95
6.10   Percussion   95
6.11   A Map for Music   97
6.12   A Fold for Music   99
6.13   Complex Rhythms   100
6.14   Crazy Recursion   101

7   Qualified Types and Type Classes   104
7.1   Motivation   104
7.2   Equality   106
7.3   Defining Our Own Type Classes   108
7.4   Haskell's Standard Type Classes   113
7.5   Other Derived Instances   118
7.6   The Type of *play*   121
7.7   Reasoning with Type Classes   122

8   From Music to MIDI   125
8.1   An Introduction to MIDI   125

| 8.2 | MIDI Streams | 128 |
| 8.3 | Euterpea's Playback Framework | 129 |

9 | **Interpretation and Performance** | **134**
9.1 | Abstract Performance | 134
9.2 | Players | 139
9.3 | Putting It All Together | 144

10 | **Self-Similar Music** | **148**
10.1 | Self-Similar Melody | 148
10.2 | Self-Similar Harmony | 152
10.3 | Other Self-Similar Structures | 153

11 | **Proof by Induction** | **156**
11.1 | Induction and Recursion | 156
11.2 | Examples of List Induction | 157
11.3 | Proving Function Equivalences | 159
11.4 | Useful Properties on Lists | 162
11.5 | Induction on the *Music* Data Type | 166
11.6 | [Advanced] Induction on Other Data Types | 170

12 | **An Algebra of Music** | **175**
12.1 | Musical Equivalence | 175
12.2 | Some Simple Axioms | 177
12.3 | The Fundamental Axiom Set | 180
12.4 | Other Musical Properties | 182

13 | **L-Systems and Generative Grammars** | **184**
13.1 | A Simple Implementation | 185
13.2 | A More General Implementation | 187
13.3 | An L-System Grammar for Music | 189

14 | **Random Numbers, Probability Distributions, and Markov Chains** | **193**
14.1 | Random Numbers | 193
14.2 | Probability Distributions | 196
14.3 | Markov Chains | 202

15 | **Basic Input/Output** | **205**
15.1 | IO in Haskell | 205
15.2 | do Syntax | 206
15.3 | Actions Are Just Values | 208
15.4 | Reading and Writing MIDI Files | 210

16   Higher-Order Types and Monads   211
16.1 The *Functor* Class   211
16.2 The *Monad* Class   213
16.3 The *MonadPlus* Class   221
16.4 State Monads   222
16.5 Type Class Type Errors   225

17   Musical User Interfaces   227
17.1 Introduction   227
17.2 Basic Concepts   228
17.3 The UISF Arrow   233
17.4 Non-Widget Signal Functions   242
17.5 Musical Examples   246
17.6 Special Purpose and Custom Widgets   251
17.7 Advanced Topics   256

18   Sound and Signals   262
18.1 The Nature of Sound   262
18.2 Digital Audio   273

19   Euterpea's Signal Functions   282
19.1 The Type of Audio Signals   282
19.2 Generating Sound   289
19.3 Clipping   290
19.4 Instruments   292

20   Spectrum Analysis   299
20.1 Fourier's Theorem   299
20.2 The Discrete Fourier Transform   305
20.3 The Fast Fourier Transform   315
20.4 Further Pragmatics   317

21   Additive and Subtractive Synthesis   318
21.1 Additive Synthesis   319
21.2 Subtractive Synthesis   326

22   Amplitude and Frequency Modulation   331
22.1 Amplitude Modulation   331
22.2 Frequency Modulation   334
22.3 Examples   334

23   Physical Modeling   336
23.1 Introduction   336

23.2   Delay Lines   336
23.3   Karplus-Strong Algorithm   340
23.4   Waveguide Synthesis   343

    Appendix A   The PreludeList Module   346

    Appendix B   Haskell's Standard Type Classes   355

    Appendix C   Built-In Types Are Not Special   365

    Appendix D   Pattern-Matching Details   367

    Appendix E   Haskell Quick Reference   370

    Appendix F   Euterpea Quick Reference   373

    Appendix G   HSoM Quick Reference   377

    Bibliography   379

    Index   381

Preface

There is a certain mind-set, a certain viewpoint of the world, and a certain approach to problem solving that collectively work best when programming in Haskell (this is true for any programming paradigm). If you teach only Haskell language details to a C programmer, he or she is likely to write ugly, incomprehensible functional programs. But if you teach how to think differently, how to see problems in a different light, functional solutions will come easily, and elegant Haskell programs will result.

Music has many ties to mathematics. Combining the elegant mathematical nature of Haskell with that of music is as natural as singing a nursery tune. Using a high-level language to express musical ideas is, of course, not new. But Haskell is unique in its insistence on purity (no side effects), and this alone makes it particularly suitable for expressing musical ideas. By focusing on *what* a musical entity is, rather than on *how* to create it, we allow musical ideas to take their natural form as Haskell expressions. Haskell's many abstraction mechanisms allow us to write computer music programs that are elegant, concise, yet powerful. We will consistently attempt to let the music express itself as naturally as possible, without encoding it in terms of irrelevant language details.

Of course, the ultimate goal of this book is not just to teach computer music concepts. Along the way you will also learn Haskell. There is no limit to what one might wish to do with computer music, and therefore the better you are at programming, the more success you will have. Many languages designed specifically for computer music – although fun to work with, easy to use, and cute in concept – face the danger of being too limited in expressiveness.

You do not need to know much, if any, music theory to read this book, and you do not need to play an instrument. Of course, the more you know about music, the more you will be able to apply the concepts learned in this text in musically creative ways.

xi

This book's general approach to introducing computer music concepts is to first provide an intuitive explanation, then a mathematically rigorous definition, and finally fully executable Haskell code. It will often be the case that there is a close correspondence between the mathematical definition and the Haskell code. Haskell features are introduced as they are needed, rather than all at once, and this interleaving of concepts and applications makes the material easier to digest.

Seasoned programmers having experience only with conventional imperative and/or object-oriented languages are encouraged to read this text with an open mind. Many things will be different, and will likely feel awkward. There will be a tendency to rely on old habits when writing new programs, and to ignore suggestions about how to approach things differently. If you can manage to resist those tendencies, you will have an enjoyable learning experience. Those who succeed in this process often find that many ideas about functional programming can be applied to imperative and object-oriented languages as well, and that their imperative coding style changes for the better.

The experienced programmer should also be patient with earlier topics, such as "syntax," "operator precedence," etc., since the intent is for this text to be readable by someone having only modest prior programming experience. With patience, the more advanced ideas will appear soon enough.

If you are a novice programmer, take your time with the book; work through the exercises, and don't rush things. If, however, you don't fully grasp an idea, feel free to move on, but try to reread difficult material at a later time when you have seen more examples of the concepts in action. For the most part, this is a "show-by-example" textbook, and you should try to execute as many of the programs in this text as you can, as well as every program that you write. Learn-by-doing is the corollary to show-by-example.

Finally, some section titles are prefaced with the parenthetical phrase "[Advanced]". These sections may be skipped upon first reading, especially if the focus is on learning computer music concepts, as opposed to programming concepts.

Prerequisites

Basic algebra and familiarity with a terminal-style environment (often called a command prompt in Windows) on your computer are also assumed as prerequisites in this text. Some prior introduction to computer science concepts and data structures (primarily lists and trees) is also strongly recommended.

This book is not a substitute for an introductory music theory course. Rather, it is intended primarily for programmers with at least a small amount of musical experience (such as having taken a music appreciation course in school or played an instrument at some point) who want to then explore music in the context of a functional programming environment. Examples of musical concepts that are considered prerequisites to this text are reading Western music notation, the naming scheme for musical pitches as letters and octave numbers, and the major and minor scales. That said, it is certainly not impossible to learn Haskell and the Euterpea library from this book as a complete musical novice – but you will likely need to consult other music-related resources to fill in the gaps as you go along using a dictionary of musical terms. A wide array of free music theory resources and tutorials for beginners are also freely available online. Links to some useful music references and tutorials can be found on the Euterpea website, www.euterpea.com.

Music Terminology

Some musical concepts have more than one term to refer to them, and which synonym is preferred differs by region. For example, the following terms are synonyms for note durations:

American English	British English
Double whole note	Breve
Whole note	Semibreve
Half note	Minim
Quarter note	Crotchet
Eight note	Quaver
Sixteenth note	Semiquaver

This book uses the American English versions of these musical terms. The reason for this is that they more closely mirror the mathematical relationships represented by the concepts they refer to, and they are also the basis for names of a number of values used in the software this text describes. The American English standard for naming note durations is both more common in computer music literature and easier to remember for those with limited musical experience – who may struggle to remember what a hemidemisemiquaver is.

Software

There are several implementations of Haskell, all available free on the Internet through the Haskell website, haskell.org. However, the one that has dominated all others, and on which Euterpea is based, is *GHC* [1], an easy-to-use and easy-to-install Haskell compiler and interpreter. GHC runs on a variety of platforms, including Windows, Linux, and Mac. The preferred way to install GHC is using *Haskell Platform* [2]. Once Haskell is installed, you will have access to what is referred to as the *Standard Prelude*, a collection of predefined definitions that are always available and do not need to be specially imported.

Two libraries are needed to code along with this textbook: Euterpea and HSoM. Euterpea is a language for representing musical structures in Haskell, and many of its features are covered in this book. HSoM is a supplemental library containing many of the longer code examples in the text and two additional features: support for modeling musical performance (Chapter 9) and music-related graphical widgets (Chapter 17).

Detailed setup information for Haskell Platform, Euterpea, and HSoM is available on the Euterpea website: www.euterpea.com. Please note: software setup details for Haskell Platform and the Euterpea library varies by architecture (32-bit vs 64-bit), operating system, and compiler version. As the exact setup details are subject to change with every new release of Euterpea's dependencies, please see www.euterpea.com for the most up-to-date installation instructions. While most installations go smoothly with the relatively simple instructions described in the next section, there are many potential differences from one machine to another that can complicate the process. The Euterpea website also contains troubleshooting information for commonly encountered installation problems.

Installation Instructions

The following setup instructions require an Internet connection.

- Download the appropriate version of Haskell Platform from www.haskell.org/platform/ and install it on your machine.
- Open a command prompt (Windows) or terminal (Mac/Linux) and run the following commands:
  cabal update
  cabal install Euterpea
  cabal install HSoM
- Mac and Linux users will also need to install a MIDI software synthesizer. Please see the Euterpea website for instructions on how to do this.

The Euterpea website also contains basic walkthroughs for getting started working with the GHC compiler and interpreter within a command prompt or terminal, loading source code files, and so on.

Quick References

Brief references for the more commonly used features of Haskell, Euterpea, and HSoM are listed in Appendices E, F, and G. These are intended to serve as a fast way to look up function and value names when you already know a bit about how to use them. A note to students: these few pages of ultra-condensed material are not a substitute for reading the chapters!

Coding and Debugging

Errors are an inevitable part of coding. The best way to minimize the number of errors you have to solve is to code a little bit and then immediately test what you've done. If it's broken, don't wait – fix it then and there! Never press onward and try to work on other things within a file that is broken elsewhere. The reason for this is that one simple error can end up masking others. When the compiler hits a serious problem, it *may not even look at the rest of your file*. As a result, continuing to code without resolving error messages often results in an explosion of new errors once the original one is fixed. You will save yourself a lot of grief by developing good habits of incremental development and not allowing errors to linger unsolved.

Coding *style* is also important. There are two reasons for this in Haskell. The first is that Haskell is *extremely* sensitive to white space characters. Do not mix spaces and tabs! Pick one and be consistent (spaces are typically recommended). Indentation matters, and a small misalignment can sometimes cause bizarre-looking error messages. Style is important, as is readability, both by other programmers and by yourself at a later date. Many novice programmers neglect good coding hygiene, which involves naming things well, laying out code cleanly, and documenting complicated parts of the code. This extra work may be tedious, but it is worthwhile. Coding large projects is often very much dependent on the immediate state of mind. Without that frame of reference, it's not impossible that you could find your own code to be impenetrable if you pick it up again later.

Acknowledgments

I wish to thank my funding agencies – the National Science Foundation, the Defense Advanced Research Projects Agency, and Microsoft Research – for their generous support of research that contributed to the foundations of Euterpea. Yale University has provided me a stimulating and flexible environment to pursue my dreams for more than thirty years, and I am especially thankful for its recent support of the Computing and the Arts initiative.

Tom Makucevich, a talented computer music practitioner and composer in New Haven, was the original motivator, and first user, of Haskore, which preceded Euterpea. Watching him toil endlessly with low-level csound programs was simply too much for me to bear! Several undergraduate students at Yale contributed to the original design and implementation of Haskore. I would like to thank in particular the contributions of Syam Gadde and Bo Whong, who coauthored the original paper on Haskore. Additionally, Matt Zamec helped me greatly in the creation of HasSound.

I wish to thank my more recent graduate students, in particular Hai (Paul) Liu, Eric Cheng, Donya Quick, and Daniel Winograd-Cort, for their help in writing much of the code that constitutes the current Euterpea library. In addition, many students in my computer music classes at Yale provided valuable feedback through earlier drafts of the manuscript.

Finally, I wish to thank my wife, Cathy Van Dyke, my best friend and ardent supporter, whose love, patience, and understanding have helped me get through some bad times, and enjoy the good.

Happy Haskell Music Making!

Paul Hudak,
January 2012

1

Computer Music, Euterpea, and Haskell

Many computer scientists and mathematicians have a serious interest in music, and it seems that those with a strong affinity or acuity in one of these disciplines is often strong in the other as well. It is quite natural then to consider how the two might interact. In fact, there is a long history of interactions between music and mathematics, dating back to the Greeks' construction of musical scales based on arithmetic relationships, and including many classical composers use of mathematical structures, the formal harmonic analysis of music, and many modern music composition techniques. Advanced music theory uses ideas from diverse branches of mathematics such as number theory, abstract algebra, topology, category theory, calculus, and so on.

There is also a long history of efforts to combine computers and music. Most consumer electronics today are digital, as are most forms of audio processing and recording. But, in addition, digital musical instruments provide new modes of expression, notation software and sequencers have become standard tools for the working musician, and those with the most computer science savvy use computers to explore new modes of composition, transformation, performance, and analysis.

This textbook explores the fundamentals of computer music using a programming-language-centric approach. In particular, the functional programming language *Haskell* is used to express all of the computer music concepts. Thus, a by-product of learning computer music concepts will be learning how to program in Haskell. The core musical ideas are collected into a Haskell library called *Euterpea*. The name "Euterpea" is derived from *Euterpe*, who was one of the nine Greek muses, or goddesses of the arts, specifically the muse of music.

1.1 The Note versus Signal Dichotomy

The field of computer music has grown astronomically over the past several decades, and the material can be structured and organized along several dimensions. A dimension that proves particularly useful with respect to a programming language is one that separates *high-level* musical concerns from *low-level* musical concerns. Since a "high-level" programming language – namely Haskell – is used to program at both of these musical levels, to avoid confusion, the terms *note level* and *signal level* will be used in the musical dimension.

At the *note level*, a *note* (i.e., pitch and duration) is the lowest musical entity that is considered, and everything else is built up from there. At this level, in addition to conventional representations of music, we can study interesting aspects of so-called algorithmic composition, including the use of fractals, grammar-based systems, stochastic processes, and so on. From this basis we can also study the harmonic and rhythmic *analysis* of music, although that is not currently an emphasis in this textbook. Haskell facilitates programming at this level through its powerful data abstraction facilities, higher-order functions, and declarative semantics.

In contrast, at the *signal level*, the focus is on the actual sound generated in a computer music application, and thus a *signal* is the lowest entity that is considered. Sound is concretely represented in a digital computer by a discrete sampling of the continuous audio signal at a high enough rate that human ears cannot distinguish the discrete from the continuous, usually 44,100 samples per second (the standard sampling rate used for CDs). But in Euterpea, these details are hidden: signals are treated abstractly as continuous quantities. This greatly eases the burden of programming with sequences of discrete values. At the signal level, we can study sound synthesis techniques (to simulate the sound of a conventional instrument, say, or something completely artificial), audio processing (e.g., determining the frequency spectrum of a signal), and special effects (reverb, panning, distortion, and so on).

Suppose that a musician is playing music using a metronome set at 96, which corresponds to 96 beats per minute. That means that one beat takes $60/96 = 0.625$ seconds. At a stereo sampling rate of 44,100 samples per second, that in turn translates into $2 \times 0.625 \times 44,100 = 55,125$ samples, and each sample typically occupies several bytes[1] of computer memory.

---

[1] The storage size of a sample is called the *bit depth*. Modern audio hardware typically supports bit depths of 16 bits (2 bytes) to 32 bits (4 bytes).

In contrast, at the note level, we only need some kind of operator or data structure that says "play this note," which requires a total of only a small handful of bytes. This dramatic difference highlights one of the key computational differences between programming at the note level and that at the signal level.

Of course, many computer music applications involve both the note level *and* the signal level, and indeed there needs to be a mechanism to mediate between the two. Although such mediation can take many forms, it is for the most part straightforward, which is another reason why the distinction between the note level and the signal level is so natural.

This textbook begins with exploration of the note level (Chapters 1–17) and follows with examination of the signal level (Chapters 18–23). If you are interested only in the signal level, you may wish to skip Chapters 9–17.

1.2 Basic Principles of Programming

Programming, in its broadest sense, is *problem solving*. It begins by recognizing problems that can and should be solved using a digital computer. Thus the first step in programming is answering the question "What problem am I trying to solve?"

Once the problem is understood, a solution must be found. This may not be easy, of course, and you may discover several solutions, so a way to measure success is needed. There are various dimensions in which to do this, including correctness ("Will I get the right answer?") and efficiency ("Will it run fast enough, or use too much memory?"). But the distinction of which solution is better is not always clear, since the number of dimensions can be large, and programs will often excel in one dimension and do poorly in others. For example, there may be one solution that is fastest, one that uses the least amount of memory, and one that is easiest to understand. Deciding which to choose can be difficult, and is one of the more interesting challenges in programming.

The last measure of success mentioned earlier, clarity of a program, is somewhat elusive, being difficult to quantify and measure. Nevertheless, in large software systems, clarity is an especially important goal, since such systems are worked on by many people over long periods of time, and evolve considerably as they mature. Having easy-to-understand code makes it much easier to modify.

In the area of computer music, there is another reason why clarity is important: namely, that the code often represents the author's thought process, musical intent, and artistic choices. A conventional musical score does not say much about what the composer thought as he or she wrote the music, but a program often does. So, when you write your programs, write them for others to see and aim for elegance and beauty, just like the musical result that you desire.

Programming is itself a creative process. Sometimes programming solutions (or artistic creations) come to mind all at once, with little effort. More often, however, they are discovered only after lots of hard work! We may write a program, modify it, throw it away and start over, give up, start again, and so on. It is important to realize that such hard work and reworking of programs is the norm, and in fact you are encouraged to get into the habit of doing so. Do not always be satisfied with your first solution, and always be prepared to go back and change or even throw away those parts of your program that you are not happy with.

1.3 Computation by Calculation

It is helpful when learning a new programming language to have a good grasp of how programs in that language are executed – in other words, an understanding of what a program *means*. The execution of Haskell programs is perhaps best understood as *computation by calculation*. Programs in Haskell can be viewed as *functions* whose input is that of the problem being solved, and whose output is the desired result – and the behavior of functions can be effectively understood as computation by calculation.

An example involving numbers might help demonstrate these ideas. Numbers are used in many applications, and computer music is no exception. For example, integers might be used to represent pitch, and floating-point numbers might be used to perform calculations involving frequency or amplitude.

Suppose we wish to perform an arithmetic calculation such as $3 \times (9 + 5)$. In Haskell this would be written as $3 * (9 + 5)$, since most standard computer keyboards and text editors do not support the special $\times$ symbol. The result can be calculated as follows:

$$3 * (9 + 5)$$
$$\Rightarrow 3 * 14$$
$$\Rightarrow 42$$

It turns out that this is not the only way to compute the result, as evidenced by this alternative calculation:[2]

---

[2] This assumes that multiplication distributes over addition in the number system being used, a point that will be returned to later in the text.

$3 * (9 + 5)$
$\Rightarrow 3 * 9 + 3 * 5$
$\Rightarrow 27 + 3 * 5$
$\Rightarrow 27 + 15$
$\Rightarrow 42$

Even though this calculation takes two extra steps, it at least gives the same, correct answer. Indeed, an important property of each and every program written in Haskell is that it will always yield the same answer when given the same inputs, regardless of the order chosen to perform the calculations.[3] This is precisely the mathematical definition of a *function*: for the same inputs, it always yields the same output.

On the other hand, the first calculation above required fewer steps than the second, and thus it is said to be more *efficient*. Efficiency in both space (amount of memory used) and time (number of steps executed) is important when searching for solutions to problems. Of course, if the computation returns the wrong answer, efficiency is a moot point. In general, it is best to search first for an elegant (and correct!) solution to a problem, and later refine it for better performance. This strategy is sometimes summarized as "Get it right first!"

The above calculations are fairly trivial, but much more sophisticated computations will be introduced soon enough. For starters, and to introduce the idea of a Haskell function, the arithmetic operations performed in the previous example can be *generalized* by defining a function to perform them for any numbers x, y, and z:

$simple \; x \; y \; z = x * (y + z)$

This equation defines *simple* as a function of three *arguments*, x, y, and z. Note the use of *spaces* in this definition to separate the function name, *simple*, from its arguments, x, y, and z. Unlike many other programming languages, Haskell functions are defined by providing first the function name and then any arguments, separated by spaces. More traditional notations for this function would look like this:

$simple(x, y, z) = x \times (y + z)$
$simple(x, y, z) = x \cdot (y + z)$
$simple(x, y, z) = x(y + z)$
$simple(x, y, z) = x * (y + z)$

---

[3] This is true as long as a non-terminating sequence of calculations is not chosen, another issue that will be addressed later.

Incidentally, the last one is also acceptable Haskell syntax – but it is not interchangeable with the previous Haskell definition. Writing *simple x y z* actually means something very different from writing *simple* (*x, y, z*) in Haskell. Usage of parentheses around Haskell function arguments indicates a tuple – a concept that will be discussed in more detail later in the text.

In any case, it should be clear that "*simple* 3 9 5" is the same as "3∗(9+5)," and that the proper way to calculate the result is:

simple 3 9 5
$\Rightarrow 3 * (9 + 5)$
$\Rightarrow 3 * 14$
$\Rightarrow 42$

The first step in this calculation is an example of *unfolding* a function definition: 3 is substituted for *x*, 9 for *y*, and 5 for *z* on the right-hand side of the definition of *simple*. This is an entirely mechanical process, not unlike what the computer actually does to execute the program.

simple 3 9 5 is said to *evaluate* to 42. To express the fact that an expression *e* evaluates (via zero, one, or possibly many more steps) to the value *v*, we will write *e* $\Longrightarrow$ *v* (this arrow is longer than that used earlier). So we can say directly, for example, that *simple* 3 9 5 $\Longrightarrow$ 42, which should be read "*simple* 3 9 5 evaluates to 42."

With *simple* now suitably defined, we can repeat the sequence of arithmetic calculations as often as we like, using different values for the arguments to *simple*. For example, *simple* 4 3 2 $\Longrightarrow$ 20.

We can also use calculation to *prove properties* about programs. For example, it should be clear that for any *a*, *b*, and *c*, *simple a b c* should yield the same result as *simple a c b*. For a proof of this, we calculate *symbolically* – that is, using the symbols *a*, *b*, and *c* rather than concrete numbers such as 3, 5, and 9:

simple a b c
$\Rightarrow a * (b + c)$
$\Rightarrow a * (c + b)$
$\Rightarrow$ *simple a c b*

Note that the same notation is used for these symbolic steps as for concrete ones. In particular, the arrow in the notation reflects the direction of formal reasoning, and nothing more. In general, if *e1* $\Rightarrow$ *e2*, then it is also true that *e2* $\Rightarrow$ *e1*.

These symbolic steps are also referred to as "calculations," even though the computer will not typically perform them when executing a program (although it might perform them *before* a program is run if it thinks that it might make the program run faster). The second step in the calculation above relies on the commutativity of addition (for any numbers x and y, $x + y = y + x$). The third step is the reverse of an unfold step, and is appropriately called a *fold* calculation. It would be particularly strange if a computer performed this step while executing a program, since it does not seem to be headed toward a final answer. But for proving properties about programs, such "backward reasoning" is quite important.

When we wish to spell out the justification for each step, whether symbolic or concrete, a calculation can be annotated with more detail, as in:

simple a b c
  ⇒ {*unfold*}
$a * (b + c)$
  ⇒ {*commutativity*}
$a * (c + b)$
  ⇒ {*fold*}
simple a c b

In most cases, however, this will not be necessary.

Proving properties of programs is another theme that will be repeated often in this text. Computer music applications often have some kind of a mathematical basis, and that mathematics must be reflected somewhere in our programs. But how do we know if we got it right? Proof by calculation is one way to connect the problem specification with the program solution.

More broadly speaking, as the world begins to rely more and more on computers to accomplish not just ordinary tasks such as writing term papers, sending e-mail, and social networking but also life-critical tasks such as controlling medical procedures and guiding spacecraft, the correctness of programs gains in importance. Proving complex properties of large, complex programs is not easy – and rarely, if ever, done in practice – but that should not deter us from proving simpler properties of the whole system, or complex properties of parts of the system, since such proofs may uncover errors, and if not, will at least give us confidence in our effort.

If you are someone who is already an experienced programmer, the idea of computing *everything* by calculation may seem odd at best and naïve at worst. How do we write to a file, play a sound, draw a picture, or respond to mouse-clicks? If you are wondering about these things, it is hoped that you have patience reading the early chapters, and that you find delight in reading the later chapters where the full power of this approach begins to shine.

In many ways this first chapter is the most difficult, since it contains the highest density of new concepts. If the reader has trouble with some of the concepts in this overview chapter, keep in mind that most of them will be revisited in later chapters, and do not hesitate to return to this chapter later to reread difficult sections; they will likely be much easier to grasp at that time.

Details: In the remainder of this textbook the need will often arise to explain some aspect of Haskell in more detail, without distracting too much from the primary line of discourse. In those circumstances the explanations will be offset in a shaded box such as this one, proceeded with the word "Details."

Exercise 1.1 Write out all of the steps in the calculation of the value of *simple* (*simple* 2 3 4) 5 6.

Exercise 1.2 Prove by calculation that *simple* $(a - b)$ a $b \Longrightarrow a^2 - b^2$.

1.4 Expressions and Values

In Haskell, the entities on which calculations are performed are called *expressions*, and the entities that result from a calculation – i.e., "the answers" – are called *values*. It is helpful to think of a value just as an expression on which no more calculation can be carried out – every value is an expression, but not the other way around.

Examples of expressions include *atomic* (meaning indivisible) values such as the integer 42 and the character 'a', which are examples of two *primitive* atomic values in Haskell. The next chapter introduces examples of *constructor* atomic values, such as the musical notes C, D, Ef, Fs, etc., which in standard music notation are written C, D, E♭, F♯, etc., and are pronounced C, D, E-flat, F-sharp, etc. (In music theory, note names are called *pitch classes*.)

In addition, there are *structured* expressions (i.e., made from smaller pieces) such as the *list* of pitches $[C, D, Ef]$, the character/number *pair* ('b', 4) (lists and pairs are different in a subtle way, to be described later), and the string "Euterpea". Each of these structured expressions is also a value, since by themselves there is no further calculation that can be carried out. As another example, $1 + 2$ is an expression, and one step of calculation yields the expression 3, which is a value, since no more calculations can be performed. As a final example, as was explained earlier, the expression *simple* 3 9 5 evaluates to the value 42.

Sometimes, however, an expression has a never-ending sequence of calculations. For example, if x is defined as:

$x = x + 1$

then here is what happens when trying to calculate the value of x:

x
$\Rightarrow x + 1$
$\Rightarrow (x + 1) + 1$
$\Rightarrow ((x + 1) + 1) + 1$
$\Rightarrow (((x + 1) + 1) + 1) + 1$
...

Similarly, if a function f is defined as:

$f\, x = f\, (x - 1)$

then an expression such as f 42 runs into a similar problem:

f 42
$\Rightarrow f$ 41
$\Rightarrow f$ 40
$\Rightarrow f$ 39
...

Both of these clearly result in a never-ending sequence of calculations. Such expressions are said to *diverge*, or not terminate. In such cases the symbol $\perp$, pronounced "bottom," is used to denote the value of the expression. This means that every diverging computation in Haskell denotes the same $\perp$ value,[4] reflecting the fact that, from an observer's point of view, there is nothing to distinguish one diverging computation from another.

1.5 Types

Every expression (and therefore every value) also has an associated *type*. It is helpful to think of types as sets of expressions (or values), in which members of the same set have much in common. Examples include the primitive atomic types *Integer* (the set of all integers) and *Char* (the set of all characters), the user-defined atomic type *PitchClass* (the set of all pitch classes, i.e., note names), as well as the structured types [*Integer*] and [*PitchClass*] (the sets of all lists of integers and lists of pitch classes, respectively), and *String* (the set of all Haskell strings).

---

[4] Technically, each type has its own version of $\perp$.

The association of an expression or value with its type is very useful, and there is a special way of expressing it in Haskell. Using the examples of values and types above:

D	:: *PitchClass*
42	:: *Integer*
'a'	:: *Char*
"Euterpea"	:: *String*
[*C, D, Ef*]	:: [*PitchClass*]
('b', 4)	:: (*Char, Integer*)

Each association of an expression with its type is called a *type signature*. Note the use of single quotes of the form 'x' or 'x' in these definitions to indicate single characters. It is important to recognize the single quote (or apostrophe) symbol as being distinct from the backquote symbol (typically found on the same key as ~), which appears as 'x' in this text and serves very specific syntactic purposes in Haskell, to be discussed later on.

Details: Note that the names of specific types are capitalized, such as *Integer* and *Char*, as are the names of some atomic values, such as *D* and *Fs*. These will never be confused in context, since things to the right of "::" are types, and things to the left are values. Note also that user-defined names of values are *not* capitalized, such as *simple* and *x*. This is not just a convention: it is required when programming in Haskell. In addition, the case of the other characters matters, too. For example, *test*, *teSt*, and *tEST* are all distinct names for values, as are *Test*, *TeST*, and *TEST* for types.

Details: Literal characters are written enclosed in single forward quotes (apostrophes), as in 'a', 'A', 'b', ',', '!', ' ' (a space), and so on. (There are some exceptions, however; see the Haskell Report for details.) Strings are written enclosed in double quote characters, as in "Euterpea" above. The connection between characters and strings will be explained in a later chapter.

The "::" should be read "has type," as in "42 has type *Integer*." Note that square braces are used both to construct a list value (the left-hand side of (::) above) and to describe its type (the right-hand side above). Analogously, the round braces used for pairs are used in the same way. But also note that all of the elements in a list, however long, must have the same type, whereas the elements of a pair can have different types.

Haskell's *type system* ensures that Haskell programs are *well-typed*; that is, that the programmer has not mismatched types in some way. For example, it does not make much sense to add together two characters, so the expression 'a' + 'b' is *ill-typed*. The best news is that Haskell's type system will tell you if your program is well-typed *before you run it*. This is a big advantage, since most programming errors are manifested as type errors.

1.6 Function Types and Type Signatures

What should the type of a function be? It seems that it should at least convey the fact that a function takes values of one type – say, *T1* – as input, and returns values of (possibly) some other type – say, *T2* – as output. In Haskell this is written $T1 \rightarrow T2$, and such a function is said to "map values of type *T1* to values of type *T2*."[5] If there is more than one argument, the notation is extended with more arrows. For example, if the intent is that the function *simple* defined in the previous section has type *Integer* → *Integer* → *Integer* → *Integer*, we can include a type signature with the definition of *simple*:

```
simple      :: Integer → Integer → Integer → Integer
simple x y z = x * (y + z)
```

> **Details:** When writing Haskell programs using a typical text editor, there will not be nice fonts and arrows as in *Integer* → *Integer*. Rather, you will have to type `Integer -> Integer`.

Haskell's type system also ensures that user-supplied type signatures such as this one are correct. Actually, Haskell's type system is powerful enough to allow us to avoid writing any type signatures at all, in which case the type system is said to *infer* the correct types.[6] Nevertheless, judicious placement of type signatures, as was done for *simple*, is a good habit, since type signatures are an effective form of documentation and help bring programming errors to light. In fact, it is a good habit to first write down the type of each function you are planning to define, as a first approximation to its full specification – a way to grasp its overall functionality before delving into its details.

The normal use of a function is referred to as *function application*. For example, *simple* 3 9 5 is the application of the function *simple* to the arguments 3, 9, and 5. Some functions, such as (+), are applied using what is known as

---

[5] In mathematics *T1* is called the *domain* of the function and *T2* the *range*.
[6] There are a few exceptions to this rule, and in the case of *simple*, the inferred type is actually a bit more general than that written in this chapter. Both of these points will be returned to later.

infix syntax; that is, the function is written between the two arguments rather than in front of them (compare $x + y$ to $f\ x\ y$).

Details: Infix functions are often called *operators*, and are distinguished by the fact that they do not contain any numbers or letters of the alphabet. Thus ^! and *# : are infix operators, whereas *thisIsAFunction* and *f9g* are not (but are still valid names for functions or other values). The only exception to this is that the symbol ' is considered to be alphanumeric; thus f' and *one's* are valid names, but not operators.

In Haskell, when referring to an infix operator as a value, it is enclosed in parentheses, such as when declaring its type, as in:

$(+) :: Integer \rightarrow Integer \rightarrow Integer$

Also, when trying to understand an expression such as $f\ x + g\ y$, there is a simple rule to remember: function application *always* has "higher precedence" than operator application, so that $f\ x + g\ y$ is the same as $(f\ x) + (g\ y)$.

Despite all of these syntactic differences, however, operators are still just functions.

Exercise 1.3 Identify the well-typed expressions in the following and, for each, give its proper type:

$[A, B, C]$
$[D, 42]$
$(-42, Ef)$
$[('a', 3), ('b', 5)]$
simple 'a' 'b' 'c'
$(simple\ 1\ 2\ 3, simple)$
$["I", "love", "Euterpea"]$

For those expressions that are ill-typed, explain why.

1.7 Abstraction, Abstraction, Abstraction

The title of this section is the answer to the question "What are the three most important ideas in programming?" Webster defines the verb "abstract" as follows:

abstract, *vt* (1) remove, separate (2) to consider apart from application to a particular instance.

In programming this happens when a pattern repeats itself and we wish to "separate" that pattern from the "particular instances" in which it appears. In this textbook this process is called the *abstraction principle*. The following sections introduce several different kinds of abstraction, using examples involving both simple numbers and arithmetic (things everyone should be familiar with) as well as musical examples (that are specific to Euterpea).

1.7.1 Naming

One of the most basic ideas in programming – for that matter, in everyday life – is to *name* things. For example, we may wish to give a name to the value of π, since it is inconvenient to retype (or remember) the value of π beyond a small number of digits. In mathematics the Greek letter π in fact *is* the name for this value, but unfortunately we do not have the luxury of using Greek letters on standard computer keyboards and/or text editors. So in Haskell we write:

> *pi* :: *Double*
> *pi* = 3.141592653589793

to associate the name *pi* with the number 3.141592653589793. The type signature in the first line declares *pi* to be a *double-precision floating-point number*, which mathematically and in Haskell is distinct from an integer.[7] Now the name *pi* can be used in expressions whenever it is in scope; it is an abstract representation, if you will, of the number 3.141592653589793. Furthermore, if there is ever a need to change a named value (which hopefully will not ever happen for *pi*, but could certainly happen for other values), we would only have to change it in one place, instead of in the possibly large number of places where it is used.

For a simple musical example, note first that in music theory, a *pitch* consists of a *pitch class* and an *octave*. For example, in Euterpea we simply write $(A, 4)$ to represent the pitch class A in the fourth octave. This particular note is called "concert A" (because it is often used as the note to which an orchestra tunes its instruments) or "A440" (because its frequency is 440 cycles per second). Because this particular pitch is so common, it may be desirable to give it a name, which is easily done in Haskell, as was done above for π:

---

[7] We will have more to say about floating-point numbers later.

$concertA, a440 :: (PitchClass, Octave)$
$concertA = (A, 4)$ -- concert A
$a440\quad = (A, 4)$ -- A440

Details: This example demonstrates the use of program *comments*. Any text to the right of "--" till the end of the line is considered to be a programmer comment and is effectively ignored. Haskell also permits *nested* comments that have the form   {-this is a comment -}   and can appear anywhere in a program, including across multiple lines.

This example demonstrates the (perhaps obvious) fact that several different names can be given to the same value – just as your brother John might have the nickname "Moose." Also note that the name *concertA* requires more typing than $(A, 4)$; nevertheless, it has more mnemonic value and, if mistyped, will more likely result in a syntax error. For example, if you type "*concrtA*" by mistake, you will likely get an error saying, "Undefined variable," whereas if you type "$(A, 5)$," you will not.

Details: This example also demonstrates that two names having the same type can be combined into the same type signature, separated by a comma. Note finally, as a reminder, that these are names of values, and thus they both begin with a lowercase letter.

Consider now a problem whose solution requires writing some larger expression more than once. For example:

$x :: Float$
$x = f\ (pi * r ** 2) + g\ (pi * r ** 2)$

Details: (**) is Haskell's floating-point exponentiation operator. Thus $pi * r ** 2$ is analogous to πr^2 in mathematics. (**) has higher precedence than (*) and the other binary arithmetic operators in Haskell.

Note in the definition of x that the expression $pi * r ** 2$ (presumably representing the area of a circle whose radius is r) is repeated – it has two instances – and thus, applying the abstraction principle, it can be separated from these instances. From the previous examples, doing this is straightforward – it is called *naming* – so we might choose to rewrite the single equation above as two:

$$area = pi * r ** 2$$
$$x \quad = f\ area + g\ area$$

If, however, the definition of *area* is not intended for use elsewhere in the program, then it is advantageous to "hide" it within the definition of *x*. This will avoid cluttering up the namespace, and prevents *area* from clashing with some other value named *area*. To achieve this, we could simply use a **let** expression:

$$x = \textbf{let}\ area = pi * r ** 2$$
$$\textbf{in}\ f\ area + g\ area$$

A **let** expression restricts the *visibility* of the names that it creates to the internal workings of the **let** expression itself. For example, if we were to write:

$$area = 42$$
$$x \quad = \textbf{let}\ area = pi * r ** 2$$
$$\textbf{in}\ f\ area + g\ area$$

then there is no conflict of names – the "outer" *area* is completely different from the "inner" one enclosed in the **let** expression. Think of the inner *area* as analogous to the first name of someone in your household. If your brother's name is John, he will not be confused with John Thompson who lives down the street when you say, "John spilled the milk."

So you can see that naming – using either top-level equations or equations within a **let** expression – is an example of the abstraction principle in action.

Details: An equation such as $c = 42$ is called a *binding*. A simple rule to remember when programming in Haskell is never to give more than one binding for the same name in a context where the names can be confused, whether at the top level of your program or nestled within a **let** expression. For example, this is not allowed:

$$a = 42$$
$$a = 43$$

nor is this:

$$a = 42$$
$$b = 43$$
$$a = 44$$

1.7.2 Functional Abstraction

The design of functions such as *simple* can be viewed as the abstraction principle in action. To see this using the example above involving the area of a circle, suppose the original program looked like this:

$$x :: Float$$
$$x = f\ (pi * r1 ** 2) + g\ (pi * r2 ** 2)$$

Note that there are now two areas involved: one of a circle whose radius is *r1*, the other *r2*. Now the expressions in parentheses have a *repeating pattern of operations*. In discerning the nature of a repeating pattern, it is sometimes helpful to first identify those things that are *not* repeating, i.e., those things that are *changing*. In the case above, it is the radius that is changing. A repeating pattern of operations can be abstracted as a *function* that takes the changing values as arguments. Using the function name *areaF* (for "area function"), we can write:

$$x = \textbf{let}\ areaF\ r = pi * r ** 2$$
$$\textbf{in}\ f\ (areaF\ r1) + g\ (areaF\ r2)$$

This is a simple generalization of the previous example, where the function now takes the "variable quantity" – in this case the radius – as an argument. A very simple proof by calculation, in which *areaF* is unfolded where it is used, can be given to demonstrate that this program is equivalent to the old one.

This application of the abstraction principle is called *functional abstraction*, since a sequence of operations is abstracted as a *function*, such as *areaF*.

For a musical example, a few more concepts from Euterpea are first introduced, concepts that are addressed more formally in the next chapter:

1. In music theory, a *note* is a *pitch* combined with a *duration*. Duration is measured in beats, and in Euterpea has type *Dur*. A note whose duration is one beat is called a whole note, one with duration $1/2$ is called a half note, and so on. A note in Euterpea is the smallest entity, besides a rest, that is actually a performable piece of music, and its type is *Music Pitch* (other variations of this type will be introduced in later chapters).
2. In Euterpea there are functions:

   $$note :: Dur \rightarrow Pitch \rightarrow Music\ Pitch$$
   $$rest\ :: Dur \rightarrow Music\ Pitch$$

   such that *note d p* is a note whose duration is *d* and pitch is *p*, and *rest d* is a rest with duration *d*. For example, *note* $(1/4)\ (A, 4)$ is a quarter note concert A.

3. In Euterpea the following infix operators combine smaller *Music* values into larger ones:

   (:+:) :: *Music Pitch* → *Music Pitch* → *Music Pitch*
   (:=:) :: *Music Pitch* → *Music Pitch* → *Music Pitch*

Intuitively:

- *m1* :+: *m2* is the music value that represents the playing of *m1* followed by *m2*.
- *m1* :=: *m2* is the music value that represents the playing of *m1* and *m2* simultaneously.

4. Euterpea also has a function *trans* :: *Int* → *Pitch* → *Pitch* such that *trans i p* is a pitch that is *i* semitones (half steps, or steps on a piano) higher than *p*.

Now for the example. Consider the simple melody:

   note qn p1 :+: *note qn p2* :+: *note qn p3*

where *qn* is a quarter note:

   $qn = 1/4$

Suppose we wish to harmonize each note with a note played a minor third lower. In music theory, a minor third corresponds to three semitones, and thus the harmonized melody can be written as:

   mel = (*note qn p1* :=: *note qn* (*trans* (−3) *p1*)) :+:
         (*note qn p2* :=: *note qn* (*trans* (−3) *p2*)) :+:
         (*note qn p3* :=: *note qn* (*trans* (−3) *p3*))

Note, as in the previous example, a repeating pattern of operations – namely, the operations that harmonize a single note with a note three semitones below it. As before, to abstract a sequence of operations such as this, a function can be defined that takes the "variable quantities" – in this case the pitch – as arguments. We can take this one step further, however, by noting that in some other context we might wish to vary the duration. To recognize this is to *anticipate* the need for abstraction. Calling this function *hNote* (for "harmonize note"), we can then write:

   hNote   :: *Dur* → *Pitch* → *Music Pitch*
   hNote d p = *note d p* :=: *note d* (*trans* (−3) *p*)

There are three instances of the pattern in *mel*, each of which can be replaced with an application of *hNote*. This leads to:

mel :: *Music Pitch*
mel = *hNote qn p1* :+: *hNote qn p2* :+: *hNote qn p3*

Again using the idea of unfolding described earlier in this chapter, it is easy to prove that this definition is equivalent to the previous one.

As with *areaF*, this use of *hNote* is an example of functional abstraction. In a sense, functional abstraction can be seen as a generalization of naming. That is, *area r1* is just a name for $pi * r1 ** 2$, *hNote d p* is just a name for *note d p* :=: *note d* (*trans* (−3) *p*), and so on. Stated another way, named quantities such as *area*, *pi*, *concertA*, and *a440* defined earlier can be thought of as functions with no arguments.

Of course, the definition of *hNote* could also be hidden within *mel* using a **let** expression as was done in the previous example:

mel :: *Music Pitch*
mel = **let** *hNote d p* = *note d p* :=: *note d* (*trans* (−3) *p*)
        in *hNote qn p1* :+: *hNote qn p2* :+: *hNote qn p3*

1.7.3 Data Abstraction

The value of *mel* is the sequential composition of three harmonized notes. But what if in another situation we must compose together five harmonized notes, or in other situations even more? In situations where the number of values is uncertain, it is useful to represent them in a *data structure*. For the example at hand, a good choice of data structure is a *list*, briefly introduced earlier, that can have any length. The use of a data structure motivated by the abstraction principle is one form of *data abstraction*.

Imagine now an entire list of pitches whose length is not known at the time the program is written. What now? It seems that a function is needed to convert a list of pitches into a sequential composition of harmonized notes. Before defining such a function, however, there is a bit more to say about lists.

Earlier the example [*C, D, Ef*] was given, a list of pitch classes whose type is thus [*PitchClass*]. A list with *no* elements is – not surprisingly – written [ ], and is called the *empty list*.

To add a single element *x* to the front of a list *xs*, we write *x* : *xs* in Haskell. (Note the naming convention used here: *xs* is the plural of *x*, and should be read that way.) For example, *C* : [*D, Ef*] is the same as [*C, D, Ef*]. In fact, this list is equivalent to *C* : (*D* : (*Ef* : [ ])), which can also be written *C* : *D* : *Ef* : [ ], since the infix operator (:) is right-associative.

Details: In mathematics we rarely worry about whether the notation $a + b + c$ stands for $(a + b) + c$ (in which case $+$ would be "left-associative") or $a + (b + c)$ (in which case $+$ would be "right-associative"). This is because, in situations where the parentheses are left out, it is usually the case that the operator is *mathematically* associative, meaning that it does not matter which interpretation is chosen. If the interpretation *does* matter, mathematicians will include parentheses to make it clear. Furthermore, in mathematics there is an implicit assumption that some operators have higher *precedence* than others; for example, $2 \times a + b$ is interpreted as $(2 \times a) + b$, not $2 \times (a + b)$.

In many programming languages, including Haskell, each operator is defined to have a particular precedence level and to be left-associative or right-associative, or to have no associativity at all. For arithmetic operators, mathematical convention is usually followed; for example, $2 * a + b$ is interpreted as $(2 * a) + b$ in Haskell. The predefined list-forming operator (:) is defined to be right-associative. Just as in mathematics, this associativity can be overridden by using parentheses: thus $(a : b) : c$ is a valid Haskell expression (assuming that it is well-typed; it must be a list of lists), and is very different from $a : b : c$. A way to specify the precedence and associativity of user-defined operators will be discussed in a later chapter.

Returning now to the problem of defining a function (call it *hList*) to turn a list of pitches into a sequential composition of harmonized notes, we should first express what its type should be:

hList :: *Dur* → [*Pitch*] → *Music Pitch*

To define its proper behavior, it is helpful to consider, one by one, all possible cases that could arise on the input. First off, the list could be empty, in which case the sequential composition should be a *Music Pitch* value that has zero duration. So:

hList d [ ] = *rest* 0

The other possibility is that the list *is not* empty – i.e., it contains at least one element, say *p*, followed by the rest of the elements, say *ps*. In this case the result should be the harmonization of *p* followed by the sequential composition of the harmonization of *ps*. Thus:

hList d (*p* : *ps*) = *hNote d p* :+: *hList d ps*

Note that this part of the definition of *hList* is *recursive* – it refers to itself! But the original problem – the harmonization of *p* : *ps* – has been reduced to the harmonization of *p* (previously captured in the function *hNote*) and the harmonization of *ps* (a slightly smaller problem than the original one).

Combining these two equations with the type signature yields the complete definition of the function *hList*:

$$hList \qquad\qquad :: Dur \rightarrow [Pitch] \rightarrow Music\ Pitch$$
$$hList\ d\ [\,] \qquad = rest\ 0$$
$$hList\ d\ (p:ps) = hNote\ d\ p \mathbin{:+:} hList\ d\ ps$$

Recursion is a powerful technique that will be used many times in this textbook. It is also an example of a general problem-solving technique where a large problem is broken down into several smaller but similar problems; solving these smaller problems one by one leads to a solution to the larger problem.

Details: Although intuitive, this example highlights an important aspect of Haskell: *pattern matching*. The left-hand sides of the equations contain *patterns* such as [ ] and *x* : *xs*. When a function is applied, these patterns are *matched* against the argument values in a fairly intuitive way ([ ] only matches the empty list, and *p* : *ps* will successfully match any list with at least one element, while naming the first element *p* and the rest of the list *ps*). If the match succeeds, the right-hand side is evaluated and returned as the result of the application. If it fails, the next equation is tried, and if all equations fail, an error results. All of the equations that define a particular function must appear together, one after the other.

Defining functions by pattern matching is quite common in Haskell, and you should eventually become familiar with the various kinds of patterns that are allowed; see Appendix D for a concise summary.

Given this definition of *hList* the definition of *mel* can be rewritten as:

$$mel = hList\ qn\ [p1, p2, p3]$$

We can prove that this definition is equivalent to the old one via calculation:

$$mel = hList\ qn\ [p1, p2, p3]$$
$$\Rightarrow hList\ qn\ (p1 : p2 : p3 : [\,])$$
$$\Rightarrow hNote\ qn\ p1 \mathbin{:+:} hList\ qn\ (p2 : p3 : [\,])$$
$$\Rightarrow hNote\ qn\ p1 \mathbin{:+:} hNote\ qn\ p2 \mathbin{:+:} hList\ qn\ (p3 : [\,])$$
$$\Rightarrow hNote\ qn\ p1 \mathbin{:+:} hNote\ qn\ p2 \mathbin{:+:} hNote\ qn\ p3 \mathbin{:+:} hList\ qn\ [\,]$$
$$\Rightarrow hNote\ qn\ p1 \mathbin{:+:} hNote\ qn\ p2 \mathbin{:+:} hNote\ qn\ p3 \mathbin{:+:} rest\ 0$$

The first step above is not really a calculation, but rather a rewriting of the list syntax. The remaining calculations each represent an unfolding of *hList*.

Lists are perhaps the most commonly used data structure in Haskell, and there is a rich library of functions that operate on them. In subsequent chapters, lists will be used in a variety of interesting computer music applications.

Exercise 1.4 Modify the definitions of *hNote* and *hList* so that they each take an extra argument that specifies the interval of harmonization (rather than being fixed at -3). Rewrite the definition of *mel* to take these changes into account.

1.8 Haskell Equality versus Musical Equality

The astute reader will have objected to the proof just completed, arguing that the original version of *mel*:

   hNote qn p1 :+: *hNote qn p2* :+: *hNote qn p3*

is not the same as the terminus of the above proof:

   hNote qn p1 :+: *hNote qn p2* :+: *hNote qn p3* :+: *rest* 0

Indeed, that reader would be right! As Haskell values, these expressions are *not* equal, and if you printed each of them you would get different results. So what happened? Did proof by calculation fail?

No, proof by calculation did not fail, since, as just pointed out, as Haskell values, these two expressions are not the same, and proof by calculation is based on the equality of Haskell values. The problem is that a "deeper" notion of equivalence is needed, one based on the notion of *musical* equality. Adding a rest of zero duration to the beginning or end of any piece of music should not change what we *hear*, and therefore it seems that the above two expressions are *musically* equivalent. But it is unreasonable to expect Haskell to figure this out for the programmer!

As an analogy, consider the use of an ordered list to represent a set (which is unordered). The Haskell values $[x1, x2]$ and $[x2, x1]$ are not equal, yet in a program that "interprets" them as sets, they *are* equal.

The way this problem is approached in Euterpea is to formally define a notion of *musical interpretation*, from which the notion of *musical equivalence* is defined. This leads to a kind of "algebra of music" that includes, among others, the following axiom:

   m :+: *rest* 0 ≡ *m*

Figure 1.1 Polyphonic versus contrapuntal interpretation.

The operator ($\equiv$) should be read "is musically equivalent to." With this axiom it is easy to see that the original two expressions above *are* in fact musically equivalent.

For a more extreme example of this idea, and to entice the reader to learn more about musical equivalence in later chapters, note that *mel*, given pitches $p1 = Ef, p2 = F, p3 = G$ and duration $d = 1/4$, generates the harmonized melody shown in Figure 1.1; we can write this concretely in Euterpea as:

> *mel1* = (*note* (1/4) (*Ef*, 4) :=: *note* (1/4) (*C*, 4)) :+:
>   (*note* (1/4) (*F*, 4) :=: *note* (1/4) (*D*, 4)) :+:
>   (*note* (1/4) (*G*, 4) :=: *note* (1/4) (*E*, 4))

The definition of *mel1* can then be seen as a *polyphonic* interpretation of the musical phrase in Figure 1.1, where each pair of notes is seen as a harmonic unit. In contrast, a *contrapuntal* interpretation sees two independent *lines*, or *voices*, in this case the line ⟨Eb,F,G⟩ and the line ⟨C,D,E⟩. In Euterpea we can write this as:

> *mel2* = (*note* (1/4) (*Ef*, 4) :+: *note* (1/4) (*F*, 4) :+: *note* (1/4) (*G*, 4))
>   :=:
>   (*note* (1/4) (*C*, 4) :+: *note* (1/4) (*D*, 4) :+: *note* (1/4) (*E*, 4))

mel1 and *mel2* are clearly not equal as Haskell values. Yet if they are played, they will *sound* the same – they are, in the sense described earlier, *musically equivalent*. But proving these two phrases musically equivalent will require far more than a simple axiom involving *rest* 0. In fact, this can be done in an elegant way using the algebra of music developed in Chapter 12.

1.9 Code Reuse and Modularity

There does not seem to be much repetition in the last definition of *hList*, so perhaps the end of the abstraction process has been reached. In fact, it is worth considering how much progress has been made. The original definition:

$$mel = (note\ qn\ p1 :=: note\ qn\ (trans\ (-3)\ p1))\ :+:$$
$$(note\ qn\ p2 :=: note\ qn\ (trans\ (-3)\ p2))\ :+:$$
$$(note\ qn\ p3 :=: note\ qn\ (trans\ (-3)\ p3))$$

was replaced with:

$$mel = hList\ qn\ [p1, p2, p3]$$

But additionally, definitions for the auxiliary functions *hNote* and *hList* were introduced:

$$hNote\qquad :: Dur \to Pitch \to Music\ Pitch$$
$$hNote\ d\ p = note\ d\ p :=: note\ d\ (trans\ (-3)\ p)$$

$$hList\qquad :: Dur \to [Pitch] \to Music\ Pitch$$
$$hList\ d\ [\,] \qquad = rest\ 0$$
$$hList\ d\ (p : ps) = hNote\ d\ p :+: hList\ d\ ps$$

In terms of code size, the final program is actually larger than the original! So has the program improved in any way?

Things have certainly gotten better from the standpoint of "removing repeating patterns," and we could argue that the resulting program therefore is easier to understand. But there is more. Now that auxiliary functions such as *hNote* and *hList* have been defined, we can *reuse* them in other contexts. Being able to reuse code is also called *modularity*, since the reused components are like little modules, or building blocks, that can form the foundation for many applications.[8] In a later chapter, techniques will be introduced – most notably *higher-order functions* and *polymorphism* – for improving the modularity of this example even more and substantially increasing the ability to reuse code.

1.10 [Advanced] Programming with Numbers

In computer music programming, it is often necessary to program with numbers. For example, it is often convenient to represent pitch on a simple absolute scale using integer values. And when computing with analog signals that represent a particular sound wave, it is necessary to use floating-point numbers as an approximation to the real numbers. So it is a good idea to understand precisely how numbers are represented inside a computer, and within a particular language such as Haskell.

---

[8] "Code reuse" and "modularity" are important software engineering principles.

In mathematics there are many different kinds of number systems. For example, there are integers, natural numbers (i.e., non-negative integers), real numbers, rational numbers, and complex numbers. These number systems possess many useful properties, such as the fact that multiplication and addition are commutative, and that multiplication distributes over addition. You have undoubtedly learned many of these properties in your studies and have used them often in algebra, geometry, trigonometry, physics, and so on.

Unfortunately, each of these number systems places great demands on computer systems. In particular, a number can, in general, require an *arbitrary amount of memory* to represent it. Clearly, for example, an irrational number such as π cannot be represented exactly; the best we can do is approximate it, or possibly write a program that computes it to whatever (finite) precision is needed in a given application. But even integers (and therefore rational numbers) present problems, since any given integer can be arbitrarily large.

Most programming languages do not deal with these problems very well. In fact, most programming languages do not have exact forms of many of these number systems. Haskell does slightly better than most, in that it has exact forms of integers (the type *Integer*) as well as rational numbers (the type *Rational*, defined in the Ratio Library). But in Haskell and most other languages, there is no exact form of real numbers, which are instead approximated by *floating-point numbers* with either single-word precision (*Float* in Haskell) or double-word precision (*Double*). Even worse, the behavior of arithmetic operations on floating-point numbers can vary somewhat depending on what kind of computer is being used, although hardware standardization in recent years has reduced the degree of this problem.

The bottom line is that, as simple as they may seem, great care must be taken when programming with numbers. Many computer errors, some quite serious and renowned, were rooted in numerical incongruities. The field of mathematics known as *numerical analysis* is concerned precisely with these problems, and programming with floating-point numbers in sophisticated applications often requires a good understanding of numerical analysis to devise proper algorithms and write correct programs.

As a simple example of this problem, consider the distributive law, expressed here as a calculation in Haskell, and used earlier in this chapter in calculations involving the function *simple*:

$$a * (b + c) \Rightarrow a * b + a * c$$

For most floating-point numbers, this law is perfectly valid. For example, in the GHC implementation of Haskell, the expressions $pi * (3 + 4) :: Float$ and $pi * 3 + pi * 4 :: Float$ both yield the same result: 21.99115. But funny things can happen when the magnitude of $b + c$ differs significantly from the magnitude of either b or c. For example, the following two calculations are from GHC:

$5 * (-0.123456 + 0.123457)$ $:: Float \Rightarrow 4.991889e{-}6$
$5 * (-0.123456) + 5 * (0.123457) :: Float \Rightarrow 5.00679e{-}6$

Although the discrepancy here is small, its very existence is worrisome, and in certain situations it could be disastrous. The precise behavior of floating-point numbers will not be discussed further in this textbook. Just remember that they are *approximations* to the real numbers. If real-number accuracy is important to your application, further study of the nature of floating-point numbers is probably warranted.

On the other hand, the distributive law (and many others) is valid in Haskell for the exact data types *Integer* and *Ratio Integer* (i.e., rationals). Although the representation of an *Integer* in Haskell is not normally something to be concerned about, it should be clear that the representation must be allowed to grow to an arbitrary size. For example, Haskell has no problem with the following number:

veryBigNumber :: *Integer*
veryBigNumber = 43208345720348593219876512372134059

and such numbers can be added, multiplied, etc., without any loss of accuracy. However, such numbers cannot fit into a single word of computer memory, most of which is limited to 32 or 64 bits. Worse, since the computer system does not know ahead of time exactly how many words will be required, it must devise a dynamic scheme to allow just the right number of words to be used in each case. The overhead of implementing this idea unfortunately causes programs to run slower.

For this reason, Haskell (and most other languages) provides another integer data type, called *Int*, that has maximum and minimum values that depend on the word size of the particular computer being used. In other words, every value of type *Int* fits into one word of memory, and the primitive machine instructions for binary numbers can be used to manipulate them efficiently.[9] Unfortunately, this means that *overflow* or *underflow* errors could occur when an *Int* value exceeds either the maximum or minimum value. Sadly, most implementations of Haskell (as well as most other languages) do not tell you when this happens. For example, in GHC running on a 32-bit processor, the following *Int* value:

---

[9] The Haskell Report requires that every implementation support *Int*s at least in the range -2^{29} to $2^{29} - 1$, inclusive. The GHC implementation running on a 32-bit processor, for example, supports the range -2^{31} to $2^{31} - 1$.

i :: *Int*
i = 1234567890

works just fine, but if you multiply it by two, GHC returns the value
−1825831516! This is because twice *i* exceeds the maximum allowed value,
so the resulting bits become nonsensical,[10] and are interpreted in this case as a
negative number of the given magnitude.

This is alarming! Indeed, why should anyone ever use *Int* when *Integer* is
available? The answer, as implied earlier, is efficiency, but clearly care should
be taken when making this choice. If you are indexing into a list, for example,
and you are confident that you are not performing index calculations that might
result in the above kind of error, then *Int* should work just fine, since a list
longer than 2^{31} will not fit into memory anyway! But if you are calculating the
number of microseconds in some large time interval or counting the number
of people living on earth, then *Integer* would most likely be a better choice.
Choose your number data types wisely!

In this textbook the numeric data types *Integer, Int, Float, Double, Rational*,
and *Complex* will be used for a variety of different applications; for a
discussion of the other number types, consult the Haskell Report. As these data
types are used, there will be little discussion about their properties – this is not,
after all, a book on numerical analysis – but a warning will be cast whenever
reasoning about, for example, floating-point numbers in a way that might not
be technically sound.

---

[10] Actually, these bits are perfectly sensible in the following way: the 32-bit binary
representation of *i* is 01001001100101100000001011010010, and twice that is
10010011001011000000010110100100. But the latter number is seen as negative, because the
32nd bit (the highest-order bit on the CPU on which this was run) is a one, which means it is a
negative number in "twos-complement" representation. The twos-complement of this number
is in turn 01101100110100111111101001011100, whose decimal representation is
1825831516.

2

Simple Music

The previous chapters introduced some of the fundamental ideas of functional programming in Haskell. Also introduced were several of Euterpea's functions and operators, such as *note*, *rest*, (:+:), (:=:), and *trans*. This chapter will reveal the actual definitions of these functions and operators, thus exposing Euterpea's underlying structure and overall design at the note level. In addition, a number of other musical ideas will be developed and, in the process, more Haskell features will be introduced as well.

2.1 Preliminaries

Sometimes it is convenient to use a built-in Haskell data type to directly represent some concept of interest. For example, we may wish to use *Int* to represent *octaves*, where by convention octave 4 corresponds to the octave containing middle C on the piano. We can express this in Haskell using a *type synonym*:

type *Octave* = *Int*

A type synonym does not create a new data type, it just gives a new name to an existing type. Type synonyms can be defined not just for atomic types such as *Int*, but also for structured types such as pairs. For example, as discussed in the last chapter, in music theory a pitch is defined as a pair consisting of a *pitch class* and an *octave*. Assuming the existence of a data type called *PitchClass* (which we will return to shortly), we can write the following type synonym:

type *Pitch* = (*PitchClass*, *Octave*)

For example, concert A (i.e., A440) corresponds to the pitch (*A*, 4) :: *Pitch*, and the lowest and highest notes on a piano correspond to (*A*, 0) :: *Pitch* and (*C*, 8) :: *Pitch*, respectively.

Another important musical concept is *duration*. Rather than using either integers or floating-point numbers, Euterpea uses *rational* numbers to denote duration:

type *Dur* = *Rational*

Rational is the data type of rational numbers expressed as ratios of *Integer*s in Haskell. The choice of *Rational* is somewhat subjective, but is justified by three observations: (1) many durations are expressed as ratios in music theory (5:4 rhythm, quarter notes, dotted notes, and so on), (2) *Rational* numbers are exact (unlike floating point numbers), which is important in many computer music applications, and (3) irrational durations are rarely needed.

Rational numbers in Haskell are printed by GHC in the form $n \% d$, where n is the numerator and d is the denominator. Even a whole number, say the number 42, will print as $42 \% 1$ if it is a *Rational* number. To create a *Rational* number in a program, however, once it is given the proper type, we can use the normal division operator, as in the following definition of a quarter note:

```
qn :: Dur
qn = 1/4   -- quarter note
```

So far, so good. But what about *PitchClass*? We might try to use integers to represent pitch classes as well, but this is not very elegant. Ideally, we would like to write something that looks more like the conventional pitch class names C, C♯, D♭, D, etc. The solution is to use an *algebraic data type* in Haskell:

```
data PitchClass = Cff | Cf | C | Dff | Cs | Df | Css | D | Eff | Ds
              | Ef | Fff | Dss | E | Ff | Es | F | Gff | Ess | Fs
              | Gf | Fss | G | Aff | Gs | Af | Gss | A | Bff | As
              | Bf | Ass | B | Bs | Bss
```

Details: All of the names to the right of the equal sign in a **data** declaration are called *constructors*, and must be capitalized. In this way they are syntactically distinguished from ordinary values. This distinction is useful, since only constructors can be used in the pattern matching that is part of a function definition, as will be described shortly.

The *PitchClass* data type declaration essentially enumerates 35 pitch class names (five for each of the note names A through G). Note that both double-sharps and double-flats are included, resulting in many enharmonics (i.e., two notes that "sound the same," such as G♯ and A♭).

(The order of the pitch classes may seem a bit odd, but the idea is that if a pitch class *pc1* is to the left of a pitch class *pc2*, then *pc1*'s pitch is "lower than" *pc2*'s. This idea will be formalized and exploited in Chapter 7.1.)

Keep in mind that *PitchClass* is a completely new, user-defined data type that is not equal to any other. This is what distinguishes a **data** declaration from a **type** declaration. As another example of the use of a **data** declaration to define a simple enumerated type, Haskell's Boolean data type, called *Bool*, is predefined in Haskell simply as:

data *Bool* = *False* | *True*

2.2 Notes, Music, and Polymorphism

We can, of course, define other data types for other purposes. For example, we will want to define the notion of a *note* and a *rest*. Both of these can be thought of as "primitive" musical values, and thus as a first attempt we might write:

data *Primitive* = *Note Dur Pitch*
      | *Rest Dur*

Analogous to our previous data type declarations, the above declaration says that a *Primitive* is either a *Note* or a *Rest*. However, it is different in that the constructors *Note* and *Rest* take arguments, like functions do. In the case of *Note*, it takes two arguments, whose types are *Dur* and *Pitch*, whereas *Rest* takes one argument, a value of type *Dur*. In other words, the types of *Note* and *Rest* are:

Note :: *Dur* → *Pitch* → *Primitive*
Rest :: *Dur* →   *Primitive*

For example, *Note qn a440* is concert A played as a quarter note, and *Rest* 1 is a whole-note rest.

This definition is not completely satisfactory, however, because we may wish to attach other information to a note, such as its loudness, or some other annotation or articulation. Furthermore, the pitch itself may actually be a percussive sound, having no true pitch at all. To resolve this, Euterpea uses an important concept in Haskell, namely *polymorphism* – the ability to parameterize, or abstract, over types (*poly* means *many* and *morphism* refers to the structure, or *form*, of objects).

Primitive can be redefined as a *polymorphic data type* as follows. Instead of fixing the type of the pitch of a note, it is left unspecified through the use of a *type variable*:

data *Primitive a = Note Dur a*
         | *Rest Dur*

Note that the type variable *a* is used as an argument to *Primitive*, and then used in the body of the declaration, just like a variable in a function. This version of *Primitive* is more general than the previous version – indeed, note that *Primitive Pitch* is the same as (or, technically, is *isomorphic to*) the previous version of *Primitive*. But additionally, *Primitive* is now more flexible than the previous version, since, for example, we can add loudness by pairing loudness with pitch, as in *Primitive (Pitch, Loudness)*. Other concrete instances of this idea will be introduced later.

Details: Type variables such as *a* above must begin with a lowercase letter, to distinguish them from concrete types such as *Dur* and *Pitch*. Since *Primitive* takes an argument, it is called a *type constructor*, whereas *Note* and *Rest* are just called constructors (or value constructors).

Another way to interpret this data declaration is to say that for any type *a*, this declaration declares the types of its constructors to be:

Note :: *Dur* $\rightarrow$ *a* $\rightarrow$ *Primitive a*
Rest :: *Dur* $\rightarrow$ *Primitive a*

Even though *Note* and *Rest* are called data constructors, they are still functions, and they have a type. Since they both have type variables in their type signatures, they are examples of *polymorphic functions*.

It is helpful to think of polymorphism as applying the abstraction principle at the type level – indeed, it is often called *type abstraction*. Many more examples of both polymorphic functions and polymorphic data types will be explored in detail in Chapter 3.

So far Euterpea's primitive notes and rests have been introduced, but how do we combine many notes and rests into a larger composition? To achieve this, Euterpea defines another polymorphic data type, perhaps the most important data type used in this textbook, which defines the fundamental structure of a note-level musical entity:

data *Music a =*
    Prim (Primitive a)   -- primitive value
    | *Music a :+: Music a*   -- sequential composition
    | *Music a :=: Music a*   -- parallel composition
    | *Modify Control (Music a)* -- modifier

Following the reasoning above, the types of these constructors are:

Prim   :: *Primitive a*   → *Music a*
(:+:)   :: *Music a* → *Music a* → *Music a*
(:=:)   :: *Music a* → *Music a* → *Music a*
Modify :: *Control* → *Music a* → *Music a*

These four constructors, then, are also polymorphic functions.

Details: Note the use of the *infix constructors* (:+:) and (:=:). Infix constructors are just like infix operators in Haskell, but they must begin with a colon. This syntactic distinction makes it clear when pattern matching is intended, and is analogous to the distinction between ordinary names (which must begin with a lowercase character) and constructor names (which must begin with an upper-case character).

The observant reader will also recall that at the very beginning of this chapter – corresponding to the module containing all the code in this chapter – the following line appeared:

infixr 5 :+:, :=:

This is called a *fixity declaration*. The "*r*" after the word "**infix**" means that the specified operators – in this case (:+:) and (:=:) – are to have *right* associativity, and the "5" specifies their *precedence level* (these operators will bind more tightly than an operator with a lower precedence). The precedence will also be equal, such that (:+:) and (:=:) will be interpreted from left to right.

The *Music* data type declaration essentially says that a value of type *Music a* has one of four possible forms:

- *Prim p* is a terminal mode, where *p* is a primitive value of type *Primitive a*, for some type *a*. For example:

    a440m :: *Music Pitch*
    a440m = *Prim (Note qn a440)*

  is the musical value corresponding to a quarter-note rendition of concert A.
- *m1* :+: *m2* is the *sequential composition* of *m1* and *m2*; i.e., *m1* and *m2* are played in sequence.
- *m1* :=: *m2* is the *parallel composition* of *m1* and *m2*; i.e., *m1* and *m2* are played simultaneously. The duration of the result is the duration of the longer of *m1* and *m2*.

(Recall that these last two operators were introduced in the last chapter. You can see now that they are actually constructors of an algebraic data type.)

• *Modify cntrl m* is an "annotated" version of *m* in which the control parameter *cntrl* specifies some way *m* is to be modified.

Details: Note that *Music a* is defined in terms of *Music a*, and thus the data type is said to be *recursive* (analogous to a recursive function). It is also often called an *inductive* data type, since it is, in essence, an inductive definition of an infinite number of values, each of which can be arbitrarily complex.

It is convenient to represent these musical ideas as a recursive data type, because it allows us to not only *construct* musical values, but also take them apart, analyze their structure, print them in a structure-preserving way, transform them, interpret them for performance purposes, and so on. Many examples of these kinds of processes will be seen in this textbook.

The *Control* data type is used by the *Modify* constructor to annotate a *Music* value with a *tempo change*, a *transposition*, a *phrase attribute*, an *instrument*, a *key signature*, or a *custom label*. This data type is unimportant at the moment, but for completeness here is its full definition:

```
data Control =
    Tempo       Rational            -- scale the tempo
  | Transpose   AbsPitch            -- transposition
  | Instrument  InstrumentName      -- instrument label
  | Phrase      [PhraseAttribute]   -- phrase attributes
  | KeySig      PitchClass Mode      -- key signature and mode
  | Custom      String              -- custom label

data Mode = Major | Minor | Ionian | Dorian | Phrygian
          | Lydian | Mixolydian | Aeolian | Locrian
          | CustomMode String
```

AbsPitch ("absolute pitch," to be defined in Section 2.4) is just a type synonym for *Int*. Instrument names are borrowed from the General MIDI standard [3, 4], and are captured as an algebraic data type in Figure 2.1. The *KeySig* constructor attaches a key signature to a *Music* value and is different from transposition. A full explanation of phrase attributes and the custom labels is deferred until Chapter 9.

data *InstrumentName =*

AcousticGrandPiano	| *BrightAcousticPiano*	| *ElectricGrandPiano*
| *HonkyTonkPiano*	| *RhodesPiano*	| *ChorusedPiano*
| *Harpsichord*	| *Clavinet*	| *Celesta*
| *Glockenspiel*	| *MusicBox*	| *Vibraphone*
| *Marimba*	| *Xylophone*	| *TubularBells*
| *Dulcimer*	| *HammondOrgan*	| *PercussiveOrgan*
| *RockOrgan*	| *ChurchOrgan*	| *ReedOrgan*
| *Accordion*	| *Harmonica*	| *TangoAccordion*
| *AcousticGuitarNylon*	| *AcousticGuitarSteel*	| *ElectricGuitarJazz*
| *ElectricGuitarClean*	| *ElectricGuitarMuted*	| *OverdrivenGuitar*
| *DistortionGuitar*	| *GuitarHarmonics*	| *AcousticBass*
| *ElectricBassFingered*	| *ElectricBassPicked*	| *FretlessBass*
| *SlapBass1*	| *SlapBass2*	| *SynthBass1*
| *SynthBass2*	| *Violin*	| *Viola*
| *Cello*	| *Contrabass*	| *TremoloStrings*
| *PizzicatoStrings*	| *OrchestralHarp*	| *Timpani*
| *StringEnsemble1*	| *StringEnsemble2*	| *SynthStrings1*
| *SynthStrings2*	| *ChoirAahs*	| *VoiceOohs*
| *SynthVoice*	| *OrchestraHit*	| *Trumpet*
| *Trombone*	| *Tuba*	| *MutedTrumpet*
| *FrenchHorn*	| *BrassSection*	| *SynthBrass1*
| *SynthBrass2*	| *SopranoSax*	| *AltoSax*
| *TenorSax*	| *BaritoneSax*	| *Oboe*
| *Bassoon*	| *EnglishHorn*	| *Clarinet*
| *Piccolo*	| *Flute*	| *Recorder*
| *PanFlute*	| *BlownBottle*	| *Shakuhachi*
| *Whistle*	| *Ocarina*	| *Lead1Square*
| *Lead2Sawtooth*	| *Lead3Calliope*	| *Lead4Chiff*
| *Lead5Charang*	| *Lead6Voice*	| *Lead7Fifths*
| *Lead8BassLead*	| *Pad1NewAge*	| *Pad2Warm*
| *Pad3Polysynth*	| *Pad4Choir*	| *Pad5Bowed*
| *Pad6Metallic*	| *Pad7Halo*	| *Pad8Sweep*
| *FX1Train*	| *FX2Soundtrack*	| *FX3Crystal*
| *FX4Atmosphere*	| *FX5Brightness*	| *FX6Goblins*
| *FX7Echoes*	| *FX8SciFi*	| *Sitar*
| *Banjo*	| *Shamisen*	| *Koto*
| *Kalimba*	| *Bagpipe*	| *Fiddle*
| *Shanai*	| *TinkleBell*	| *Agogo*
| *SteelDrums*	| *Woodblock*	| *TaikoDrum*
| *MelodicDrum*	| *SynthDrum*	| *ReverseCymbal*
| *GuitarFretNoise*	| *BreathNoise*	| *Seashore*
| *BirdTweet*	| *TelephoneRing*	| *Helicopter*
| *Applause*	| *Gunshot*	| *Percussion*
| *CustomInstrument String*		

Figure 2.1 General MIDI instrument names.

2.3 Convenient Auxiliary Functions

For convenience, and in anticipation of their frequent use, a number of
functions are defined in Euterpea to make it easier to write certain kinds of
musical values. For starters:

$$
\begin{array}{ll}
note & :: Dur \rightarrow a \rightarrow Music\ a \\
note\ d\ p & = Prim\ (Note\ d\ p) \\[4pt]
rest & :: Dur \rightarrow Music\ a \\
rest\ d & = Prim\ (Rest\ d) \\[4pt]
tempo & :: Dur \rightarrow Music\ a \rightarrow Music\ a \\
tempo\ r\ m & = Modify\ (Tempo\ r)\ m \\[4pt]
transpose & :: AbsPitch \rightarrow Music\ a \rightarrow Music\ a \\
transpose\ i\ m & = Modify\ (Transpose\ i)\ m \\[4pt]
instrument & :: InstrumentName \rightarrow Music\ a \rightarrow Music\ a \\
instrument\ i\ m & = Modify\ (Instrument\ i)\ m \\[4pt]
phrase & :: [PhraseAttribute] \rightarrow Music\ a \rightarrow Music\ a \\
phrase\ pa\ m & = Modify\ (Phrase\ pa)\ m \\[4pt]
keysig & :: PitchClass \rightarrow Mode \rightarrow Music\ a \rightarrow Music\ a \\
keysig\ pc\ mo\ m & = Modify\ (KeySig\ pc\ mo)\ m
\end{array}
$$

Note that each of these functions is polymorphic, a trait inherited from the data
types that it uses. Also recall that the first two of these functions were used in
an example in the last chapter.

We can also create simple names for familiar notes, durations, and rests, as
shown in Figures 2.2 and 2.3. Despite the large number of them, these names
are sufficiently "unusual" that name clashes are unlikely.

Details: Figures 2.2 and 2.3 demonstrate that at the top level of a
program, more than one equation can be placed on one line, as long as
they are separated by semicolons. This allows us to save vertical space on
the page, and is useful whenever each line is relatively short. A semicolon
is not needed at the end of a single equation, or at the end of the last
equation on a line. This convenient feature is part of Haskell's *layout*
rule, and will be explained in more detail later.

More than one equation can also be placed on one line in a **let** expression,
as demonstrated in the following:

> **let** $x = 1; y = 2$
> **in** $x + y$

$cff, cf, c, cs, css, dff, df, d, ds, dss, eff, ef, e, es, ess, fff, ff, f,$
$\quad fs, fss, gff, gf, g, gs, gss, aff, af, a, as, ass, bff, bf, b, bs, bss ::$
$\qquad Octave \rightarrow Dur \rightarrow Music\ Pitch$

$cff\ o\ d = note\ d\ (Cff,\ o); cf\ \ o\ d = note\ d\ (Cf,\ o)$
$c\ \ \ o\ d = note\ d\ (C,\ \ \ o); cs\ \ o\ d = note\ d\ (Cs,\ o)$
$css\ o\ d = note\ d\ (Css, o); dff\ o\ d = note\ d\ (Dff, o)$
$df\ \ o\ d = note\ d\ (Df,\ \ o); d\ \ \ o\ d = note\ d\ (D,\ \ \ o)$
$ds\ \ o\ d = note\ d\ (Ds,\ \ o); dss\ o\ d = note\ d\ (Dss, o)$
$eff\ o\ d = note\ d\ (Eff,\ o); ef\ \ o\ d = note\ d\ (Ef,\ \ o)$
$e\ \ \ o\ d = note\ d\ (E,\ \ \ o); es\ \ o\ d = note\ d\ (Es,\ \ o)$
$ess\ o\ d = note\ d\ (Ess,\ o); fff\ o\ d = note\ d\ (Fff,\ o)$
$ff\ \ o\ d = note\ d\ (Ff,\ \ o); f\ \ \ o\ d = note\ d\ (F,\ \ \ o)$
$fs\ \ o\ d = note\ d\ (Fs,\ \ o); fss\ o\ d = note\ d\ (Fss, o)$
$gff\ o\ d = note\ d\ (Gff,\ o); gf\ \ o\ d = note\ d\ (Gf,\ \ o)$
$g\ \ \ o\ d = note\ d\ (G,\ \ \ o); gs\ \ o\ d = note\ d\ (Gs,\ o)$
$gss\ o\ d = note\ d\ (Gss, o); aff\ o\ d = note\ d\ (Aff,\ o)$
$af\ \ o\ d = note\ d\ (Af,\ \ o); a\ \ \ o\ d = note\ d\ (A,\ \ \ o)$
$as\ \ o\ d = note\ d\ (As,\ \ o); ass\ o\ d = note\ d\ (Ass, o)$
$bff\ o\ d = note\ d\ (Bff,\ o); bf\ \ o\ d = note\ d\ (Bf,\ \ o)$
$b\ \ \ o\ d = note\ d\ (B,\ \ \ o); bs\ \ o\ d = note\ d\ (Bs,\ o)$
$bss\ o\ d = note\ d\ (Bss, o)$

Figure 2.2 Convenient shorthand for creating *Note* values. The standard adopted is that "x sharp" is *xs*, "x double sharp" is *xss*, "x flat" is *xf*, and "x double flat" is *xff*. This is quite convenient for the vast majority of notes, with one caveat for those who are more musically inclined: *ff* means "f flat" and *fff* means "f double flat" – these names refer to *Note* values, not to the dynamic or loudness values double forte and triple forte, which are often written using those abbreviations on musical scores. Fortunately, the use of these notes is rather rare, and typically their enharmonic equivalents are used instead (*e* and *ef*, respectively).

2.3.1 A Simple Example

As a simple example, suppose we wish to generate a ii-V-I chord progression in a particular major key. In music theory, such a chord progression begins with a minor chord on the second degree of the major scale, followed by a major chord on the fifth degree, and ends in a major chord on the first degree. We can write this in Euterpea, using triads in the key of C major, as follows:

```
t251 :: Music Pitch
t251 = let dMinor = d 4 wn :=: f 4 wn :=: a 4 wn
           gMajor = g 4 wn :=: b 4 wn :=: d 5 wn
           cMajor = c 4 bn :=: e 4 bn :=: g 4 bn
       in dMinor :+: gMajor :+: cMajor
```

bn, wn, hn, qn, en, sn, tn, sfn, dwn, dhn,
  dqn, den, dsn, dtn, ddhn, ddqn, dden :: *Dur*

bnr, wnr, hnr, qnr, enr, snr, tnr, sfnr, dwnr, dhnr,
  dqnr, denr, dsnr, dtnr, ddhnr, ddqnr, ddenr :: *Music Pitch*

bn	= 2;	*bnr*	= *rest bn*	-- brevis or double whole note rest
wn	= 1;	*wnr*	= *rest wn*	-- whole note rest
hn	= 1/2;	*hnr*	= *rest hn*	-- half note rest
qn	= 1/4;	*qnr*	= *rest qn*	-- quarter note rest
en	= 1/8;	*enr*	= *rest en*	-- eighth note rest
sn	= 1/16;	*snr*	= *rest sn*	-- sixteenth note rest
tn	= 1/32;	*tnr*	= *rest tn*	-- thirty-second note rest
sfn	= 1/64;	*sfnr*	= *rest sfn*	-- sixty-fourth note rest
dwn	= 3/2;	*dwnr*	= *rest dwn*	-- dotted whole note rest
dhn	= 3/4;	*dhnr*	= *rest dhn*	-- dotted half note rest
dqn	= 3/8;	*dqnr*	= *rest dqn*	-- dotted quarter note rest
den	= 3/16;	*denr*	= *rest den*	-- dotted eighth note rest
dsn	= 3/32;	*dsnr*	= *rest dsn*	-- dotted sixteenth note rest
dtn	= 3/64;	*dtnr*	= *rest dtn*	-- dotted thirty-second note rest
ddhn	= 7/8;	*ddhnr*	= *rest ddhn*	-- double-dotted half note rest
ddqn	= 7/16;	*ddqnr*	= *rest ddqn*	-- double-dotted quarter note rest
dden	= 7/32;	*ddenr*	= *rest dden*	-- double-dotted eighth note rest

Figure 2.3 Convenient shorthand for creating *Duration* and *Rest* values. Notice that these adhere closely to the American English standard for naming durations, with the exception of *bn* and *bnr*. This design choice was made because the dotted whole note already occupies the *dwn* and *dwnr* names.

Details: Note that more than one equation is allowed in a **let** expression, just like at the top level of a program. The first characters of each equation, however, must line up vertically, and if an equation takes more than one line, then the subsequent lines must be to the right of the first characters. For example, this is legal:

let *a* = *aLongName*
         + *anEvenLongerName*
      b = 56
  in ...

but neither of these is:

let   *a* = *aLongName*
     + *anEvenLongerName*
       b = 56
  in ...

let *a* = *aLongName*
           + *anEvenLongerName*
      b = 56
  in ...

(The second line in the first example is too far to the left, as is the third line in the second example.)

Although this rule, called the *layout rule*, may seem a bit ad hoc, it avoids having to use special syntax (such as inserting a semicolon) to denote the end of one equation and the beginning of the next, thus enhancing readability. In practice, use of layout is rather intuitive. Just remember two things:

First, the first character following **let** (and a few other keywords that will be introduced later) is what determines the starting column for the set of equations being written. Thus we can begin the equations on the same line as the keyword, the next line, or whatever.

Second, be sure that the starting column is farther to the right than the starting column associated with any immediately surrounding **let** clause (otherwise it would be ambiguous). The "termination" of an equation happens when something appears at or to the left of the starting column associated with that equation.

We can play this simple example using Euterpea's *play* function by simply typing:

play t251

at the GHCi command line. Default instruments and tempos are used to convert *t251* into MIDI and then play the result through your computer's standard sound card.

Details: It is important when using *play* that the type of its argument is made clear. In the case of *t251*, it is clear from the type signature in its definition. But for reasons to be explained in Chapter 7, if we write even something very simple such as *play (note qn (C, 4))*, Haskell cannot infer exactly what kind of number 4 is, and therefore cannot infer that (C, 4) is intended to be a *Pitch*. We can get around this by writing:

m :: Music Pitch
m = note qn (C, 4)

in which case *play m* will work just fine, or we can include the type signature "in-line" with the expression, as in
play (note qn ((C, 4) :: Pitch)).

Exercise 2.1 The above example is fairly concrete, in that, for one, it is rooted in C major, and furthermore it has a fixed tempo. Define a function *twoFiveOne* :: *Pitch* → *Dur* → *Music Pitch* such that *twoFiveOne p d* constructs a ii-V-I chord progression in the key whose major scale begins on the pitch *p* (i.e., the first degree of the major scale on which the progression is being constructed), where the duration of each of the first two chords is *d*, and the duration of the last chord is 2 * *d*.

To verify your code, prove by calculation that *twoFiveOne* (*C*, 4) *wn* = *t251*.

Exercise 2.2 The *PitchClass* data type implies the use of standard Western harmony, in particular the use of a *12-tone equal temperament scale*. But there are many other scale possibilities. For example, the *pentatonic blues scale* consists of five notes (thus "pentatonic"), and in the key of C approximately corresponds to the notes C, E♭, F, G, and B♭. More abstractly, let's call these the root, minor third, fourth, fifth, and minor seventh, respectively. Your job is to:

1. Define a new algebraic data type called *BluesPitchClass* that captures this scale (for example, you may wish to use the constructor names *Ro*, *MT*, *Fo*, *Fi*, and *MS*).
2. Define a type synonym *BluesPitch*, akin to *Pitch*.
3. Define the auxiliary functions *ro*, *mt*, *fo*, *fi*, and *ms*, akin to those in Figure 2.2, that make it easy to construct notes of type *Music BluesPitch*.
4. In order to play a value of type *Music BluesPitch* using MIDI, it will have to be converted into a *Music Pitch* value. Define a function *fromBlues* :: *Music BluesPitch* → *Music Pitch* to do this, using the "approximate" translation described at the beginning of this exercise.

   Hint: To do this properly, you will have to pattern match against the *Music* value, something like this:

   ```
   fromBlues (Prim (Note d p)) = ...
   fromBlues (Prim (Rest d))   = ...
   fromBlues (m1 :+: m2)       = ...
   fromBlues (m1 :=: m2)       = ...
   fromBlues (Modify...)       = ...
   ```

5. Write out a few melodies of type *Music BluesPitch*, and play them using *fromBlues* and *play*.

2.4 Absolute Pitches

Treating pitches simply as integers is useful in many settings, so Euterpea uses a type synonym to define the concept of an "absolute pitch":

type *AbsPitch = Int*

The absolute pitch of a (relative) pitch can be defined mathematically as 12 times the octave plus the index of the pitch class. We can express this in Haskell as follows:

$$absPitch \qquad :: Pitch \rightarrow AbsPitch$$
$$absPitch\ (pc, oct) = 12 * (oct + 1) + pcToInt\ pc$$

Details: Note the use of pattern matching to match the argument of *absPitch* to a pair.

---

pcToInt is a function that converts a particular pitch class to an index, easily but tediously expressed, as shown in Figure 2.4. But there is a subtlety: according to music theory convention, pitches are assigned integers in the range 0–11, i.e., modulo 12, starting on pitch class C. In other words, the index of C is 0, C♭ is 11, and B♯ is 0. However, that would mean the absolute pitch of $(C, 4)$, say, would be 60, whereas $(Cf, 4)$ would be 71. Somehow the latter does

$$
\begin{aligned}
&pcToInt :: PitchClass \rightarrow Int \\
&pcToInt\ Cff\ = -2;\ pcToInt\ Dff\ = 0;\ pcToInt\ Eff\ = 2 \\
&pcToInt\ Cf\ \ = -1;\ pcToInt\ Df\ \ = 1;\ pcToInt\ Ef\ \ = 3 \\
&pcToInt\ C\ \ \ = 0;\ \ \ pcToInt\ D\ \ \ = 2;\ pcToInt\ E\ \ \ = 4 \\
&pcToInt\ Cs\ \ = 1;\ \ \ pcToInt\ Ds\ \ = 3;\ pcToInt\ Es\ \ = 5 \\
&pcToInt\ Css\ = 2;\ \ \ pcToInt\ Dss\ = 4;\ pcToInt\ Ess\ = 6 \\
\\
&pcToInt\ Fff\ = 3;\ \ \ pcToInt\ Gff\ = 5;\ pcToInt\ Aff\ = 7 \\
&pcToInt\ Ff\ \ = 4;\ \ \ pcToInt\ Gf\ \ = 6;\ pcToInt\ Af\ \ = 8 \\
&pcToInt\ F\ \ \ = 5;\ \ \ pcToInt\ G\ \ \ = 7;\ pcToInt\ A\ \ \ = 9 \\
&pcToInt\ Fs\ \ = 6;\ \ \ pcToInt\ Gs\ \ = 8;\ pcToInt\ As\ \ = 10 \\
&pcToInt\ Fss\ = 7;\ \ \ pcToInt\ Gss\ = 9;\ pcToInt\ Ass\ = 11 \\
\\
&pcToInt\ Bff\ = 9 \\
&pcToInt\ Bf\ \ = 10 \\
&pcToInt\ B\ \ \ = 11 \\
&pcToInt\ Bs\ \ = 12 \\
&pcToInt\ Bss\ = 13
\end{aligned}
$$

Figure 2.4 Converting pitch classes to integers.

not seem right; 59 would be a more logical choice. Therefore, the definition in Figure 2.4 is written in such a way that the wrap-around does not happen, i.e., numbers outside the range 0–11 are used. With this definition, *absPitch* (*Cf*, 4) yields 59, as desired.

Details: The repetition of "*pcToInt*" above can be avoided by using a Haskell **case** expression, resulting in a more compact definition:

$$pcToInt \quad :: PitchClass \rightarrow Int$$
$$pcToInt\ pc = \textbf{case}\ pc\ \textbf{of}$$
$$\quad Cff \rightarrow -2; Cf \rightarrow -1; C \rightarrow 0; \quad Cs \rightarrow 1; \quad Css \rightarrow 2;$$
$$\quad Dff \rightarrow 0; \quad Df \rightarrow 1; \quad D \rightarrow 2; \quad Ds \rightarrow 3; \quad Dss \rightarrow 4;$$
$$\quad Eff \rightarrow 2; \quad Ef \rightarrow 3; \quad E \rightarrow 4; \quad Es \rightarrow 5; \quad Ess \rightarrow 6;$$
$$\quad Fff \rightarrow 3; \quad Ff \rightarrow 4; \quad F \rightarrow 5; \quad Fs \rightarrow 6; \quad Fss \rightarrow 7;$$
$$\quad Gff \rightarrow 5; \quad Gf \rightarrow 6; \quad G \rightarrow 7; \quad Gs \rightarrow 8; \quad Gss \rightarrow 9;$$
$$\quad Aff \rightarrow 7; \quad Af \rightarrow 8; \quad A \rightarrow 9; \quad As \rightarrow 10; Ass \rightarrow 11;$$
$$\quad Bff \rightarrow 9; \quad Bf \rightarrow 10; B \rightarrow 11; Bs \rightarrow 12; Bss \rightarrow 13$$

As you can see, a **case** expression allows multiple pattern matches on an expression without using equations. Note that layout applies to the body of a case expression and can be overriden as before, using a semicolon. (As in a function type signature, the right-pointing arrow in a **case** expression must be typed as "->" on your computer keyboard.)

The body of a **case** expression observes layout just as a **let** expression, including that semicolons can be used, as above, to place more than one pattern match on the same line.

Converting an absolute pitch to a pitch is a bit more tricky because of enharmonic equivalences. For example, the absolute pitch 15 might correspond to either (*Ds*, 1) or (*Ef*, 1). Euterpea takes the approach of always returning a sharp in such ambiguous cases:

$$pitch \quad :: AbsPitch \rightarrow Pitch$$
$$pitch\ ap =$$
$$\quad \textbf{let}\ (oct, n) = divMod\ ap\ 12$$
$$\quad \textbf{in}\ ([C, Cs, D, Ds, E, F, Fs, G, Gs, A, As, B]\ !!\ n, oct - 1)$$

Details: (!!) is Haskell's zero-based list-indexing function; *list* !! *n* returns the (*n* + 1)th element in *list*. *divMod* *x* *n* returns a pair (*q*, *r*), where *q* is the integer quotient of *x* divided by *n*, and *r* is the value of *x* modulo *n*.

Given *pitch* and *absPitch*, it is now easy to define a function *trans* that transposes pitches:

$$trans \quad :: Int \rightarrow Pitch \rightarrow Pitch$$
$$trans \; i \; p = pitch \; (absPitch \; p + i)$$

With this definition, all of the operators and functions introduced in the previous chapter have been covered.

Exercise 2.3 Show that *abspitch* (*pitch ap*) $=$ *ap* and, up to enharmonic equivalences, *pitch* (*abspitch p*) $= p$.

Exercise 2.4 Show that *trans i* (*trans j p*) $=$ *trans* $(i + j)$ *p*.

Exercise 2.5 *Transpose* is part of the *Control* data type, which in turn is part of the *Music* data type. Its use in transposing a *Music* value is thus a kind of "annotation" – it doesn't really change the *Music* value, it just annotates it as something that is transposed.

Define instead a recursive function *transM* :: *AbsPitch* $\rightarrow$ *Music Pitch* $\rightarrow$ *Music Pitch* that actually changes each note in a *Music Pitch* value by transposing it by the interval represented by the first argument.

Hint: To do this properly, you will have to pattern match against the *Music* value, something like this:

$$transM \; ap \; (Prim \; (Note \; d \; p)) = ...$$
$$transM \; ap \; (Prim \; (Rest \; d)) \quad = ...$$
$$transM \; ap \; (m1 :+: m2) \qquad = ...$$
$$transM \; ap \; (m1 :=: m2) \qquad = ...$$
$$transM \; ap \; (Modify...) \qquad\quad = ...$$

3

Polymorphic and Higher-Order Functions

Several examples of polymorphic data types were introduced in the first couple of chapters. In this chapter the focus is on *polymorphic functions*, which are most commonly defined over polymorphic data types.

The already familiar *list* is the protoypical example of a polymorphic data type, and it will be studied in depth in this chapter. Although lists have no direct musical connection, they are perhaps the most commonly used data type in Haskell and have many applications in computer music programming. But in addition, the *Music* data type is polymorphic, and several new functions that operate on it polymorphically will also be defined.

(A more detailed discussion of predefined polymorphic functions that operate on lists can be found in Appendix A.)

This chapter also introduces *higher-order functions*, which take one or more functions as arguments or return a function as a result (functions can also be placed in data structures). Higher-order functions permit the elegant and concise expression of many musical concepts. Together with polymorphism, higher-order functions substantially increase the programmer's expressive power and ability to reuse code.

Both of these new ideas naturally follow the foundations that have already been established.

3.1 Polymorphic Types

In previous chapters, examples of lists containing several different kinds of elements – integers, characters, pitch classes, and so on – were introduced, and we can well imagine situations requiring lists of other element types. Sometimes, however, it is not necessary to be so particular about the type of the elements. For example, suppose we wish to define a function *length* that determines the number of elements in a list. It does not really matter whether the list contains integers, pitch classes, or even other lists – we can imagine computing the length in exactly the same way in each case. The obvious definition is:

$$length\ [\,] \quad\quad = 0$$
$$length\ (x : xs) = 1 + length\ xs$$

This recursive definition is self-explanatory. Indeed, we can read the equations as saying: "The length of the empty list is 0, and the length of a list whose first element is x and remainder is xs is 1 plus the length of xs."

But what should the type of *length* be? Intuitively, we would like to say that, for *any* type a, the type of *length* is $[a] \rightarrow Integer$. In mathematics we might write this as:

$$length :: (\forall a)\ [a] \rightarrow Integer$$

But in Haskell this is written simply as:

$$length :: [a] \rightarrow Integer$$

In other words, the universal quantification of the type variable a is implicit.

Details: Generic names for types, such as a above, are called *type variables*, and are uncapitalized to distinguish them from concrete types such as *Integer*.

So *length* can be applied to a list containing elements of *any* type. For example:

$$length\ [1, 2, 3] \quad\quad\quad \Longrightarrow 3$$
$$length\ [C, D, Ef] \Longrightarrow 3$$
$$length\ [[1], [\,], [2, 3, 4]] \Longrightarrow 3$$

Note that the type of the argument to *length* in the last example is $[[Integer]]$; that is, a list of lists of integers.

Here are two other examples of polymorphic list functions, which happen to be predefined in Haskell:

$$head \quad\quad :: [a] \rightarrow a$$
$$head\ (x : \_) = x$$
$$tail \quad\quad :: [a] \rightarrow [a]$$
$$tail\ (\_ : xs) = xs$$

Details: The _ on the left-hand side of these equations is called a
wildcard pattern. It matches any value and binds no variables. It is useful
as a way of documenting the fact that we do not care about the value in
that part of the pattern. Note that we could (perhaps should) have used a
wildcard in place of the variable *x* in the definition of *length*.

These two functions take the "head" and "tail," respectively, of any non-empty list. For example:

head $[1, 2, 3] \Rightarrow 1$
head $[C, D, Ef] \Rightarrow C$
tail $[1, 2, 3] \Rightarrow [2, 3]$
tail $[C, D, Ef] \Rightarrow [D, Ef]$

Note that, for any non-empty list *xs*, *head* and *tail* obey the following law:

head xs : *tail xs* = *xs*

Functions such as *length*, *head*, and *tail* are said to be *polymorphic*.
Polymorphic functions arise naturally when defining functions on lists and
other polymorphic data types, including the *Music* data type defined in the
last chapter.

3.2 Abstraction over Recursive Definitions

Given a list of pitches, suppose we wish to convert each pitch into an absolute
pitch. We could define a function:

toAbsPitches   :: $[Pitch] \rightarrow [AbsPitch]$
toAbsPitches [ ]   = [ ]
toAbsPitches $(p : ps) = absPitch\ p : toAbsPitches\ ps$

We might also want to convert a list of absolute pitches to a list of pitches:

toPitches   :: $[AbsPitch] \rightarrow [Pitch]$
toPitches [ ]   = [ ]
toPitches $(a : as) = pitch\ a : toPitches\ as$

These two functions are different but share something in common: there
is a repeating pattern of operations. But the pattern is not quite like any
of the examples studied earlier, and therefore it is unclear how to apply
the abstraction principle. What distinguishes this situation is that there is a
repeating pattern of *recursion*.

In discerning the nature of a repeating pattern, recall that it is sometimes helpful to first identify those things that *are not* repeating – i.e., those things that are *changing* – since these will be the sources of *parameterization*: those values that must be passed as arguments to the abstracted function. In the case above, these changing values are the functions *absPitch* and *pitch*; consider them instances of a new name, f. Rewriting either of the above functions as a new function – call it *map* – that takes an extra argument f yields:

$$map\ f\ [\ ] \qquad = [\ ]$$
$$map\ f\ (x : xs) = f\ x : map\ f\ xs$$

This recursive pattern of operations is so common that *map* is predefined in Haskell (and is why the name *map* was chosen in the first place).

With *map*, we can now redefine *toAbsPitches* and *toPitches* as:

$$toAbsPitches \quad :: [Pitch] \rightarrow [AbsPitch]$$
$$toAbsPitches\ ps = map\ absPitch\ ps$$

$$toPitches \quad :: [AbsPitch] \rightarrow [Pitch]$$
$$toPitches\ as = map\ pitch\ as$$

Note that these definitions are non-recursive; the common pattern of recursion has been abstracted away and isolated in the definition of *map*. They are also very succinct; so much so, that it seems unnecessary to create new names for these functions at all! One of the powers of higher-order functions is that they permit concise yet easy-to-understand definitions such as this, and you will see many similar examples throughout the remainder of the text.

A proof that the new versions of these two functions are equivalent to the old ones can be done via calculation, but requires a proof technique called *induction*, because of the recursive nature of the original function definitions. Inductive proofs are discussed in detail, including for these two examples, in Chapter 11.

3.2.1 Map Is Polymorphic

What should the type of *map* be? Looking first at its use in *toAbsPitches*, note that it takes the function *absPitch* :: *Pitch* → *AbsPitch* as its first argument and a list of *Pitch*s as its second argument, returning a list of *AbsPitch*s as its result. So its type must be:

$$map :: (Pitch \rightarrow AbsPitch) \rightarrow [Pitch] \rightarrow [AbsPitch]$$

Yet a similar analysis of its use in *toPitches* reveals that *map*'s type should be:

$$map :: (AbsPitch \rightarrow Pitch) \rightarrow [AbsPitch] \rightarrow [Pitch]$$

This apparent anomaly can be resolved by noting that *map*, like *length*, *head*, and *tail*, does not really care what its list element types are, *as long as its functional argument can be applied to them*. Indeed, *map* is *polymorphic*, and its most general type is:

$$map :: (a \rightarrow b) \rightarrow [a] \rightarrow [b]$$

This can be read as "*map* is a function that takes a function from any type *a* to any type *b*, and a list of *a*'s, and returns a list of *b*'s." The correspondence between the two *a*'s and between the two *b*'s is important: a function that converts *Int*'s to *Char*'s, for example, cannot be mapped over a list of *Char*'s. It is easy to see that in the case of *toAbsPitches*, *a* is instantiated as *Pitch* and *b* as *AbsPitch*, whereas in *toPitches*, *a* and *b* are instantiated as *AbsPitch* and *Pitch*, respectively.

Note, as we did in Section 2.2, that the above reasoning can be viewed as the abstraction principle at work at the type level.

Details: In Chapter 1 it was mentioned that every expression in Haskell has an associated type. But with polymorphism, we might wonder if there is just one type for every expression. For example, *map* could have any of these types:

$$(a \rightarrow b) \rightarrow [a] \rightarrow [b]$$
$$(Integer \rightarrow b) \rightarrow [Integer] \rightarrow [b]$$
$$(a \rightarrow Float) \rightarrow [a] \rightarrow [Float]$$
$$(Char \rightarrow Char) \rightarrow [Char] \rightarrow [Char]$$

and so on, depending on how it will be used. However, notice that the first of these types is in some fundamental sense more general than the other three. In fact, every expression in Haskell has a unique type, known as its *principal type*, the least general type that captures all valid uses of the expression. The first type above is the principal type of *map*, since it captures all valid uses of *map* yet is less general than, for example, the type $a \rightarrow b \rightarrow c$. As another example, the principal type of *head* is $[a] \rightarrow a$; the types $[b] \rightarrow a$, $b \rightarrow a$, and even *a* are too general, whereas something like $[Integer] \rightarrow Integer$ is too specific. (The existence of unique principal types is the hallmark feature of the *Hindley-Milner type system* [5, 6] that forms the basis of the type systems of Haskell, ML [7], and several other functional languages [8].)

3.2.2 Using *map*

For a musical example involving *map*, consider the task of generating a six-note whole-tone scale starting at a given pitch:[1]

wts :: *Pitch* → [*Music Pitch*]
wts p = **let** *f ap* = *note qn* (*pitch* (*absPitch p* + *ap*))
          in *map f* [0, 2, 4, 6, 8]

For example:

wts a440
⟹ [*note qn* (*A*, 4), *note qn* (*B*, 4), *note qn* (*C#*, 4),
        note qn (*D#*, 4), *note qn* (*F*, 4), *note qn* (*G*, 4)]

Exercise 3.1 Using *map*, define:

1. A function *f1* :: *Int* → [*Pitch*] → [*Pitch*] that transposes each pitch in its second argument by the amount specified in its first argument.
2. A function *f2* :: [*Dur*] → [*Music a*] that turns a list of durations into a list of rests, each having the corresponding duration.
3. A function *f3* :: [*Music Pitch*] → [*Music Pitch*] that takes a list of music values (that are assumed to be single notes) and, for each such note, halves its duration and places a rest of that same duration after it. For example:

    f3 [*c* 4 *qn*, *d* 4 *en*, *e* 4 *hn*]
    ⟹ [*c* 4 *en* :+: *rest en*, *d* 4 *sn* :+: *rest sn*, *e* 4 *qn* :+: *rest qn*]

    You can think of this as giving a staccato interpretation of the notes.

3.3 Append

Consider now the problem of *concatenating* or *appending* two lists together; that is, creating a third list that consists of all of the elements from the first list followed by all of the elements of the second. Once again, the type of list elements does not matter, so we can define this as a polymorphic infix operator (++):

(++) :: [*a*] → [*a*] → [*a*]

---

[1] A whole-tone scale is a sequence of six ascending notes, with each adjacent pair of notes separated by two semitones, i.e., a whole note.

For example, here are two uses of ($+\!\!\!+$) on different types:

$$[1,2,3] +\!\!\!+ [4,5,6] \implies [1,2,3,4,5,6]$$
$$[C,E,G] +\!\!\!+ [D,F,A] \implies [C,E,G,D,F,A]$$

As usual, we can approach this problem by considering the various possibilities that could arise as input. But in the case of ($+\!\!\!+$), there are *two* inputs – so which should be considered first? In general this is not an easy question to answer, so we could just try the first list first: it could be empty or non-empty. If it is empty, the answer is easy:

$$[\,] +\!\!\!+ ys = ys$$

and if it is not empty, the answer is also straightforward:

$$(x : xs) +\!\!\!+ ys = x : (xs +\!\!\!+ ys)$$

Note the recursive use of ($+\!\!\!+$). The full definition is thus:

$$(+\!\!\!+) \qquad :: [a] \rightarrow [a] \rightarrow [a]$$
$$[\,] \qquad +\!\!\!+ ys = ys$$
$$(x : xs) +\!\!\!+ ys = x : (xs +\!\!\!+ ys)$$

Details: Note that an infix operator can be defined just as any other function, including pattern matching, except that on the left-hand side it is written using its infix syntax.

Also be aware that this textbook takes liberty in typesetting by displaying the append operator as $+\!\!\!+$. When you type your code, however, you will need to write ++. Recall that infix operators in Haskell must not contain any numbers or letters, and also must not begin with a colon (because those are reserved for infix constructors).

If we were to consider instead the second list first, then the first equation would still be easy:

$$xs +\!\!\!+ [\,] = xs$$

but the second is not so obvious:

$$xs +\!\!\!+ (y : ys) = \,??$$

So it seems that the right choice was made to begin with.

Like *map*, the concatenation operator ($+\!\!\!+$) is used so often that it is predefined in Haskell.

3.3.1 [Advanced] The Efficiency and Fixity of Append

In Chapter 11 the following simple property about ($+\!\!\!+$) will be proved:

$(xs +\!\!\!+ ys) +\!\!\!+ zs = xs +\!\!\!+ (ys +\!\!\!+ zs)$

That is, ($+\!\!\!+$) is *associative*.

But what about the efficiency of the left-hand and right-hand sides of this equation? It is easy to see via calculation that appending two lists together takes a number of steps proportional to the length of the first list (indeed, the second list is not evaluated at all). For example:

$[1, 2, 3] +\!\!\!+ xs$
$\Rightarrow 1 : ([2, 3] +\!\!\!+ xs)$
$\Rightarrow 1 : 2 : ([3] +\!\!\!+ xs)$
$\Rightarrow 1 : 2 : 3 : ([\,] +\!\!\!+ xs)$
$\Rightarrow 1 : 2 : 3 : xs$

Therefore, the evaluation of $xs +\!\!\!+ (ys +\!\!\!+ zs)$ takes a number of steps proportional to the length of xs plus the length of ys. But what about $(xs +\!\!\!+ ys) +\!\!\!+ zs$? The leftmost append will take a number of steps proportional to the length of xs, but then the rightmost append will require a number of steps proportional to the length of xs plus the length of ys, for a total cost of:

$2 * length\ xs + length\ ys$

Thus $xs +\!\!\!+ (ys +\!\!\!+ zs)$ is more efficient than $(xs +\!\!\!+ ys) +\!\!\!+ zs$. This is why the Standard Prelude defines the fixity of ($+\!\!\!+$) as:

infixr 5 $+\!\!\!+$

In other words, if you just write $xs +\!\!\!+ ys +\!\!\!+ zs$, you will get the most efficient association, namely the right association $xs +\!\!\!+ (ys +\!\!\!+ zs)$. In the next section, a more dramatic example of this property will be introduced.

3.4 Fold

Suppose we wish to take a list of notes (each of type *Music a*) and convert them into a *line*, or *melody*. We can define a recursive function to do this as follows:

```
line          :: [Music a] → Music a
line [ ]       = rest 0
line (m : ms) = m :+: line ms
```

Note that this function is polymorphic – the first example so far, in fact, of a polymorphic function involving the *Music* data type.

We might also wish to have a function *chord* that operates in an analogous way, but using (:=:) instead of (:+:):

> *chord*   :: [*Music a*] → *Music a*
> *chord* [ ]   = *rest* 0
> *chord* (*m* : *ms*) = *m* :=: *chord ms*

This function is also polymorphic.

In a completely different context, we might wish to compute the highest pitch in a list of pitches, which we might capture in the following way:

> *maxPitch*   :: [*Pitch*] → *Pitch*
> *maxPitch* [ ]   = *pitch* 0
> *maxPitch* (*p* : *ps*) = *p* ! ! ! *maxPitch ps*

where (! ! !) is defined as:

> *p1* ! ! ! *p2* = **if** *absPitch p1* > *absPitch p2* **then** *p1* **else** *p2*

Details: An expression **if** *pred* **then** *cons* **else** *alt* is called a *conditional expression*. If *pred* (called the *predicate*) is true, then *cons* (called the *consequence*) is the result; if *pred* is false, then *alt* (called the *alternative*) is the result.

Once again, we have a situation where several definitions share something in common: a repeating recursive pattern. Using the process used earlier to discover *map*, we first identify those things that are changing. There are two situations: the *rest* 0 and *pitch* 0 values (for which the generic name *init*, for "initial value," will be used), and the (:+:), (:=:), and (! ! !) operators (for which the generic name *op*, for "operator," will be used). Now, rewriting any of the above three functions as a new function – call it *fold* – that takes extra arguments *op* and *init*, we arrive at:[2]

> *fold op init* [ ]   = *init*
> *fold op init* (*x* : *xs*) = *x* ‘*op*‘ *fold op init xs*

---

[2] The use of the name "*fold*" for this function is historical (within the functional programming community), and has nothing to do with the use of "fold" and "unfold" in Chapter 1 to describe steps in a calculation.

> **Details:** Any normal binary function name can be used as an infix
> operator by enclosing it in backquotes; x 'f' y is equivalent to f x y. Using
> infix application here for *op* better reflects the structure of the repeating
> pattern that is being abstracted, but it could also be written
> *op x (fold op init xs)*.

With this definition of *fold*, we can now rewrite the definitions of *line*, *chord*,
and *maxPitch* as:

```
line, chord :: [Music a] → Music a
line   ms = fold (:+:) (rest 0) ms
chord ms = fold (:=:) (rest 0) ms

maxPitch    :: [Pitch] → Pitch
maxPitch ps = fold (!!!) (pitch 0) ps
```

> **Details:** Just as we can turn a function into an operator by enclosing it in
> backquotes, we can turn an operator into a function by enclosing it in
> parentheses. This is required in order to pass an operator as a value to
> another function, as in the examples above. (If we wrote *fold* ! ! ! 0 *ps*
> instead of *fold* (! ! !) 0 *ps*, it would look like we were trying to apply
> (! ! !) to *fold* and 0 *ps*, which is nonsensical and ill-typed.)

In Chapter 11 we will use induction to prove that these new definitions are
equivalent to the old.

fold, like *map*, is a highly useful, and reusable, function, as will be seen
through several other examples later in the text. Indeed, it too is polymorphic,
for note that it does not depend on the type of the list elements. Its most general
type – somewhat trickier than that for *map* – is:

$$fold :: (a → b → b) → b → [a] → b$$

This allows us to use *fold* whenever we need to "collapse" a list of elements
using a binary (i.e., two-argument) operator.

As a final example, recall the definition of *hList* from Chapter 1:

```
hList             :: Dur → [Pitch] → Music Pitch
hList d [ ]       = rest 0
hList d (p : ps) = hNote d p :+: hList d ps
```

A little thought should convince the reader that this can be rewritten as:

hList d ps = **let** *f p* = *hNote d p*
              in *line* (*map f ps*)

This version is more modular, in that it avoids explicit recursion and is instead built up from smaller building blocks, namely *line* (which uses *fold*) and *map*.

3.4.1 Haskell's Folds

Haskell actually defines two versions of *fold* in the Standard Prelude. The first is called *foldr* ("fold-from-the-right"), whose definition is the same as that of *fold* given earlier:

foldr $:: (a \to b \to b) \to b \to [a] \to b$
foldr op init [ ]   = *init*
foldr op init (*x* : *xs*) = *x* '*op*' *foldr op init xs*

A good way to think about *foldr* is that it replaces all occurrences of the list operator (:) with its first argument (a function), and replaces [ ] with its second argument. In other words:

foldr op init (*x1* : *x2* : ... : *xn* : [ ])
   $\Longrightarrow$ *x1* '*op*' (*x2* '*op*' (...(*xn* '*op*' *init*)...))

This might help in better understanding the type of *foldr*, and also explains its name: the list is "folded from the right." Stated another way, for any list *xs*, the following always holds:[3]

foldr (:) [ ] *xs* $\Longrightarrow$ *xs*

Haskell's second version of *fold* is called *foldl*:

foldl $:: (b \to a \to b) \to b \to [a] \to b$
foldl op init [ ]   = *init*
foldl op init (*x* : *xs*) = *foldl op* (*init* '*op*' *x*) *xs*

A good way to think about *foldl* is to imagine "folding the list from the left":

foldl op init (*x1* : *x2* : ... : *xn* : [ ])
   $\Longrightarrow$ (...((*init* '*op*' *x1*) '*op*' *x2*)...) '*op*' *xn*

3.4.2 [Advanced] Why Two Folds?

Note that if we used *foldl* instead of *foldr* in the definitions given earlier, then not much would change; *foldr* and *foldl* would give the same result. Indeed,

---

[3] This will be formally proved in Chapter 11.

judging from their types, it looks like the only difference between *foldr* and *foldl* is that the operator takes its arguments in a different order.

So why does Haskell have two versions of *fold*? It turns out that there are situations where using one is more efficient and possibly more "defined" (that is, the function terminates on more values of its input domain) than the other.

Probably the simplest example of this is a generalization of the associativity of (++) discussed in the last section. Suppose we wish to collapse a list of lists into one list. The Standard Prelude defines the polymorphic function *concat* for this purpose:

> *concat* $:: [[a]] \rightarrow [a]$
> *concat xss* $= foldr$ (++) [ ] *xss*

For example:

> *concat* $[[1], [3, 4], [ ], [5, 6]]$
> $\implies [1] ++ ([3, 4] ++ ([ ] ++ ([5, 6] ++ [ ])))$
> $\implies [1, 3, 4, 5, 6]$

More generally, we have that:

> *concat* $[xs1, xs2, ..., xsn]$
> $\implies$ *foldr* (++) [ ] $[xs1, xs2, ..., xsn]$
> $\implies xs1 ++ (xs2 ++ (...(xsn ++ [ ]))...)$

The total cost of this computation is proportional to the sum of the lengths of all of the lists. If each list has the same length *len*, and there are *n* lists, then this cost is $n * len$.

On the other hand, if we defined *concat* this way:

> *slowConcat xss* $= foldl$ (++) [ ] *xss*

then:

> *slowConcat* $[xs1, xs2, ..., xsn]$
> $\implies$ *foldl* (++) [ ] $[xs1, xs2, ..., xsn]$
> $\implies (...(([ ] ++ xs1) ++ xs2)...) ++ xsn$

If each list has the same length *len*, then the cost of this computation will be:

> $len + (len + len) + (len + len + len) + \cdots + (n - 1) * len$
> $= n * (n - 1) * len / 2$

which is considerably worse than $n * len$. Thus the choice of *foldr* in the definition of *concat* is quite important.

Similar examples can be given to demonstrate that *foldl* is sometimes more efficient than *foldr*. On the other hand, in many cases the choice does not matter at all (consider, for example, $(+)$). The moral of all this is that care must be taken in the choice between *foldr* and *foldl* if efficiency is a concern.

3.4.3 Fold for Non-Empty Lists

In certain contexts, it may be understood that the functions *line* and *chord* should not be applied to an empty list. For such situations, the Standard Prelude provides the functions *foldr1* and *foldl1*, which return an error if applied to an empty list. And thus we may also desire to define versions of *line* and *chord* that adopt this behavior:

> *line12, chord1* :: [*Music a*] → *Music a*
> *line1 ms*   = *foldr1* (:+:) *ms*
> *chord1 ms* = *foldr1* (:=:) *ms*

Note that *foldr1* and *foldl1* do not take an *init* argument.

In the case of *maxPitch*, we could go a step further and say that the previous definition is in fact flawed, for who is to say what the maximum pitch of an empty list is? The choice of 0 is indeed arbitrary, and in a way it is nonsensical – how can 0 be the maximum if it is not even in the list? In such situations we might wish to define only one function, and to have that function return an error when presented with an empty list. For consistency with *line* and *chord*, however, that function is defined here with a new name:

> *maxPitch1*   :: [*Pitch*] → *Pitch*
> *maxPitch1 ps* = *foldr1* (!!!) *ps*

3.5 [Advanced] A Final Example: Reverse

As a final example of a useful list function, consider the problem of *reversing* a list, which will be captured in a function called *reverse*. This could be useful, for example, when constructing the *retrograde* of a musical passage, i.e., the music as if it were played backwards. For example, *reverse* [C, D, Ef] is [Ef, D, C].

Thus *reverse* takes a single list argument, whose possibilities are the normal ones for a list: either it is empty or it is not. And thus:

> *reverse*   :: [a] → [a]
> *reverse* []   = []
> *reverse* ($x : xs$) = *reverse xs* ++ [x]

This, in fact, is a perfectly good definition for *reverse* – it is certainly clear, except for one small problem: it is terribly inefficient! To see why, first recall that the number of steps needed to compute $xs \mathbin{+\!\!+} ys$ is proportional to the length of xs. Now suppose that the list argument to *reverse* has length n. The recursive call to *reverse* will return a list of length $n - 1$, which is the first argument to (+). Thus the cost to reverse a list of length of n will be proportional to $n - 1$ plus the cost to reverse a list of length $n - 1$. So the total cost is proportional to $(n - 1) + (n - 2) + \cdots + 1 = n(n - 1)/2$, which in turn is proportional to the square of n.

Can we do better than this? In fact, yes.

There is another algorithm for reversing a list, which can be described intuitively as follows: take the first element and put it at the front of an empty auxiliary list, then take the next element and add it to the front of the auxiliary list (thus the auxiliary list now consists of the first two elements in the original list, but in reverse order), then do this again and again until the end of the original list is reached. At that point the auxiliary list will be the reverse of the original one.

This algorithm can be expressed recursively, but the auxiliary list implies the need for a function that takes *two* arguments – the original list and the auxiliary one – yet *reverse* takes only one. This can be solved by creating an auxiliary function *rev*:

$$\text{reverse } xs = \textbf{let } rev \; acc \; [\,] \quad = acc$$
$$rev \; acc \; (x : xs) = rev \; (x : acc) \; xs$$
$$\textbf{in } rev \; [\,] \; xs$$

The auxiliary list is the first argument to *rev* and is called *acc*, since it behaves as an "accumulator" of the intermediate results. Note how it is returned as the final result once the end of the original list is reached.

A little thought should convince the reader that this function does not have the quadratic (n^2) behavior of the first algorithm, and indeed can be shown to execute a number of steps that is directly proportional to the length of the list, which we can hardly expect to improve upon.

But now compare the definition of *rev* with the definition of *foldl*:

$$\text{foldl } op \; init \; [\,] \quad = init$$
$$\text{foldl } op \; init \; (x : xs) = foldl \; op \; (init \; `op` \; x) \; xs$$

They are somewhat similar. In fact, suppose we were to slightly revise the definition of *rev* as follows:

$$\text{rev } op \; acc \; [\,] \quad = acc$$
$$\text{rev } op \; acc \; (x : xs) = rev \; op \; (acc \; `op` \; x) \; xs$$

Now *rev* looks strongly like *foldl*, and the question becomes whether or not there is a function that can be substituted for *op* that would make the latter definition of *rev* equivalent to the former one. Indeed there is:

$$\text{revOp } a \; b = b : a$$

For note that:

> acc '$revOp$' x
> $\Rightarrow revOp\ acc\ x$
> $\Rightarrow x : acc$

So *reverse* can be rewritten as:

> $reverse\ xs =$ **let** $rev\ op\ acc\ [\ ] \qquad = acc$
> $\qquad\qquad\qquad\qquad rev\ op\ acc\ (x : xs) = rev\ op\ (acc$ 'op' $x)\ xs$
> $\qquad\qquad$ **in** $rev\ revOp\ [\ ]\ xs$

which is the same as:

> $reverse\ xs = foldl\ revOp\ [\ ]\ xs$

If all of this seems like magic, well, you are starting to see the beauty of functional programming!

3.6 Currying

We can further improve upon some of the definitions given in this chapter using a technique called *currying simplification*. To understand this idea, first look closer at the notation used to write function applications, such as *simple x y z*. Although, as noted earlier, this is similar to the mathematical notation *simple*(x, y, z), in fact there is an important difference, namely that *simple x y z* is actually shorthand for $(((simple\ x)\ y)\ z)$. In other words, function application is *left associative*, taking one argument at a time.

Now look at the expression $(((simple\ x)\ y)\ z)$ a bit closer: there is an application of *simple* to x, the result of which is applied to y, so $(simple\ x)$ must be a function! The result of this application, $((simple\ x)\ y)$, is then applied to z, so $((simple\ x)\ y)$ must also be a function!

Since each of these intermediate applications yields a function, it seems perfectly reasonable to define a function such as:

> $multSumByFive = simple\ 5$

What is *simple* 5? From the above argument, it is clear that it must be a function. And from the definition of *simple* in Section 1, we might guess that this function takes two arguments and returns 5 times their sum. Indeed, we can *calculate* this result as follows:

> $multSumByFive\ a\ b$
> $\Rightarrow (simple\ 5)\ a\ b$
> $\Rightarrow simple\ 5\ a\ b$
> $\Rightarrow 5 * (a + b)$

The intermediate step with parentheses is included just for clarity. This method of applying functions to one argument at a time, yielding intermediate functions along the way, is called *currying*, after the logician Haskell B. Curry, who popularized the idea.[4] It is helpful to look at the types of intermediate functions as arguments are applied:

> *simple*   :: *Float → Float → Float → Float*
> *simple 5*   :: *Float → Float → Float*
> *simple 5 a* :: *Float → Float*
> *simple 5 a b* :: *Float*

For a musical example of this idea, recall the function *note* :: *Dur → Pitch → Music Pitch*. So *note qn* is a function that, given a pitch, yields a quarter note rendition of that pitch. A common use of this idea is simplifying something like:

> *note qn p1* :+: *note qn p2* :+: ... :+: *note qn pn*

to:

> *line (map (note qn) [p1, p2, ..., pn])*

Indeed, this idea is used extentively in the larger example in the next chapter.

A note for beginners: It is possible to write a lot of Haskell code without using currying – the code is just longer and a bit less elegant-looking. If you are new to functional programming, you may find it easier to code for a while without using this language feature. If you find yourself struggling when trying to use currying, it can be useful to first write a definition that does *not* use currying and then look carefully for opportunities to introduce it as a second step.

3.6.1 Currying Simplification

We can also use currying to improve some of the previous function definitions as follows. Suppose that the values of f x and g x are the same for all values of x. Then it seems clear that the functions f and g are equivalent.[5] So, if we wish to define f in terms of g, instead of writing:

> f $x = g$ x

We could instead simply write:

> $f = g$

---

[4] It was actually Schönfinkel who first called attention to this idea [9], but the word "schönfinkelling" is rather a mouthful!

[5] In mathematics, we would say that the two functions are *extensionally equivalent*.

We can apply this reasoning to the definitions of *line* and *chord* from Section 3.4:

> *line ms* $= fold$ (:+:) (*rest* 0) *ms*
> *chord ms* $= fold$ (:=:) (*rest* 0) *ms*

Since function application is left associative, we can rewrite these as:

> *line ms*　$= (fold$ (:+:) (*rest* 0)) *ms*
> *chord ms* $= (fold$ (:=:) (*rest* 0)) *ms*

But now applying the same reasoning here that we used for *f* and *g* above means that we can write these simply as:

> *line*　$= fold$ (:+:) (*rest* 0)
> *chord* $= fold$ (:=:) (*rest* 0)

Similarly, the definitions of *toAbsPitches* and *toPitches* from Section 3.2:

> *toAbsPitches ps* $= map\ absPitch\ ps$
> *toPitches*　　*as* $= map\ pitch\ as$

can be rewritten as:

> *toAbsPitches* $= map\ absPitch$
> *toPitches*　$= map\ pitch$

Furthermore, the definition *hList*, most recently defined as:

> *hList d ps* $=$ **let** *f p* $= hNote\ d\ p$
> 　　　　　　**in** *line* (*map f ps*)

can be rewritten as:

> *hList d ps* $=$ **let** *f* $= hNote\ d$
> 　　　　　　**in** *line* (*map f ps*)

and since the definition of *f* is now so simple, we might as well "in-line" it:

> *hList d ps* $= line$ (*map* (*hNote d*) *ps*)

This kind of simplification will be referred to as "currying simplification" or just "currying."[6]

> **Details:** Some care should be taken when using this simplification idea. In particular, note that an equation such as $f\ x = g\ x\ y\ x$ cannot be simplified to $f = g\ x\ y$, since the remaining x on the right-hand side would become undefined!

---

[6] In the Lambda calculus this is called "eta contraction."

3.6.2 [Advanced] Simplification of *reverse*

Here is a more interesting example, in which currying simplification is used three times. Recall from Section 3.5 the definition of *reverse* using *foldl*:

> *reverse xs* = **let** *revOp acc x* = *x* : *acc*
>   **in** *foldl revOp* [ ] *xs*

Using the polymorphic function *flip*, which is defined in the Standard Prelude as:

> *flip*   :: $(a \rightarrow b \rightarrow c) \rightarrow (b \rightarrow a \rightarrow c)$
> *flip f x y* = *f y x*

it should be clear that *revOp* can be rewritten as:

> *revOp acc x* = *flip* (:) *acc x*

But now currying simplification can be used twice to reveal that:

> *revOp* = *flip* (:)

This, along with a third use of currying, allows us to rewrite the definition of *reverse* simply as:

> *reverse* = *foldl* (*flip* (:)) [ ]

This is, in fact, the way *reverse* is defined in the Standard Prelude.

Exercise 3.2 Show that *flip* (*flip f*) is the same as *f*.

Exercise 3.3 Define the type of *ys* in:

> *xs* = [1, 2, 3] :: [*Integer*]
> *ys* = *map* (+) *xs*

Exercise 3.4 Define a function *applyEach* that, given a list of functions, applies each to some given value. For example:

> *applyEach* [*simple* 2 2, (+3)] 5 $\Longrightarrow$ [14, 8]

where *simple* is as defined in Chapter 1.

Exercise 3.5 Define a function *applyAll* that, given a list of functions [*f1,f2, ...,fn*] and a value *v*, returns the result *f1* (*f2* (...(*fn v*)...)). For example:

> *applyAll* [*simple* 2 2, (+3)] 5 $\Longrightarrow$ 20

Exercise 3.6 Recall the discussion about the efficiency of (++) and *concat* in Chapter 3. Which of the following functions is more efficient, and why?

$appendr, appendl :: [[a]] \rightarrow [a]$
$appendr = foldr\ (flip\ (+\!\!+))\ [\,]$
$appendl = foldl\ (flip\ (+\!\!+))\ [\,]$

3.7 Errors

The last section suggested the idea of "returning an error" when the argument to *foldr1* is the empty list. As you might imagine, there are other situations where an error result is also warranted.

There are many ways to deal with such situations, depending on the application, but sometimes all we want to do is stop the program, signaling to the user that some kind of an error has occurred. In Haskell this is done with the Standard Prelude function *error* :: *String* $\rightarrow$ *a*. Note that *error* is polymorphic, meaning that it can be used with any data type. The value of the expression *error s* is $\bot$, the completely undefined, or "bottom," value that was discussed in Section 1.4. As an example of its use, here is the definition of *foldr1* from the Standard Prelude:

$foldr1$ $:: (a \rightarrow a \rightarrow a) \rightarrow [a] \rightarrow a$
$foldr1\ f\ [x]$ $= x$
$foldr1\ f\ (x : xs) = f\ x\ (foldr1\ f\ xs)$
$foldr1\ f\ [\,]$ $= error$ `"Prelude.foldr1: empty list"`

Thus, if the anomalous situation arises, the program will terminate immediately and the string `"Prelude.foldr1: empty list"` will be printed.

Exercise 3.7 Rewrite the definition of *length* non-recursively.

Exercise 3.8 Define a function that behaves as each of the following:

a) Doubles each number in a list. For example:

$doubleEach\ [1, 2, 3] \Longrightarrow [2, 4, 6]$

b) Pairs each element in a list with that number and one plus that number. For example:

$pairAndOne\ [1, 2, 3] \Longrightarrow [(1, 2), (2, 3), (3, 4)]$

c) Adds together each pair of numbers in a list. For example:

$addEachPair\ [(1, 2), (3, 4), (5, 6)] \Longrightarrow [3, 7, 11]$

d) Adds "pointwise" the elements of a list of pairs. For example:

$addPairsPointwise\ [(1, 2), (3, 4), (5, 6)] \Longrightarrow (9, 12)$

Exercise 3.9 Define a polymorphic function *fuse* :: [*Dur*] → [*Dur* → *Music a*] → [*Music a*] that combines a list of durations with a list of notes lacking a duration, to create a list of complete notes. For example:

fuse [*qn, hn, sn*] [*c* 4, *d* 4, *e* 4]
⟹ [*c* 4 *qn, d* 4 *hn, e* 4 *sn*]

You may signal an error if the lists have unequal lengths.

In the next two exercises, give both recursive and (if possible) non-recursive definitions, and be sure to include type signatures.

Exercise 3.10 Define a function *maxAbsPitch* that determines the maximum absolute pitch of a list of absolute pitches. Define *minAbsPitch* analogously. Both functions should return an error if applied to the empty list.

Exercise 3.11 Define a function *chrom* :: *Pitch* → *Pitch* → *Music Pitch* such that *chrom p1 p2* is a chromatic scale of quarter notes whose first pitch is *p1* and last pitch is *p2*. If *p1* > *p2*, the scale should be descending, otherwise it should be ascending. If *p1* == *p2*, then the scale should contain just one note. (A chromatic scale is one whose successive pitches are separated by one absolute pitch (i.e., one semitone).)

Exercise 3.12 Abstractly, a scale can be described by the intervals between successive notes. For example, the 7-note major scale can be defined as the sequence of 6 intervals [2, 2, 1, 2, 2, 2], and the 12-note chromatic scale by 11 intervals [1, 1, 1, 1, 1, 1, 1, 1, 1, 1, 1]. Define a function *mkScale* :: *Pitch* → [*Int*] → *Music Pitch* such that *mkScale p ints* is the scale beginning at pitch *p* and having the intervallic structure *ints*.

Exercise 3.13 Define an enumerated data type that captures each of the standard major scale modes: Ionian, Dorian, Phrygian, Lydian, Mixolydian, Aeolian, and Locrian. Then define a function *genScale* that, given one of these constructors, generates a scale in the intervalic form described in Exercise 3.12.

Exercise 3.14 Write the melody of "Frère Jacques" (or "Are You Sleeping?") in Euterpea. Try to make it as succinct as possible. Then, using functions already defined, generate a traditional four-part round, i.e., four identical voices, each delayed successively by two measures. Use a different instrument to realize each voice.

Exercise 3.15 Freddie the Frog wants to communicate privately with his girlfriend, Francine, by *encrypting* messages he sends to her. Frog brains are not that large, so they agree on this simple strategy: each character in the text shall be converted to the character "one greater" than it, based on the representation described below (with wrap-around from 255 to 0). Define the functions *encrypt* and *decrypt* that will allow Freddie and Francine to communicate using this strategy.

Details: Characters are often represented inside a computer as some kind of an integer; in the case of Haskell, a 16-bit unicode representation is used. However, the standard keyboard is adequately represented by a standard byte (eight bits), and thus we only need to consider the first 256 codes in the unicode representation. For the above exercise, you will want to use two Haskell functions, *toEnum* and *fromEnum*. The first will convert an integer into a character, the second will convert a character into an integer.

4

A Musical Interlude

At this point, enough detail about Haskell and Euterpea has been covered that it
is worth developing a small but full application or two. In this chapter, we will
first look at transcribing existing music into Euterpea, thus exemplifying how
to express conventional musical ideas in Euterpea. We will also take a look
at Haskell's modules system, which is important for creating larger projects.
Finally, a simple form of algorithmic composition will be presented, where it
will become apparent that more exotic things can be easily expressed as well
as simpler structures.

4.1 Transcribing an Existing Score

Let's start with something simple and likely musically familiar: the melody for
"Twinkle Twinkle Little Star," a score for which is shown in Figure 4.1. This
is a fairly straightforward melody to transcribe. One way to do it is to simply
write out all the notes as they are on the score using Euterpea's shorthand for
creating *Note*s.

twinkle =
    c 4 *qn* :+: *c* 4 *qn* :+: *g* 4 *qn* :+: *g* 4 *qn* :+: *a* 4 *qn* :+: *a* 4 *qn* :+: *g* 4 *hn* :+:
    f 4 *qn* :+: *f* 4 *qn* :+: *e* 4 *qn* :+: *e* 4 *qn* :+: *d* 4 *qn* :+: *d* 4 *qn* :+: *c* 4 *hn* :+:
    g 4 *qn* :+: *g* 4 *qn* :+: *f* 4 *qn* :+: *f* 4 *qn* :+: *e* 4 *qn* :+: *e* 4 *qn* :+: *d* 4 *hn* :+:
    g 4 *qn* :+: *g* 4 *qn* :+: *f* 4 *qn* :+: *f* 4 *qn* :+: *e* 4 *qn* :+: *e* 4 *qn* :+: *d* 4 *hn* :+:
    c 4 *qn* :+: *c* 4 *qn* :+: *g* 4 *qn* :+: *g* 4 *qn* :+: *a* 4 *qn* :+: *a* 4 *qn* :+: *g* 4 *hn* :+:
    f 4 *qn* :+: *f* 4 *qn* :+: *e* 4 *qn* :+: *e* 4 *qn* :+: *d* 4 *qn* :+: *d* 4 *qn* :+: *c* 4 *hn*

How verbose! This process would be extremely tedious if we were trying to transcribe a more complex piece of music. Fortunately, we can do
better here.

Figure 4.1 The melody of "Twinkle Twinkle Little Star."

First, observe that this is a purely sequential pattern, which makes it a good candidate for using *line* to join up a list of notes. However, this by itself won't save us much, and the resulting definition would still involve a very long list of notes. Two other points to notice are the repeating refrains (the song has an overall ABA format) and the prevalence of quarter notes that are all within the same octave. Now, let's use these points in combination with some of the language features covered in earlier chapters to create a much more concise definition.

To start, we can define a helper or auxiliary function to address the fact that we have so many notes of the form *x* 4 *qn*. Remember that there are many ways to define a note, and that all of the following are equivalent:

Prim (Note qn (C, 4))
note qn (C, 4)
c 4 qn

We can make use of the *note* function to turn *PitchClass*es into single notes as *Music Pitch* values.

pcToQN :: PitchClass → Music Pitch
pcToQN pc = note qn (pc, 4)

Then, we can use this to shrink the horizontal sprawl of the code by (1) reducing much of the melody to *PitchClass* values, (2) using *map* to turn those into notes with *pcToQN*, and finally (3) using *line* to combine lists of *Music Pitch* values.

twinkle1 =
   line (map pcToQN [C, C, G, G, A, A]) :+: g 4 hn :+:
   line (map pcToQN [F, F, E, E, D, D]) :+: c 4 hn :+:
   line (map pcToQN [G, G, F, F, E, E]) :+: d 4 hn :+:
   line (map pcToQN [G, G, F, F, E, E]) :+: d 4 hn :+:
   line (map pcToQN [C, C, G, G, A, A]) :+: g 4 hn :+:
   line (map pcToQN [F, F, E, E, D, D]) :+: c 4 hn

Now let's address the larger-scale repetition in the music. We can use a **let** statement to create definitions for individual refrains that repeat in multiple places.

$twinkle2 =$
   let $m1 = line \ (map \ pcToQN \ [C, C, G, G, A, A]) :+: g \ 4 \ hn$
      $m2 = line \ (map \ pcToQN \ [F, F, E, E, D, D]) :+: c \ 4 \ hn$
      $m3 = line \ (map \ pcToQN \ [G, G, F, F, E, E]) :+: d \ 4 \ hn$
   in $line \ [m1, m2, m3, m3, m1, m2]$

There are ways to make this definition even more concise using features described in later chapters (for example, the *pcToQN* helper function can actually be eliminated!), although when striving to reduce character count, there is something important to consider: that which is maximally concise is not necessarily maximally readable to another person. Additionally, that which is maximally concise is typically not maximally editable. For example, if we wished to have slight variations in repeats of the refrains, the last simplification we used here would defeat that. Keep these trade-offs in mind as you write code to create your own music.

4.2 Modules

But before tackling more complex examples, it's worth examining Haskell's *modules* in more detail, as these are an important aspect of code organization and structuring larger projects.

Haskell programs are partitioned into *modules* that capture common types, functions, etc., that naturally comprise an application. The first part of a module is called the module *header*, which declares what the name of the module is and what other modules it might import. For this chapter, the module's name is *Interlude*, into which the module *Euterpea* is imported:

   module *Interlude* **where**
   import *Euterpea*

Details: Module names must always be capitalized (just like type names).

Maintaining the name space of modules in a large software system can be a daunting task. So, Haskell provides a way to structure module names *hierarchically*. Indeed, because the *Interlude* module is part of the overall HSoM library, the actual module declaration that is used is:

module *HSoM.Examples.Interlude* **where**
import *Euterpea*

This says that the *Interlude* module is part of the *Examples* folder in the overall *HSoM* library. In general, these hierarchical names correspond to the folder (directory) structure of a particular implementation. Similarly, the name of the file containing the module is generally the same as the module name, plus the file extension (in this case, the name of the file is *Interlude.lhs*).

If we wish to use this module in another module, say *M*, it may be imported into *M*, just as was done above in importing *Euterpea* into *Interlude*:

module *M* **where**
import *HSoM.Examples.Interlude*

This will make available in *M* all of the names of functions, types, and so on that are defined at the top level of *Interlude*.

But this is not always what the programmer would like. Another purpose of a module is to manage the overall name space of an application. Modules allow us to structure an application in such a way that only the functionality intended for the end user is visible – everything else needed to implement the system is effectively hidden. In the case of *Interlude*, there are only two names whose visibility is desirable: *childSong6* and *prefix*. This can be achieved by writing the module header as follows:

module *HSoM.Examples.Interlude* (*childSong6*, *prefix*) **where**
import *Euterpea*

This set of visible names is sometimes called the *export list* of the module. If the list is omitted, as was done initially, then *all* names defined at the top level of the module are exported.

Although explicit type signatures in export lists are not allowed, it is sometime useful to add them as comments at least, as in:

module *HSoM.Examples.Interlude*
      (*childSong6*,   -- :: Music Pitch,

        ...

) **where**
import *Euterpea*

In this case, the list of names is sometimes called the *interface* to the module.

There are several other rules concerning the import and export of names to and from modules. Rather than introducing them all at once, they will be introduced as needed in future chapters.

4.3 Transcribing a More Complex Score

Figure 4.2 shows the first 28 bars of Chick Corea's "Children's Songs No. 6," written for electric piano [10]. Analyzing the structure of this tune explores several basic issues that arise in the transcription of an existing score into Euterpea, including repeating phrases, grace notes, triplets, tempo, and specifying an instrument. To begin, however, we will define a couple of auxiliary functions to make our job easier.

4.3.1 Auxiliary Functions

For starters, note that there are several repeating patterns of notes in this composition, each enclosed in a rectangle in Figure 4.2. In fact, the bass line

Figure 4.2 Excerpt from Chick Corea's "Children's Songs No. 6."

consists *entirely* of three repeating phrases. In anticipation of this, a function
can be defined that repeats a phrase a particular number of times:

$$times \quad :: Int \rightarrow Music\ a \rightarrow Music\ a$$
$$times\ 0\ m = rest\ 0$$
$$times\ n\ m = m :+: times\ (n-1)\ m$$

Details: Note that pattern-matching can be used on numbers. As
mentioned earlier, when there is more than one equation that defines a
function, the first equation is tried first. If it fails, the second equation is
tried, and so on. In the case above, if the first argument to *times* is not 0,
the first equation will fail. The second equation is then tried, which
always succeeds.

So, for example, *times* 3 *b1* will repeat the baseline *b1* (to be defined
shortly) three times.

To motivate the second auxiliary function, note in Figure 4.2 that there
are many melodic lines that consist of a sequence of consecutive notes
having the same duration (for example, eighth notes in the melody and dotted
quarter notes in the bass). To avoid having to write each of these durations
explicitly, we will define a function that specifies them just once. To do this,
recall that *a* 4 *qn* is a concert A quarter note. Then note that because of currying, *a* 4 is a function that can be applied to any duration – i.e., its type is *Dur* →
Music a. In other words, it is a note whose duration has not been specified yet.

With this thought in mind, we can return to the original problem and define
a function that takes a duration and a *list* of notes with the aforementioned type,
returning a *Music* value with the duration attached to each note appropriately.
In Haskell:

$$addDur \quad :: Dur \rightarrow [Dur \rightarrow Music\ a] \rightarrow Music\ a$$
$$addDur\ d\ ns = \textbf{let}\ f\ n = n\ d$$
$$\textbf{in}\ line\ (map\ f\ ns)$$

(Compare this idea with Exercise 3.9 in Chapter 3.)

Finally, a function to add a grace note to a note is defined. Grace notes can
approach the principal note from above or below, sometimes starting a half-
step away and sometimes a whole step, and can have a rhythmic interpretation
that is to a large extent up to the performer. In the case of the six uses of grace
notes in "Children's Songs No. 6," we will assume that the grace note begins
on the downbeat of the principal note, and thus its duration will subtract from

that of the principal note. We will also assume that the grace note duration is one-eighth of that of the principal note. Thus the goal is to define a function:

graceNote :: Int → Music Pitch → Music Pitch

such that *graceNote n* (*note d p*) is a *Music* value consisting of two notes, the first being the grace note whose duration is *d*/8 and whose pitch is *n* semitones higher (or lower if *n* is negative) than *p*, and the second being the principal note at pitch *p* but now with duration 7*d*/8. In Haskell:

graceNote n (*Prim* (*Note d p*)) =
  note (*d* / 8) (*trans n p*) :+: *note* (7 ∗ *d* / 8) *p*
graceNote n _   =
  error "Can only add a grace note to a note."

Note that pattern-matching is performed against the nested constructors of *Prim* and *Note*, not the lowercase function name *note*. Haskell does not permit pattern-matching against function applications. Although functions can be passed as arguments, matching against them must be done in a generic fashion, not by their particular name. Therefore,

myFunction (*Prim* (*Note d p*)) = ...

is acceptable syntax, but

myFunction (*note d p*) = ...

will cause an error message.

On the subject of errors, it is also worth noting the use of Haskell's *error* function in *graceNote*'s definition to print a customized error message – programs are not expected to ever apply *graceNote* to something other than a single note, but it is good programming practice to handle all possible cases in some way, even if it is simply to inform the user that the function was used inappropriately. In Chapter 6, a slightly more general form of *graceNote* will be defined.

The only special cases that will not be handled using auxiliary functions are the single staccato on note four of bar fifteen and the single portamento on note three of bar sixteen. These situations will be addressed differently in a later chapter.

4.3.2 Bass Line

With these auxilary functions now defined, the base line in Figure 4.2 can be defined by first noting the three repeating phrases (enclosed in rectangular boxes), which can be captured as follows:

$b1 = addDur\ dqn\ [b\ 3,\ fs\ 4,\ g\ 4,\ fs\ 4]$
$b2 = addDur\ dqn\ [b\ 3,\ es\ 4, fs\ 4, es\ 4]$
$b3 = addDur\ dqn\ [as\ 3, fs\ 4,\ g\ 4,\ fs\ 4]$

Using *times*, it is then easy to define the entire 28 bars of the base line:

$bassLine = times\ 3\ b1 :\!+\!: times\ 2\ b2 :\!+\!:$
$\qquad\qquad times\ 4\ b3 :\!+\!: times\ 5\ b1$

4.3.3 Main Voice

The upper voice of this composition is a bit more tedious to define, but is still straightforward. At the highest level, it consists of the phrase *v1* in the first two bars (in the rectangular box) repeated three times, followed by the remaining melody, which will be named *v2*:

$mainVoice = times\ 3\ v1 :\!+\!: v2$

The repeating phrase *v1* is defined by:

$v1\ = v_{1a} :\!+\!: graceNote\ (-1)\ (d\ 5\ qn) :\!+\!: v_{1b}$ -- bars 1-2
$v_{1a} = addDur\ en\ [a\ 5, e\ 5, d\ 5, fs\ 5, cs\ 5, b\ 4, e\ 5, b\ 4]$
$v_{1b} = addDur\ en\ [cs\ 5, b\ 4]$

Note the treatment of the grace note.

The remainder of the main voice, *v2*, is defined in seven pieces:

$v2 = v_{2a} :\!+\!: v_{2b} :\!+\!: v_{2c} :\!+\!: v_{2d} :\!+\!: v_{2e} :\!+\!: v_{2f} :\!+\!: v_{2g}$

with each of the pieces defined in Figure 4.3. Note that:

- The phrases are divided so as to (for the most part) line up with bar lines, for convenience. But it may be that this is not the best way to organize the music – for example, we could argue that the last two notes in bar 20 form a "pickup" to the phrase that follows, and thus more logically fall with that following phrase. The organization of the Euterpea code in this way is at the discretion of the composer.
- The staccato is treated by playing the quarter note as an eighth note; the portamento is ignored. As mentioned earlier, these ornamentations will be addressed differently in a later chapter.
- The triplet of eighth notes in bar 25 is addressed by scaling the tempo by a factor of $3/2$.

$v_{2a} = line \ [cs \ 5 \ (dhn + dhn), d \ 5 \ dhn,$
$\qquad\qquad f \ 5 \ hn, gs \ 5 \ qn, fs \ 5 \ (hn + en), g \ 5 \ en]$ -- bars 7–11
$v_{2b} = addDur \ en \ [fs \ 5, e \ 5, cs \ 5, as \ 4] :+: a \ 4 \ dqn :+:$
$\qquad\qquad addDur \ en \ [as \ 4, cs \ 5, fs \ 5, e \ 5, fs \ 5]$ -- bars 12–13
$v_{2c} = line \ [g \ 5 \ en, as \ 5 \ en, cs \ 6 \ (hn + en), d \ 6 \ en, cs \ 6 \ en] :+:$
$\qquad\ e \ 5 \ en :+: enr :+:$
$\qquad\quad line \ [as \ 5 \ en, a \ 5 \ en, g \ 5 \ en, d \ 5 \ qn, c \ 5 \ en, cs \ 5 \ en]$
$\qquad\qquad\qquad\qquad\qquad\qquad\qquad\qquad\qquad$ -- bars 14–16
$v_{2d} = addDur \ en \ [fs \ 5, cs \ 5, e \ 5, cs \ 5,$
$\qquad\qquad\qquad a \ 4, as \ 4, d \ 5, e \ 5, fs \ 5]$ -- bars 17–18.5
$v_{2e} = line \ [graceNote \ 2 \ (e \ 5 \ qn), d \ 5 \ en, graceNote \ 2 \ (d \ 5 \ qn), cs \ 5 \ en,$
$\qquad\quad graceNote \ 1 \ (cs \ 5 \ qn), b \ 4 \ (en + hn), cs \ 5 \ en, b \ 4 \ en]$
$\qquad\qquad\qquad\qquad\qquad\qquad\qquad\qquad\qquad$ -- bars 18.5–20
$v_{2f} = line \ [fs \ 5 \ en, a \ 5 \ en, b \ 5 \ (hn + qn), a \ 5 \ en, fs \ 5 \ en, e \ 5 \ qn,$
$\qquad\quad d \ 5 \ en, fs \ 5 \ en, e \ 5 \ hn, d \ 5 \ hn, fs \ 5 \ qn]$ -- bars 21–23
$v_{2g} = tempo \ (3/2) \ (line \ [cs \ 5 \ en, d \ 5 \ en, cs \ 5 \ en]) :+:$
$\qquad\quad b \ 4 \ (3 * dhn + hn)$ -- bars 24–28

Figure 4.3 Bars 7–28.

4.3.4 Putting It All Together

In the Preface to *Children's Songs: 20 Pieces for Keyboard* [10], Chick Corea notes, "Songs 1 through 15 were composed for the Fender Rhodes." Therefore, the MIDI instrument *RhodesPiano* is a logical choice for the transcription of his composition. Furthermore, note in the score that a dotted half note is specified to have a metronome value of 69. By default, the *play* function in Euterpea uses a tempo equivalent to a quarter note with a metronome value of 120. Therefore, the tempo should be scaled by a factor of (dhn / qn) $* (69 / 120)$.

These two observations lead to the final definition of the transcription of "Children's Songs No. 6" into Euterpea:

$childSong6 :: Music \ Pitch$
$childSong6 = \mathbf{let} \ t = (dhn / qn) * (69 / 120)$
$\qquad\qquad\qquad \mathbf{in} \ instrument \ RhodesPiano$
$\qquad\qquad\qquad\qquad\quad (tempo \ t \ (bassLine :=: mainVoice))$

The intent is that this is the only value that will be of interest to users of this module, and thus *childSong6* is the only name exported from this section of the module, as discussed in Section 4.2.

This example can be played through the command *play childSong6*.

Exercise 4.1 Find a simple piece of music written by your favorite composer and transcribe it into Euterpea. In doing so, look for repeating patterns, transposed phrases, etc., and reflect this in your code, thus revealing deeper structural aspects of the music than that found in common practice notation.

4.4 Simple Algorithmic Composition

Algorithmic composition is the process of designing an algorithm (or heuristic) for generating music. There are unlimited possibilities, with some trying to duplicate a particular style of music, others exploring more exotic styles; some based on traditional notions of music theory, others not; some completely deterministic, others probabilistic; and some requiring user interaction, others being completely automatic. Some even are based simply on "interpreting" data – like New York Stock Exchange numbers – in interesting ways! In this textbook, a number of algorithmic composition techniques are explored, but the possibilities are endless. Hopefully what is presented will motivate the reader to invent new, exciting algorithmic composition techniques.

To give a very tiny glimpse into algorithmic composition, we end this chapter with a very simple example. We will call this example "prefix," for reasons that will become clear shortly.

The user of this algorithm provides an initial melody (or "motif") represented as a list of notes. The main idea is to play every proper (meaning non-empty) prefix of the given melody in succession. So the first thing we do is define a polymorphic function *prefixes* :: $[a] \rightarrow [[a]]$ that returns all proper prefixes of a list:

$$
\begin{array}{ll}
prefixes & :: [a] \rightarrow [[a]] \\
prefixes\ [\,] & = [\,] \\
prefixes\ (x : xs) & = \textbf{let}\ f\ pf = x : pf \\
& \quad\ \textbf{in}\ [x] : map\ f\ (prefixes\ xs)
\end{array}
$$

We can use this to play all prefixes of a given melody *mel* in succession as follows:

$$play\ (line\ (concat\ (prefixes\ mel)))$$

But let's do a bit more. Let's create two voices (each using a different instrument), one the reverse of the other, and play them in parallel. And then let's play the whole thing once, then transposed up a perfect fourth (i.e., five semitones), then repeat the whole thing a final time. And let's package it all into one function:

prefix :: [*Music a*] → *Music a*
prefix mel = **let** *m1* = *line* (*concat* (*prefixes mel*))
                m2 = *transpose* 12 (*line* (*concat* (*prefixes* (*reverse mel*))))
              m   = *instrument Flute m1* :=: *instrument VoiceOohs m2*
        in *m* :+: *transpose* 5 *m* :+: *m*

Here are two melodies (differing only in rhythm) that you can try with this algorithm:

mel1 = [*c* 5 *en*, *e* 5 *sn*, *g* 5 *en*, *b* 5 *sn*, *a* 5 *en*, *f* 5 *sn*, *d* 5 *en*, *b* 4 *sn*, *c* 5 *en*]
mel2 = [*c* 5 *sn*, *e* 5 *sn*, *g* 5 *sn*, *b* 5 *sn*, *a* 5 *sn*, *f* 5 *sn*, *d* 5 *sn*, *b* 4 *sn*, *c* 5 *sn*]

Although not very sophisticated at all, *prefix* can generate some interesting music from a very small seed.

Another typical approach to algorithmic composition is to specify some constraints on the solution space and then generate lots of solutions that satisfy those constraints. The user can then choose one of the solutions based on aesthetic preference.

As a simple example of this, how do we choose the original melody in the prefix program above? We could require that all solutions be a multiple of some preferred meter. For example, in triple meter (say 3/4 time) we might wish for the solutions to be multiples of three quarter-note beats (i.e., one measure), or in 4/4 time, multiples of four beats. In this way, the result is always an integer number of measures. If the original melody consists of notes all of the same duration, say one beat, then the prefixes, when played sequentially, will have a total duration that is the sum of the numbers 1 through n, where n is the length of melody in beats. That sum is $n*(n+1)/2$. The first 10 sums in this series are:

$$1, 3, 6, 10, 15, 21, 28, 36, 45, 55, ...$$

The second, third, fifth, sixth, eighth, and ninth of these are divisible by three, and the seventh and eighth are divisible by four. When rendering the result, we could, for example, place an accent on the first note in each of these implied measures, thus giving the result more of a musical feel. (Placing an accent on a note will be explained in Chapters 6 and 9.)

Exercise 4.2 Try using *prefix* on your own melodies. Indeed, note that the list of notes could, in general, be a list of any *Music* values.

Exercise 4.3 Try making the following changes to *prefix*:

1. Use different instruments.
2. Change the definition of *m* in some way.
3. Compose the result in a different way.

5

Syntactic Magic

This chapter introduces several more of Haskell's syntactic devices that facilitate writing concise and intuitive programs. These devices will be used frequently in the remainder of the text.

5.1 Sections

The use of currying was introduced in Chapter 3 as a way to simplify programs. This is a syntactic device that relies on the way that normal functions are applied and how those applications are parsed.

With a bit more syntax, we can also curry applications of infix operators such as $(+)$. This syntax is called a *section*, and the idea is that in an expression such as $(x + y)$, we can omit either the x or the y and the result (with the parentheses still intact) is a function of that missing argument. If *both* variables are omitted, it is a function of *two* arguments. In other words, the expressions $(x+)$, $(+y)$, and $(+)$ are equivalent, respectively, to the functions:

$$f1\ y\ \ = x + y$$
$$f2\ x\ \ = x + y$$
$$f3\ x\ y = x + y$$

For example, suppose we wish to remove all absolute pitches greater than 99 from a list, perhaps because everything above that value is assumed to be unplayable on a particular instrument. There is a predefined function in Haskell that can help to achieve this:

$$filter :: (a \rightarrow Bool) \rightarrow [a] \rightarrow [a]$$

filter p xs returns a list for which each element x satisfies the predicate p; i.e., $p\ x$ is *True*.

Using *filter*, we can then write:

playable   :: [*AbsPitch*] → [*AbsPitch*]
playable xs = **let** *test ap* = *ap* < 100
                in *filter test xs*

But using a section, we can write this more succinctly as:

playable   :: [*AbsPitch*] → [*AbsPitch*]
playable xs = *filter* (<100) *xs*

which can be further simplified using currying:

playable :: [*AbsPitch*] → [*AbsPitch*]
playable = *filter* (<100)

This is an extremely concise definition. As you gain experience with higher-order functions, you will not only be able to start writing definitions such as this directly, but you will also start *thinking* in "higher-order" terms. Many more examples of this kind of reasoning will appear throughout the text.

Exercise 5.1 Define a function *twice* that, given a function *f*, returns a function that applies *f* twice to its argument. For example:

(*twice* (+1)) 2 ⇒ 4

What is the principal type of *twice*? Describe what *twice twice* does and give an example of its use. Also consider the functions *twice twice twice* and *twice* (*twice twice*).

Exercise 5.2 Generalize *twice* defined in the previous exercise by defining a function *power* that takes a function *f* and an integer *n* and returns a function that applies the function *f* to its argument *n* times. For example:

power (+2) 5 1 ⟹ 11

Use *power* in a musical context to define something useful.

5.2 Anonymous Functions

Another way to define a function in Haskell is in some sense the most fundamental: it is called an *anonymous function*, or *lambda expression* (since the concept is drawn directly from Church's lambda calculus [11]). The idea is that functions are values, just like numbers and characters and strings, and therefore there should be a way to create them without having to give them a name.

As a simple example, suppose we have the function $f\ x = x + 1$. Using lambda notation, we can also write the function this way: $f = \lambda x \rightarrow x + 1$, where the right-hand side of the equation would be read as "given an x, return $x+1$." Anonymous functions are most useful in situations where one wishes to avoid giving a new name to some operation in a larger context, hence making it "anonymous" instead. Anonymity is a property also shared by sections, but sections can only be derived from an existing infix operator.

Consider the use of the simple incrementing function above in a *map* statement. If the function is named, we must do this:

$f\ x = x + 1$
$ys = map\ f\ zs$

However, as an anonymous function, we only need one line:

$ys = map\ (\lambda x \rightarrow x + 1)\ zs$

Details: The typesetting used in this textbook prints an actual Greek lambda character, such as: $\lambda x \rightarrow x + 1$. However, in your programs, you will have to type "`\x -> x+1`" instead.

As another example, to raise the pitch of every element in a list of pitches *ps* by an octave, we could write:

$map\ (\lambda p \rightarrow pitch\ (absPitch\ p + 12))\ ps$

An even better example is an anonymous function that pattern-matches its argument, as in the following, which doubles the duration of every note in a list of notes *ns*:

$map\ (\lambda(Note\ d\ p) \rightarrow Note\ (2 * d)\ p)\ ns$

Details: Anonymous functions can only perform one match against an argument. That is, you cannot stack together several anonymous functions to define one function, as you can with equations. Be careful using anonymous functions over data types with multiple constructors, such as *Music*, since you can only pattern-match against a single constructor (which leaves the potential for non-exhaustive pattern-matching errors at runtime).

Anonymous functions are considered fundamental, because definitions such as that for *simple* given in Chapter 1:

$simple\ x\ y\ z = x * (y + z)$

can be written instead as:

$simple = \lambda x\ y\ z \rightarrow x * (y + z)$

Details: $\lambda x\ y\ z \rightarrow exp$ is shorthand for $\lambda x \rightarrow \lambda y \rightarrow \lambda z \rightarrow exp$.

We can also use anonymous functions to explain precisely the behavior of sections. In particular, note that:

$(x+) \Rightarrow \lambda y \rightarrow x + y$
$(+y) \Rightarrow \lambda x \rightarrow x + y$
$(+) \quad \Rightarrow \lambda x\ y \rightarrow x + y$

Exercise 5.3 Suppose we define a function *fix* as:

$fix\ f = f\ (fix\ f)$

What is the principal type of *fix*? (This is tricky!) Suppose further that we have a recursive function:

$remainder \quad :: Integer \rightarrow Integer \rightarrow Integer$
$remainder\ a\ b = \textbf{if}\ a < b\ \textbf{then}\ a$
$\qquad\qquad\qquad\quad \textbf{else}\ remainder\ (a - b)\ b$

Rewrite this function using *fix* so that there is no recursive call to *remainder*. (Also tricky!) Do you think that this process can be applied to *any* recursive function?

5.3 List Comprehensions

Haskell has a convenient and intuitive way to define a list in such a way that it resembles the definition of a *set* in mathematics. For example, recall in the last chapter the definition of the function *addDur*:

$addDur \quad :: Dur \rightarrow [Dur \rightarrow Music\ a] \rightarrow Music\ a$
$addDur\ d\ ns = \textbf{let}\ f\ n = n\ d$
$\qquad\qquad\qquad \textbf{in}\ line\ (map\ f\ ns)$

Here *ns* is a list of notes, each of which does not have a duration yet assigned to it. If we think of this as a set, we might be led to write the following solution in mathematical notation:

$$\{n\ d \mid n \in ns\}$$

which can be read as "the set of all notes *n d* such that *n* is an element of *ns*." Indeed, using a Haskell *list comprehension*, we can write almost exactly the same thing:

$$[n\ d \mid n \leftarrow ns]$$

The difference, of course, is that the above expression generates an ordered list in Haskell, not an unordered set in mathematics.

List comprehensions allow us to rewrite the definition of *addDur* much more succinctly and elegantly:

$$addDur \quad :: Dur \rightarrow [Dur \rightarrow Music\ a] \rightarrow Music\ a$$
$$addDur\ d\ ns = line\ [n\ d \mid n \leftarrow ns]$$

Details: Liberty is again taken in typesetting by using the symbol $\leftarrow$ to mean "is an element of." When writing your programs, you will have to type "`<-`" instead.

The expression $[exp \mid x \leftarrow xs]$ is actually shorthand for the expression *map* $(\lambda x \rightarrow exp)\ xs$. The form $x \leftarrow xs$ is called a *generator*, and in general more than one is allowed, as in:

$$[(x, y) \mid x \leftarrow [0, 1, 2], y \leftarrow ['a', 'b']]$$

which evaluates to the list:

$$[(0, 'a'), (0, 'b'), (1, 'a'), (1, 'b'), (2, 'a'), (2, 'b')]$$

The order here is important; that is, note that the leftmost generator changes the least quickly.

It is also possible to *filter* values as they are generated; for example, we can modify the above example to eliminate the odd integers in the first list:

$$[(x, y) \mid x \leftarrow [0, 1, 2], even\ x, y \leftarrow ['a', 'b']]$$

where *even n* returns *True* if *n* is even. This example evaluates to:

$$[(0, 'a'), (0, 'b'), (2, 'a'), (2, 'b')]$$

> **Details:** When reasoning about list comprehensions (e.g., when doing proof by calculation), we can use the following syntactic translation into pure functions:
>
> $$[e \mid True] \qquad = [e]$$
> $$[e \mid q] \qquad\quad = [e \mid q, True]$$
> $$[e \mid b, qs] \qquad = \textbf{if } b \textbf{ then } [e \mid qs] \textbf{ else } [\,]$$
> $$[e \mid p \leftarrow xs, qs] = \textbf{let } ok\ p = [e \mid qs]$$
> $$ok\ \_ = [\,]$$
> $$\textbf{in } concatMap\ ok\ xs$$
> $$[e \mid \textbf{let } decls, qs] = \textbf{let } decls \textbf{ in } [e \mid qs]$$
>
> where q is a single qualifier, qs is a sequence of qualifiers, b is a Boolean, p is a pattern, and $decls$ is a sequence of variable bindings (a feature of list comprehensions not explained earlier).

5.3.1 Arithmetic Sequences

Another convenient syntax for lists whose elements can be enumerated is called an *arithmetic sequence*. For example, the arithmetic sequence $[1 \ldots 10]$ is equivalent to the list:

$$[1, 2, 3, 4, 5, 6, 7, 8, 9, 10]$$

There are actually four different versions of arithmetic sequences, some of which generate *infinite* lists (whose use will be discussed in a later chapter). In the following, let $a = n' - n$:

$$[n \mathrel{..}] \qquad\quad \text{-- infinite list } n, n + 1, n + 2, \ldots$$
$$[n, n' \mathrel{..}] \qquad \text{-- infinite list } n, n + a, n + 2 * a, \ldots$$
$$[n \mathrel{..} m] \qquad\; \text{-- finite list } n, n + 1, n + 2, \ldots, m$$
$$[n, n' \mathrel{..} m] \quad \text{-- finite list } n, n + a, n + 2 * a, \ldots, m$$

Arithmetic sequences are discussed in greater detail in Appendix B.

Exercise 5.4 Using list comprehensions, define a function:

$$apPairs :: [AbsPitch] \rightarrow [AbsPitch] \rightarrow [(AbsPitch, AbsPitch)]$$

such that *apPairs aps1 aps2* is a list of all combinations of the absolute pitches in *aps1* and *aps2*. Furthermore, for each pair $(ap1, ap2)$ in the result, the absolute value of $ap1 - ap2$ must be greater than two and less than eight.

Finally, write a function to turn the result of *apPairs* into a *Music Pitch* value by playing each pair of pitches in parallel and stringing them all together sequentially. Try varying the rhythm by, for example, using an eighth note when the first absolute pitch is odd and a sixteenth note when it is even, or some other criterion.

Test your functions by using arithmetic sequences to generate the two lists of arguments given to *apPairs*.

5.4 Function Composition

An example of polymorphism that has nothing to do with data structures arises from the desire to take two functions *f* and *g* and "glue them together," yielding another function *h* that first applies *g* to its argument, and then applies *f* to that result. This is called function *composition* (just as in mathematics), and Haskell predefines a simple infix operator (∘) to achieve it, as follows:

$$(\circ) \qquad :: (b \to c) \to (a \to b) \to a \to c$$
$$(f \circ g)\ x = f\ (g\ x)$$

> **Details:** The symbol for function composition is typeset in this textbook as ∘, which is consistent with mathematical convention. When writing your programs, however, you will have to use a period, as in "f . g".

Note the type of the operator (∘); it is completely polymorphic. Note also that the result of the first function to be applied – some type *b* – must be the same as the type of the argument to the second function to be applied. Pictorially, if we think of a function as a black box that takes input at one end and returns some output at the other, function composition is like connecting two boxes together, end to end, as shown in Figure 5.1.

The ability to compose functions using (∘) is quite handy. For example, recall the last version of *hList*:

$$hList\ d\ ps = line\ (map\ (hNote\ d)\ ps)$$

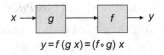

$$y = f\ (g\ x) = (f \circ g)\ x$$

Figure 5.1 Gluing two functions together.

We can do two simplifications here. First, rewrite the right-hand side using function composition:

hList d ps = (line ∘ map (hNote d)) ps

Then, use currying simplification:

hList d = line ∘ map (hNote d)

5.5 Higher-Order Thinking

It is worth taking a deep breath here and contemplating what has been done with *hList*, which has gone through quite a few transformations. Here is the original definition given in Chapter 1:

hList d [] = rest 0
hList d (p : ps) = hNote d p :+: hList d ps

Compare this to the definition above. You may be distressed to think that you have to go through all of these transformations just to write a relatively simple function! There are two points to make about this: First, you do not have to make *any* of these transformations if you do not want to. All of these versions of *hList* are correct, and they all run about equally fast. They are explained here for pedagogical purposes, so that you understand the full power of Haskell. Second, with practice, you will find that you can write the concise higher-order versions of many functions straight away, without going through all of the steps presented here.

As mentioned earlier, one thing that helps is to start *thinking* in "higher-order" terms. To facilitate this way of thinking, it is helpful to write type signatures that more closely reflect their higher-order nature. For example, recall these type signatures for *map*, *filter*, and (∘):

map :: $(a \rightarrow b) \rightarrow [a] \rightarrow [b]$
filter :: $(a \rightarrow Bool) \rightarrow [a] \rightarrow [a]$
(∘) :: $(b \rightarrow c) \rightarrow (a \rightarrow b) \rightarrow a \rightarrow c$

Also recall that the arrow in function types is right-associative. Therefore, another completely equivalent way to write the above type signatures is:

map :: $(a \rightarrow b) \rightarrow ([a] \rightarrow [b])$
filter :: $(a \rightarrow Bool) \rightarrow ([a] \rightarrow [a])$
(∘) :: $(b \rightarrow c) \rightarrow (a \rightarrow b) \rightarrow (a \rightarrow c)$

Although equivalent, the latter versions emphasize the fact that each of these functions returns a function as its result. *map* essentially "lifts" a function on elements to a function on lists of elements. *filter* converts a predicate into a function on lists. And (∘) returns a function that is the composition of its two functional arguments.

So, for example, using higher-order thinking, *map* (+12) is a function that transposes a list of absolute pitches by one octave, and *filter* (<100) is a function that removes all absolute pitches greater than or equal to 100 (as discussed earlier). Therefore, *map* (+12) ∘ *filter* (<100) first does the filtering, and then does the transposition. All very concise and very natural using higher-order thinking.

In the remainder of this textbook, definitions such as this will be written directly, using a small set of rich polymorphic functions such as *foldl*, *map*, *filter*, (∘), and a few other functions drawn from the Standard Prelude and other standard libraries.

5.6 Infix Function Application

Haskell predefines an infix operator to apply a function to a value:

$$f \ \$ \ x = f \ x$$

At first glance, this does not seem very useful – after all, why not simply write $f \ x$ instead of $f \ \$ \ x$?

But in fact, this operator has a very useful purpose: to eliminate parentheses! In the Standard Prelude, ($) is defined to be right-associative and to have the lowest precedence level, via the fixity declaration:

infixr 0 $

Therefore, note that $f \ (g \ x)$ is the same as $f \ \$ \ g \ x$ (remember that normal function application always has higher precedence than infix operator application), and $f \ (x + 1)$ is the same as $f \ \$ \ x + 1$. This "trick" is especially useful when there is a sequence of nested parenthesized expressions. For example, recall the following definition from the last chapter:

$childSong6 = $ **let** $t = (dhn / qn) * (69 / 120)$
               in *instrument RhodesPiano*
                        $(tempo \ t \ (bassLine :=: mainVoice))$

We can rewrite the last few lines a bit more clearly, as follows:

$childSong6 = $ **let** $t = (dhn / qn) * (69 / 120)$
               in *instrument RhodesPiano* $
                        tempo t $
                        $bassLine :=: mainVoice$

Or, on a single line, instead of:

   instrument RhodesPiano (*tempo t* (*bassLine* :=: *mainVoice*))

we can write:

   instrument RhodesPiano $ *tempo t* $ *bassLine* :=: *mainVoice*

Exercise 5.5 The last definition of *hList* still has an argument *d* on the left-hand side and one occurrence of *d* on the right-hand side. Is there some way to eliminate it using currying simplification? (Hint: The answer is yes, but the solution is a bit perverse, and is not recommended as a way to write your code!)

Exercise 5.6 Use *line*, *map*, and ($) to give a concise definition of *addDur*.

Exercise 5.7 Rewrite this example:

   $map\ (\lambda x \rightarrow (x+1)/2)\ xs$

using a composition of sections.

Exercise 5.8 Consider the expression:

   $map\ f\ (map\ g\ xs)$

Rewrite this using function composition and a single call to *map*. Then rewrite the earlier example:

   $map\ (\lambda x \rightarrow (x+1)/2)\ xs$

as a "map of a map" (i.e., using two maps).

Exercise 5.9 Go back to any exercises prior to this chapter and simplify your solutions using ideas learned here.

Exercise 5.10 Using higher-order functions introduced in this chapter, fill in the two missing functions, *f1* and *f2*, in the evaluation below so that it is valid:

   $f1\ (f2\ (*)\ [1,2,3,4])\ 5 \Rightarrow [5,10,15,20]$

6

More Music

This chapter explores a number of simple strategies for manipulating Euterpea's musical structures. The operations described here mirror common tactics used in music composition to transform musical material, such as the notion of inverting a melody.

6.1 Delay and Repeat

We can *offset* the start of a music value in time simply by inserting a rest in front of it, which can be packaged in a function as follows:

offset $:: Dur \rightarrow Music\ a \rightarrow Music\ a$
offset d m = rest d :+: m

With *offset*, it is easy to write canon-like structures such as $m :=:$ *offset d m*, a song written in rounds (see Exercise 3.14), and so on.

Recall from Chapter 4 the function *times* that repeats a musical phrase a certain number of times:

times $:: Int \rightarrow Music\ a \rightarrow Music\ a$
times $0\ m =$ *rest* 0
times n m = m :+: times $(n - 1)\ m$

More interestingly, Haskell's non-strict semantics allows us to define *infinite* musical values. For example, a musical value may be repeated *forever* using this simple function:

forever $:: Music\ a \rightarrow Music\ a$
forever m = m :+: forever m

Thus, for example, an infinite ostinato can be expressed in this way, and then used in different contexts that automatically extract only the portion that is actually needed. Functions that create such contexts will be described shortly.

6.2 Inversion and Retrograde

The notions of inversion, retrograde, retrograde inversion, etc., as used in 12-tone theory are also easily captured in Euterpea. These terms are usually applied only to a "line" of notes, i.e., a melody (in 12-tone theory, it is called a "row"). The *retrograde* of a line is simply its reverse – i.e., the notes played in the reverse order. The *inversion* of a line is with respect to a given pitch (by convention, usually the first pitch), where the intervals between successive pitches are inverted, i.e., negated. If the absolute pitch of the first note is *ap*, then each pitch *p* is converted into an absolute pitch $ap - (absPitch\ p - ap)$, in other words, $2 * ap - absPitch\ p$.

To do all this in Haskell, a transformation from a line created by *line* to a list is defined:

```
lineToList                    :: Music a → [Music a]
lineToList (Prim (Rest 0)) = [ ]
lineToList (n :+: ns)       = n : lineToList ns
lineToList _                  =
    error "lineToList: argument not created by function line"
```

Using this function, it is then straightforward to define *invert*:

```
invert :: Music Pitch → Music Pitch
invert m =
    let l@(Prim (Note _ r) : _) = lineToList m
        inv (Prim (Note d p)) =
                note d (pitch (2 * absPitch r − absPitch p))
        inv (Prim (Rest d))   = rest d
    in line (map inv l)
```

Details: The pattern *l*@(*Prim* (*Note* _ r) : _) is called an *as pattern*. It behaves just like the pattern *Prim* (*Note* _ r) : _ but additionally binds *l* to the value of a successful match to that pattern. *l* can then be used wherever it is in scope, such as in the last line of the function definition.

Figure 6.1 A simple melody and four transformations.

With *lineToList* and *invert*, it is then easy to define the remaining functions via composition:

retro, *retroInvert*, *invertRetro* :: *Music Pitch* → *Music Pitch*
retro   = *line* ○ *reverse* ○ *lineToList*
retroInvert = *retro* ○ *invert*
invertRetro = *invert* ○ *retro*

As an example of these concepts, Figure 6.1 shows a simple melody (not a complete 12-tone row) and four transformations of it.

Exercise 6.1 Show that *retro* ○ *retro*, *invert* ○ *invert*, and *retroInvert* ○ *invertRetro* are the identities on values created by *line*. (You may use the lemma that *reverse* (*reverse l*) = *l*.)

Exercise 6.2 Define a function *properRow* :: *Music Pitch* → *Bool* that determines whether or not its argument is a "proper" 12-tone row, meaning that: (a) it must have exactly 12 notes, and (b) each unique pitch class is used exactly once (regardless of the octave). Enharmonically equivalent pitch classes are *not* considered unique. You may assume that the *Music Pitch* value is generated by the function *line*, but note that rests are allowed.

Exercise 6.3 Define a function *palin* :: *Music Pitch* → *Bool* that determines whether or not a given line (as generated by the *line* function) is a palindrome or not. You should ignore rests and disregard note durations – the main question is whether or not the melody is a palindrome.

Exercise 6.4 Define a function *retroPitches* :: *Music Pitch* → *Music Pitch* that reverses the pitches in a line but maintains the durations in the same order from beginning to end. For example:

retroPitches (*line* [*c* 4 *en*, *d* 4 *qn*])
⟹ (*line* [*d* 4 *en*, *c* 4 *qn*])

6.3 Computing Duration

It is often desirable to compute the *duration*, in whole notes, of a musical value; we can do so as follows:

$$dur \qquad\qquad :: Music\ a \to Dur$$
$$dur\ (Prim\ (Note\ d\ \_)) \quad = d$$
$$dur\ (Prim\ (Rest\ d)) \qquad = d$$
$$dur\ (m1 :\!+\!: m2) \qquad = dur\ m1 + dur\ m2$$
$$dur\ (m1 :\!=\!: m2) \qquad = dur\ m1\ \text{`}max\text{`}\ dur\ m2$$
$$dur\ (Modify\ (Tempo\ r)\ m) = dur\ m/r$$
$$dur\ (Modify\ \_\ m) \qquad = dur\ m$$

The duration of a primitive value is obvious. The duration of $m1 :\!+\!: m2$ is the sum of the two, and the duration of $m1 :\!=\!: m2$ is the maximum of the two. The only tricky case is the duration of a music value that is modified by the *Tempo* attribute – in this case, the duration must be scaled appropriately.

Note that the duration of a music value that is conceptually infinite in duration will be $\bot$, since *dur* will not terminate. (Similarly, taking the length of an infinite list is $\bot$.) For example:

$$dur\ (forever\ (a\ 4\ qn))$$
$$\Rightarrow dur\ (a\ 4\ qn :\!+\!: forever\ (a\ 4\ qn))$$
$$\Rightarrow dur\ (a\ 4\ qn) + dur\ (forever\ (a\ 4\ qn))$$
$$\Rightarrow qn + dur\ (forever\ (a\ 4\ qn))$$
$$\Rightarrow qn + qn + dur\ (forever\ (a\ 4\ qn))$$
$$\Rightarrow \ ...$$
$$\Rightarrow \bot$$

6.4 Super-Retrograde

Using *dur*, we can redefine *retro* that reverses any *Music* value whose duration is finite (and is thus considerably more useful than the version defined earlier):

$$retro \qquad\qquad :: Music\ a \to Music\ a$$
$$retro\ n@(Prim\ \_) = n$$
$$retro\ (Modify\ c\ m) = Modify\ c\ (retro\ m)$$
$$retro\ (m1 :\!+\!: m2) = retro\ m2 :\!+\!: retro\ m1$$
$$retro\ (m1 :\!=\!: m2) =$$
$$\quad \textbf{let}\ d1 = dur\ m1$$
$$\qquad d2 = dur\ m2$$

in if $d1 > d2$ **then** *retro m1* :=: (*rest* $(d1 - d2)$:+: *retro m2*)
                        else (*rest* $(d2 - d1)$:+: *retro m1*) :=: *retro m2*

The first three cases are easy, but the last case is a bit tricky. The parallel constructor (:=:) implicitly begins each of its music values at the same time. But if one is shorter than the other, then, when reversed, a *rest* must be inserted before the shorter one, to account for the difference.

Note that *retro* of a *Music* value whose duration is infinite is ⊥. (Analogously, reversing an infinite list is ⊥.)

6.5 *cut* and *remove*

Two other useful operations on *Music* values are the ability to take or *cut* some duration (in whole notes) of music from the beginning, discarding the rest, and, conversely, the ability to *remove* some duration of music from the beginning, returning what is left. We will first define a function *cut* :: *Dur* → *Music a* → *Music a* such that *cut d m* is a *prefix* of *m* having duration *d*. In other words, it "takes" only the first *d* beats (in whole notes) of *m*. We can define this function as follows:

cut :: *Dur* → *Music a* → *Music a*
cut d m | $d \leqslant 0$ = *rest* 0
cut d (*Prim* (*Note oldD p*)) = *note* (*min oldD d*) *p*
cut d (*Prim* (*Rest oldD*))   = *rest* (*min oldD d*)
cut d (*m1* :=: *m2*)   = *cut d m1* :=: *cut d m2*
cut d (*m1* :+: *m2*)   = **let** *m'1* = *cut d m1*
                                          m'2 = *cut* $(d - dur\ m'1)$ *m2*
                                   in *m'1* :+: *m'2*
cut d (*Modify* (*Tempo r*) *m*) = *tempo r* (*cut* $(d * r)$ *m*)
cut d (*Modify c m*)   = *Modify c* (*cut d m*)

This definition is fairly straightforward, except for the case of sequential composition, where two cases arise: (1) if *d* is greater than *dur m1*, then we return *all* of *m1* (i.e., *m'1* = *m1*), followed by $d - dur\ m'1$ beats of *m2*, and (2) if *d* is less than *dur m1*, then we return *d* beats of *m1* (i.e., *m'1*), followed by nothing (since $d - dur\ m'1$ will be zero). Note that this strategy will work even if *m1* or *m2* is infinite.

Similarly, we can define a function *remove* :: *Dur* → *Music a* → *Music a* such that *remove d m* is a *suffix* of *m* where the first *d* beats (in whole notes) of *m* have been "dropped":

remove :: *Dur* → *Music a* → *Music a*
remove d m | *d* ≤ 0   = *m*
remove d (*Prim* (*Note oldD p*)) = *note* (*max* (*oldD* − *d*) 0) *p*
remove d (*Prim* (*Rest oldD*))   = *rest* (*max* (*oldD* − *d*) 0)
remove d (*m1* :=: *m2*)   = *remove d m1* :=: *remove d m2*
remove d (*m1* :+: *m2*)   = **let** *m′1* = *remove d m1*
                                         m′2 = *remove* (*d* − *dur m1*) *m2*
                                      in *m′1* :+: *m′2*
remove d (*Modify* (*Tempo r*) *m*) = *tempo r* (*remove* (*d* ∗ *r*) *m*)
remove d (*Modify c m*)   = *Modify c* (*remove d m*)

This definition is also straightforward, except for the case of sequential composition. Again, two cases arise: (1) if *d* is greater than *dur m1*, then we drop *m1* altogether (i.e., *m′1* will be *rest* 0) and simply drop *d* − *dur m1* from *m2*, and (2) if *d* is less than *dur m1*, then we return *m′1*, followed by all of *m2* (since *d* − *dur m1* will be negative). This definition, too, will work for infinite values of *m1* or *m2*.

6.6 Removing Zeros

Note that functions such as *times*, *line*, *retro*, *cut*, and *remove* occasionally insert rests of zero duration and, in the case of *cut* and *remove*, may insert notes of zero duration. Doing this makes the code simpler and more elegant, and since we cannot hear the effect of the zero-duration events, the musical result is the same.

On the other hand, these extraneous notes and rests (which we will call "zeros") can be annoying when viewing the textual (rather than hearing the audible) representation of the result. To alleviate this problem, we define a function that removes them from a given *Music* value:

removeZeros :: *Music a* → *Music a*
removeZeros (*Prim p*)   = *Prim p*
removeZeros (*m1* :+: *m2*) =
   let *m′1* = *removeZeros m1*
      m′2 = *removeZeros m2*
   in case (*m′1*, *m′2*) **of**
      (*Prim* (*Note* 0 *p*), *m*) → *m*
      (*Prim* (*Rest* 0), *m*)   → *m*
      (*m*, *Prim* (*Note* 0 *p*)) → *m*

$$(m, Prim\ (Rest\ 0))\quad \rightarrow\ m$$
$$(m1, m2)\qquad\qquad\quad \rightarrow\ m1\ :+:\ m2$$
$$removeZeros\ (m1\ :=:\ m2)\ =$$

let $m'1\ =\ removeZeros\ m1$
      $m'2\ =\ removeZeros\ m2$
in case $(m'1, m'2)$ **of**
      $(Prim\ (Note\ 0\ p), m)\ \rightarrow\ m$
      $(Prim\ (Rest\ 0), m)\quad \rightarrow\ m$
      $(m, Prim\ (Note\ 0\ p))\ \rightarrow\ m$
      $(m, Prim\ (Rest\ 0))\quad \rightarrow\ m$
      $(m1, m2)\qquad\qquad \rightarrow\ m1\ :=:\ m2$
$removeZeros\ (Modify\ c\ m)\ =\ Modify\ c\ (removeZeros\ m)$

Details: A **case** expression can only match against one value. To match against more than one value, we can place them in a tuple of the appropriate length. In the case above, *removeZeros* matches against $m'1$ and $m'2$ by placing them in a pair $(m'1, m'2)$.

This function depends on the "musical axiom" that if *m1* in either *m1* :+: *m2* or *m1* :=: *m2* is a zero, then the latter expressions are equivalent to just *m2*. Similarly, if *m2* is a zero, they are equivalent to just *m1*. Although this is intuitive, a formal proof of these axioms is deferred until Chapter 12.

As an example of using *removeZeros*, consider the *Music* value:

$$m\ =\ c\ 4\ en\ :+:\ forever\ (d\ 4\ en)$$

Then note that:

$$cut\ hn\ (remove\ hn\ m)$$
$$\Longrightarrow$$

$Prim\ (Note\ (0\ \%\ 1)\ (C, 4))\ :+:\ (Prim\ (Note\ (0\ \%\ 1)\ (D, 4))\ :+:$
$(Prim\ (Note\ (0\ \%\ 1)\ (D, 4))\ :+:\ (Prim\ (Note\ (0\ \%\ 1)\ (D, 4))\ :+:$
$(Prim\ (Note\ (1\ \%\ 8)\ (D, 4))\ :+:\ (Prim\ (Note\ (1\ \%\ 8)\ (D, 4))\ :+:$
$(Prim\ (Note\ (1\ \%\ 8)\ (D, 4))\ :+:\ (Prim\ (Note\ (1\ \%\ 8)\ (D, 4))\ :+:$
$Prim\ (Rest\ (0\ \%\ 1)))))))))$

Note the zero-duration notes and rests. But if we apply *removeZeros* to the result, we get:

removeZeros (*cut hn* (*remove hn m*))

$\Longrightarrow$

Prim (*Note* (1 % 8) (*D*, 4)) :+: (*Prim* (*Note* (1 % 8) (*D*, 4)) :+:

(*Prim* (*Note* (1 % 8) (*D*, 4)) :+: *Prim* (*Note* (1 % 8) (*D*, 4))))

Both the zero-duration rests and notes have been removed.

6.7 Truncating Parallel Composition

The duration of *m1* :=: *m2* is the maximum of the durations of *m1* and *m2* (and thus if one is infinite, so is the result). However, sometimes it is useful to have the result be of a duration equal to the *shorter* of the two. Defining a function to achieve this is not as easy as it sounds, since it may require truncating the longer one in the middle of a note (or notes), and it may be that one (or both) of the *Music* values is infinite.

The goal is to define a "truncating parallel composition" operator (/=:) :: *Music a* → *Music a* → *Music a*. Using *cut*, we can make an initial attempt at a suitable definition for (/=:) as follows:

(/=:)   :: *Music a* → *Music a* → *Music a*

m1 /=: *m2* = *cut* (*dur m2*) *m1* :=: *cut* (*dur m1*) *m2*

Unfortunately, whereas *cut* can handle infinite-duration music values, (/=:) cannot. This is because (/=:) computes the duration of both of its arguments, but if one of them, say *m1*, has infinite duration, then *dur m1* $\Rightarrow$ $\bot$. If, in a particular context, we know that only one of the two arguments is infinite, and we know which one (say *m1*), it is always possible to write:

cut (*dur m2*) *m1* :=: *m2*

But somehow this seems unsatisfactory.

6.7.1 Lazy Evaluation to the Rescue

The root of this problem is that *dur* uses a conventional number type, namely the type *Rational* (which is a ratio of *Integers*), to compute with, which does not have a value for infinity ($\bot$ is not the same as infinity!). But what if we were to somehow compute the duration *lazily* – meaning that we only compute as much of the duration that is needed to perform some arithmetic result of interest. In particular, if we have one number n that we know is "at least" x, and another number m that is exactly y, then if $x > y$, we know that $n > m$, even if n's actual value is infinity!

To realize this idea, let's first define a type synonym for "lazy durations":

type $LazyDur = [Dur]$

The intent is that a value $d :: LazyDur$ is a non-decreasing list of durations such that the last element in the list is the actual duration, and an infinite list implies an infinite duration.

Now let's define a new version of dur that computes the $LazyDur$ of its argument:

$$
\begin{aligned}
&durL :: Music\ a \rightarrow LazyDur \\
&durL\ m@(Prim\ \_) && = [dur\ m] \\
&durL\ (m1 :+: m2) && = \textbf{let}\ d1 = durL\ m1 \\
& && \quad \textbf{in}\ d1 \mathbin{+\!\!+} map\ (+(last\ d1))\ (durL\ m2) \\
&durL\ (m1 :=: m2) && = mergeLD\ (durL\ m1)\ (durL\ m2) \\
&durL\ (Modify\ (Tempo\ r)\ m) = map\ (/r)\ (durL\ m) \\
&durL\ (Modify\ \_\ m) && = durL\ m
\end{aligned}
$$

where $mergeLD$ merges two $LazyDur$ values into one:

$$
\begin{aligned}
&mergeLD :: LazyDur \rightarrow LazyDur \rightarrow LazyDur \\
&mergeLD\ [\ ]\ ld = ld \\
&mergeLD\ ld\ [\ ] = ld \\
&mergeLD\ ld1@(d1 : ds1)\ ld2@(d2 : ds2) = \\
&\quad \textbf{if}\ d1 < d2\ \textbf{then}\ d1 : mergeLD\ ds1\ ld2 \\
&\qquad\qquad\quad \textbf{else}\quad d2 : mergeLD\ ld1\ ds2
\end{aligned}
$$

We can then define a function $minL$ to compare a $LazyDur$ with a regular Dur, returning the least Dur as a result:

$$
\begin{aligned}
&minL :: LazyDur \rightarrow Dur \rightarrow Dur \\
&minL\ [\ ] \qquad d' = 0 \\
&minL\ [d] \qquad d' = min\ d\ d' \\
&minL\ (d : ds)\ d' = \textbf{if}\ d < d'\ \textbf{then}\ minL\ ds\ d'\ \textbf{else}\ d'
\end{aligned}
$$

And with $minL$, we can then define a new version of cut:

$$
\begin{aligned}
&cutL :: LazyDur \rightarrow Music\ a \rightarrow Music\ a \\
&cutL\ [\ ]\ m && = rest\ 0 \\
&cutL\ (d : ds)\ m\ |\ d \leqslant 0 && = cutL\ ds\ m \\
&cutL\ ld\ (Prim\ (Note\ oldD\ p)) && = note\ (minL\ ld\ oldD)\ p \\
&cutL\ ld\ (Prim\ (Rest\ oldD)) && = rest\ (minL\ ld\ oldD) \\
&cutL\ ld\ (m1 :=: m2) && = cutL\ ld\ m1 :=: cutL\ ld\ m2
\end{aligned}
$$

cutL ld (*m1* :+: *m2*)   =
  let *m'1* = *cutL ld m1*
      m'2 = *cutL* (*map* (λ*d* → *d* − *dur m'1*) *ld*) *m2*
  in *m'1* :+: *m'2*
cutL ld (*Modify* (*Tempo r*) *m*) = *tempo r* (*cutL* (*map* (∗*r*) *ld*) *m*)
cutL ld (*Modify c m*)   = *Modify c* (*cutL ld m*)

Compare this definition with that of *cut* – they are very similar.

Finally, we can define a correct (meaning it works properly on infinite *Music* values) version of (/=:) as follows:

(/=:)   :: *Music a* → *Music a* → *Music a*
m1 /=: *m2* = *cutL* (*durL m2*) *m1* :=: *cutL* (*durL m1*) *m2*

Whew! This may seem like a lot of effort, but the new code is actually not much different from the old, and now we can freely use (/=:) without worrying about which, if any, of its arguments are infinite.

Exercise 6.5 Try using (/=:) with some infinite *Music* values (such as created by *forever*) to assure yourself that it works properly. When using it with *two* infinite values, it should return an infinite value, which you can test by applying *cut* to the result.

6.8 Trills

A *trill* is an ornament that alternates rapidly between two (usually adjacent) pitches. Two versions of a trill function will be defined, both of which take the starting note and an interval for the trill note as arguments (the interval is usually one or two, but can actually be anything). One version will additionally have an argument that specifies how long each trill note should be, whereas the other will have an argument that specifies how many trills should occur. In both cases, the total duration will be the same as the duration of the original note.

Here is the first trill function:

trill :: *Int* → *Dur* → *Music Pitch* → *Music Pitch*
trill i sDur (*Prim* (*Note tDur p*)) =
  if *sDur* ⩾ *tDur* **then** *note tDur p*
              else *note sDur p* :+:
                  trill (*negate i*) *sDur*
                      (*note* (*tDur* − *sDur*) (*trans i p*))
trill i d (*Modify* (*Tempo r*) *m*) = *tempo r* (*trill i* (*d* ∗ *r*) *m*)

ssfMel :: *Music Pitch*
ssfMel = *line* (*l1* ++ *l2* ++ *l3* ++ *l4*)
   where *l1* = [*trilln* 2 5 (*bf* 6 *en*), *ef* 7 *en*, *ef* 6 *en*, *ef* 7 *en*]
          l2 = [*bf* 6 *sn*, *c* 7 *sn*, *bf* 6 *sn*, *g* 6 *sn*, *ef* 6 *en*, *bf* 5 *en*]
          l3 = [*ef* 6 *sn*, *f* 6 *sn*, *g* 6 *sn*, *af* 6 *sn*, *bf* 6 *en*, *ef* 7 *en*]
          l4 = [*trill* 2 *tn* (*bf* 6 *qn*), *bf* 6 *sn*, *denr*]
starsAndStripes :: *Music Pitch*
starsAndStripes = *instrument Flute ssfMel*

Figure 6.2 Trills in "The Stars and Stripes Forever."

trill i d (*Modify c m*) = *Modify c* (*trill i d m*)
trill _ _ _   =
   error "trill: input must be a single note."

Using this function, it is simple to define a version that starts on the trill note rather than the start note:

trill' :: *Int* → *Dur* → *Music Pitch* → *Music Pitch*
trill' i sDur m = *trill* (*negate i*) *sDur* (*transpose i m*)

The second way to define a trill is in terms of the number of subdivided notes to be included in the trill. We can use the first trill function to define this new one:[1]

trilln :: *Int* → *Int* → *Music Pitch* → *Music Pitch*
trilln i nTimes m = *trill i* (*dur m*/*fromIntegral nTimes*) *m*

This, too, can be made to start on the other note.

trilln' :: *Int* → *Int* → *Music Pitch* → *Music Pitch*
trilln' i nTimes m = *trilln* (*negate i*) *nTimes* (*transpose i m*)

Finally, a *roll* can be implemented as a trill whose interval is zero. This feature is particularly useful for percussion.

roll :: *Dur* → *Music Pitch* → *Music Pitch*
rolln :: *Int* → *Music Pitch* → *Music Pitch*

roll dur m = *trill* 0 *dur m*
rolln nTimes m = *trilln* 0 *nTimes m*

Figure 6.2 shows a nice use of the trill functions in encoding the opening lines of John Philip Sousa's "The Stars and Stripes Forever."

---

[1] Note that we must introduce a new function here: *fromIntegral*. This is necessary to convert between Haskell's numerical types, since division, (/), requires floating point numbers rather than integers.

Details: *ssfMel* uses a **where** clause, which is similar to a **let** expression, except that the equations appear after the result rather than before.

6.9 Grace Notes

Recall from Chapter 4 the function *graceNote* to generate grace notes. A more general version is defined below, which takes a *Rational* argument that specifies the fraction of the principal note's duration to be used for the grace note's duration:

> *grace* :: *Int* → *Rational* → *Music Pitch* → *Music Pitch*
> *grace n r (Prim (Note d p))* =
>   *note (r * d) (trans n p) :+: note ((1 − r) * d) p*
> *grace n r _*   =
>   *error* "grace: can only add a grace note to a note"

Thus *grace n r (note d p)* is a *Music* value consisting of two notes, the first being the grace note whose duration is *r * d* and whose pitch is *n* semitones higher (or lower if *n* is negative) than *p*, and the second being the principal note at pitch *p* but now with duration (1 − *r*) * *d*.

Note that *grace* places the downbeat of the grace note at the point written for the principal note. Sometimes the interpretation of a grace note is such that the downbeat of the principal note is to be unchanged. In that case, the grace note reduces the duration of the *previous* note. We can define a function *grace2* that takes two notes as arguments and places the grace note appropriately:

> *grace2* :: *Int* → *Rational* →
>   *Music Pitch* → *Music Pitch* → *Music Pitch*
> *grace2 n r (Prim (Note d1 p1)) (Prim (Note d2 p2))* =
>   *note (d1 − r * d2) p1 :+: note (r * d2) (trans n p2) :+: note d2 p2*
> *grace2 _ _ _ _* =
>   *error* "grace2: can only add a grace note to a note"

Exercise 6.6 Related to trills and grace notes in Western classical music are the notions of *mordent*, *turn*, and *appoggiatura*. Define functions to realize these musical ornamentations.

6.10 Percussion

Percussion is a difficult notion to represent in the abstract. On the one hand, a percussion instrument is just another instrument, so why should it be

data *PercussionSound* =
    AcousticBassDrum   -- MIDI Key 35
    | *BassDrum1*   -- MIDI Key 36
    | *SideStick*   -- ...

AcousticSnare	*HandClap*	*ElectricSnare*	*LowFloorTom*
ClosedHiHat	*HighFloorTom*	*PedalHiHat*	*LowTom*
OpenHiHat	*LowMidTom*	*HiMidTom*	*CrashCymbal1*
HighTom	*RideCymbal1*	*ChineseCymbal*	*RideBell*
Tambourine	*SplashCymbal*	*Cowbell*	*CrashCymbal2*
Vibraslap	*RideCymbal2*	*HiBongo*	*LowBongo*
MuteHiConga	*OpenHiConga*	*LowConga*	*HighTimbale*
LowTimbale	*HighAgogo*	*LowAgogo*	*Cabasa*
Maracas	*ShortWhistle*	*LongWhistle*	*ShortGuiro*
LongGuiro	*Claves*	*HiWoodBlock*	*LowWoodBlock*
MuteCuica	*OpenCuica*	*MuteTriangle*	
OpenTriangle	-- MIDI Key 82		

Figure 6.3 General MIDI percussion names.

treated differently? On the other hand, even common practice notation treats it specially, although it has much in common with non-percussive notation. The MIDI standard is equally ambiguous about the treatment of percussion: on the one hand, percussion sounds are chosen by specifying an octave and a pitch, just like any other instrument; on the other hand, these pitches have no tonal meaning whatsoever: they are just a convenient way to select from a large number of percussion sounds. Indeed, part of the General MIDI Standard is a set of names for commonly used percussion sounds.

Since MIDI is such a popular platform, it is worth defining some handy functions for using the General MIDI Standard. In Figure 6.3, a data type is defined that borrows its constructor names from the General MIDI Standard. The comments reflecting the "MIDI Key" numbers will be explained later, but basically a MIDI Key is the equivalent of an absolute pitch in Euterpea terminology. So all that remains to be done is to convert these percussion sound names into a *Music* value; i.e., a *Note*:

perc :: *PercussionSound* → *Dur* → *Music Pitch*
perc ps dur = *instrument Percussion* $ *note dur* (*pitch* (*fromEnum ps*+35))

Details: *fromEnum* is an operator in the *Enum* class, which is all about enumerations, and will be discussed in more detail in Chapter 7. A data type that is a member of this class can be *enumerated* – i.e., the elements of the data type can be listed in order. *fromEnum* maps each value to its index in this enumeration. Thus *fromEnum AcousticBassDrum* is 0, *fromEnum BassDrum1* is 1, and so on.

Note that the *Percussion* instrument is assigned in the definition above to enforce that the correct sound is produced. Notes that have no assigned instruments will be interpreted as piano.

For example, here are eight bars of a simple rock tune or "funk groove" that uses *perc* and *roll*:

```
funkGroove :: Music Pitch
funkGroove
    = let p1 = perc LowTom       qn
          p2 = perc AcousticSnare en
      in tempo 3 $ cut 8 $ forever
         ((p1 :+: qnr :+: p2 :+: qnr :+: p2 :+:
           p1 :+: p1 :+: qnr :+: p2 :+: enr)
          :=: roll en (perc ClosedHiHat 2))
```

Exercise 6.7 Write a program that generates all of the General MIDI percussion sounds, playing through each of them one at a time.

Exercise 6.8 Find a drum beat that you like, and express it in Euterpea. Then use *forever*, *cut*, and (:=:) to add a simple melody to it.

6.11 A Map for Music

Recall from Chapter 3 the definition of *map*:

```
map         :: (a → b) → [a] → [b]
map f [ ]    = [ ]
map f (x : xs) = f x : map f xs
```

This function is defined on the list data type. Is there something analogous for *Music*? That is, a function:[2]

$$mMap :: (a → b) → Music\ a → Music\ b$$

Such a function is indeed straightforward to define, but it helps to first define a map-like function for the *Primitive* type:

```
pMap             :: (a → b) → Primitive a → Primitive b
pMap f (Note d x) = Note d (f x)
pMap f (Rest d)   = Rest d
```

---

[2] The name *mapM* would perhaps have been a better choice here, to be consistent with previous names. However, *mapM* is a predefined function in Haskell, and thus *mMap* is used instead. Similarly, Haskell's *Monad* library defines a function *foldM*, and thus in the next section the name *mFold* is used instead.

With *pMap* in hand, we can now define *mMap*:

$$
\begin{array}{ll}
mMap & :: (a \rightarrow b) \rightarrow Music\ a \rightarrow Music\ b \\
mMap\ f\ (Prim\ p) & = Prim\ (pMap\ f\ p) \\
mMap\ f\ (m1 :+: m2) & = mMap\ f\ m1 :+: mMap\ f\ m2 \\
mMap\ f\ (m1 :=: m2) & = mMap\ f\ m1 :=: mMap\ f\ m2 \\
mMap\ f\ (Modify\ c\ m) & = Modify\ c\ (mMap\ f\ m)
\end{array}
$$

Just as *map f xs* for lists replaces each polymorphic element x in *xs* with $f\ x$, *mMap f m* for *Music* replaces each polymorphic element p in *m* with $f\ p$.

As an example of how *mMap* can be used, let's introduce a *Volume* type for a note:

type *Volume* = *Int*

The goal is to convert a value of type *Music Pitch* into a value of type *Music* (*Pitch*, *Volume*) – that is, to pair each pitch with a volume attribute. We can define a function to do so as follows:

$$
\begin{array}{l}
addVolume \quad :: Volume \rightarrow Music\ Pitch \rightarrow Music\ (Pitch, Volume) \\
addVolume\ v = mMap\ (\lambda p \rightarrow (p, v))
\end{array}
$$

For MIDI, the variable v can range from 0 (softest) to 127 (loudest).

For example, compare the loudness of these two phrases:

$$
\begin{array}{l}
m1, m2 :: Music\ (Pitch, Volume) \\
m1 = addVolume\ 100\ (c\ 4\ qn :+: d\ 4\ qn :+: e\ 4\ qn :+: c\ 4\ qn) \\
m2 = addVolume\ 30\ (c\ 4\ qn :+: d\ 4\ qn :+: e\ 4\ qn :+: c\ 4\ qn)
\end{array}
$$

using the *play* function. (Recall from Section 2.3 that the type of the argument to *play* must be made clear, as is done here with the type signature.)

Details: Note that the name *Volume* is used both as a type synonym and as a constructor. Haskell allows this, since they can always be distinguished by context.

Exercise 6.9 Using *mMap*, define a function:

$$
\begin{array}{l}
scaleVolume :: Rational \rightarrow Music\ (Pitch, Volume) \\
\qquad\qquad\qquad \rightarrow Music\ (Pitch, Volume)
\end{array}
$$

such that *scaleVolume s m* scales the volume of each note in *m* by the factor *s*.

(This problem requires multiplying a *Rational* number by an *Int* [i.e., *Volume*]. To do this, some coercions between number types are needed, which in Haskell is done using *qualified types*, which are discussed in Chapter 7.

For now, you can simply do the following: If v is the volume of a note, then *round* ($s * fromIntegral\ v$) is the desired scaled volume.)

6.12 A Fold for Music

We can also define a fold-like operator for *Music*. But whereas the list data type has only two constructors (the nullary constructor [ ] and the binary constructor (:)), *Music* has *four* constructors (*Prim*, (:+:), (:=:), and *Modify*). Thus the following function takes four arguments in addition to the *Music* value it is transforming instead of two:

$mFold$ :: ($Primitive\ a \rightarrow b$) $\rightarrow$ ($b \rightarrow b \rightarrow b$) $\rightarrow$ ($b \rightarrow b \rightarrow b$) $\rightarrow$
          ($Control \rightarrow b \rightarrow b$) $\rightarrow$ $Music\ a \rightarrow b$
$mFold\ f$ (+:) (=:) $g\ m =$
  let rec $= mFold\ f$ (+:) (=:) g
  in case m **of**
    $Prim\ p$ $\rightarrow f\ p$
    $m1$:+: $m2$ $\rightarrow$ **rec** $m1$ +: **rec** $m2$
    $m1$:=: $m2$ $\rightarrow$ **rec** $m1$ =: **rec** $m2$
    $Modify\ c\ m \rightarrow g\ c$ (**rec** m)

This somewhat unwieldy function basically takes apart a *Music* value and puts it back together with different constructors. Indeed, note that:

$mFold\ Prim$ (:+:) (:=:) $Modify\ m == m$

Although it is intuitive, proving this property requires induction, a proof technique discussed in Chapter 11.

To see how *mFold* might be used, note first of all that it is more general than *mMap* – indeed, *mMap* can be defined in terms of *mFold* like this:

$mMap$ :: ($a \rightarrow b$) $\rightarrow$ $Music\ a \rightarrow Music\ b$
$mMap\ f = mFold\ g$ (:+:) (:=:) $Modify$ **where**
  g ($Note\ d\ x$) $= note\ d$ ($f\ x$)
  g ($Rest\ d$) $= rest\ d$

More interestingly, we can use *mFold* to more succinctly define functions such as *dur* from Section 6.3:

dur :: $Music\ a \rightarrow Dur$
$dur = mFold\ getDur$ (+) $max\ modDur$ **where**
  $getDur$ ($Note\ d$ _) $= d$
  $getDur$ ($Rest\ d$) $= d$

$$modDur \ (Tempo \ r) \ d = d/r$$
$$modDur \ \_ \ d \qquad\quad = d$$

Exercise 6.10 Redefine *retro* from Section 6.4 using *mFold*.

Exercise 6.11 Define a function *insideOut* that inverts the role of serial and parallel composition in a *Music* value. Using *insideOut*, see if you can (a) find a non-trivial value $m :: Music \ Pitch$ such that m is "musically equivalent" to (i.e., sounds the same as) *insideOut* m and (b) find a value $m :: Music \ Pitch$ such that $m :+: insideOut \ m :+: m$ sounds interesting. (You are free to define what "sounds interesting" means.)

6.13 Complex Rhythms

Euterpea's *Tempo* modifier has the potential to do more than simply speed up or slow down a piece of music. One of its uses is to create triplets out of eighth notes. For example, compare the sound of *v1* and *v2* in the following:

$$x1 = g \ 4 \ qn :=: (c \ 4 \ en :+: d \ 4 \ en :+: e \ 4 \ en)$$
$$x2 = g \ 4 \ qn :=: tempo \ (3/2) \ (c \ 4 \ en :+: d \ 4 \ en :+: e \ 4 \ en)$$

Notice that the use of *tempo* (3/2) causes the three eighth notes to sound like triplets. Because *tempo* inserts *Modify Tempo* node into the musical tree, this operation also preserves the symbolic way of representing triplets on a score, which is fundamentally as eighth notes under a speed modifier. This strategy can also be used to create other interesting rhythmic textures, such as those based on fifths or sevenths.

Another interesting use of the *Tempo* modifier is to create what is referred to as a *phase composition*: a simple motif is repeated in parallel with itself, but each part is played at a slightly different speed. Phase compositions are repetitive, but demonstrate subtle changes in rhythmic texture over time. The difference in tempo between parts typically must be very small to achieve this effect. Listen to the following and observe how the degree of tempo change affects the result.

$$phaseIt \ factor \ m = m :=: tempo \ factor \ m$$
$$phase1 = phaseIt \ 1.5 \ (times \ 4 \ twinkle)$$
$$phase2 = phaseIt \ 1.1 \ (times \ 4 \ twinkle)$$
$$phase3 = phaseIt \ 1.01 \ (times \ 4 \ twinkle)$$

6.14 Crazy Recursion

With all the functions and data types that have been defined, and the power of recursion and higher-order functions well understood, we can start to do some wild and crazy things with music. Here is just one such idea.

The goal is to define a function to recursively apply transformations f (to elements in a sequence) and g (to accumulated phrases) some specified number of times:

$$rep :: (Music\ a \rightarrow Music\ a) \rightarrow (Music\ a \rightarrow Music\ a) \rightarrow Int$$
$$\rightarrow Music\ a \rightarrow Music\ a$$
$$rep\ f\ g\ 0\ m = rest\ 0$$
$$rep\ f\ g\ n\ m = m :=: g\ (rep\ f\ g\ (n-1)\ (f\ m))$$

With this simple function, we can create some interesting phrases of music with very little code. For example, rep can be used three times, nested together, to create a "cascade" of sounds:

$$run\quad = rep\ (transpose\ 5)\ (offset\ tn)\ 8\ (c\ 4\ tn)$$
$$cascade\ = rep\ (transpose\ 4)\ (offset\ en)\ 8\ run$$
$$cascades = rep\ id\ (offset\ sn)\ 2\ cascade$$

We can then make the cascade run up and then down:

$$final = cascades :+: retro\ cascades$$

What happens if the f and g arguments are reversed?

$$run'\quad = rep\ (offset\ tn)\ (transpose\ 5)\ 8\ (c\ 4\ tn)$$
$$cascade'\ = rep\ (offset\ en)\ (transpose\ 4)\ 8\ run'$$
$$cascades' = rep\ (offset\ sn)\ id\ 2\ cascade'$$
$$final'\quad = cascades' :+: retro\ cascades'$$

Exercise 6.12 Consider this sequence of eight numbers:

$$s1 = [1, 5, 3, 6, 5, 0, 1, 1]$$

We might interpret this as a sequence of pitches, i.e., a melody. Another way to represent this sequence is as a sequence of seven intervals:

$$s2 = [4, -2, 3, -1, -5, 1, 0]$$

Together with the starting pitch (i.e., 1), this sequence of intervals can be used to reconstruct the original melody. But with a suitable transposition to eliminate negative numbers, it can also be viewed as another melody. Indeed, we can repeat the process: $s2$ can be represented by this sequence of six intervals:

$$s3 = [-6, 5, -4, -4, 6, -1]$$

Together with the starting number (i.e., 4), $s3$ can be used to reconstruct $s2$. Continuing the process:

$$s4 = [11, -9, 0, 10, -7]$$
$$s5 = [-20, 9, 10, -17]$$
$$s6 = [29, 1, -27]$$
$$s7 = [-28, -28]$$
$$s8 = [0]$$

Now, if we take the first element of each of these sequences to form this eight-number sequence:

$$ic = [0, -28, 29, -20, 11, -6, 4, 1]$$

then it alone can be used to recreate the original eight-number sequence in its entirety. Of course, it can also be used as the original melody was used and we could derive another eight-note sequence from it – and so on. The list ic will be referred to as the "interval closure" of the original list $s1$.

Your job is to:

a) Define a function *toIntervals* that takes a list of n numbers and generates a list of n lists, such that the ith list is the sequence s_i as defined above.

b) Define a function *getHeads* that takes a list of n lists and returns a list of n numbers such that the ith element is the head of the ith list.

c) Compose the above two functions in a suitable way to define a function *intervalClosure* that takes an n-element list and returns its interval closure.

d) Define a function *intervalClosures* that takes an n-element list and returns an infinite sequence of interval closures.

e) Now for the open-ended part of this exercise: Interpret the outputs of any of the functions above to create some "interesting" music.

Exercise 6.13 Write a Euterpea program that sounds like an infinitely descending (in pitch) sequence of musical lines. Each descending line should fade into the audible range as it begins its descent, and then fade out as it descends further. So the beginning and end of each line will be difficult to hear. And there will be many such lines, each starting at a different time, some perhaps descending a little faster than others, or perhaps using different instrument sounds, and so on. The effect will be that as you listen to the music, everything will seem to be falling, falling, falling with no end, but no beginning either. (This illusion is called the *Shepard tone*, or *Shepard scale*, first introduced by Roger Shepard in 1964 [12].)

Use higher-order functions, recursion, and whatever other abstraction techniques you have learned to write an elegant solution to this problem. Try to parameterize things in such a way that, for example, with a simple change, you could generate an infinite *ascension* as well. The *Volume* constructor in the *NoteAttribute* type, as used in the definition of *addVol*, should be used to set the volumes.

Exercise 6.14 Do something wild and crazy with Euterpea.

7

Qualified Types and Type Classes

This chapter introduces the notions of *qualified types* and *type classes*. These concepts can be viewed as a refinement of the notion of polymorphism, and they increase the ability to write modular programs.

7.1 Motivation

A polymorphic type such as ($a \rightarrow a$) can be viewed as shorthand for $\forall(a)a \rightarrow a$, which can be read as "*for all* types a, functions mapping elements of type a to elements of type a." Note the emphasis on "*for all*."

In practice, however, there are times when we would prefer to limit a polymorphic type to a smaller number of possibilities. A good example is a function such as (+). It is probably not a good idea to limit (+) to a *single* (that is, *monomorphic*) type such as *Integer* $\rightarrow$ *Integer* $\rightarrow$ *Integer*, since there are other kinds of numbers, such as rational and floating-point numbers, that we would like to perform addition on as well. Nor is it a good idea to have a different addition function for each number type, since that would require giving each a different name, such as *addInteger*, *addRational*, *addFloat*, etc. And, unfortunately, giving (+) a type such as $a \rightarrow a \rightarrow a$ will not work, since this would imply that we could add things other than numbers, such as characters, pitch classes, lists, tuples, functions, and any type that we might define on our own!

Haskell provides a solution to this problem through the use of *qualified types*. Conceptually, it is helpful to think of a qualified type just as a polymorphic type, except that in place of "*for all* types a" it will be possible to say "for all types a *that are members of the type class C*," where the type class *C* can be thought of as a set of types. For example, suppose there is a type class *Num* with members *Integer*, *Rational*, and *Float*. Then an accurate type for (+) would be $\forall(a{\in}Num)a \to a \to a$. But in Haskell, instead of writing $\forall(a \in Num) \cdots$, the notation *Num* $a \Rightarrow \cdots$ is used. So the proper type signature for (+) is:

(+) :: *Num* $a \Rightarrow a \to a \to a$

which should be read as "for all types *a* that are members of the type class *Num*, (+) has type $a \to a \to a$." Members of a type class are also called *instances* of the class, and these two terms will be used interchangeably in the remainder of the text. The *Num* $a \Rightarrow \cdots$ part of the type signature is often called a *context*, or *constraint*.

Details: It is important not to confuse *Num* with a data type or a constructor within a data type, even though the same syntax ("*Num a*") is used. *Num* is a *type class*, and the context of its use (to the left of a $\Rightarrow$) is always sufficient to determine this fact.

Recall now the type signature given for the function *simple* in Chapter 1:

simple   :: *Integer* $\to$ *Integer* $\to$ *Integer* $\to$ *Integer*
simple x y z = $x * (y + z)$

Note that *simple* uses the operator (+) discussed above. It also uses (∗), whose type is the same as that for (+):

(∗) :: *Num* $a \Rightarrow a \to a \to a$

This suggests that a more general type for *simple* is:

simple   :: *Num* $a \Rightarrow a \to a \to a \to a$
simple x y z = $x * (y + z)$

Indeed, this is the preferred, most general type that can be given for *simple*. It can now be used with any type that is a member of the *Num* class, which includes *Integer*, *Int*, *Rational*, *Float*, and *Double*, among others.

The ability to qualify polymorphic types is a unique feature of Haskell and, as we will soon see, provides great expressiveness. In the following sections, the idea is explored much more thoroughly, and in particular it is shown how a programmer can define his or her own type classes and their instances. To begin, let's take a closer look at one of the predefined type classes in Haskell having to do with equality.

7.2 Equality

Equality between two expressions *e1* and *e2* in Haskell means that the value
of *e1* is the same as the value of *e2*. Another way to view equality is that we
should be able to substitute *e1* for *e2*, or vice versa, wherever they appear in a
program, without affecting the result of that program.

In general, however, it is not possible for a program to determine the
equality of two expressions. Consider, for example, determining the equality
of two infinite lists, two infinite *Music* values, or two functions of type
Integer $\rightarrow$ *Integer*.[1] The property of computing the equality of two values
is called *computational equality*. Even though by the above simple examples
it is clear that computational equality is strictly weaker than full equality, it is
still an operation that we would like to use in many ordinary programs.

Haskell's operator for computational equality is (==). Partly because of
the problem mentioned earlier, there are many types for which we would like
equality defined, but some for which it might not make sense. For example, it is
common to compare two characters, two integers, two floating-point numbers,
etc. On the other hand, comparing the equality of infinite data structures, or
functions, is difficult, and in general not possible. Thus Haskell has a type class
called *Eq*, so that the equality operator (==) can be given the qualified type:

$$(==) :: Eq\ a \Rightarrow a \rightarrow a \rightarrow Bool$$

In other words, (==) is a function that, for any type *a* in the class *Eq*, tests
two values of type *a* for equality, returning a Boolean (*Bool*) value as a result.
Among *Eq*'s instances are the types *Char* and *Integer*, so that the following
calculations hold:

```
42  == 42  ⇒ True
42  == 43  ⇒ False
'a' == 'a' ⇒ True
'a' == 'b' ⇒ False
```

Furthermore, the expression 42 == 'a' is *ill-typed*; Haskell is clever enough
to know when qualified types are ill-formed.

One of the nice things about qualified types is that they work in the presence
of ordinary polymorphism. In particular, the type constraints can be made to
propagate through polymorphic data types. For example, because *Integer* and
Float are members of *Eq*, so are the types (*Integer, Char*), [*Integer*], [*Float*],
etc. Thus:

---

[1] This is the same as determining *program equivalence*, a well-known example of an *undecidable
problem* in the theory of computation.

$$[42, 43] \; == [42, 43] \; \Rightarrow \textit{True}$$
$$[4.2, 4.3] \; == [4.3, 4.2] \; \Rightarrow \textit{False}$$
$$(42, 'a') == (42, 'a') \Rightarrow \textit{True}$$

This will be elaborated upon in a later section.

Type constraints also propagate through function definitions. For example, consider this definition of the function $\in$ that tests for membership in a list:

$$x \in [\,] \qquad = \textit{False}$$
$$x \in (y : ys) = x == y \lor x \in ys$$

Details: ($\in$) is actually written *elem* in Haskell; i.e., it is a normal function, not an infix operator. Of course, it can be used in an infix manner by enclosing it with backquotes: x 'f' y is the same as $f \; x \; y$. Note that the backquote character is sometimes called a backtick; it is not the same as an apostrophe! On a standard qwerty keyboard, the backquote is typically found on the same key as the $\sim$ character.

Note the use of (==) on the right-hand side of the second equation. The principal type for ($\in$) is thus:

$$\in \; :: Eq \; a \Rightarrow a \to [a] \to \textit{Bool}$$

This should be read as: "For every type a that is an instance of the class *Eq*, ($\in$) has type $a \to [a] \to \textit{Bool}$." This is exactly what we would hope for – it expresses the fact that ($\in$) is not defined on all types, just those for which computational equality is defined.

The above type for ($\in$) is also its principal type, and Haskell will infer this type if no signature is given. Indeed, if we were to write the type signature:

$$(\in) :: a \to [a] \to \textit{Bool}$$

a type error would result, because this type is fundamentally *too general*, and the Haskell type system will complain.

Details: On the other hand, we could write:

$$(\in) :: \textit{Integer} \to [\textit{Integer}] \to \textit{Bool}$$

if we expect to use ($\in$) only on lists of integers. In other words, using a type signature to constrain a value to be less general than its principal type is OK.

As another example of this idea, a function that squares its argument:

square x = x ∗ x

has principal type *Num a ⇒ a → a*, since (∗), like (+), has type
Num a ⇒ a → a → a. Thus:

> *square* 42 ⇒ 1764
> *square* 4.2 ⇒ 17.64

The *Num* class will be discussed in greater detail shortly.

7.3 Defining Our Own Type Classes

Haskell provides a mechanism by which we can create our own qualified types, by defining a new type class and specifying which types are members, or "instances," of it. Indeed, the type classes *Num* and *Eq* are not built in as primitives in Haskell, but rather are simply predefined in the Standard Prelude.

To see how this is done, consider the *Eq* class. It is created by the following *type class declaration*:

> **class** *Eq a* **where**
> (==) :: *a → a → Bool*

The connection between (==) and *Eq* is important: the above declaration should be read as "a type *a* is an instance of the class *Eq* only if there is an operation (==) :: *a → a → Bool* defined on it." (==) is called an *operation* in the class *Eq*, and in general more than one operation is allowed in a class. More examples of this will be introduced shortly.

So far, so good. But how do we specify which types are instances of the class *Eq* and the actual behavior of (==) on each of those types? This is done with an *instance declaration*. For example:

> **instance** *Eq Integer* **where**
> *x* == *y* = *integerEq x y*

The definition of (==) is called a *method*. The function *integerEq* happens to be the primitive function that compares integers for equality, but in general any valid expression is allowed on the right-hand side, just as for any other function definition. The overall instance declaration is essentially saying: "The type *Integer* is an instance of the class *Eq*, and here is the method corresponding to the operation (==)." Given this declaration, we can now compare fixed-precision integers for equality using (==). Similarly:

instance *Eq Float* **where**
    $x == y = floatEq \; x \; y$

allows us to compare floating-point numbers using ($==$).

More importantly, data types that we have defined on our own can also be made instances of the class *Eq*. Consider, for example, the *PitchClass* data type defined in Chapter 2:

data *PitchClass* = *Cff* | *Cf* | *C* | *Dff* | *Cs* | *Df* | *Css* | *D* | *Eff* | *Ds*
    | *Ef* | *Fff* | *Dss* | *E* | *Ff* | *Es* | *F* | *Gff* | *Ess* | *Fs*
    | *Gf* | *Fss* | *G* | *Aff* | *Gs* | *Af* | *Gss* | *A* | *Bff* | *As*
    | *Bf* | *Ass* | *B* | *Bs* | *Bss*

We can declare *PitchClass* to be an instance of *Eq* as follows:

instance *Eq PitchClass* **where**
    $Cff == Cff = True$
    $Cf == Cf = True$
    $C == C = True$
    ...
    $Bs == Bs = True$
    $Bss == Bss = True$
    $\_ == \_ = False$

where ... refers to the other 30 equations needed to make this definition complete. Indeed, this is rather tedious! Not only is it tedious, it is also dead obvious how ($==$) should be defined.

7.3.1 Derived Instances

To alleviate the burden of defining instances such as those above, Haskell provides a convenient way to *automatically derive* such instance declarations from data type declarations for certain predefined type classes. This is done using a **deriving** clause. For example, in the case of *PitchClass*, we can simply write:

data *PitchClass* = *Cff* | *Cf* | *C* | *Dff* | *Cs* | *Df* | *Css* | *D* | *Eff* | *Ds*
    | *Ef* | *Fff* | *Dss* | *E* | *Ff* | *Es* | *F* | *Gff* | *Ess* | *Fs*
    | *Gf* | *Fss* | *G* | *Aff* | *Gs* | *Af* | *Gss* | *A* | *Bff* | *As*
    | *Bf* | *Ass* | *B* | *Bs* | *Bss*
    deriving *Eq*

With this declaration, Haskell will automatically derive the instance declaration given above, so that ($==$) behaves in the way we would expect it to.

Consider now a polymorphic type, such as the *Primitive* type from Chapter 2:

data *Primitive a* = *Note Dur a*
                    | *Rest Dur*

What should an instance for this type in the class *Eq* look like? Here is a first attempt:

instance *Eq* (*Primitive a*) **where**
    Note d1 x1 == *Note d2 x2* = (*d1* == *d2*) ∧ (*x1* == *x2*)
    Rest d1   == *Rest d2*   = *d1* == *d2*
    _   == _   = *False*

Note the use of (==) on the right-hand side in several places. Two of those places involve *Dur*, which a type synonym for *Rational*. The *Rational* type is in fact a predefined instance of *Eq*, so all is well there. (If it were not an instance of *Eq*, a type error would result.)

But what about the term *x1* == *x2*? *x1* and *x2* are values of the polymorphic type *a*, but how do we know that equality is defined on *a*, i.e., that the type *a* is an instance of *Eq*? In fact, this is not known in general. The simple fix is to add a constraint to the instance declaration as follows:

instance *Eq a* ⇒ *Eq* (*Primitive a*) **where**
    Note d1 x1 == *Note d2 x2* = (*d1* == *d2*) ∧ (*x1* == *x2*)
    Rest d1   == *Rest d2*   = *d1* == *d2*
    _   == _   = *False*

This can be read as: "For any type *a* in the class *Eq*, the type *Primitive a* is also in the class *Eq*, and here is the definition of (==) for that type." Indeed, if we wrote the original type declaration like this:

data *Primitive a* = *Note Dur a*
                    | *Rest Dur*
    deriving *Eq*

then Haskell would derive the above correct instance declaration automatically.

So, for example, (==) is defined on the type *Primitive Pitch*, because *Pitch* is a type synonym for (*PitchClass, Octave*) and (a) *PitchClass* is an instance of *Eq* by the effort above, (b) *Octave* is a synonym for *Int*, which is a predefined instance of *Eq*, and (c) as mentioned earlier, the pair type is a predefined instance of *Eq*. Indeed, now that an instance for a polymorphic type has been seen, we can understand what the predefined instance for polymorphic pairs must look like, namely:

instance (*Eq a, Eq b*) ⇒ *Eq* (*a, b*) **where**
    (*x1, y1*) == (*x2, y2*) = (*x1* == *x2*) ∧ (*y1* == *y2*)

About the only thing not considered is a *recursive* data type. For example, recall the *Music* data type, also from Chapter 2:

data *Music a* = *Prim* (*Primitive a*)
            | *Music a* :+: *Music a*
            | *Music a* :=: *Music a*
            | *Modify Control* (*Music a*)

Its instance declaration for *Eq* seems obvious:

instance *Eq a* $\Rightarrow$ *Eq* (*Music a*) **where**
  Prim p1   == *Prim p2*   = *p1* == *p2*
  (*m1* :+: *m2*)   == (*m3* :+: *m4*)   = (*m1* == *m3*) $\land$ (*m2* == *m4*)
  (*m1* :=: *m2*)   == (*m3* :=: *m4*)   = (*m1* == *m3*) $\land$ (*m2* == *m4*)
  Modify c1 m1 == *Modify c2 m2* = (*c1* == *c2*) $\land$ (*m1* == *m2*)

Indeed, assuming that *Control* is an instance of *Eq*, this is just what is expected, and it can be automatically derived by adding a **deriving** clause to the data type declaration for *Music*.

7.3.2 Default Methods

In reality, the class *Eq* as defined in Haskell's Standard Prelude is slightly richer than what is defined above. Here it is in its exact form:

class *Eq a* **where**
  (==), ($\neq$) :: $a \to a \to Bool$
  $x \neq y$ = $\neg$ (x == y)
  x == y = $\neg$ ($x \neq y$)

This is an example of a class with two operations: one for equality, the other for inequality. It also demonstrates the use of a *default method*, one for each operator. If a method for a particular operation is omitted in an instance declaration, then the default one defined in the class declaration, if it exists, is used instead. For example, all of the instances of *Eq* defined earlier will work perfectly well with the above class declaration, yielding just the right definition of inequality that we would expect: the logical negation of equality.

> **Details:** Both the inequality and logical negation operators are shown here using the mathematical notations $\neq$ and $\neg$, respectively. When writing your Haskell programs, you instead will have to use the operator / = and the function name not, respectively.

A useful slogan that helps to distinguish type classes from ordinary polymorphism is this: Polymorphism captures similar structure over different values, while type classes capture similar operations over different structures. For example, a sequence of integers, sequence of characters, etc., can be captured as a polymorphic *List*, whereas equality of integers, equality of trees, etc., can be captured by a type class such as *Eq*.

7.3.3 Inheritance

Haskell also supports a notion called *inheritance*. For example, we may wish to define a class *Ord* that "inherits" all of the operations in *Eq*, but in addition has a set of comparison operations and minimum and maximum functions (a fuller definition of *Ord*, as taken from the Standard Prelude, is given in Appendix B):

class $Eq\ a \Rightarrow Ord\ a$ **where**
$\quad (<), (\leqslant), (\geqslant), (>) :: a \to a \to Bool$
$\quad max, min \qquad\quad :: a \to a \to a$

Note the constraint $Eq\ a \Rightarrow$ in the **class** declaration. *Eq* is a *superclass* of *Ord* (conversely, *Ord* is a *subclass* of *Eq*), and any type that is an instance of *Ord* must also be an instance of *Eq*. The reason that this extra constraint makes sense is that performing comparisons such as $a \leqslant b$ and $a \geqslant b$ implies that we know how to compute $a == b$.

For example, following the strategy used for *Eq*, we could declare *Music* an instance of *Ord* as follows (note the constraint $Ord\ a \Rightarrow ...$):

instance $Ord\ a \Rightarrow Ord\ (Music\ a)$ **where**
$\quad Prim\ p1 \qquad\quad < Prim\ p2 \qquad\quad = p1 < p2$
$\quad (m1 :+: m2) \quad < (m3 :+: m4) \quad = (m1 < m3) \wedge (m2 < m4)$
$\quad (m1 :=: m2) \quad < (m3 :=: m4) \quad = (m1 < m3) \wedge (m2 < m4)$
$\quad Modify\ c1\ m1 < Modify\ c2\ m2 = (c1 < c2) \quad \wedge (m1 < m2)$
$\quad ...$

Although this is a perfectly well-defined definition for $<$, it is not clear that it exhibits the desired behavior, an issue that will be returned to in Section 7.7.

Another benefit of inheritance is shorter constraints. For example, the type of a function that uses operations from both the *Eq* and *Ord* classes can use just the constraint $(Ord\ a)$ rather than $(Eq\ a, Ord\ a)$, since *Ord* "implies" *Eq*.

As an example of the use of *Ord*, a generic *sort* function should be able to sort lists of any type that is an instance of *Ord*, and thus its most general type should be:

$sort :: Ord\ a \Rightarrow [a] \to [a]$

This typing for *sort* would naturally arise through the use of comparison operators such as < and ⩾ in its definition.

Details: Haskell also permits *multiple inheritance*, since classes may have more than one superclass. Name conflicts are avoided by the constraint that a particular operation can be a member of at most one class in any given scope. For example, the declaration:

  class (*Eq a, Show a*) ⇒ *C a* **where** ...

creates a class *C* that inherits operations from both *Eq* and *Show*.

Finally, class methods may have additional class constraints on any type variable except the one defining the current class. For example, in this class:

  class *C a* **where**
    m :: *Eq b* ⇒ *a* → *b*

the method *m* requires that type *b* is in class *Eq*. However, additional class constraints on type *a* are not allowed in the method *m*; these would instead have to be part of the overall constraint in the class declaration.

7.4 Haskell's Standard Type Classes

The Standard Prelude defines many useful type classes, including *Eq* and *Ord*. They are described in detail in Appendix B. In addition, the Haskell Report and the Library Report contain useful examples and discussions of type classes; you are encouraged to read through them.

Most of the standard type classes in Haskell are shown in Figure 7.1, along with their key instances. Since these have various default methods defined, also shown is the minimal set of methods that must be defined – the rest are taken care of by the default methods. For example, for *Ord*, all we have to provide is a definition for (⩽).

The *Num* class, which has been used implicitly throughout much of the text, is described in more detail in the next section. With this explanation, a few more of Haskell's secrets will be revealed.

7.4.1 The *Num* Class

As we know, Haskell provides several kinds of numbers, some of which have already been introduced: *Int*, *Integer*, *Rational*, and *Float*. These numbers are

Type Class	**Key functions**	**Key instances**
Num	$(+), (-), (*) :: Num\ a \Rightarrow a \rightarrow a \rightarrow a$ $negate :: Num\ a \Rightarrow a \rightarrow a$ minimal set: all but $(-)$ or *negate*	*Integer, Int, Float, Double, Rational*
Eq	$(==), (\neq) :: Eq\ a \Rightarrow a \rightarrow a \rightarrow Bool$ minimal set: either $(==)$ or $(\neq)$	*Integer, Int, Float, Double, Rational, Char, Bool, ...*
Ord	$(>), (<), (\geqslant), (\leqslant) ::$ $\quad Ord\ a \Rightarrow a \rightarrow a \rightarrow Bool$ $max, min :: Ord\ a \Rightarrow a \rightarrow a \rightarrow a$ minimal set: $(\leqslant)$	*Integer, Int, Float, Double, Rational, Char, Bool, ...*
Enum	$succ, pred :: Enum\ a \Rightarrow a \rightarrow a$ $fromEnum :: Enum\ a \Rightarrow a \rightarrow Int$ $toEnum :: Enum\ a \Rightarrow Int \rightarrow a$ also enables arithmetic sequences minimal set: *toEnum* and *fromEnum*	*Integer, Int, Float, Double, Rational, Char, Bool, ...*
Bounded	$minBound, maxBound :: a$	*Int, Char, Bool*
Show	$show :: Show\ a \Rightarrow a \rightarrow String$	Almost every type except for functions
Read	$read :: Read\ a \Rightarrow String \rightarrow a$	Almost every type except for functions

Figure 7.1　Common type classes and their instances.

instances of various type classes arranged in a rather complicated hierarchy. The reason for this is that there are many operations, such as $(+)$, *abs*, and *sin*, that are common among some of these number types. For example, we would expect $(+)$ to be defined on every kind of number, whereas *sin* might only be applicable to either single-precision (*Float*) or double-precision (*Double*) floating-point numbers.

Control over which numerical operations are allowed and which are not is the purpose of the numeric type class hierarchy. At the top of the hierarchy, and therefore containing operations that are valid for all numbers, is the class *Num*. It is defined as:

```
class (Eq a, Show a) ⇒ Num a where
    (+), (−), (∗) :: a → a → a
    negate        :: a → a
    abs, signum   :: a → a
    fromInteger   :: Integer → a
```

Note that (/) is *not* an operation in this class. *negate* is the negation function, *abs* is the absolute value function, and *signum* is the sign function, which returns -1 if its argument is negative, 0 if it is 0, and 1 if it is positive. *fromInteger* converts an *Integer* into a value of type $Num\ a \Rightarrow a$, which is useful for certain coercion tasks.

Details: Haskell also has a negation operator, which is its only prefix operator. However, it is just shorthand for *negate*. That is, $-e$ in Haskell is shorthand for *negate e*.

The operation *fromInteger* also has a special purpose. How is it that we can write the constant 42, say, both in a context requiring an *Int* and in one requiring, say, a *Float*. Somehow Haskell "knows" which version of 42 is required in a given context. But what is the type of 42 itself? The answer is that it has type *Num a* $\Rightarrow$ *a*, for some *a* to be determined by its context. (If this seems strange, remember that [ ] by itself is also somewhat ambiguous; it is a list, but a list of what? The most we can say about its type is that it is [*a*] for some *a* yet to be determined.)

The way this is achieved in Haskell is that literal numbers such as 42 are actually considered to be shorthand for *fromInteger* 42. Since *fromInteger* has type *Num a* $\Rightarrow$ *Integer* $\rightarrow$ *a*, then *fromInteger* 42 has type *Num a* $\Rightarrow$ *a*.

The complete hierarchy of numeric classes is shown in Figure 7.2; note that some of the classes are subclasses of certain non-numeric classes, such as *Eq* and *Show*. The comments below each class name refer to the Standard Prelude types that are instances of that class. See Appendix B for more details.

The Standard Prelude actually defines only the most basic numeric types: *Int*, *Integer*, *Float*, and *Double*. Other numeric types, such as rational numbers (*Ratio a*) and complex numbers (*Complex a*), are defined in libraries. The connection between these types and the numeric classes is given in Figure 7.3. The instance declarations implied by this table can be found in the Haskell Report.

7.4.2 The *Show* Class

It is very common to want to convert a data type value into a string. In fact, it happens all the time when we interact with GHCi at the command prompt, and GHCi will complain if it does not "know" how to "show" a value. The type of anything that GHCi prints must be an instance of the *Show* class.

Not all of the operations in the *Show* class will be discussed here; in fact, the only one of interest is *show*:

class *Show a* **where**
    show :: *a* $\rightarrow$ *String*
        ...

Instances of *Show* can be derived, so normally we do not have to worry about the details of the definition of *show*.

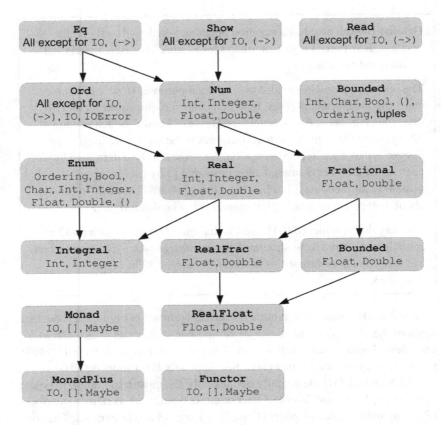

Figure 7.2 Numeric class hierarchy.

Numeric Type	Type Class	Description
Int	*Integral*	Fixed-precision integers
Integer	*Integral*	Arbitrary-precision integers
Integral a ⇒		
Ratio a	*RealFrac*	Rational numbers
Float	*RealFloat*	Real floating point, single precision
Double	*RealFloat*	Real floating point, double precision
RealFloat a ⇒		
Complex a	*Floating*	Complex floating point

Figure 7.3 Standard numeric types.

Lists also have a *Show* instance, but it is not derived, since, after all, lists have special syntax. Also, when *show* is applied to a string such as `"Hello"`, it should generate a string that, when printed, will look like `"Hello"`. This means that it must include characters for the quotation marks themselves, which in Haskell is achieved by prefixing the quotation mark with the "escape" character \. Given the following data declaration:

data *Hello* = *Hello*
    deriving *Show*

it is then instructive to ponder over the following calculations:

show Hello $\Longrightarrow$ `"Hello"`
show (*show Hello*) $\Longrightarrow$ *show* `"Hello"` $\Longrightarrow$ `"\"Hello\""`
show (*show* (*show Hello*)) $\Longrightarrow$ `"\"\\"Hello\\\"\""`

Details: To refer to the escape character itself, it must also be escaped, thus `"\\"` prints as \.

For further pondering, consider the following program. See if you can figure out what it does, and why![2]

main = *putStr* (*quine q*)
quine s = *s* ++ *show s*
q   = `"main = putStr (quine q)\nquine s`
             `= s ++ show s\nq = "`

Details: The `"\n"` that appears twice in the string *q* is a "newline" character; that is, when *q* is printed (or displayed on a console), the string starting to the right of `"\n"` will appear on a new line.

Derived *Show* instances are possible for all types whose component types also have *Show* instances. *Show* instances for most of the standard types are provided in the Standard Prelude.

---

[2] The essence of this idea is due to Willard Van Orman Quine [13], and its use in a computer program is discussed by Hofstadter [14]. It was adapted for Haskell by Jón Fairbairn.

7.4.3 The Functor Class

The *Functor* type class, which contains the *fmap* function, is for polymorphic data types that can benefit from map-like operations.

class *Functor f* **where**
    fmap :: $(a \to b) \to f\,a \to f\,b$
    ...

To see the utility of *Functor*, consider one of its instances, the *Maybe* data type:

data *Maybe a = Nothing | Just a*

Maybe is useful for situations where there may or may not be a value. Suppose we wish to transform the value of the *Just* constructor in a particular context. One option is to pattern-match against the two constructors with a **case** statement. However, it is far more concise to use *Maybe*'s *Functor* instance, which allows an arbitrary *Maybe* value to be transformed without requiring pattern-matching.

instance *Functor Maybe* **where**
    fmap f Nothing = Nothing
    fmap f (Just a) = Just (f a)

Euterpea's *Primitive* and *Music* data types are also instances of *Functor*. See Chapter 16 for the details.

7.5 Other Derived Instances

In addition to *Eq* and *Ord*, instances of *Enum, Bounded, Ix, Read,* and *Show* (see Appendix B) can also be generated by the **deriving** clause. These type classes are widely used in Haskell programming, making the deriving mechanism very useful.

The textual representation defined by a derived *Show* instance is consistent with the appearance of constant Haskell expressions (i.e., values) of the type involved. For example, from:

data *Color = Black*
    | Blue
    | Green
    | Cyan
    | Red

| *Magenta*
| *Yellow*
| *White*
   deriving (*Show, Eq, Ord, Enum, Bounded*)

we can expect that:

show [*Red* ..]
$\Longrightarrow$ "[Red,Magenta,Yellow,White]"

We can also expect that:

minBound :: *Color* $\Longrightarrow$ *Black*
maxBound :: *Color* $\Longrightarrow$ *White*

Note that the type signature "::*Color*" is given explicitly in this case, because, out of any context at least, Haskell does not know the type for which you are trying to determine the minimum and maximum bounds.

Further details about derived instances can be found in the Haskell Report.

Many of the predefined data types in Haskell have **deriving** clauses, even ones with special syntax. For example, if we could write a data type declaration for lists (the reason we cannot do this is that lists have special syntax, both at the value and type level) it would look something like this:

data [*a*] = [ ]
      | *a* : [*a*]
   deriving (*Eq, Ord*)

The derived *Eq* and *Ord* instances for lists are the usual ones; in particular, character strings, as lists of characters, are ordered as determined by the underlying *Char* type, with an initial sub-string being smaller than a longer string; for example, "cat" < "catalog" is *True*.

In practice, *Eq* and *Ord* instances are almost always derived rather than user-defined. In fact, you should provide your own definitions of equality and ordering predicates only with some trepidation, being careful to maintain the expected algebraic properties of equivalence relations and total orders, respectively (more on this later). An intransitive (==) predicate, for example, would be problematic, confusing readers of the program who expect (==) to be transitive. Nevertheless, it is sometimes necessary to provide *Eq* or *Ord* instances different from those that would be derived.

The data type declarations for *PitchClass, Primitive, Music,* and *Control* given in Chapter 1 are not the ones actually used in Eutperpea. The actual definitions each use a **deriving** clause, and are shown in Figure 7.4. The

data *PitchClass* = *Cff* | *Cf* | *C* | *Dff* | *Cs* | *Df* | *Css* | *D* | *Eff* | *Ds*
                  | *Ef* | *Fff* | *Dss* | *E* | *Ff* | *Es* | *F* | *Gff* | *Ess* | *Fs*
                  | *Gf* | *Fss* | *G* | *Aff* | *Gs* | *Af* | *Gss* | *A* | *Bff* | *As*
                  | *Bf* | *Ass* | *B* | *Bs* | *Bss*
    deriving (*Eq, Ord, Show, Read, Enum, Bounded*)

data *Primitive a* = *Note Dur a*
                  | *Rest Dur*
    deriving (*Show, Eq, Ord*)

data *Music a* =
      Prim (*Primitive a*)   -- primitive value
    | *Music a* :+: *Music a*   -- sequential composition
    | *Music a* :=: *Music a*   -- parallel composition
    | *Modify Control* (*Music a*)   -- modifier
    deriving (*Show, Eq, Ord*)

data *Control* =
      Tempo   *Rational*   -- scale the tempo
    | *Transpose AbsPitch*   -- transposition
    | *Instrument InstrumentName*   -- instrument label
    | *Phrase*   [*PhraseAttribute*]   -- phrase attributes
    | *Player*   *PlayerName*   -- player label
    deriving (*Show, Eq, Ord*)

Figure 7.4 Euterpea's data types with deriving clauses.

InstrumentName data type from Chapter 1 also has a deriving clause for *Show*, *Eq*, and *Ord* (but is omitted here to save space).

Details: When instances of more than one type class are derived for the same data type, they appear grouped in parentheses, as in Figure 7.4. Also, in this case *Eq must* appear if *Ord* does (unless an explicit instance for *Eq* is given), since *Eq* is a superclass of *Ord*.

Note that with single and double sharps and flats, there are many enharmonic equivalences. Thus in the data declaration for *PitchClass*, the constructors are ordered such that, if $pc1 < pc2$, then $pcToInt\ pc1 \leqslant pcToInt\ pc2$.

For some examples, the *Show* class allows us to convert values to strings:

show Cs $\Longrightarrow$ "Cs"
show concertA $\Longrightarrow$ "(A,4)"

The *Read* class allows us to go the other way around:

read "Cs" $\Longrightarrow$ *Cs*
read "(A,4)" $\Longrightarrow$ (A,4)

The *Eq* class allows testing values for equality:

$concertA == a440 \implies True$
$concertA == (A, 5) \implies False$

And the *Ord* class has relational operators for types whose values can be ordered:

$C < G \quad \implies True$
$max\ C\ G \implies G$

The *Enum* class is for "enummerable" types. For example:

$succ\ C \qquad \implies Dff$
$pred\ 1 \qquad \implies 0$
$fromEnum\ C \implies 2$
$toEnum\ 3 \quad \implies Dff$

The *Enum* class is also the basis on which *arithmetic sequences* (defined earlier in Section 5.3.1) are defined.

7.6 The Type of *play*

Ever since the *play* function was introduced in Chapter 2, we have been using it to "play" the results of our *Music* values, i.e., to listen to their rendering through MIDI. However, it is just a function like any other function in Haskell, but we never discussed what its type is. In fact, here it is:

$play :: (ToMusic1\ a, NFData\ a) \implies Music\ a \rightarrow IO\ ()$

The type of the result, *IO* (), is the type of a *command* in Haskell, i.e., something that "does I/O." We will have more to say about this in a later chapter.

But of more relevance to this chapter, note the constraint *ToMusic1 a*. You might guess that *ToMusic1* is a type class, and indeed it is the type class of values that can be reasonably converted to *Music1*, which is a type synonym for *Music* (*Pitch*, [*NoteAttribute*]). If a given type is a member of (i.e. an instance of) *ToMusic1*, then it can be performed or rendered as sound using Euterpea's various playback functions. Some things we would not expect to be possible to convert to *Music1* – for example, an arbitrary list, string, or function. So the type signature for *play* can be read as "for any type *T* that is a member of the class *ToMusic1*, *play* has type *Music T* → *IO* ()."[3]

---

[3] The NFData class is also required for use with the strict-timing playback option in Euterpea, accessible via the function *playS*.

Currently the types *Pitch*, *(Pitch, Volume)*, and *(Pitch,* [*NoteAttribute*]),
a type synonym for *Note1*, are members of the class *ToMusic1*. (The
NoteAttribute data type will be introduced in Chapter 9.) Indeed, we used
play on the first two of these types, i.e., on values of type *Music Pitch* and
Music (Pitch, Volume) in previous examples, and you might wonder how both
could possibly be properly typed – hopefully now it is clear. Chapter 9 also
introduces another, similar type class called *Performable*.

7.7 Reasoning with Type Classes

Type classes often imply a set of *laws* that govern the use of the operators in
the class. For example, for the *Eq* class, we can expect the following laws to
hold for every instance of the class:

$$x == x$$
$$x == y \qquad\qquad \supseteq y == x$$
$$(x == y) \wedge (y == z) \supseteq x == z$$
$$(x \neq y) \qquad\qquad \supseteq \neg (x == y)$$

where $\supseteq$ should be read "implies that."[4]

However, there is no way to guarantee these laws. A user may create an
instance of *Eq* that violates them, and in general Haskell has no way to enforce
them. Nevertheless, it is useful to state the laws of interest for a particular class,
and to state the expectation that all instances of the class be "law-abiding."
Then, as diligent functional programmers, we should ensure that every instance
that is defined, whether for our own type class or someone else's, is in fact
law-abiding.

As another example, consider the *Ord* class, whose instances are intended
to be *totally ordered*, which means that the following laws should hold for all
a, *b*, and *c*:

$$a \leqslant a$$
$$(a \leqslant b) \wedge (b \leqslant c) \supseteq (a \leqslant c)$$
$$(a \leqslant b) \wedge (b \leqslant a) \supseteq (a == b)$$
$$(a \neq b) \qquad\qquad \supseteq (a < b) \vee (b < a)$$

Similar laws should hold for ($>$).

---

[4] Mathematically, the first three of these laws are the same as those for an *equivalence relation*.

But alas, the instance of *Music* in the class *Ord* given in Section 7.3.3 does not satisfy all of these laws! To see why, consider two *Primitive* values $p1$ and $p2$ such that $p1 < p2$. Now consider these two *Music* values:

$m1 = Prim\ p1 :+: Prim\ p2$
$m2 = Prim\ p2 :+: Prim\ p1$

Clearly $m1 == m2$ is false, but the problem is, so are $m1 < m2$ and $m2 < m1$, thus violating the last law above.

To fix the problem, a *lexicographic ordering* should be used on the *Music* type, as is used in a dictionary. For example, "polygon" comes before "poly-morphic," using a left-to-right comparison of the letters. The new instance declaration looks like this:

instance *Ord a* $\Rightarrow$ *Ord* (*Music a*) **where**
  Prim p1   < *Prim p2*   = *p1 < p2*
  Prim p1   < _   = *True*
  (*m1 :+: m2*)   < *Prim* _   = *False*
  (*m1 :+: m2*)   < (*m3 :+: m4*)   = (*m1 < m3*) $\vee$
                          (*m1 == m3*) $\wedge$ (*m2 < m4*)
  (*m1 :+: m2*)   < _   = *True*
  (*m1 :=: m2*)   < *Prim* _   = *False*
  (*m1 :=: m2*)   < (*m3 :+: m4*) = *False*
  (*m1 :=: m2*)   < (*m3 :=: m4*) = (*m1 < m3*) $\vee$
                          (*m1 == m3*) $\wedge$ (*m2 < m4*)
  (*m1 :=: m2*)   < _   = *True*
  Modify c1 m1 < *Modify c2 m2* = (*c1 < c2*) $\vee$
                          (*c1 == c2*) $\wedge$ (*m1 < m2*)
  Modify c1 m1 < _   = *False*

This example shows the value of checking to be sure that each instance obeys the laws of its class. Of course, that check should come by way of a proof. This example also highlights the utility of derived instances, since the derived instance of *Music* for the class *Ord* is equivalent to that above, yet is done automatically.

Exercise 7.1 Prove that the instance of *Music* in the class *Eq* satisfies the laws of its class. Also prove that the modified instance of *Music* in the class *Ord* satisfies the laws of its class.

Exercise 7.2 Write out appropriate instance declarations for the *Color* type in the classes *Eq*, *Ord*, and *Enum*. (For simplicity, you may define *Color* to have fewer constructors, say just *Red*, *Green*, and *Blue*.)

Exercise 7.3 Define a type class called *Temporal* whose members are types that can be interpreted as having temporal duration. *Temporal* should have three operations, namely:

$durT :: Temporal\ a \Rightarrow a \rightarrow Dur$
$cutT :: Temporal\ a \Rightarrow Dur \rightarrow a \rightarrow a$
$removeT :: Temporal\ a \Rightarrow Dur \rightarrow a \rightarrow a$

Then define instances of *Temporal* for the types *Music* and *Primitive*. (Hint: This is not as hard as it sounds, because you can *reuse* some function names previously defined to do these sorts of operations.)

Can you think of other types that are temporal?

Exercise 7.4 Functions are not members of the *Eq* class, because, in general, determining whether two functions are equal is undecidable. But functions whose domains are finite and can be completely enumerated *can* be tested for equality. We just need to test that each function, when applied to each element in the domain, returns the same result.

Define an instance of *Eq* for functions. For this to be possible, note that if the function type is $a \rightarrow b$, then:

- the type a must be *enumerable* (i.e., a member of the *Enum* class),
- the type a must be *bounded* (i.e., a member of *Bounded* class), and
- the type b must admit *equality* (i.e., be a member of the *Eq* class).

These constraints must therefore be part of the instance declaration.

Hint: Using the minimum and maximum bounds of a type, enumerate all the elements of that type using an arithmetic sequence (recall Section 5.3.1), which, despite its name, works for any enumerable type.

Test your implementation by defining some functions on existing Euterpea types that are finite and bounded (such as *PitchClass* and *Color*), or by defining some functions on your own data type(s).

8

From Music to MIDI

MIDI is short for "Musical Instrument Digital Interface" and is a standard protocol for controlling electronic musical instruments [3, 4]. This chapter describes the process Euterpea uses to convert *Music* values to MIDI files and streams.

8.1 An Introduction to MIDI

MIDI is a standard adopted by most manufacturers of electronic instruments and personal computers. At its core is a protocol for communicating *musical events* (such as "note on" and "note off") and so-called *meta events* (select synthesizer patch, change tempo, etc.). Beyond the logical protocol, the MIDI standard also specifies electrical signal characteristics and cabling details, as well as a *standard MIDI file*.

MIDI files and MIDI streams only deal with *abstract* musical information, much like Euterpea's *Music* values. Information exists regarding when to start and stop pitches on various instruments, but the actual implementation of those instruments is subject to interpretation. MIDI contains no information on the actual *sound* you hear, and, as a result, playing the same MIDI file on different computers or even within different software on the same computer will produce different sounds. Software and hardware responsible for turning MIDI data into sound are called *synthesizers*. There are also hardware MIDI *controllers* that are user interfaces for sending MIDI data to a computer or hardware synthesizer. Some pieces of MIDI equipment have both of these functionalities combined.

General MIDI is a standard that introduced a convention for indicating when to use common instrument sounds, such as "acoustic grand piano," "electric piano," "violin," and "acoustic bass," as well as more exotic sounds,

125

Table 8.1. *General MIDI instrument families.*

Family	Program #	Family	Program #
Piano	1–8	Reed	65–72
Chromatic Percussion	9–16	Pipe	73–80
Organ	17–24	Synth Lead	81–88
Guitar	25–32	Synth Pad	89–96
Bass	33–40	Synth Effects	97–104
Strings	41–48	Ethnic	105–112
Ensemble	49–56	Percussive	113–120
Brass	57–64	Sound Effects	121–128

such as "choir aahs," "voice oohs," "bird tweet," and "helicopter." The General MIDI Standard establishes standard names for 128 sounds (also called "patches") and assigns an integer, called the *program number* (also called "program change number"), to each of them. The instrument names and their program numbers are grouped into "families" of instrument sounds, as shown in Table 8.1. However, the software interpreting these patch numbers is under no obligation to adhere to any particular interpretation of them. For virtual instrument libraries capturing exotic and rare instruments, it is common to repurpose patch numbers to refer to different things.

Recall that in Chapter 2 we defined a set of instruments via the *InstrumentName* data type (see Figure 2.1). All of the names chosen for that data type come directly from the General MIDI Standard, except for two, *Percussion* and *CustomInstrument*, which were added for convenience and extensibility within Euterpea: *Percussion* is used to address a peculiarity in General MIDI format to be described shortly, and *CustomInstrument* is for use with Euterpea's signal processing framework (see Chapter 19).

8.1.1 Channels, Instruments, and Tracks

A MIDI *channel* is similar in some ways to a staff on a paper score. You can have up to 16 channels, numbered 0 through 15, each assigned a different program number (corresponding to an instrument sound, see previous section). All of the dynamic "Note On" and "Note Off" messages (to be defined shortly) are tagged with a channel number, so up to 16 different instruments can be controlled independently and simultaneously.

Every channel can be assigned a single instrument at any given point in time, and it is possible to change which instrument appears on a given channel partway through a MIDI file through the use of a *program change*.

Thus, even though there can be at most 16 instruments simultaneously, it is possible to have a MIDI file that uses many more in total throughout its duration.

One oddity of the General MIDI Standard is that Channel 10 (9 in Euterpea's 0-based numbering) is dedicated to *percussion*, which is different from the "percussive instruments" described in Table 8.1. Instead, "percussion" in this case refers to a standard drum kit and other miscellaneous small percussive instruments that have only one or two sounds associated with them. Unlike regular instruments, percussion on channel 10 uses pitch numbers to refer to distinct sounds, such as a bass kick drum (pitch number 36) or close hi-hat (pitch number 42). Recall that in Chapter 6 we captured these percussion sounds through the *PercussionSound* data type, and we defined a way to convert such a sound into a pitch number or absolute pitch (*AbsPitch*). This mirrors the General MIDI Standard.

Except for percussion, the MIDI channel used to represent a particular instrument is completely arbitrary. Euterpea's playback functions support the notion of a *channel assignment policy*: a function that maps instrument names to channel numbers over the duration of a *Music* value. Euterpea's default behavior is to use a *linear* policy that simply assigns instruments as they are encountered to channels 0 to 15 (accounting for channel 9's oddities). Under this policy, the same instrument will always appear on the same channel, but *Music* values with more than 16 instruments will cause an error. Alternatively, Euterpea also offers a *dynamic* policy that assigns instruments to channels in a FIFO (first in, first out) fashion: the oldest instrument is replaced with a newer one if more than 16 instruments are encountered, and program changes are used to alter the current instrument on a given channel. This allows playback of *Music* values with many more instruments, but instruments may end up distributed across multiple channels over time. If a particular instrument is "pushed out" to make room for newer instruments but comes back in later, it is unlikely that it will later end up back on its original channel.

MIDI file format also contains the notion of a *track*, which is a collection of ordered, *timestamped musical events*. Timestamps are relative, indicating how much time should elapse between two events. In some software, tracks have a one-to-one relationship with channels and thus there is no real need to distinguish between the two. However, this is not the case for all software. MIDI supports a many-to-one relationship between tracks and channels, and information for a single channel can be distributed across multiple tracks. This type of structure can be beneficial for organizational purposes, but it is somewhat irrelevant to Euterpea. Therefore, Euterpea takes the one-to-one model of a single track per channel.

8.1.2 MIDI Files

The General MIDI Standard defines the precise format of a *standard MIDI file*. When the General MIDI Standard was first created, disk space was at a premium, and thus a compact file structure was important. Standard MIDI files are thus defined at the bit and byte level, and are quite compact.

There are three types of Midi files:

- A Format 0, or *single-track*, file stores its information in a single track of events and is best used only for monophonic music.
- A Format 1, or *multi-track*, file stores its information in multiple tracks that are played simultaneously, where each track normally corresponds to a single MIDI channel.
- A Format 2, or *multi-pattern*, file also has multiple tracks, but they are temporally independent.

Euterpea only makes use of single- and multi-track files, depending on the number of channels needed to represent a given *Music* value.

Rather than dealing directly with the low-level file representations, Euterpea converts *Music* values to MIDI using two intermediate types that mirror MIDI format at different levels of abstraction: one representation is for event lists, and the other is essentially a Haskell representation of the MIDI file format.

8.2 MIDI Streams

MIDI format also supports the notion of *event streams*. These are used to send MIDI information over physical cables, such as when connecting a MIDI keyboard controller to a synthesizer. MIDI streams still adhere to the other principles discussed so far regarding channels, and the types of musical events that can be sent are the same as those that can be stored in a MIDI file. However, for MIDI streams, the events are *not timestamped*. For software that streams MIDI messages, control over timing must happen within the program, typically using buffers to accumulate messages before sending them out at the appropriate time.

MIDI streams can be sent to any MIDI device that accepts input. This can be a hardware device with physical five-pin MIDI connections, or it can be a software device with a *virtual MIDI port*. Computers can have many MIDI devices sending and receiving MIDI streams simultaneously, although care must be taken in complex, multi-device systems to avoid feedback loops (such loops are particularly easy to create with virtual MIDI ports).

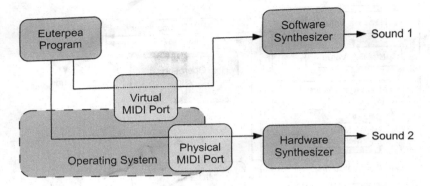

Figure 8.1 Illustration of a multi-device system involving Euterpea. Euterpea can send to any MIDI device registered with the operating system, whether it is a physical device or a virtual one. Because synthesizers often have different virtual instrument implementations, sending the same MIDI stream to a different output device typically produces a different sound.

Euterpea's playback functions stream MIDI messages to an output device, which can be either the default device or a user-specified device, depending on the particular function used. The musical user interfaces, or MUIs, presented in Chapter 17 also support a MIDI streaming framework. Figure 8.1 shows at a high level how message routing works in these situations.

8.3 Euterpea's Playback Framework

Euterpea has several playback functions, each with a slightly different purpose:

- *play* provides lazy playback to the default MIDI output device that permits sequentially infinite *Music* values.
- *playS* provides strict[1] playback to the default MIDI output device for finite *Music* values.
- *playDev* is like *play*, but for a user-specified MIDI output device.
- *playDevS* is like *playS*, but for a user-specified MIDI output device.
- *playC* allows maximum customization of the playback behavior, including selection of a channel assignment policy.[2] The other four functions are simply different front ends to *playC*.

---

[1] Strictness is the opposite of laziness: everything must be evaluated before use.
[2] See euterpea.com for complete specifications.

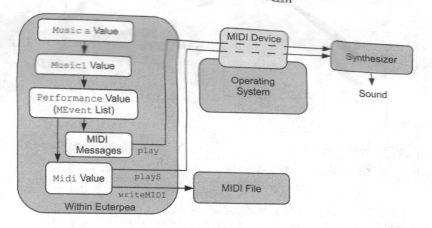

Figure 8.2 Illustration of the transformations that take place to convert a *Music a* value to either a MIDI stream or a MIDI file. Note that *playS* and *writeMidi* share the step of converting a *Music* value to a *Midi* value despite diverging in functionality thereafter.

Figure 8.2 shows the overall process involved in converting a *Music* value to a MIDI stream (or file). *Music* values must go through a series of transformations before being streamed as MIDI messages. The first step is to transform a given *Music a* into a *Music1*. There is a type class for this conversion, called *ToMusic1*, with a single function, *toMusic1*. *Music Pitch*, *Music (Pitch, Volume)*, and *Music1* are all instances of the *ToMusic1* type class:

class *ToMusic1 a* **where**
  toMusic1 :: Music a → Music1

instance *ToMusic1 Pitch* **where**
  toMusic1 = mMap (λp → (p, [ ]))

instance *ToMusic1 (Pitch, Volume)* **where**
  toMusic1 = mMap (λ(p, v) → (p, [Volume v]))

instance *ToMusic1 (Note1)* **where**
  toMusic1 = id

The next transformation involves flattening a *Music1* structure into an event list. *Music* has a tree structure, and this is linearized into a time-stamped series of events, with one event per note. This is captured with the following data structure and type synonyms:

```
data MEvent = MEvent {
    eTime   :: PTime,            -- onset time
    eInst   :: InstrumentName,   -- assigned instrument
    ePitch  :: AbsPitch,         -- pitch number from 0–127
    eDur    :: DurT,             -- note duration
    eVol    :: Volume,           -- volume from 0–127
    eParams :: [Double]}         -- optional other parameters
    deriving (Show, Eq, Ord)
type Performance = [MEvent]
type PTime = Rational
type DurT = Rational
```

Details: The data declaration for *MEvent* uses Haskell's *field label* syntax, also called *record* syntax, and is equivalent to:

```
data MEvent = MEvent PTime InstrumentName
                     AbsPitch DurT Volume [Double]
    deriving (Show, Eq, Ord)
```

except that the former also defines "field labels" *eTime*, *eInst*, *ePitch*, *eDur*, *eVol*, and *eParams*, which can be used to create, update, and select from *MEvent* values. For example, this equation:

$$e = MEvent \ 0 \ Cello \ 27 \ (1/4) \ 50 \ [\,]$$

is equivalent to:

$$e = MEvent \ \{eTime = 0, ePitch = 27, eDur = 1/4,$$
$$eInst = Cello, eVol = 50, eParams = [\,]\}$$

Although more verbose, the latter is also more descriptive, and the order of the fields does not matter (indeed, the order here is not the same as above).

Field labels can be used to *select* fields from an *MEvent* value; for example, using the value of e above, $eInst \ e \Rightarrow Cello$, $eDur \ e \Rightarrow 1/4$, and so on. They can also be used to selectively *update* fields of an existing *MEvent* value. For example:

$$e \ \{eInst = Flute\} \Rightarrow MEvent \ 0 \ Flute \ 27 \ (1/4) \ 50 \ [\,]$$

Finally, they can be used selectively in pattern-matching:

$$f \ (MEvent \ \{eDur = d, ePitch = p\}) = ...d ... p ...$$

Field labels do not change the basic nature of a data type; they are simply a convenient syntax for referring to the components of a data type by name rather than by position.

The process of turning a *Music1* value into a *Performance* is more complex than simply determining the start times and instruments for each *Note* in the tree. Recall that Euterpea allows various performance-related annotations through the use of *Modify*: accents, accelerandos, and so on. These are fuzzy concepts that would normally be subject to interpretation by a performer. Euterpea provides a *default performance interpretation* of these annotations. Chapter 9 provides more detail on the subject as well as a more customizable approach to performance using the notion of *players*, or algorithms that interpret the *Music* value in different ways. The remaining transformations to the MIDI level remain the same in both cases.

Once a *Music1* value has been "performed," the resulting event list can be handled in one of two ways:

1. Direct conversion to a stream of MIDI messages to be sent to a MIDI output device.
2. Conversion to a *Midi*[3] value, the various fields of which have a one-to-one correspondence to the byte-level representation of a MIDI file. A *Midi* value can be either streamed or written to a file.

8.3.1 Infinite Values and Timing Correctness

The laziness of the *play* function allows it to accommodate sequentially infinite *Music* values, such as $m = c \ 4 \ qn :+: m$. However, this comes at the expense of timing accuracy. Because lazy evaluation computes values on demand rather than in advance, the possibility exists of hitting a substantial "computation bubble" in the middle of playback that can throw off the timing. To make a musical analogy, the basic premise for *play*'s implementation is much like having a musician sight-read a score – if he or she hits an exceptionally difficult part, there will likely be a pause while contemplation takes place.

For *Music* values that require substantial computation time or for situations where exact timing is required, *playS* will have superior performance, since it

---

[3] The *Midi* datatype is defined in the Codec.Midi library, which Euterpea imports.

fully computes ... *usic* value before playback and uses an alternative MIDI ... .hm that is more accurate. To give another musical analogy, streaming ... *to* allowing a musician to memorize a score before playing it. *playS* ...ness involved in *playS* is partly due to the use of the intermediate ... data type, which is not possible to construct "on the fly" and instead ...quires traversal of the entire *Music* structure before it can be finalized. This in turn introduces the constraint that playback cannot start until the entire *Music* structure has been evaluated.

Typically, it is safest to work with *play* in most situations involving simple music values. In the event that the observed timing is unsatisfactory, it is easy to switch to *playS*. For sequentially infinite values, one can simply use *playS* $ *cut d m* to play *d* amount of *Music* value *m*.

Infinite parallelism, of course, is not supported and will simply hang regardless of the playback function used. However, such structures make no musical sense at the score level. Most synthesizers also have a *polyphony limit*, which is a cap on the number of notes that can be played simultaneously.[4]

---

[4] Although the polyphony limit on multi-instrument synthesizers is typically quite large, such as 127, for many hardware synthesizers it is smaller. In the analog domain, it is common to have a mono synth, which is a synthesizer that can only play a single note at a time!

9
Interpretation and Performance

So far, our presentation of musical values in Haskell has been mostly structural, i.e., *syntactic*. Although we have given an interpretation of the duration of *Music* values (as manifested in *dur*, *cut*, *remove*, and so on), we have not given any deeper musical interpretation. What do these musical values actually *mean*, i.e., what is their *semantics*, or *interpretation*? The formal process of giving a semantic interpretation for syntactic constructs is very common in computer science, especially in programming language theory. But it is obviously also common in music: the interpretation of music is the very essence of musical performance. However, in conventional music this process is usually informal, appealing to aesthetic judgments and values. What we would like to do is make the process formal, but still flexible, so that more than one interpretation is possible, just as in the human performance of music.

Details: To use the *arrow syntax* described in this chapter, it is necessary to use the following compiler pragmas in GHC:

{-# LANGUAGE FlexibleInstances, TypeSynonymInstances #-}

The first line of code in a Haskell source file can specify pragmas this way. In this case, the pragmas relax certain constraints on instance declarations. Specifically, instances cannot normally be declared for type synonyms, but the above pragma overrides that constraint.

9.1 Abstract Performance

To begin, we need to say exactly what an abstract *performance* is. Our approach is to consider a performance to be a time-ordered sequence of musical *events*, where each event captures the playing of one individual note. Recall the following definitions from Chapter 8:

```
data MMEvent = MMEvent {
  eTime   :: PTime,              -- onset time
  eInst   :: InstrumentName,     -- assigned instrument
  ePitch  :: AbsPitch,           -- pitch number from 0–127
  eDur    :: DurT,               -- note duration
  eVol    :: Volume,             -- volume from 0–127
  eParams :: [Double]}           -- optional other parameters
  deriving (Show, Eq, Ord)

type Performance = [MMEvent]
type PTime = Rational
type DurT = Rational
```

An event *MEvent* $\{eTime = s, eInst = i, ePitch = p, eDur = d, eVol = v\}$ captures the fact that at start time s, instrument i sounds pitch p with volume v for duration d (where now duration is measured in seconds rather than beats). (The *eParams* of an event is for instruments other than MIDI, in particular instruments that we might design using the techniques described in Chapter 19.)

9.1.1 Context

To generate a complete performance of or give an interpretation for a musical value, we must know the time to begin the performance and the proper instrument, volume, starting pitch offset, and tempo. We can think of this as the "context" in which a musical value is interpreted. This context can be captured formally in Haskell as a data type:

```
data Context a = Context {cTime   :: PTime,
                          cPlayer :: Player a,
                          cInst   :: InstrumentName,
                          cDur    :: DurT,
                          cPch    :: AbsPitch,
                          cVol    :: Volume,
                          cKey    :: (PitchClass, Mode)}
  deriving Show
```

When a *Music* value is interpreted, it will be given an inital context, but as the *Music* value is recursively interpreted, the context will be updated to reflect things like tempo change, transposition, and so on. This will be made clear shortly.

The *DurT* component of the context is the duration, in seconds, of one whole note. To make it easier to compute, we can define a "metronome" function that, given a standard metronome marking (in beats per minute) and the note type associated with one beat (quarter note, eighth note, etc.), generates the duration of one whole note:

$$metro \qquad \qquad :: Int \to Dur \to DurT$$
$$metro\ setting\ dur = 60\,/\,(fromIntegral\ setting * dur)$$

Thus, for example, *metro 96 qn* creates a tempo of 96 quarter notes per minute.

Details: *fromIntegral* :: *(Integral a, Num b)* $\Rightarrow a \to b$ coerces a value whose type is a member of the *Integral* class to a value whose type is a member of the *Num* class. As used here, it is effectively converting the *Int* value *setting* to a *Rational* value, because *dur* is a *Rational* value, *Rational* is a member of the *Num* class, and multiplication has type $(*) :: Num\ a \Rightarrow a \to a \to a.$

9.1.2 Player Map

In addition to the context, we also need to know what *player* to use; that is, we need a mapping from each *PlayerName* (a string) in a *Music* value to the actual player to be used.[1] The details of what a player is will be explained later in this chapter (Section 9.2). For now, we simply define a type synonym to capture the mapping of *PlayerName* to *Player*:

type *PMap a = PlayerName $\to$ Player a*

9.1.3 Interpretation

Euterpea defines a playerless default performance function called *perform*, which turns a *Music* value into a *Performance*. We will broaden Euterpea's existing functionality by creating a new performance function, *hsomPerform*:

hsomPerform :: *PMap a $\to$ Context a $\to$ Music a $\to$ Performance*

So *hsomPerform pm c m* is the *Performance* that results from interpreting *m* using player map *pm* in the initial context *c*. Conceptually, *hsomPerform* is perhaps the most important function defined in this textbook, and it is shown

---

[1] We do not need a mapping from *InstrumentNames* to instruments, since that is handled in the translation from a performance into MIDI, which is discussed in Chapter 8.

$hsomPerform :: PMap\ a \to Context\ a \to Music\ a \to Performance$
$hsomPerform\ pm$
  $c@Context\ \{cTime = t, cPlayer = pl, cDur = dt, cPch = k\}\ m =$
case m **of**
    $Prim\ (Note\ d\ p)$ $\to playNote\ pl\ c\ d\ p$
    $Prim\ (Rest\ d)$ $\to [\,]$
    $m1 \mathbin{:+:} m2$ $\to$
      let $c' = c\ \{cTime = t + dur\ m1 * dt\}$
      in $hsomPerform\ pm\ c\ m1 \mathbin{+\!\!+} hsomPerform\ pm\ c'\ m2$
    $m1 \mathbin{:=:} m2$ $\to merge\ (hsomPerform\ pm\ c\ m1)$
                                    $(hsomPerform\ pm\ c\ m2)$
    $Modify\ (Tempo\ r)$ $m \to hsomPerform\ pm\ (c\ \{cDur = dt/r\})$ m
    $Modify\ (Transpose\ p)$ $m \to hsomPerform\ pm\ (c\ \{cPch = k + p\})$ m
    $Modify\ (Instrument\ i)$ $m \to hsomPerform\ pm\ (c\ \{cInst = i\})$ m
    $Modify\ (KeySig\ pc\ mo)\ m \to hsomPerform\ pm\ (c\ \{cKey = (pc, mo)\})\ m$
    $Modify\ (Phrase\ pa)$ $m \to interpPhrase\ pl\ pm\ c\ pa\ m$
      if $take\ 7\ s == $ `"Player "` **then** $hsomPerform\ pm\ (c\ \{cPlayer = pm\ \$\ drop\ 7\ s\})\ m$
      else $perf\ pm\ c\ m$

Figure 9.1 An abstract performance function.

in Figure 9.1. To help in understanding the definition of *hsomPerform*, let's step through the equations one at a time.

1. The interpretation of a note is player-dependent. This is handled in *hsomPerform* using the *playNote* function, which takes the player as an argument. Precisely how the *playNote* function works is described in Section 9.2, but for now you can think of it as returning a *Performance* (a list of events) with just one event: the note being played.
2. In the interpretation of (:+:), note that the *Performances* of the two arguments are appended together, with the start time of the second *Performance* delayed by the duration of the first (as captured in the context c'). The function *dur* (defined in Section 6.3) is used to compute this duration. Note that the interpretation of (:+:) is well-defined even for infinite *Music* values.
3. In the interpretation of (:=:), the *Performances* derived from the two arguments are merged into a time-ordered stream. The definition of *merge* is given below:

$merge :: Performance \to Performance \to Performance$

$merge\ [\,]$ $es2$ $= es2$
$merge\ es1$ $[\,]$ $= es1$
$merge\ a@(e1 : es1)\ b@(e2 : es2) =$
    if $e1 < e2$ **then** $e1 : merge\ es1\ b$
               else $e2 : merge\ a\ es2$

Note that *merge* is esssentially the same as the *mergeLD* function defined in Section 6.7.1.

4. In the interpretation of *Modify*, first recall the definition of *Control* from Chapter 2:

data *Control* =
    Tempo   *Rational*   -- scale the tempo
    | *Transpose* *AbsPitch*   -- transposition
    | *Instrument* *InstrumentName* -- instrument label
    | *Phrase*   [*PhraseAttribute*] -- phrase attributes
    | *KeySig*   *PitchClass Mode* -- key signature and mode
    | *Custom*   *String*   -- for user-specified controls
  deriving (*Show, Eq, Ord*)

The *Custom* constructor is used to hold information on the current player by using a *String* of the form "Player playerName." Each of these six constructors is handled by a separate equation in the definition of *hsomPerform*. Note how the context is updated in each case – the *Context*, in general, is the running "state" of the performance and gets updated in several different ways.

Also of note is the treatment of *Phrase*. Like the playing of a note, the playing of a phrase is player-dependent. This is captured with the function *interpPhrase*, which takes the player as an argument. Like *playNote*, this too, along with the *PhraseAttribute* data type, will be described in full detail in Section 9.2.

9.1.4 Efficiency Concerns

The use of *dur* in the treatment of (:+:) can, in the worst case, result in a quadratic time complexity for *hsomPerform*. (Why?) A more efficient solution is to have *hsomPerform* compute the duration directly, returning it as part of its result. This version of *hsomPerform* is shown in Figure 9.2.

Aside from efficiency, there is a more abstract reason for including duration in the result of *hsomPerform*: the performance of a rest is not just nothing; it is a period of "silence" equal in duration to that of the rest. Indeed, John Cage's famous composition *4'33"*, in which the performer is instructed to play nothing, would otherwise be meaningless.[2]

---

[2] In reality, this piece is meant to capture extemporaneously the sound of the environment during that period of "silence" [15].

```
hsomPerform :: PMap a → Context a → Music a → Performance
hsomPerform pm c m = fst (perf pm c m)

perf :: PMap a → Context a → Music a → (Performance, DurT)
perf pm
  c@Context {cTime = t, cPlayer = pl, cDur = dt, cPch = k} m =
  case m of
    Prim (Note d p)             → (playNote pl c d p, d ∗ dt)
    Prim (Rest d)               → ([ ], d ∗ dt)
    m1 :+: m2                   →
        let (pf1, d1) = perf pm c m1
            (pf2, d2) = perf pm (c {cTime = t + d1}) m2
        in (pf1 ++ pf2, d1 + d2)
    m1 :=: m2                   →
        let (pf1, d1) = perf pm c m1
            (pf2, d2) = perf pm c m2
        in (merge pf1 pf2, max d1 d2)
    Modify (Tempo r)     m → perf pm (c {cDur = dt/r})      m
    Modify (Transpose p) m → perf pm (c {cPch = k + p})     m
    Modify (Instrument i) m → perf pm (c {cInst = i})       m
    Modify (KeySig pc mo) m → perf pm (c {cKey = (pc, mo)}) m
    Modify (Phrase pas)  m → interpPhrase pl pm c pas       m
    Modify (Custom s) m →
        if take 7 s == "Player  " then perf pm (c {cPlayer = pm $ drop 7 s}) m
        else perf pm c m
```

Figure 9.2 A more efficient *hsomPerform* function.

Also note that *merge* compares entire events rather than just start times. This is to ensure that it is commutative, a desirable condition for some of the proofs used later in the text. Here is a more efficient version of *merge* that will work just as well in practice:

```
merge :: Performance → Performance → Performance
merge [ ]              es2              = es2
merge es1              [ ]              = es1
merge a@(e1 : es1) b@(e2 : es2) =
    if eTime e1 < eTime e2 then e1 : merge es1 b
                           else e2 : merge a es2
```

9.2 Players

Recall from Section 2.2 that the *Phrase* constructor in the *Control* data type takes a list of *PhraseAttribute*s as an argument:

```
data Control = ...
  | Phrase [PhraseAttribute]    -- phrase attributes
  ...
```

It is now time to unveil the definition of *PhraseAttribute*! Shown fully in Figure 9.3, these attributes give us great flexibility in the interpretation process, because they can be interpreted by different players in different ways. For example, how should "legato" be interpreted in a performance? Or "diminuendo"? Different human players interpret things in different ways, of course, but even more fundamental is the fact that a pianist, for example, realizes legato in a way fundamentally different from the way a violinist does, because of differences in their instruments. Similarly, diminuendo on a piano and diminuendo on a harpsichord are very different concepts.

In addition to phrase attributes, Euterpea has a notion of *note attributes* that can similarly be interpreted in different ways by different players. This is done

```
data PhraseAttribute = Dyn Dynamic
                     |  Tmp Tempo
                     |  Art Articulation
                     |  Orn Ornament
  deriving (Show, Eq, Ord)

data Dynamic = Accent Rational | Crescendo Rational
             | Diminuendo Rational | StdLoudness StdLoudness
             | Loudness Rational
  deriving (Show, Eq, Ord)

data StdLoudness = PPP | PP | P | MP | SF | MF | NF | FF | FFF
  deriving (Show, Eq, Ord, Enum)

data Tempo = Ritardando Rational | Accelerando Rational
  deriving (Show, Eq, Ord)

data Articulation =  Staccato Rational | Legato Rational
                  |  Slurred Rational | Tenuto | Marcato | Pedal
                  |  Fermata | FermataDown | Breath | DownBow
                  |  UpBow | Harmonic | Pizzicato | LeftPizz
                  |  BartokPizz | Swell | Wedge | Thumb | Stopped
  deriving (Show, Eq, Ord)

data Ornament = Trill | Mordent | InvMordent | DoubleMordent
              | Turn | TrilledTurn | ShortTrill
              | Arpeggio | ArpeggioUp | ArpeggioDown
              | Instruction String | Head NoteHead
              | DiatonicTrans Int
  deriving (Show, Eq, Ord)

data NoteHead = DiamondHead | SquareHead | XHead | TriangleHead
              | TremoloHead | SlashHead | ArtHarmonic | NoHead
  deriving (Show, Eq, Ord)
```

Figure 9.3 Phrase attributes.

by exploiting polymorphism to define a version of *Music* that, in addition to pitch, carries a list of note attributes for each individual note:

data *NoteAttribute* =
  Volume Int   -- MIDI convention: 0=min, 127=max
  | *Fingering Integer*
  | *Dynamics String*
  | *Params* [*Double*]
  deriving (*Show*, *Eq*)

Our goal, then, is to define a player for music values of type:

type *Note1*   = (*Pitch*, [*NoteAttribute*])
type *Music1* = *Music Note1*

Recall the definition of the *ToMusic1* type class from Chapter 8:

class *ToMusic1 a* **where**
  toMusic1 :: *Music a → Music1*

Music Pitch and *Music* (*Pitch*, *Volume*) are instances of *ToMusic1*, allowing them to be converted to *Music1* before calling *hsomPerform*.

To handle different levels of interpretation, Euterpea has a notion of a *player* that "knows" about differences with respect to performance and notation. A Euterpean *Player* is a three-tuple consisting of a name and two functions: one for interpreting notes, and one for phrases.

data *Player a* = *MkPlayer* {*pName*   :: *PlayerName*,
                        playNote   :: *NoteFun a*,
                        interpPhrase :: *PhraseFun a*}

type *NoteFun a*   = *Context a → Dur → a → Performance*
type *PhraseFun a* = *PMap a → Context a →* [*PhraseAttribute*]
                  → *Music a →* (*Performance*, *DurT*)

instance *Show a ⇒ Show* (*Player a*) **where**
  show p = "Player " ++ *pName p*

Note the instance declaration for a *Player* – since its components are mostly functions, which are not default instances of *Show*, we define a simple way to return the *PlayerName*.

9.2.1 Example of Player Construction

In this section, we define a "default player" called *defPlayer* (not to be confused with a "deaf player"!) for use when no other is specified in a score; it also functions as a basis from which other players can be derived.

$defPlayNote :: (Context\ (Pitch, [a]) \rightarrow a \rightarrow MEvent \rightarrow MEvent)$
$\qquad\qquad\qquad \rightarrow NoteFun\ (Pitch, [a])$
$defPlayNote\ nasHandler$
$\quad c@(Context\ cTime\ cPlayer\ cInst\ cDur\ cPch\ cVol\ cKey)\ d\ (p, nas) =$
$\qquad \textbf{let}\ initEv = MEvent\ \{eTime = cTime, eInst = cInst,$
$\qquad\qquad eDur\quad = d * cDur, eVol = cVol,$
$\qquad\qquad ePitch\quad = absPitch\ p + cPch,$
$\qquad\qquad eParams = [\,]\}$
$\qquad \textbf{in}\ [foldr\ (nasHandler\ c)\ initEv\ nas]$

$defNasHandler :: Context\ a \rightarrow NoteAttribute \rightarrow MEvent \rightarrow MEvent$
$defNasHandler\ c\ (Volume\ v)\quad ev = ev\ \{eVol = v\}$
$defNasHandler\ c\ (Params\ pms)\ ev = ev\ \{eParams = pms\}$
$defNasHandler\ \_\qquad\qquad \_\quad\ \ ev = ev$

$defInterpPhrase ::$
$\quad (PhraseAttribute \rightarrow Performance \rightarrow Performance) \rightarrow$
$\quad (PMap\ a \rightarrow Context\ a \rightarrow [PhraseAttribute] \rightarrow \quad$ -- PhraseFun
$\quad\ Music\ a \rightarrow (Performance, DurT))$
$defInterpPhrase\ pasHandler\ pm\ context\ pas\ m =$
$\quad \textbf{let}\ (pf, dur) = perf\ pm\ context\ m$
$\quad \textbf{in}\ (foldr\ pasHandler\ pf\ pas, dur)$

$defPasHandler :: PhraseAttribute \rightarrow Performance \rightarrow Performance$
$defPasHandler\ (Dyn\ (Accent\ x))\quad =$
$\quad map\ (\lambda e \rightarrow e\ \{eVol = round\ (x * fromIntegral\ (eVol\ e))\})$
$defPasHandler\ (Art\ (Staccato\ x)) =$
$\quad map\ (\lambda e \rightarrow e\ \{eDur = x * eDur\ e\})$
$defPasHandler\ (Art\ (Legato\ x))\quad =$
$\quad map\ (\lambda e \rightarrow e\ \{eDur = x * eDur\ e\})$
$defPasHandler\ \_\qquad\qquad\qquad = id$

Figure 9.4 Definition of the default player *defPlayer*.

At the uppermost level, *defPlayer* is defined as a three-tuple:

$defPlayer :: Player\ Note1$
$defPlayer = MkPlayer$
$\qquad\quad \{pName\qquad\quad = \texttt{"Default"},$
$\qquad\quad\ \ playNote\quad\ = defPlayNote\quad defNasHandler,$
$\qquad\quad\ \ interpPhrase = defInterpPhrase\ defPasHandler\}$

The remaining functions are defined in Figure 9.4. Before reading this code, first review how players are invoked by the *hsomPerform* function defined in the last section; in particular, note the calls to *playNote* and *interpPhrase*. We will define *defPlayer* to respond only to the *Volume* note attribute and to the *Accent*, *Staccato*, and *Legato* phrase attributes.

Then note:

1. *defPlayNote* is the only function (even in the definition of *hsomPerform*) that actually generates an event. It also modifies that event based on an interpretation of each note attribute by the function *defNasHandler*.
2. *defNasHandler* only recognizes the *Volume* attribute, which it uses to set the event volume accordingly.
3. *defInterpPhrase* calls (mutually recursively) *perf* to interpret a phrase, and then modifies the result based on an interpretation of each phrase attribute by the function *defPasHandler*.
4. *defPasHandler* only recognizes the *Accent*, *Staccato*, and *Legato* phrase attributes. For each of these, it uses the numeric argument as a "scaling" factor of the volume (for *Accent*) and duration (for *Staccato* and *Legato*). Thus *Modify* (*Phrase* [*Legato* (5/4)]) *m* effectively increases the duration of each note in *m* by 25% (without changing the tempo).

9.2.2 Deriving New Players from Old Ones

It should be clear that much of the code in Figure 9.4 can be reused in defining a new player. For example, to define a player *newPlayer* that interprets note attributes just like *defPlayer* but behaves differently with respect to certain phrase attributes, we could write:

newPlayer :: *Player* (*Pitch*, [*NoteAttribute*])
newPlayer = *MkPlayer*
    {*pName*   = "NewPlayer",
     playNote   = *defPlayNote defNasHandler*,
     interpPhrase = *defInterpPhrase myPasHandler*}

and then supply a suitable definition of *myPasHandler*. Better yet, we could just do this:

newPlayer :: *Player* (*Pitch*, [*NoteAttribute*])
newPlayer = *defPlayer*
    {*pName*   = "NewPlayer",
     interpPhrase = *defInterpPhrase myPasHandler*}

This version uses the "record update" syntax to directly derive the new player from *defPlayer*.

The definition of *myPasHandler* can also reuse code, in the following sense: suppose we wish to add an interpretation for *Crescendo*, but otherwise have *myPasHandler* behave just like *defPasHandler*.

myPasHandler :: *PhraseAttribute* → *Performance* → *Performance*
myPasHandler (*Dyn* (*Crescendo x*)) *pf* = ...
myPasHandler pa   *pf* = *defPasHandler pa pf*

9.2.3 A Fancy Player

Figure 9.5 defines a more sophisticated player called *fancyPlayer* that knows
all that *defPlayer* knows, and more. Note that *Slurred* is different from *Legato*,
in that it does not extend the duration of the *last* note(s). The behavior of
Ritardando x can be explained as follows. We would like to "stretch" the time
of each event by a factor from 0 to x, linearly interpolated based on how far
along the musical phrase the event occurs. That is, given a start time t_0 for the
first event in the phrase, total phrase duration D, and event time t, the new event
time t' is given by:

$$t' = \left(1 + \frac{t - t_0}{D}x\right)(t - t_0) + t_0$$

Further, if d is the duration of the event, then the end of the event $t + d$ gets
stretched to a new time t'_d given by:

$$t'_d = \left(1 + \frac{t + d - t_0}{D}x\right)(t + d - t_0) + t_0$$

The difference $t'_d - t'$ gives us the new stretched duration d', which after
simplification is:

$$d' = \left(1 + \frac{2(t - t_0) + d}{D}x\right)d$$

Accelerando behaves in exactly the same way, except that it shortens event
times rather than lengthening them. And a similar but simpler strategy explains
the behaviors of *Crescendo* and *Diminuendo*.

9.3 Putting It All Together

Euterpea's *play* function does not include the notion of players discussed in this
chapter. To accomodate players, the HSoM library accompanying this textbook
includes a function called *playA* that allows specification of players. Default
player maps and context are supplied as follows:

```
fancyPlayer :: Player (Pitch, [NoteAttribute])
fancyPlayer = MkPlayer {pName       = "Fancy",
                        playNote     = defPlayNote defNasHandler,
                        interpPhrase = fancyInterpPhrase,
                        notatePlayer = ()}

fancyInterpPhrase                    :: PhraseFun a
fancyInterpPhrase pm c [] m = perf pm c m
fancyInterpPhrase pm
  c@Context {cTime = t, cPlayer = pl, cInst = i,
             cDur = dt, cPch = k, cVol = v}
  (pa : pas) m =
  let pfd@(pf, dur) = fancyInterpPhrase pm c pas m
      loud x        = fancyInterpPhrase pm c (Dyn (Loudness x) : pas) m
      stretch x     = let  t0 = eTime (head pf); r = x / dur
                           upd (e@MEvent {eTime = t, eDur = d}) =
                             let dt = t - t0
                                 t' = (1 + dt * r) * dt + t0
                                 d' = (1 + (2 * dt + d) * r) * d
                             in e {eTime = t', eDur = d'}
                      in (map upd pf, (1 + x) * dur)
      inflate x     = let  t0 = eTime (head pf);
                           r  = x / dur
                           upd (e@MEvent {eTime = t, eVol = v}) =
                             e {eVol = round ((1 + (t - t0) * r) *
                                       fromIntegral v)}
                      in (map upd pf, dur)
  in case pa of
  Dyn (Accent x) →
     (map (λe → e {eVol = round (x * fromIntegral (eVol e))}) pf, dur)
  Dyn (StdLoudness l) →
      case l of
          PPP → loud 40; PP → loud 50; P   → loud 60
          MP  → loud 70; SF → loud 80; MF  → loud 90
          NF  → loud 100; FF → loud 110; FFF → loud 120
  Dyn (Loudness x)    → fancyInterpPhrase pm
                          c {cVol = round x} pas m
  Dyn (Crescendo x)  → inflate x; Dyn (Diminuendo x) → inflate (−x)
  Tmp (Ritardando x) → stretch x; Tmp (Accelerando x) → stretch (−x)
  Art (Staccato x)    → (map (λe → e {eDur = x * eDur e}) pf, dur)
  Art (Legato x)      → (map (λe → e {eDur = x * eDur e}) pf, dur)
  Art (Slurred x)     →
      let  lastStartTime = foldr (λe t → max (eTime e) t) 0 pf
           setDur e      = if eTime e < lastStartTime
                           then e {eDur = x * eDur e}
                           else e
      in (map setDur pf, dur)
  Art _               → pfd
  Orn _               → pfd
```

Figure 9.5 Definition of the player *fancyPlayer*.

$$
\begin{aligned}
&\textit{defPMap} && :: \textit{PMap Note1} \\
&\textit{defPMap "Fancy"} && = \textit{fancyPlayer} \\
&\textit{defPMap "Default"} && = \textit{defPlayer} \\
&\textit{defPMap n} && = \textit{defPlayer \{pName = n\}}
\end{aligned}
$$

$$
\textit{defCon} :: \textit{Context Note1}
$$

$$
\begin{aligned}
\textit{defCon} = \textit{Context } \{ \textit{cTime} \;\;&= 0, \\
\textit{cPlayer} &= \textit{fancyPlayer}, \\
\textit{cInst} &= \textit{AcousticGrandPiano}, \\
\textit{cDur} &= \textit{metro } 120 \; \textit{qn}, \\
\textit{cPch} &= 0, \\
\textit{cKey} &= (C, \textit{Major}), \\
\textit{cVol} &= 127 \}
\end{aligned}
$$

Note that if anything other than a "Fancy" or "Default" player is specified in the *Music* value, such as *player* "Strange" *m*, then the default player *defPlayer* is used and is given the name "Strange".

If instead we wish to use our own player, say *newPlayer* defined in Section 9.2.2, then a new player map can be defined, such as:

$$
\begin{aligned}
&\textit{myPMap} && :: \textit{PlayerName} \rightarrow \textit{Player Note1} \\
&\textit{myPMap "NewPlayer"} && = \textit{newPlayer} \\
&\textit{myPMap p} && = \textit{defPMap p}
\end{aligned}
$$

Similarly, different versions of the context can be defined based on the user's needs.

We could, then, use these versions of player maps and contexts to invoke the *hsomPerform* function to generate an abstract *Performance*. Of course, we ultimately want to hear our music, not just see an abstract *Performance* displayed on our computer screen.

The type signature of *playA* is as follows:[3]

$$
\begin{aligned}
\textit{playA} :: (\textit{Performable } a, \textit{NFData } a) \Rightarrow \\
\textit{PMap Note1} \rightarrow \textit{Context Note1} \rightarrow \textit{Music } a \rightarrow \textit{IO } ()
\end{aligned}
$$

For example, to play a *Music* value *m* using *myPMap* defined above and the default context *defCon*, we can do:

$$
\textit{playA myPMap defCon m}
$$

The way this function converts a *Performance* to a MIDI stream follows the same transformation as described in Chapter 8.

---

[3] The NFData type class is required for the timing-strict playback option Euterpea includes.

Exercise 9.1 Fill in the ... in the definition of *myPasHandler* according to the following strategy: Gradually scale the volume of each event in the performance by a factor of 1 through $1 + x$ using linear interpolation.

Exercise 9.2 Choose some of the other phrase attributes and provide interpretations for them.

(Hint: As in *fancyPlayer*, you may not be able to use the "*pasHandler*" approach to implement some of the phrase attributes. For example, for a proper treatment of *Trill* [and similar ornaments], you will need to access the *cKey* field in the context.)

Exercise 9.3 Define a player *myPlayer* that appropriately handles the *Pedal* articulation and both the *ArpeggioUp* and *ArpeggioDown* ornamentations. You should define *myPlayer* as a derivative of *defPlayer* or *newPlayer*.

Exercise 9.4 Define a player *jazzMan* (or *jazzWoman* if you prefer) that plays a melody using a jazz "swing" feel. Since there are different kinds and degrees of swing, we can be more specific as follows: whenever there is a sequence of two eighth notes, they should be interpreted instead as a quarter note followed by an eighth note, but with tempo 3/2. In essence, the first note is lengthened and the second note is shortened, so that the first note is twice as long as the second, but they still take up the same amount of overall time.

(Hint: There are several ways to solve this problem. One surprisingly effective and straightforward solution is to implement *jazzMan* as a *NoteFun*, not a *PhraseFun*. In jazz, if an eighth note falls on a quarter-note beat, it is said to fall on the "downbeat," and the eighth notes that are in between are said to fall on the "upbeat." For example, in the phrase *c* 4 *en* :+: *d* 4 *en* :+: *e* 4 *en* :+: *f* 4 *en*, the C and E fall on the downbeat, and the D and F fall on the upbeat. So to get a "swing" feel, the notes on the downbeat need to be lengthened, and the ones on the upbeat need to be delayed and shortened. Whether an event falls on a downbeat or an upbeat can be determined from the *cTime* and *cDur* of the context.)

Exercise 9.5 Implement the ornamentation *DiatonicTrans*, which is intended to be a "diatonic tranposition" of a phrase within a particular key. The argument to *DiatonicTrans* is an integer representing the number of *scale degrees* to do the transposition. For example, the diatonic transposition of *c* 4 *en*:+:*d* 4 *en*:+: *e* 4 *en* in C major by two scale degrees should yield *e* 4 *en*:+:*f* 4 *en*:+:*g* 4 *en*, whereas in G major should yield *e* 4 *en* :+: *fs* 4 *en* :+: *g* 4 *en*.

(Hint: You will need to access the key from the context [using *cKey*]. Thus, as with *fancyPlayer*, you may not be able to use the "*pasHandler*" approach to solve this problem.)

10

Self-Similar Music

In this chapter we will explore the notion of *self-similar* music – i.e., musical structures that have patterns that repeat themselves recursively in interesting ways. There are many approaches to generating self-similar structures, the most well-known being *fractals*, which have been used to generate not just music, but also graphical images. We will delay a general treatment of fractals, however, and instead focus on more specialized notions of self-similarity, notions that we conceive of musically and then manifest as Haskell programs.

10.1 Self-Similar Melody

For the first notion of self-similarity we will consider, we will begin with a very simple melody of n notes. Next, we will duplicate this melody n times, playing each in succession, but first performing the following transformations: transpose the ith melody by an amount proportional to the pitch of the ith note in the original melody, and scale its tempo by a factor proportional to the duration of the ith note. For example, Figure 10.1 shows the result of applying this process once to a four-note melody (the first four notes form the original melody). Now imagine that this process is repeated infinitely often. For a melody whose notes are all shorter than a whole note, it yields an infinitely dense melody of infinitesimally shorter notes. To make the result playable, however, we must stop the process at some predetermined level.

How can this be represented in Haskell? A *tree* seems like it would be a logical choice; let's call it a *Cluster*:

```
data Cluster = Cluster SNote [Cluster]
type SNote   = (Dur, AbsPitch)
```

148

Figure 10.1 An example of several iterations of creating self-similar music. A pitch transformation of 0, +5, −2, and 0 is applied to each note in the music, splitting the original note's duration each time.

This particular kind of tree happens to be called a *rose tree*. An *SNote* is just a *simple note*: a duration paired with an absolute pitch. It is simpler to stick with absolute pitches when creating a self-similar structure, and so we will convert the result into a normal *Music* value only after we are done.

The sequence of *SNote*s at each level of the cluster is the melodic fragment for that level. The very top cluster will contain a "dummy" note, whereas the next level will contain the original melody, the next level will contain one iteration of the process described above (e.g., the melody in Figure 10.1), and so forth.

To achieve this, we will define a function *selfSim* that takes the initial melody as argument and generates an infinitely deep cluster:

selfSim   :: [*SNote*] → *Cluster*
selfSim pat = *Cluster* (0, 0) (*map mkCluster pat*)
   where *mkCluster note* =
    Cluster note (*map* (*mkCluster* ∘ *addMult note*) *pat*)

addMult   :: *SNote* → *SNote* → *SNote*
addMult (*d0, p0*) (*d1, p1*) = (*d0* ∗ *d1, p0* + *p1*)

Note that *selfSim* itself is not recursive, but *mkCluster* is. This code should be studied carefully. In particular, the recursion in *mkCluster* is different from what we have seen before, as it is not a direct invocation of *mkCluster*, but rather a high-order argument to *map* (which in turn invokes *mkCluster* an arbitrary number of times).

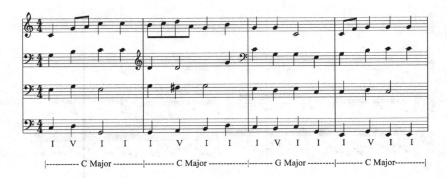

Figure 10.2 Self-similarity doesn't have to sound strange or artificial. This phase, produced by Kulitta [16], demonstrates a distinctly self-similar pattern in the harmony. However, it is somewhat "hidden" from the ear, as it appears at a more abstract level in the music: even though the surface-level notes are quite varied, the relationship between the keys of C major and G major is much like the relationship of I and V chords within a key.

Next, we define a function to skim off the notes at the nth level, or nth "fringe," of a cluster:

$fringe$ :: $Int \rightarrow Cluster \rightarrow [SNote]$
$fringe$ 0 $(Cluster\ note\ cls) = [note]$
$fringe\ n\ (Cluster\ note\ cls) = concatMap\ (fringe\ (n-1))\ cls$

Details: *concatMap* is defined in the Standard Prelude as:

$concatMap$ :: $(a \rightarrow [b]) \rightarrow [a] \rightarrow [b]$
$concatMap\ f = concat \circ map\ f$

Recall that *concat* appends together a list of lists, and is defined in the Prelude as:

$concat :: [[a]] \rightarrow [a]$
$concat = foldr\ (+\!\!+)\ [\ ]$

All that is left to do is convert this into a *Music* value that we can play:

$simToMusic$ :: $[SNote] \rightarrow Music\ Pitch$
$simToMusic\ ss =$ **let** $mkNote\ (d, ap) = note\ d\ (pitch\ ap)$
             in $line\ (map\ mkNote\ ss)$

We can define this with a bit more elegance, as follows:

$$simToMusic \quad :: [SNote] \to Music\ Pitch$$
$$simToMusic \quad = line \circ map\ mkNote$$

$$mkNote \quad :: (Dur, AbsPitch) \to Music\ Pitch$$
$$mkNote\ (d, ap) = note\ d\ (pitch\ ap)$$

The increased modularity will allow us to reuse *mkNote* later in the chapter.

Putting it all together, we can define a function that takes an initial pattern, a level, a number of pitches to transpose the result, and a tempo scaling factor to yield a final result:

$$ss\ pat\ n\ tr\ te =$$
$$transpose\ tr\ \$\ tempo\ te\ \$\ simToMusic\ \$\ fringe\ n\ \$\ selfSim\ pat$$

10.1.1 Sample Compositions

Let's start with a melody with no rhythmic variation.

$$m0 :: [SNote]$$
$$m0 = [(1, 2), (1, 0), (1, 5), (1, 7)]$$

$$tm0 = instrument\ Vibraphone\ (ss\ m0\ 4\ 50\ 20)$$

One fun thing to do with music like this is to combine it with variations of itself. For example:

$$ttm0 = tm0 :=: transpose\ (12)\ (retro\ tm0)$$

We could also try the opposite: a simple percussion instrument with no melodic variation, i.e., all rhythm:

$$m1 :: [SNote]$$
$$m1 = [(1, 0), (0.5, 0), (0.5, 0)]$$

$$tm1 = instrument\ Percussion\ (ss\ m1\ 4\ 43\ 2)$$

Note that the pitch is transposed by 43, which is the MIDI key number for a "high floor tom" (i.e., percussion sound *HighFloorTom*; recall the discussion in Section 6.10).

Here is a very simple melody with two different pitches and two different durations:

$$m2 :: [SNote]$$
$$m2 = [(dqn, 0), (qn, 4)]$$

$$tm2 = ss\ m2\ 6\ 50\ (1/50)$$

Here are some more exotic compositions combining melody and rhythm:

m3 :: [*SNote*]

m3 = [$(hn, 3), (qn, 4), (qn, 0), (hn, 6)$]

tm3 = *ss m3* 4 50 (1/4)

ttm3 = **let** *l1* = *instrument Flute tm3*

　　　　　　l2 = *instrument AcousticBass* $

　　　　　　　　　transpose (−9) (*retro tm3*)

　　　in *l1* :=: *l2*

m4 :: [*SNote*]

m4 = [$(hn, 3), (hn, 8), (hn, 22), (qn, 4), (qn, 7), (qn, 21),$

　　　　$(qn, 0), (qn, 5), (qn, 15), (wn, 6), (wn, 9), (wn, 19)$]

tm4 = *ss m4* 3 50 8

Exercise 10.1 Experiment with this idea further using other melodic seeds, exploring different depths of the clusters, and so on.

Exercise 10.2 Note that *concat* is defined as *foldr* (++) [ ], which means that it takes a number of steps proportional to the sum of the lengths of the lists being concatenated; we cannot do any better than this. (If *foldl* were used instead, the number of steps would be proportional to the number of lists times their average length.)

　　However, *fringe* is not very efficient, for the following reason: *concat* is being used over and over again, like this:

concat [*concat* [...], *concat* [...], *concat* [...]]

This causes a number of steps proportional to the depth of the tree times the length of the sub-lists; clearly not optimal.

　　Define a version of *fringe* that is linear in the total length of the final list.

10.2 Self-Similar Harmony

In the last section we used a melody as a seed and created longer melodies from it. Another idea is to stack the melodies vertically. Specifically, suppose we redefine *fringe* in such a way that it does not concatenate the sub-clusters together:

fringe'　　　　　　　　　　:: *Int* → *Cluster* → [[*SNote*]]

fringe' 0 (*Cluster note cls*) = [[*note*]]

fringe' n (*Cluster note cls*) = *map* (*fringe* (n − 1)) *cls*

Note that this strategy is only applied to the top level – below that we use *fringe*. Thus the type of the result is [[*SNote*]], i.e., a list of lists of notes.

We can convert the individual lists into melodies and play the melodies all together, like this:

simToMusic' :: [[*SNote*]] → *Music Pitch*
simToMusic' = *chord* ∘ *map* (*line* ∘ *map mkNote*)

Finally, we can define a function akin to *ss* defined earlier:

ss' pat n tr te =
    transpose tr $ *tempo te* $ *simToMusic'* $ *fringe' n* $ *selfSim pat*

Using some of the same patterns used earlier, here are some sample compositions (with not necessarily a great outcome...):

ss1 = *ss' m2* 4 50 (1/8)
ss2 = *ss' m3* 4 50 (1/2)
ss3 = *ss' m4* 3 50 2

Here is a new one, based on a major triad:

m5 = [(*en*, 4), (*sn*, 7), (*en*, 0)]
ss5 = *ss m5* 4 45 (1/500)
ss6 = *ss' m5* 4 45 (1/1000)

Note the need to scale the tempo back drastically, due to the short durations of the starting notes.

10.3 Other Self-Similar Structures

The reader will observe that our notion of "self-similar harmony" does not involve changing the structure of the *Cluster* data type or the algorithm for computing the sub-structures (as captured in *selfSim*). All we do is interpret the result differently. This is a common characteristic of algorithmic music composition – the same mathematical or computational structure is interpreted in different ways to yield musically different results.

For example, instead of the above strategy for playing melodies in parallel, we could play entire levels of the *Cluster* in parallel, where the number of levels that we choose is given as a parameter. If aligned properly in time, there will be a harmonic relationship between the levels, which could yield pleasing results.

The *Cluster* data type is conceptually useful in that it represents the infinite solution space of self-similar melodies. It is also computationally useful, in that it is computed to a desired depth only once, and thus can be inspected and reused without recomputing each level of the tree. This idea might be useful in the application mentioned above, namely combining two or more levels of the result in interesting ways.

However, the *Cluster* data type is strictly unnecessary, in that, for example, if we are interested in computing a specific level, we could define a function that recursed to that level and gave the result directly, without saving the intermediate levels.

A final point about the notion of self-similarity captured in this chapter is that the initial pattern is used as the basis with which to transform each successive level. Another strategy would be to use the entirety of each new level as the seed for transforming itself into the next level. This will result in an exponential blow-up in the size of each level, but may be worth pursuing – in some sense it is a simpler notion of self-similarity than what we have used in this chapter.

All of the ideas in this section, and others, we leave as exercises for the reader.

Exercise 10.3 Experiment with the self-similar programs in this chapter. Compose an interesting piece of music through a judicious choice of starting melody, depth of recursion, instrumentation, etc.

Exercise 10.4 Devise an interpretation of a *Cluster* that plays multiple levels of the *Cluster* in parallel. Try to get the levels to align properly in time so that each level has the same duration. You may choose to play all the levels up to a certain depth in parallel or levels within a certain range, say levels 3 through 5.

Exercise 10.5 Define an alternative version of *simToMusic* that interprets the music differently. For example:

- Interpret the pitch as an index into a scale – e.g., as an index into the C major scale, so that 0 corresponds to C, 1 to D, 2 to E, 3 to F, . . . , 6 to B, 7 to C in the next octave, and so on.
- Interpret the pitch as duration and the duration as pitch.

Exercise 10.6 Modify the self-similar code in the following ways:

- Add a Volume component to *SNote* – in other words, define it as a triple instead of a pair – and redefine *addMult* so that it takes two of these triples and combines them in a suitable way. Then modify the rest of the code so that the result is a *Music1* value. With these modifications, compose something interesting that highlights the changes in volume.

- Change the *AbsPitch* field in *SNote* to be a list of *AbsPitchs*, to be interpreted ultimately as a chord. Figure out some way to combine them in *addMult* and compose something interesting.

Exercise 10.7 Devise some other variant of self-similar music and encode it in Haskell. In particular, consider structures that are different from those generated by the *selfSim* function.

Exercise 10.8 Define a function that gives the same result as *ss*, but without using a data type such as *Cluster*.

Exercise 10.9 Define a version of self-similarity similar to that defined in this chapter, but that uses the entire melody generated at one level to transform itself into the next level (rather than using the original seed pattern).

11

Proof by Induction

In this chapter we will study a powerful proof technique based on *mathematical induction*. With it we will be able to prove complex and important properties of programs that cannot be accomplished with proof-by-calculation alone. The inductive proof method is one of the most powerful and common methods for proving program properties.

11.1 Induction and Recursion

Induction is very closely related to *recursion*. In fact, in certain contexts the terms are used interchangeably; in others, one is preferred over the other primarily for historical reasons. Think of them as being duals of each other: induction is used to describe the process of starting with something small and simple and building up from there, whereas recursion describes the process of starting with something large and complex and working backward to the simplest case.

For example, although we have previously used the phrase *recursive data type*, in fact data types are often described *inductively*, such as a list:

A *list* is either empty or is a pair consisting of a value and another list.

On the other hand, we usually describe functions that manipulate lists, such as *map* and *foldr*, as being recursive. This is because when you apply a function such as *map*, you apply it initially to the whole list and work backward toward [ ].

But these differences between induction and recursion run no deeper; they are really just two sides of the same coin.

This chapter is about *inductive properties* of programs (but based on the above argument could just as rightly be called *recursive properties*) that are not usually proven via calculation alone. Proving inductive properties usually involves the inductive nature of data types and the recursive nature of functions defined on the data types.

As an example, suppose that p is an inductive property of a list. In other words, p (l) for some list l is either true or false (no middle ground!). To prove this property inductively, we do so based on the length of the list: starting with length 0, we first prove p ([ ]) (using our standard method of proof-by-calculation).

Now for the key step: assume for the moment that p (xs) is true for any list xs whose length is less than or equal to n. Then, if we can prove (via calculation) that p ($x : xs$) is true for any x – i.e., that p is true for lists of length $n + 1$ – the claim is that p is true for lists of any (finite) length.

Why is this so? Well, from the first step above we know that p is true for length 0, so the second step tells us that it is also true for length 1. But if it is true for length 1, then it must also be true for length 2; similarly for lengths 3, 4, etc. So p is true for lists of any length!

(It is important to realize, however, that a property being true for every finite list does not necessarily imply that it is true for every infinite list. The property "the list is finite" is a perfect example of this!)

To summarize, to prove a property p by induction on the length of a list, we proceed in two steps:

1. Prove p ([ ]) (this is called the *base case*).
2. Assume that p (xs) is true (this is called the *induction hypothesis*), and prove that p ($x : xs$) is true (this is called the *induction step*).

11.2 Examples of List Induction

OK, enough talk, let's see this idea in action. Recall in Section 3.1 the following property about *foldr*:

$(\forall xs)$ *foldr* (:) [ ] $xs \implies xs$

We will prove this by induction on the length of xs. Following the ideas above, we begin with the base case by proving the property for length 0; i.e., for $xs = [\,]$:

foldr (:) [ ] [ ]
$\implies$ {*unfold foldr*}
[ ]

This step is immediate from the definition of *foldr*. Now for the induction step: we first *assume* that the property is true for all lists *xs* of length *n*, and then prove the property for list $x : xs$. Again proceeding by calculation:

> *foldr* (:) [ ] (*x* : *xs*)
> ⇒ {*unfold foldr*}
> *x* : *foldr* (:) [ ] *xs*
> ⇒ {*induction hypothesis*}
> *x* : *xs*

And we are done; the induction hypothesis is what justifies the second step.

Now let's do something a bit harder. Suppose we are interested in proving the following property:

(∀*xs*, *ys*) *length* (*xs* ++ *ys*) = *length xs* + *length ys*

Our first problem is to decide which list to perform the induction over. A little thought (in particular, a look at how the definitions of *length* and (++) are structured) should convince you that *xs* is the right choice. (If you do not see this, you are encouraged to try the proof by induction over the length of *ys*!) Again following the ideas above, we begin with the base case by proving the property for length 0; i.e., for *xs* = [ ]:

> *length* ([ ] ++ *ys*)
> ⇒ {*unfold* (++)}
> *length ys*
> ⇒ {*fold* (+)}
> 0 + *length ys*
> ⇒ {*fold length*}
> *length* [ ] + *length ys*

For the induction step, we first assume that the property is true for all lists *xs* of length *n*, and then prove the property for list $x : xs$. Again proceeding by calculation:

> *length* ((*x* : *xs*) ++ *ys*)
> ⇒ {*unfold* (++)}
> *length* (*x* : (*xs* ++ *ys*))
> ⇒ {*unfold length*}
> 1 + *length* (*xs* ++ *ys*)
> ⇒ {*induction hypothesis*}
> 1 + (*length xs* + *length ys*)
> ⇒ {*associativity* **of** (+)}
> (1 + *length xs*) + *length ys*
> ⇒ {*fold length*}
> *length* (*x* : *xs*) + *length ys*

And we are done. The transition from the third line to the fourth is where the induction hypothesis is used.

11.3 Proving Function Equivalences

At this point it is a simple matter to return to Chapter 3 and supply the proofs that functions defined using *map* and *fold* are equivalent to the recursively defined versions. In particular, recall these two definitions of *toAbsPitches*:

toAbsPitches1 [ ]   = [ ]
toAbsPitches1 (*p* : *ps*) = *absPitch p* : *toAbsPitches1 ps*
toAbsPitches2 = *map absPitch*

We want to prove that *toAbsPitches1* = *toAbsPitches2*. To do so, we use the extensionality principle (briefly discussed in Section 3.6.1), which says that two functions are equal if, when applied to the same value, they always yield the same result. We can change the specification slightly to reflect this. For any finite list *ps*, we want to prove:

toAbsPitches1 ps = *toAbsPitches2 ps*

We proceed by induction, starting with the base case *ps* = [ ]:

toAbsPitches1 [ ]
$\Rightarrow$ [ ]
$\Rightarrow$ *map absPitch* [ ]
$\Rightarrow$ *toAbsPitches2* [ ]

Next we assume that *toAbsPitches1 ps* = *toAbsPitches2 ps* holds, and try to prove that *toAbsPitches1* (*p* : *ps*) = *toAbsPitches2* (*p* : *ps*):

toAbsPitches1 (*p* : *ps*)
$\Rightarrow$ *absPitch p* : *toAbsPitches1 ps*
$\Rightarrow$ *absPitch p* : *toAbsPitches2 ps*
$\Rightarrow$ *absPitch p* : *map absPitch ps*
$\Rightarrow$ *map absPitch* (*p* : *ps*)

Note the use of the induction hypothesis in the second step.

For a proof involving *foldr*, recall from Chapter 3 this recursive definition of *line*:

line1 [ ]   = *rest* 0
line1 (*m* : *ms*) = *m* :+: *line1 ms*

and this non-recursive version:

line2 = *foldr* (:+:) (*rest* 0)

We can prove that these two functions are equivalent by induction. First the base case:

line1 [ ]
⇒ *rest* 0
⇒ *foldr* (:+:) (*rest* 0) [ ]
⇒ *line2* [ ]

Then the induction step:

line1 (*m* : *ms*)
⇒ *m* :+: *line1 ms*
⇒ *m* :+: *line2 ms*
⇒ *m* :+: *foldr* (:+:) (*rest* 0) *ms*
⇒ *foldr* (:+:) (*rest* 0) (*m* : *ms*)
⇒ *line2* (*m* : *ms*)

The proofs of equivalence of the definitions of *toPitches*, *chord*, *maxPitch*, and *hList* from Chapter 3 are similar, and are left as an exercise.

Exercise 11.1 From Chapter 3, prove that the original recursive versions of the following functions are equivalent to the versions using *map* or *fold*: *toPitches*, *chord*, *maxPitch*, and *hList*.

11.3.1 [Advanced] Reverse

The proofs of function equivalence in the last section were fairly straightforward. For something more challenging, consider the definition of *reverse* given in Section 3.5:

reverse1 [ ]   = [ ]
reverse1 (*x* : *xs*) = *reverse1 xs* ++ [*x*]

and the version given in Section 3.6:

reverse2 xs = *foldl* (*flip* (:)) [ ] *xs*

We would like to show that these are the same; i.e., that *reverse1 xs* = *reverse2 xs* for any finite list *xs*. In carrying out this proof, one new idea will be demonstrated, namely the need for an *auxiliary property* that is proved independently of the main result.

The base case is easy, as it often is:

reverse1 [ ]
⇒ [ ]
⇒ *foldl* (*flip* (:)) [ ] [ ]
⇒ *reverse2* [ ]

Assume now that *reverse1 xs = reverse2 xs*. The induction step proceeds as follows:

> *reverse1* (*x* : *xs*)
> ⇒ *reverse1 xs* ⧺ [*x*]
> ⇒ *reverse2 xs* ⧺ [*x*]
> ⇒ *foldl* (*flip* (:)) [ ] *xs* ⧺ [*x*]
> ⇒ ???

But now what do we do? Intuitively, it seems that the following property, which we will call property (1), should hold:

> *foldl* (*flip* (:)) [ ] *xs* ⧺ [*x*]
> ⇒ *foldl* (*flip* (:)) [ ] (*x* : *xs*)

in which case we could complete the proof as follows:

> ...
> ⇒ *foldl* (*flip* (:)) [ ] *xs* ⧺ [*x*]
> ⇒ *foldl* (*flip* (:)) [ ] (*x* : *xs*)
> ⇒ *reverse2* (*x* : *xs*)

The ability to see that if we could just prove one thing, then perhaps we could prove another, is useful in conducting proofs. In this case we reduced the overall problem to one of proving property (1), which simplifies the structure of the proof, although not necessarily the difficulty. These auxiliary properties are often called *lemmas* in mathematics, and in many cases their proofs become the most important contributions, since they are often at the heart of a problem.

In fact, if you try to prove property (1) directly, you will run into a problem, namely that it is not *general* enough. So first let's generalize property (1) (while renaming *x* as *y*), as follows:

> *foldl* (*flip* (:)) *ys xs* ⧺ [*y*]
> ⇒ *foldl* (*flip* (:)) (*ys* ⧺ [*y*]) *xs*

Let's call this property (2). If (2) is true for any finite *xs* and *ys*, then property (1) is also true, because:

> *foldl* (*flip* (:)) [ ] *xs* ⧺ [*x*]
> ⇒ {*property* (2)}
> *foldl* (*flip* (:)) ([ ] ⧺ [*x*]) *xs*
> ⇒ {*unfold* (⧺)}
> *foldl* (*flip* (:)) [*x*] *xs*
> ⇒ {*fold* (*flip* (:))}
> *foldl* (*flip* (:)) (*flip* (:) [ ] *x*) *xs*
> ⇒ {*fold foldl*}
> *foldl* (*flip* (:)) [ ] (*x* : *xs*)

You are encouraged to try proving property (1) directly, in which case you will likely come to the same conclusion, namely that the property needs to be generalized. This is not always easy to see, but is sometimes an important step is constructing a proof, because despite being somewhat counterintuitive, it is often the case that making a property more general (and therefore more powerful) makes it easier to prove.

In any case, how do we prove property (2)? Using induction, of course! Setting xs to $[\,]$, the base case is easy:

> $foldl\ (flip\ (:))\ ys\ [\,] +\!\!+ [y]$
> $\Rightarrow \{unfold\ foldl\}$
> $ys +\!\!+ [y]$
> $\Rightarrow \{fold\ foldl\}$
> $foldl\ (flip\ (:))\ (ys +\!\!+ [y])\ [\,]$

and the induction step proceeds as follows:

> $foldl\ (flip\ (:))\ ys\ (x : xs) +\!\!+ [y]$
> $\Rightarrow \{unfold\ foldl\}$
> $foldl\ (flip\ (:))\ (flip\ (:)\ ys\ x)\ xs +\!\!+ [y]$
> $\Rightarrow \{unfold\ flip\}$
> $foldl\ (flip\ (:))\ (x : ys)\ xs +\!\!+ [y]$
> $\Rightarrow \{induction\ hypothesis\}$
> $foldl\ (flip\ (:))\ ((x : ys) +\!\!+ [y])\ xs$
> $\Rightarrow \{unfold\ (+\!\!+)\}$
> $foldl\ (flip\ (:))\ (x : (ys +\!\!+ [y]))\ xs$
> $\Rightarrow \{fold\ foldl\}$
> $foldl\ (flip\ (:))\ (ys +\!\!+ [y])\ (x : xs)$

11.4 Useful Properties on Lists

There are many useful properties of functions on lists that require inductive proofs. Figures 11.1 and 11.2 list a number of them involving functions used in this text, but their proofs are left as exercises (except for one). You may assume that these properties are true and use them freely in proving other properties of your programs. In fact, some of these properties can be used to simplify the proof that *reverse1* and *reverse2* are the same; see if you can find them![1]

---

[1] More thorough discussions of these properties and their proofs may be found in [17, 18].

Properties of *map*:

$$map \ (\lambda x \to x) \quad = \lambda x \to x$$
$$map \ (f \circ g) \quad\quad = map \ f \circ map \ g$$
$$map \ f \circ tail \quad\quad = tail \circ map \ f$$
$$map \ f \circ reverse \ = reverse \circ map \ f$$
$$map \ f \circ concat \ = concat \circ map \ (map \ f)$$
$$map \ f \ (xs \ +\!\!+ \ ys) = map \ f \ xs \ +\!\!+ \ map \ f \ ys$$

For all strict f:

$$f \circ head = head \circ map \ f$$

Properties of the *fold* **functions:**

1. If *op* is associative, and $e \ `op` \ x = x$ and $x \ `op` \ e = x$ for all x, then for all finite xs:

   $$foldr \ op \ e \ xs = foldl \ op \ e \ xs$$

2. If the following are true:

   $$x \ `op1` \ (y \ `op2` \ z) = (x \ `op1` \ y) \ `op2` \ z$$
   $$x \ `op1` \ e \quad\quad = e \ `op2` \ x$$

   then for all finite xs:

   $$foldr \ op1 \ e \ xs = foldl \ op2 \ e \ xs$$

3. For all finite xs:

   $$foldr \ op \ e \ xs = foldl \ (flip \ op) \ e \ (reverse \ xs)$$

Figure 11.1 Some useful properties of *map* and *fold*.

(Note, by the way, that in the first rule for *map* in Figure 11.1, the type of $\lambda x \to x$ on the left-hand side is $a \to b$, whereas on the right-hand side it is $[a] \to [b]$; i.e., these are really two different functions.)

11.4.1 [Advanced] Function Strictness

Note that the last rule for *map* in Figure 11.1 is only valid for *strict* functions. A function f is said to be strict if $f \perp = \perp$. Recall from Section 1.4 that $\perp$ is the value associated with a non-terminating computation. So another way to think about a strict function is that it is one that, when applied to a non-terminating computation, results in a non-terminating computation. For example, the successor function $(+1)$ is strict, because $(+1) \perp = \perp + 1 = \perp$. In other words, if you apply $(+1)$ to a non-terminating computation, you end up with a non-terminating computation.

Not all functions in Haskell are strict, and we have to be careful to say on which argument a function is strict. For example, $(+)$ is strict on both of its

Properties of (++):

For all *xs*, *ys*, and *zs*:
$$(xs \mathbin{+\!\!+} ys) \mathbin{+\!\!+} zs = xs \mathbin{+\!\!+} (ys \mathbin{+\!\!+} zs)$$
$$xs \mathbin{+\!\!+} [\,] \qquad = [\,] \mathbin{+\!\!+} xs = xs$$

Properties of *take* and *drop*:

$$take\ m \circ take\ n\ = take\ (min\ m\ n)$$
$$drop\ m \circ drop\ n = drop\ (m+n)$$
$$take\ m \circ drop\ n\ = drop\ n \circ take\ (m+n)$$
For all non-negative *m* and *n* such that $n \geqslant m$:
$$drop\ m \circ take\ n = take\ (n-m) \circ drop\ m$$
For all non-negative *m* and *n*, and finite *xs*:
$$take\ n\ xs \mathbin{+\!\!+} drop\ n\ xs = xs$$

Properties of *reverse*:

For all finite *xs*:
$$reverse\ (reverse\ xs) = xs$$
$$head\ (reverse\ xs)\ \ = last\ xs$$
$$last\ (reverse\ xs)\ \ \ = head\ xs$$

Figure 11.2 Useful properties of other functions over lists

arguments, which is why the section (+1) is also strict. On the other hand, the constant function:

$$const\ x\ y = x$$

is strict on its first argument (why?) but not its second, because $const\ x \perp = x$, for any *x*.

Details: Understanding strictness requires a careful understanding of Haskell's pattern-matching rules. For example, consider the definition of (∧) from the Standard Prelude:

$$(\wedge) \qquad :: Bool \rightarrow Bool \rightarrow Bool$$
$$True \wedge x\ = x$$
$$False \wedge \_ = False$$

When choosing a pattern to match, Haskell starts with the top leftmost pattern and works to the right and downward. So in the above, (∧) first evaluates its left argument. If that value is *True*, then the first equation succeeds and the second argument gets evaluated, because that is the value that is returned. But if the first argument is *False*, the second equation succeeds. In particular, *it does not bother to evaluate the second argument at all*, and simply returns *False* as the answer. This means that $(\wedge)$ is strict in its first argument but not its second.

A more detailed discussion of pattern matching is found in Appendix D.

Let's now look more closely at the last law for *map*, which says that for all strict f:

$f \circ head = head \circ map\ f$

Let's try to prove this property, starting with the base case but ignoring for now the strictness constraint on f:

$f\ (head\ [\ ])$
$\Rightarrow f\ \bot$

head [ ] is an error, which you will recall has value $\bot$. So you can see immediately that the issue of strictness might play a role in the proof, because without knowing anything about f, there is no further calculation to be done here. Similarly, if we start with the right-hand side:

$head\ (map\ f\ [\ ])$
$\Rightarrow head\ [\ ]$
$\Rightarrow \bot$

It should be clear that for the base case to be true, it must be that $f\ \bot = \bot$; i.e., f must be strict. Thus we have essentially "discovered" the constraint on the theorem through the process of trying to prove it! (This is not an uncommon phenomenon.)

The induction step is less problematic:

$f\ (head\ (x : xs))$
$\Rightarrow f\ x$
$\Rightarrow head\ (f\ x : map\ f\ xs)$
$\Rightarrow head\ (map\ f\ (x : xs))$

and we are done.

Exercise 11.2 Prove as many of the properties in Figures 11.1 and 11.2 as you can.

Exercise 11.3 Determine which of the following functions are strict (if the function takes more than one argument, specify on which arguments it is strict): *reverse*, *simple*, *map*, *tail*, *dur*, *retro*, $(\wedge)$, $(True\ \wedge)$, $(False\ \wedge)$, and:

$ifFun$ $:: Bool \rightarrow a \rightarrow a \rightarrow a$
$ifFun\ pred\ cons\ alt = $ **if** *pred* **then** *cons* **else** *alt*

11.5 Induction on the *Music* Data Type

Proof by induction is not limited to lists. In particular, we can use it to reason about *Music* values.

For example, recall this property intuitively conjectured in Section 6.12:

   mFold Prim (:+:) (:=:) *Modify m = m*

Alternatively, we can view this as:

   mFold Prim (:+:) (:=:) *Modify = id*

To prove this property, we again use the extensionality principle, and then proceed by induction. But what is the base case? Recall that the *Music* data type is defined as:

   data *Music a =*
       Prim (*Primitive a*)
       | *Music a* :+: *Music a*
       | *Music a* :=: *Music a*
       | *Modify Control* (*Music a*)

The only constructor that does not take a *Music* value as an argument is *Prim*, so that in fact is the only base case.

So, starting with this base case:

   mFold Prim (:+:) (:=:) *Modify* (*Prim p*)
   ⇒ *Prim p*
   ⇒ *id* (*Prim p*)

That was easy! Next, we develop an induction step for each of the three non-base cases:

   mFold Prim (:+:) (:=:) *Modify* (*m1* :+: *m2*)
   ⇒ *mFold Prim* (:+:) (:=:) *Modify m1* :+:
       mFold Prim (:+:) (:=:) *Modify m2*
   ⇒ *m1* :+: *m2*
   ⇒ *id* (*m1* :+: *m2*)

   mFold Prim (:+:) (:=:) *Modify* (*m1* :=: *m2*)
   ⇒ *mFold Prim* (:+:) (:=:) *Modify m1* :=:
       mFold Prim (:+:) (:=:) *Modify m2*
   ⇒ *m1* :=: *m2*
   ⇒ *id* (*m1* :=: *m2*)

mFold Prim (:+:) (:=:) *Modify* (*Modify c m*)
$\Rightarrow$ *Modify c* (*mFold Prim* (:+:) (:=:) *Modify m*)
$\Rightarrow$ *Modify c m*
$\Rightarrow$ *id* (*Modify c m*)

These three steps are quite easy as well, but this is not something we can do without induction.

For something more challenging, let's consider the following:

dur (*retro m*) = *dur m*

Again we proceed by induction, starting with the base case:

dur (*retro* (*Prim p*))
$\Rightarrow$ *dur* (*Prim p*)

Sequential composition is straightforward:

dur (*retro* (*m1* :+: *m2*))
$\Rightarrow$ *dur* (*retro m2* :+: *retro m1*)
$\Rightarrow$ *dur* (*retro m2*) + *dur* (*retro m1*)
$\Rightarrow$ *dur m2* + *dur m1*
$\Rightarrow$ *dur m1* + *dur m2*
$\Rightarrow$ *dur* (*m1* :+: *m2*)

But things get more complex with parallel composition:

dur (*retro* (*m1* :=: *m2*))
$\Rightarrow$ *dur* (**let** *d1* = *dur m1*
          d2 = *dur m2*
      in if *d1* > *d2* **then** *retro m1* :=: (*rest* (*d1* − *d2*) :+: *retro m2*)
                 else (*rest* (*d2* − *d1*) :+: *retro m1*) :=: *retro m2*)
$\Rightarrow$ **let** *d1* = *dur m1*
     d2 = *dur m2*
  in if *d1* > *d2* **then** *dur* (*retro m1* :=: (*rest* (*d1* − *d2*) :+: *retro m2*))
             else *dur* ((*rest* (*d2* − *d1*) :+: *retro m1*) :=: *retro m2*)
  ...

At this point, to make things easier to understand, we will consider each branch of the conditional in turn. First the consequent branch:

dur (*retro m1* :=: (*rest* (*d1* − *d2*) :+: *retro m2*))
$\Rightarrow$ *max* (*dur* (*retro m1*)) (*dur* (*rest* (*d1* − *d2*) :+: *retro m2*))
$\Rightarrow$ *max* (*dur m1*) (*dur* (*rest* (*d1* − *d2*) :+: *retro m2*))

$\Rightarrow max \ (dur \ m1) \ (dur \ (rest \ (d1 - d2)) + dur \ (retro \ m2))$
$\Rightarrow max \ (dur \ m1) \ ((d1 - d2) + dur \ m2)$
$\Rightarrow max \ (dur \ m1) \ (dur \ m1)$
$\Rightarrow dur \ m1$

And then the alternative:

$dur \ ((rest \ (d2 - d1) :+: retro \ m1) :=: retro \ m2)$
$\Rightarrow max \ (dur \ ((rest \ (d2 - d1) :+: retro \ m1)) \ (dur \ (retro \ m2))$
$\Rightarrow max \ (dur \ ((rest \ (d2 - d1) :+: retro \ m1)) \ (dur \ m2)$
$\Rightarrow max \ (dur \ (rest \ (d2 - d1)) + dur \ (retro \ m1)) \ (dur \ m2)$
$\Rightarrow max \ ((d2 - d1) + dur \ m1) \ (dur \ m2)$
$\Rightarrow max \ (dur \ m2) \ (dur \ m2)$
$\Rightarrow dur \ m2$

Now we can continue the proof from above:

...
$\Rightarrow$ **let** $d1 = dur \ m1$
       $d2 = dur \ m2$
  in if $d1 > d2$ **then** $dur \ m1$
                else $dur \ m2$
$\Rightarrow max \ (dur \ m1) \ (dur \ m2)$
$\Rightarrow dur \ (m1 :=: m2)$

The final inductive step involves the *Modify* constructor, but recall that *dur* treats a *Tempo* modification specially, and thus we treat it specially as well:

$dur \ (retro \ (Modify \ (Tempo \ r) \ m))$
$\Rightarrow dur \ (Modify \ (Tempo \ r) \ (retro \ m))$
$\Rightarrow dur \ (retro \ m)/r$
$\Rightarrow dur \ m/r$
$\Rightarrow dur \ (Modify \ (Tempo \ r) \ m)$

Finally, we consider the case that $c \neq Tempo \ r$:

$dur \ (retro \ (Modify \ c \ m))$
$\Rightarrow dur \ (Modify \ c \ (retro \ m))$
$\Rightarrow Modify \ c \ (dur \ (retro \ m))$
$\Rightarrow Modify \ c \ (dur \ m)$
$\Rightarrow dur \ (Modify \ c \ m)$

And we are done.

Exercise 11.4 Recall Exercises 3.11 and 3.12. Prove that if $p2 \geqslant p1$:

  chrom p1 p2 = mkScale p1 (take (absPitch p2 − absPitch p1)
                                         (repeat 1))

using the lemma:

  $[m .. n] = scanl \ (+) \ m \ (take \ (n − m) \ (repeat \ 1))$

Exercise 11.5 Prove the following facts involving *dur*:

  dur (timesM n m) = n ∗ dur m
  dur (cut d m) = d, **if** $d \leqslant dur \ m$

Exercise 11.6 Prove the following facts involving *mMap*:

  mMap id m   = m
  mMap f (mMap g m) = mMap (f ∘ g) m

Exercise 11.7 Prove that for all *pmap, c,* and *m*:

  perf pmap c m = (perform pmap c m, dur m)

where *perform* is the function defined in Figure 9.1.

11.5.1 The Need for Musical Equivalence

In Chapter 1 we discussed the need for a notion of *musical equivalence*, noting that, for example, *m :+: rest 0* "sounds the same" as *m*, even if the two *Music* values are not equal as Haskell values. That same issue can strike us here as we try to prove intuitively natural properties such as:

  retro (retro m) = m

To see why this property cannot be proved without a notion of musical equivalence, note that:

  retro (retro (c 4 en :=: d 4 qn))
  $\Longrightarrow$ *retro ((rest en :+: c 4 en) :=: d 4 qn)*
  $\Longrightarrow$ *(rest 0 :+: c 4 en :+: rest en) :=: d 4 qn*

Clearly the last line above is not equal, as a Haskell value, to *c 4 en :=: d 4 qn*. But somehow we need to show that these two values "sound the same" as musical values. In the next chapter we will formally develop the notion of musical equivalence, and with it be able to prove the validity of our intuitions regarding *retro*, as well as many other important musical properties.

11.6 [Advanced] Induction on Other Data Types

Proof by induction can be used to reason about many data types. For example, we can use it to reason about natural numbers.[2] Suppose we define an exponentiation function as follows:

$(^\wedge)$ :: $Integer \to Integer \to Integer$
$x^\wedge 0 = 1$
$x^\wedge n = x * x^\wedge(n - 1)$

Details: $(*)$ is defined in the Standard Prelude to have precedence level 7, and recall that if no **infix** declaration is given for an operator, it defaults to precedence level 9, which means that $(^\wedge)$ has precedence level 9, which is higher than that for $(*)$. Therefore no parentheses are needed to disambiguate the last line in the definition above, which corresponds nicely to mathematical convention.

Now suppose that we want to prove that:

$(\forall x, n \geqslant 0, m \geqslant 0)$ $x^\wedge(n + m) = x^\wedge n * x^\wedge m$

We proceed by induction on n, beginning with $n = 0$:

$x^\wedge(0 + m)$
$\Rightarrow x^\wedge m$
$\Rightarrow 1 * (x^\wedge m)$
$\Rightarrow x^\wedge 0 * x^\wedge m$

Next we assume that the property is true for numbers less than or equal to n, and prove it for $n + 1$:

$x^\wedge((n + 1) + m)$
$\Rightarrow x * x^\wedge(n + m)$
$\Rightarrow x * (x^\wedge n * x^\wedge m)$
$\Rightarrow (x * x^\wedge n) * x^\wedge m$
$\Rightarrow x^\wedge(n + 1) * x^\wedge m$

and we are done.

Or are we? What if, in the definition of $(^\wedge)$, x or n is *negative*? Since a negative integer is not a natural number, we could dispense with the problem

---

[2] Indeed, one could argue that a proof by induction over finite lists is really an induction over natural numbers, since it is an induction over the *length* of the list, which is a natural number.

by saying that these situations fall beyond the bounds of the property we are trying to prove. But let's look a little closer. If x is negative, the property we are trying to prove still holds (why?). But if n is negative, $x^\wedge n$ will not terminate (why?). As diligent programmers we may wish to defend against the latter situation by writing:[3]

```
(^)                :: Integer → Integer → Integer
x^0                = 1
x^n | n < 0        = error "negative exponent"
    | otherwise    = x * x^(n − 1)
```

If we consider non-terminating computations and ones that produce an error to both have the same value, namely ⊥, then these two versions of (^) are equivalent. Pragmatically, however, the latter is clearly superior.

Note that the above definition will test for $n < 0$ on every recursive call, when actually the only call in which it could happen is the first. Therefore a slightly more efficient version of this program would be:

```
(^) :: Integer → Integer → Integer
x^n | n < 0        = error "negative exponent"
    | otherwise    = f x n
  where f x 0 = 1
        f x n = x * f x (n − 1)
```

Proving the property stated earlier for this version of the program is straightforward, with one minor distinction: what we really need to prove is that the property is true for f; that is:

$$(\forall x, n \geqslant 0, m \geqslant 0)\ f\ x\ (n + m) = f\ x\ n * f\ x\ m$$

from which the proof for the whole function follows trivially.

11.6.1 A More Efficient Exponentiation Function

But in fact there is a more serious inefficiency in our exponentiation function: we are not taking advantage of the fact that, for any even number n, $x^n = (x * x)^{n/2}$. Using this fact, here is a more clever way to accomplish the exponentiation task, using the names (^!) and $f\!f$ for our functions to distinguish them from the previous versions:

---

[3] This code uses Haskell's guard notation, which is analogous to piecewise function notation in regular mathematics.

$(\verb|^|!) :: Integer \rightarrow Integer \rightarrow Integer$

$x \verb|^|! \ n \mid n < 0 \qquad = error \ \verb|"negative exponent"|$

$\qquad \mid otherwise = ff \ x \ n$

$\quad$ **where** $ff \ x \ n \mid n == 0 \quad = 1$

$\qquad\qquad\qquad \mid even \ n \quad = ff \ (x * x) \ (n \ `quot` \ 2)$

$\qquad\qquad\qquad \mid otherwise = x * ff \ x \ (n - 1)$

Details: *quot* is Haskell's *quotient* operator, which returns the integer quotient of the first argument divided by the second, rounded toward zero.

You should convince yourself that, intuitively at least, this version of exponentiation is not only correct, but also more efficient. More precisely, $(\verb|^|)$ executes a number of steps proportional to n, whereas $(\verb|^|!)$ executes a number of steps proportional to the $\log_2$ of n. The Standard Prelude defines $(\verb|^|)$ similarly to the way in which $(\verb|^|!)$ is defined here.

Since intuition is not always reliable, let's *prove* that this version is equivalent to the old. That is, we wish to prove that $x\verb|^|n = x \verb|^|! \ n$ for all x and n.

A quick look at the two definitions reveals that what we really need to prove is that $f \ x \ n = ff \ x \ n$, from which it follows immediately that $x\verb|^|n = x\verb|^|! \ n$. We do this by induction on n, beginning with the base case $n = 0$:

$f \ x \ 0 \Rightarrow 1 \Rightarrow ff \ x \ 0$

so the base case holds trivially. The induction step, however, is considerably more complicated. We must consider two cases: $n + 1$ is either even or odd. If it is odd, we can show that:

$f \ x \ (n + 1)$
$\Rightarrow x * f \ x \ n$
$\Rightarrow x * ff \ x \ n$
$\Rightarrow ff \ x \ (n + 1)$

and we are done (note the use of the induction hypothesis in the second step).

If $n + 1$ is even, we might try proceeding in a similar way:

$f \ x \ (n + 1)$
$\Rightarrow x * f \ x \ n$
$\Rightarrow x * ff \ x \ n$

But now what shall we do? Since n is odd, we might try unfolding the call to ff:

$x * ff \ x \ n$
$\Rightarrow x * (x * ff \ x \ (n - 1))$

but this does not seem to be getting us anywhere. Furthermore, *folding* the call to *ff* (as we did in the odd case) would involve *doubling* n and taking the square root of *x*, neither of which seems like a good idea!

We could also try going in the other direction:

$ff\ x\ (n+1)$
$\Rightarrow ff\ (x*x)\ ((n+1)\ \text{`}quot\text{`}\ 2)$
$\Rightarrow f\ (x*x)\ ((n+1)\ \text{`}quot\text{`}\ 2)$

The use of the induction hypothesis in the second step needs to be justified, because the first argument to *f* has changed from *x* to $x*x$. But recall that the induction hypothesis states that for *all* values *x*, and all natural numbers up to *n*, *f x n* is the same as *ff x n*. So this is OK.

But even allowing this, we seem to be stuck again!

Instead of pushing this line of reasoning further, let's pursue a different tactic tack based on the (valid) assumption that if *m* is even, then:

$m = m\ \text{`}quot\text{`}\ 2 + m\ \text{`}quot\text{`}\ 2$

Let's use this fact together with the property that we proved in the last section:

$f\ x\ (n+1)$
$\Rightarrow f\ x\ ((n+1)\ \text{`}quot\text{`}\ 2 + ((n+1)\ \text{`}quot\text{`}\ 2)$
$\Rightarrow f\ x\ ((n+1)\ \text{`}quot\text{`}\ 2) * f\ x\ ((n+1)\ \text{`}quot\text{`}\ 2)$

Next, as with the proof in the last section involving *reverse*, let's make an assumption about a property that will help us along. Specifically, what if we could prove that $f\ x\ n * f\ x\ n$ is equal to $f\ (x*x)\ n$? If so, we could proceed as follows:

$f\ x\ ((n+1)\ \text{`}quot\text{`}\ 2) * f\ x\ ((n+1)\ \text{`}quot\text{`}\ 2)$
$\Rightarrow f\ (x*x)\ ((n+1)\ \text{`}quot\text{`}\ 2)$
$\Rightarrow ff\ (x*x)\ ((n+1)\ \text{`}quot\text{`}\ 2)$
$\Rightarrow ff\ x\ (n+1)$

and we are finally done. Note the use of the induction hypothesis in the second step, as justified earlier. The proof of the auxiliary property is not difficult, but also requires induction; it is shown in Figure 11.3.

Aside from improving efficiency, one of the pleasant outcomes of proving that (^) and (^!) are equivalent is that *anything that we prove about one function will be true for the other*. For example, the validity of the property that we proved earlier:

$x\char`^(n+m) = x\char`^n * x\char`^m$

immediately implies the validity of:

$x\ \char`^!\ (n+m) = x\ \char`^!\ n * x\ \char`^!\ m$

Base case ($n = 0$):

$$f \, x \, 0 * f \, x \, 0$$
$$\Rightarrow 1 * 1$$
$$\Rightarrow 1$$
$$\Rightarrow f \, (x * x) \, 0$$

Induction step ($n + 1$):

$$f \, x \, (n + 1) * f \, x \, (n + 1)$$
$$\Rightarrow (x * f \, x \, n) * (x * f \, x \, n)$$
$$\Rightarrow (x * x) * (f \, x \, n * f \, x \, n)$$
$$\Rightarrow (x * x) * f \, (x * x) \, n$$
$$\Rightarrow f \, (x * x) \, (n + 1)$$

Figure 11.3 Proof that $f \, x \, n * f \, x \, n = f \, (x * x) \, n$.

Although ($\wedge!$) is more efficient than ($\wedge$), it is also more complicated, so it makes sense to try proving new properties for ($\wedge$), since the proofs will likely be easier.

The moral of this story is that you should not throw away old code that is simpler but less efficient than a newer version. That old code can serve at least two good purposes: First, if it is simpler, it is likely to be easier to understand, and thus serves a useful purpose in documenting your effort. Second, as we have just discussed, if it is provably equivalent to the new code, then it can be used to simplify the task of proving properties about the new code.

Exercise 11.8 The function ($\wedge!$) can be made more efficient by noting that in the last line of the definition of *ff*, n is odd, and therefore $n - 1$ must be even, so the test for n being even on the next recursive call could be avoided. Redefine ($\wedge!$) so that it avoids this (minor) inefficiency.

Exercise 11.9 Consider this definition of the *factorial* function:[4]

```
fac1   :: Integer → Integer
fac1 0 = 1
fac1 n = n * fac1 (n − 1)
```

and this alternative definition that uses an "accumulator":

```
fac2   :: Integer → Integer
fac2 n = fac' n 1
   where fac' 0 acc = acc
         fac' n acc = fac' (n − 1) (n * acc)
```

Prove that *fac1* = *fac2*.

---

[4] The factorial function is defined mathematically as:

$$factorial(n) = \begin{cases} 1 & \text{if } n = 0 \\ n * factorial(n - 1) & \text{otherwise} \end{cases}$$

12

An Algebra of Music

In this chapter we will explore a number of properties of the *Music* data type and functions defined on it, properties that collectively form an *algebra of music* [19]. With this algebra we can reason about, transform, and optimize computer music programs in a meaning-preserving way.

12.1 Musical Equivalence

Suppose we have two values *m1* :: *Music Pitch* and *m2* :: *Music Pitch* and we want to know if they are equal. If we treat them simply as Haskell values, we could easily write a function that compares their structures recursively to see if they are the same at every level, all the way down to the *Primitive* rests and notes. This is in fact what the Haskell function (==) does. For example, if:

$m1 = c\ 4\ en :+: d\ 4\ qn$
$m2 = retro\ (retro\ m1)$

then *m1 == m2* is *True*.

Unfortunately, as we saw in the last chapter, if we reverse a parallel composition, things do not work out as well. For example:

$retro\ (retro\ (c\ 4\ en :=: d\ 4\ qn))$
$\Rightarrow (rest\ 0 :+: c\ 4\ en :+: rest\ en) :=: d\ 4\ qn$

In addition, as we discussed briefly in Chapter 1, there are musical properties that standard Haskell equivalence is insufficient to capture. For example, we would expect the following two musical values to *sound* the same, regardless of the actual values of *m1*, *m2*, and *m3*:

$(m1 :+: m2) :+: m3$
$m1 :+: (m2 :+: m3)$

175

In other words, we expect the operator $(:\!+\!:)$ to be *associative*.

The problem is that, as data structures, these two values are *not* equal in general; in fact, there are no finite values that can be assigned to *m1*, *m2*, and *m3* to make them equal.[1]

The obvious way out of this dilemma is to define a new notion of equality that captures the fact that the *performances* are the same – i.e., if two things *sound* the same, they must be musically equivalent.

And thus we define a formal notion of musical equivalence:

Definition: Two musical values *m1* and *m2* are *equivalent*, written $m1 \equiv m2$, if and only if:

$$(\forall pm, c) \; perf \; pm \; c \; m1 = perf \; pm \; c \; m2$$

We will study a number of properties in this chapter that capture musical equivalences, similar in spirit to the associativity of $(:\!+\!:)$ above. Each of them can be thought of as an *axiom*, and the set of valid axioms collectively forms an *algebra of music*. By proving the validity of each axiom, we not only confirm our intuitions about how music is interpreted, but also gain confidence that our *hsomPerform* function actually does the right thing. Furthermore, with these axioms in hand, we can *transform* musical values in meaning-preserving ways.

Speaking of the *hsomPerform* function, recall from Chapter 9 that we defined *two* versions of *hsomPerform*, and the definition above uses the function *perf*, which includes the duration of a musical value in its result. The following lemma captures the connection between these functions:

Lemma 12.1.1 For all *pm*, *c*, and *m*:

$$perf \; pm \; c \; m = (hsomPerform \; pm \; c \; m, dur \; m * cDur \; c)$$

where *hsomPerform* is the function defined in Figure 9.1.

To see the importance of including duration in the definition of equivalence, we first note that if two musical values are equivalent, we should be able to substitute one for the other in any valid musical context. But if duration is not taken into account, then all rests are equivalent (because their performances are just the empty list). This means that, for example, $m1 :\!+\!: rest \; 1 :\!+\!: m2$ is equivalent to $m1 :\!+\!: rest \; 2 :\!+\!: m2$, which is surely not what we want.[2]

---

[1] If $m1 = m1 :\!+\!: m2$ and $m3 = m2 :\!+\!: m3$, then the two expressions are equal, but these are infinite values that cannot be reversed or even performed.

[2] A more striking example of this point is John Cage's composition *4'33"*, which consists basically of four minutes and thirty-three seconds of silence [].

Note that we could have defined *perf* as above, i.e., in terms of *hsomPerform* and *dur*, but as mentioned in Section 9.1, it would have been computationally inefficient to do so. On the other hand, if the lemma above is true, then our proofs might be simpler if we first proved the property using *hsomPerform*, then using *dur*. That is, to prove $m1 \equiv m2$, we need to prove:

perf pm c m1 = perf pm c m2

Instead of doing this directly using the definition of *perf*, we could instead prove both of the following:

hsomPerform pm c m1 = hsomPerform pm c m2
dur m1 = dur m2

12.1.1 Literal Player

The only problem with this strategy for defining musical equivalence is that the notion of a *player* can create situations where certain properties that we would like to hold in fact do not. After all, a player may interpret a note or phrase in whatever way it (or he or she) may desire. For example, it seems that this property should hold:

tempo 1 m $\equiv$ m

However, a certain (rather perverse) player might interpret anything tagged with a *Tempo* modifier as an empty performance – in which case the above property will fail! To solve this problem, we will assume players that take a *musically sound* approach to interpretation, such as the default and fancy players shown in Chapter 9. In other words, we will assume players that treat a *Tempo* marking as indicating that durations need to be scaled in some way, a *Transpose* marking as indicating adding or subtracting pitch numbers, and so on. Euterpea's built-in performance algorithm (which does not include the notion of players) also enforces the same kinds of interpretations.

12.2 Some Simple Axioms

Let's look at a few simple axioms, and see how we can prove each of them using the proof techniques that we have developed so far.

(Note: In the remainder of this chapter we will use the functions *tempo r* and *trans p* to represent their unfolded versions, *Modify* (*Tempo r*) and *Modify* (*Transpose t*), respectively. In the proofs we will not bother with the intermediate steps of unfolding these functions.)

Here is the first axiom that we will consider:

Axiom 12.2.1 For any *r1*, *r2*, and *m*:

$$tempo\ r1\ (tempo\ r2\ m) \equiv tempo\ (r1 * r2)\ m$$

In other words, *tempo scaling is multiplicative*.

We can prove this by calculation, starting with the definition of musical equivalence. For clarity, we will first prove the property for *hsomPerform*, and then for *dur*, as suggested in the last section:

> **let** *dt* = *cDur c*
>
> *hsomPerform pm c (tempo r1 (tempo r2 m))*
> $\Rightarrow$ {*unfold hsomPerform*}
> *hsomPerform pm (c {cDur = dt/r1}) (tempo r2 m)*
> $\Rightarrow$ {*unfold hsomPerform*}
> *hsomPerform pm (c {cDur = (dt/r1)/r2}) m*
> $\Rightarrow$ {*arithmetic*}
> *hsomPerform pm (c {cDur = dt/(r1 * r2)}) m*
> $\Rightarrow$ {*fold hsomPerform*}
> *hsomPerform pm c (tempo (r1 * r2) m)*
>
> *dur (tempo r1 (tempo r2 m))*
> $\Rightarrow$ {*unfold dur*}
> *dur (tempo r2 m)/r1*
> $\Rightarrow$ {*unfold dur*}
> *(dur m/r2)/r1*
> $\Rightarrow$ {*arithmetic*}
> *dur m/(r1 * r2)*
> $\Rightarrow$ {*fold dur*}
> *dur (tempo (r1 * r2) m)*

Here is another useful axiom and its proof:

Axiom 12.2.2 For any *r*, *m1*, and *m2*:

$$tempo\ r\ (m1 :+: m2) \equiv tempo\ r\ m1 :+: tempo\ r\ m2$$

In other words, *tempo scaling distributes over sequential composition*.

Proof:

> **let** *t* = *cTime c*; *dt* = *cDur c*
> *t1* = *t* + *dur m1* * (*dt*/*r*)
> *t2* = *t* + (*dur m1*/*r*) * *dt*
> *t3* = *t* + *dur (tempo r m1)* * *dt*

$hsomPerform\ pm\ c\ (tempo\ r\ (m1 :+: m2))$
$\Rightarrow \{unfold\ hsomPerform\}$
$hsomPerform\ pm\ (c\ \{cDur = dt/r\})\ (m1 :+: m2)$
$\Rightarrow \{unfold\ hsomPerform\}$
$hsomPerform\ pm\ (c\ \{cDur = dt/r\})\ m1$
$\quad +\!\!+\ hsomPerform\ pm\ (c\ \{cTime = t1, cDur = dt/r\})\ m2$
$\Rightarrow \{fold\ hsomPerform\}$
$hsomPerform\ pm\ c\ (tempo\ r\ m1)$
$\quad +\!\!+\ hsomPerform\ pm\ (c\ \{cTime = t1\})\ (tempo\ r\ m2)$
$\Rightarrow \{arithmetic\}$
$hsomPerform\ pm\ c\ (tempo\ r\ m1)$
$\quad +\!\!+\ hsomPerform\ pm\ (c\ \{cTime = t2\})\ (tempo\ r\ m2)$
$\Rightarrow \{fold\ dur\}$
$hsomPerform\ pm\ c\ (tempo\ r\ m1)$
$\quad +\!\!+\ hsomPerform\ pm\ (c\ \{cTime = t3\})\ (tempo\ r\ m2)$
$\Rightarrow \{fold\ hsomPerform\}$
$hsomPerform\ pm\ c\ (tempo\ r\ m1 :+: tempo\ r\ m2)$

$dur\ (tempo\ r\ (m1 :+: m2))$
$\Rightarrow dur\ (m1 :+: m2)/r$
$\Rightarrow (dur\ m1 + dur\ m2)/r$
$\Rightarrow dur\ m1/r + dur\ m2/r$
$\Rightarrow dur\ (tempo\ r\ m1) + dur\ (tempo\ r\ m2)$
$\Rightarrow dur\ (tempo\ r\ m1 :+: tempo\ r\ m2)$

An even simpler axiom is given by:

Axiom 12.2.3 For any m, $tempo\ 1\ m \equiv m$.

In other words, *unit tempo scaling is the identity function for type Music.*

Proof:

let $dt = cDur\ c$
$hsomPerform\ pm\ c\ (tempo\ 1\ m)$
$\Rightarrow \{unfold\ hsomPerform\}$
$hsomPerform\ pm\ (c\ \{cDur = dt/1\})\ m$
$\Rightarrow \{arithmetic\}$
$hsomPerform\ pm\ c\ m$

$dur\ (tempo\ 1\ m)$
$\Rightarrow dur\ m/1$
$\Rightarrow dur\ m$

Note that the above three proofs, being used to establish axioms, all involve the definitions of *hsomPerform* and *dur*. In contrast, we can also establish *theorems* whose proofs involve only the axioms. For example, Axioms 1, 2, and 3 are all needed to prove the following:

Theorem 12.2.1 For any *r*, *m1*, and *m2*:

$$tempo\ r\ m1 :+: m2 \equiv tempo\ r\ (m1 :+: tempo\ (1/r)\ m2)$$

Proof:

$tempo\ r\ m1 :+: m2$
$\Rightarrow \{Axiom\ 3\}$
$tempo\ r\ m1 :+: tempo\ 1\ m2$
$\Rightarrow \{arithmetic\}$
$tempo\ r\ m1 :+: tempo\ (r * (1/r))\ m2$
$\Rightarrow \{Axiom\ 1\}$
$tempo\ r\ m1 :+: tempo\ r\ (tempo\ (1/r)\ m2)$
$\Rightarrow \{Axiom\ 2\}$
$tempo\ r\ (m1 :+: tempo\ (1/r)\ m2)$

12.3 The Fundamental Axiom Set

There are many other useful axioms, but we do not have room to include all of their proofs here. They are listed below, including the axioms from the previous section as special cases, and the proofs are left as exercises.

Axiom 12.3.1 *Tempo* is *multiplicative* and *Transpose* is *additive*. That is, for any *r1*, *r2*, *p1*, *p2*, and *m*:

$$tempo\ r1\ (tempo\ r2\ m) \equiv tempo\ (r1 * r2)\ m$$
$$trans\ p1\ (trans\ p2\ m)\ \ \equiv trans\ (p1 + p2)\ m$$

Axiom 12.3.2 Function composition is *commutative* with respect to both tempo scaling and transposition. That is, for any *r1*, *r2*, *p1*, and *p2*:

$$tempo\ r1 \circ tempo\ r2 \equiv tempo\ r2 \circ tempo\ r1$$
$$trans\ p1 \circ trans\ p2\ \ \equiv trans\ p2 \circ trans\ p1$$
$$tempo\ r1 \circ trans\ p1\ \equiv trans\ p1 \circ tempo\ r1$$

Axiom 12.3.3 Tempo scaling and transposition are *distributive* over both sequential and parallel composition. That is, for any *r*, *p*, *m1*, and *m2*:

$tempo\ r\ (m1 :+: m2) \equiv tempo\ r\ m1 :+: tempo\ r\ m2$

$tempo\ r\ (m1 :=: m2) \equiv tempo\ r\ m1 :=: tempo\ r\ m2$

$trans\ p\ (m1 :+: m2) \equiv trans\ p\ m1 :+: trans\ p\ m2$

$trans\ p\ (m1 :=: m2) \equiv trans\ p\ m1 :=: trans\ p\ m2$

Axiom 12.3.4 Sequential and parallel composition are *associative*. That is, for any *m0*, *m1*, and *m2*:

$m0 :+: (m1 :+: m2) \equiv (m0 :+: m1) :+: m2$

$m0 :=: (m1 :=: m2) \equiv (m0 :=: m1) :=: m2$

Axiom 12.3.5 Parallel composition is *commutative*. That is, for any *m0* and *m1*:

$m0 :=: m1 \equiv m1 :=: m0$

Axiom 12.3.6 *rest* 0 is a *unit* for *tempo* and *trans*, and a *zero* for sequential and parallel composition. That is, for any *r*, *p*, and *m*:

$tempo\ r\ (rest\ 0) \equiv rest\ 0$

$trans\ p\ (rest\ 0) \equiv rest\ 0$

$m :+: rest\ 0 \quad \equiv m \equiv rest\ 0 :+: m$

$m :=: rest\ 0 \quad \equiv m \equiv rest\ 0 :=: m$

Axiom 12.3.7 A rest can be used to "pad" a parallel composition. That is, for any *m1* and *m2* such that $diff = dur\ m1 - dur\ m2 \geqslant 0$, and any $d \leqslant diff$:

$m1 :=: m2 \equiv m1 :=: (m2 :+: rest\ d)$

Axiom 12.3.8 There is a duality between (:+:) and (:=:), namely that for any *m0*, *m1*, *m2*, and *m3* such that $dur\ m0 = dur\ m2$:

$(m0 :+: m1) :=: (m2 :+: m3) \equiv (m0 :=: m2) :+: (m1 :=: m3)$

Exercise 12.1 Prove Lemma 12.1.1.

Exercise 12.2 Establish the validity of each of the above axioms.

Exercise 12.3 Recall the polyphonic and contrapuntal melodies *mel1* and *mel2* from Chapter 1. Prove that $mel1 \equiv mel2$.

12.4 Other Musical Properties

Aside from the axioms discussed so far, there are many other properties of the values of *Music* and its various operators, just as we saw in Chapter 11 for lists. For example, this property of *map* taken from Figure 11.1:

$$map\ (f \circ g) = map\ f \circ map\ g$$

suggests an analogous property for *mMap*:

$$mMap\ (f \circ g) = mMap\ f \circ mMap\ g$$

Not all of the properties in Figures 11.1 and 11.2 have analogous musical renditions, and there are also others that are special only to *Music* values. Figure 12.1 summarizes the most important of these properties, including the

Properties of *mMap*:

$$mMap\ (\lambda x \to x) = \lambda x \to x$$
$$mMap\ (f \circ g) \quad = mMap\ f \circ mMap\ g$$
$$mMap\ f \circ remove\ d = remove\ d \circ mMap\ f$$
$$mMap\ f \circ cut\ d = cut\ d \circ mMap\ f$$

Properties of *cut* and *remove*:

For all non-negative *d1* and *d2*:
$$cut\ d1 \circ cut\ d2 = cut\ (min\ d1\ d2)$$
$$remove\ d1 \circ remove\ d2 = remove\ (d1 + d2)$$
$$cut\ d1 \circ remove\ d2 = remove\ d1 \circ cut\ (d1 + d2)$$
For all non-negative *d1* and *d2* such that $d2 \geqslant d1$:
$$remove\ d1 \circ cut\ d2 = cut\ (d2 - d1) \circ remove\ d1$$

Properties of *retro*:

For all finite-duration *m*:
$$retro\ (retro\ m) \quad \equiv m$$
$$retro\ (cut\ d\ m) \equiv remove\ (dur\ m - d)\ (retro\ m)$$
$$retro\ (remove\ d\ m) \equiv cut\ (dur\ m - d)\ (retro\ m)$$
$$cut\ d\ (retro\ m) \equiv retro\ (remove\ (dur\ m - d)\ m)$$
$$remove\ d\ (retro\ m) \equiv retro\ (cut\ (dur\ m - d)\ m)$$

Properties of *dur*:

$$dur\ (retro\ m) \quad = dur\ m$$
$$dur\ (cut\ d\ m) = min\ d\ (dur\ m)$$
$$dur\ (remove\ d\ m) = max\ 0\ (dur\ m - d)$$

Figure 12.1 Useful properties of other musical functions.

one above. Note that some of the properties are expressed as strict equality – that is, the left-hand and right-hand sides are equivalent as Haskell values. But others are expressed using musical equivalence – that is, using ($\equiv$). We leave the proofs of all these properties as an exercise.

Exercise 12.4 Prove that *timesM a m* :+: *timesM b m* $\equiv$ *timesM* $(a + b)$ *m*.

Exercise 12.5 Prove as many of the axioms from Figure 12.1 as you can.

13

L-Systems and Generative Grammars

A *grammar* describes a *formal language*. One can either design a *recognizer* (or *parser*) for that language, or design a *generator* that generates sentences in that language. We are interested in using grammars to generate music, and thus we are only interested in generative grammars.

A generative grammar is a four-tuple (N, T, n, P), where:

- N is the set of *non-terminal symbols*.
- T is the set of *terminal symbols*.
- n is the *initial symbol*.
- P is a set of *production rules*, where each production rule is a pair (X, Y), often written $X \rightarrow Y$. X and Y are sentences (or *sentential forms*) formed over the alphabet $N \cup T$, and X contains at least one non-terminal.

A *Lindenmayer system*, or *L-system*, is an example of a generative grammar, but is different in two ways:

1. The *sequence* of sentences is as important as the individual sentences, and
2. A new sentence is generated from the previous one by applying as many productions as possible on each step – a kind of "parallel production."

Lindenmayer was a biologist and mathematician, and he used L-systems to describe the growth of certain biological organisms (such as plants, in particular, algae).

We will limit our discussion to L-systems that have the following additional characteristics:

1. They are *context-free*: the left-hand side of each production (i.e., X above) is a single non-terminal.
2. No distinction is made between terminals and non-terminals (with no loss of expressive power – why?).

We will consider both *deterministic* and *non-deterministic* grammars. A deterministic grammar has exactly one production corresponding to each non-terminal symbol in the alphabet, whereas a non-deterministic grammar may have more than one, and thus we will need some way to choose between them.

13.1 A Simple Implementation

A framework for simple, context-free, deterministic grammars can be designed in Haskell as follows. We represent the set of productions as a list of symbol/list-of-symbol pairs:

data *DetGrammar a = DetGrammar a*   -- start symbol
                                    $[(a,[a])]$ -- productions
   deriving *Show*

To generate a succession of "sentential forms," we need to define a function that, given a grammar, returns a list of lists of symbols:

detGenerate :: Eq a $\Rightarrow$ DetGrammar a $\rightarrow$ [[a]]
detGenerate (DetGrammar st ps) = iterate (concatMap f) [st]
   where *f a = maybe [a] id (lookup a ps)*

Details: *maybe* is a convenient function for conditionally giving a result based on the structure of a value of type *Maybe a*. It is defined in the Standard Prelude as:

maybe $:: b \rightarrow (a \rightarrow b) \rightarrow Maybe\ a \rightarrow b$
maybe _f (Just x) = f x
maybe z _ Nothing = z

lookup :: Eq a $\Rightarrow$ a $\rightarrow$ [(a,b)] $\rightarrow$ Maybe b is a convenient function for finding the value associated with a given key in an association list. For example:

lookup 'b' $[('a',0),('b',1),('c',2)] \Rightarrow$ *Just 1*
lookup 'd' $[('a',0),('b',1),('c',2)] \Rightarrow$ *Nothing*

Note that we expand each symbol "in parallel" at each step, using *concatMap*. The repetition of this process at each step is achieved using *iterate*. Note also that a list of productions is essentially an *association list*, and thus the *Data.List* library function *lookup* works quite well in finding the production rule that we seek. Finally, note once again how the use of higher-order functions makes this definition concise yet efficient.

As an example of the use of this simple program, consider the following Lindenmayer grammar inspired by growth patterns in algae:

```
redAlgae = DetGrammar 'a'
  [('a',"b|c"),  ('b',"b"),('c',"b|d"),
   ('d',"e\\d"),('e',"f"),('f',"g"),
   ('g',"h(a)"),('h',"h"),('|',"|"),
   ('(',"("),      (')',")"),('/',"\\"),
   ('\\',"/")
  ]
```

Details: Recall that `'\\'` is how the backslash character is written in Haskell, because a single backslash is the "escape" character for writing special characters such as newline (`'\n'`), tab (`'\t'`), and so on. Since the backslash is used in this way, it is also a special character, and must be escaped using itself, i.e. `'\\'`.

Then *detGenerate redAlgae* gives us the result that we want – or, to make it look nicer, we could do:

t n g = sequence_ (map putStrLn (take n (detGenerate g)))

For example, *t 10 redAlgae* yields:

```
a
b|c
b|b|d
b|b|e\d
b|b|f/e\d
b|b|g\f/e\d
b|b|h(a)/g\f/e\d
b|b|h(b|c)\h(a)/g\f/e\d
b|b|h(b|b|d)/h(b|c)\h(a)/g\f/e\d
b|b|h(b|b|e\d)\h(b|b|d)/h(b|c)\h(a)/g\f/e\d
```

Exercise 13.1 Define a function *strToMusic :: AbsPitch → Dur → String → Music Pitch* that interprets the strings generated by *redAlgae* as music. Specifically, *strToMusic ap d str* interprets the string *str* in the following way:

1. Characters ′a′ through ′h′ are interpreted as notes, each with duration d and absolute pitch ap, $ap + 2$, $ap + 4$, $ap + 5$, $ap + 7$, $ap + 9$, $ap + 11$, and $ap + 12$, respectively (i.e., a major scale).
2. ′|′ is interpreted as a no-op.
3. ′/′ and ′\\′ are both interpreted as a rest of length d.
4. ′(′ is interpreted as a transposition by 5 semitones (a perfect fourth).
5. ′)′ is interpreted as a transposition by −5 semitones.

Exercise 13.2 Design a function $testDet :: Grammar\ a \rightarrow Bool$ such that $testDet\ g$ is $True$ if g has exactly one rule for each of its symbols; i.e., it is deterministic. Then modify the $generate$ function above so that it returns an error if a grammar not satisfying this constraint is given as argument.

13.2 A More General Implementation

The design given in the last section only captures deterministic context-free grammars, and the generator considers only parallel productions that are characteristic of L-systems.

We would also like to consider non-deterministic grammars, where a user can specify the probability that a particular rule is selected, as well as possibly non–context-free (i.e., context-sensitive) grammars. Thus we will represent a generative grammar a bit more abstractly, as a data structure that has a starting sentence in an (implicit, polymorphic) alphabet and a list of production rules:

```
data Grammar a = Grammar a          -- start sentence
                         (Rules a)   -- production rules
  deriving Show
```

The production rules are instructions for converting sentences in the alphabet to other sentences in the alphabet. A rule set is either a set of uniformly distributed rules (meaning that those with the same left-hand side have an equal probability of being chosen) or a set of stochastic rules (each of which is paired with a probability). A specific rule consists of a left-hand side and a right-hand side.

```
data Rules a = Uni [Rule a]
             | Sto [(Rule a, Prob)]
  deriving (Eq, Ord, Show)
```

```
data Rule a = Rule {lhs :: a, rhs :: a}
   deriving (Eq, Ord, Show)
type Prob = Double
```

One of the key sub-problems that we will have to solve is how to probabilistically select a rule from a set of rules, and use that rule to expand a non-terminal. We define the following type to capture this process:

```
type ReplFun a = [[(Rule a, Prob)]] → (a, [Rand]) → (a, [Rand])
type Rand      = Double
```

The idea here is that a function $f :: ReplFun\ a$ is such that $f\ rules\ (s, rands)$ will return a new sentence s' in which each symbol in s has been replaced according to some rule in *rules* (which are grouped by common left-hand sides). Each rule is chosen probabilistically based on the random numbers in *rands*, and thus the result also includes a new list of random numbers to account for those "consumed" by the replacement process.

With such a function in hand, we can now define a function that, given a grammar, generates an infinite list of the sentences produced by this replacement process. Because the process is non-deterministic, we also pass a seed (an integer) to generate the initial pseudo-random number sequence to give us repeatable results.

```
gen :: Ord a ⇒ ReplFun a → Grammar a → Int → [a]
gen f (Grammar s rules) seed =
   let Sto newRules = toStoRules rules
       rands        = randomRs (0.0, 1.0) (mkStdGen seed)
   in if checkProbs newRules
       then generate f newRules (s, rands)
       else (error "Stochastic rule-set is malformed.")
```

toStoRules converts a list of uniformly distributed rules to an equivalent list of stochastic rules. Each set of uniform rules with the same LHS is converted to a set of stochastic rules in which the probability of each rule is one divided by the number of uniform rules.

```
toStoRules :: (Ord a, Eq a) ⇒ Rules a → Rules a
toStoRules (Sto rs) = Sto rs
toStoRules (Uni rs) =
   let rs' = groupBy (λr1 r2 → lhs r1 == lhs r2) (sort rs)
   in Sto (concatMap insertProb rs')
insertProb :: [a] → [(a, Prob)]
insertProb rules = let prb = 1.0/fromIntegral (length rules)
                   in zip rules (repeat prb)
```

> **Details:** *groupBy* :: $(a \to a \to Bool) \to [a] \to [[a]]$ is a *Data.List*
> library function that behaves as follows: *groupBy eqfn xs* returns a list of
> lists such that all elements in each sublist are "equal" in the sense defined
> by *eqfn*.

checkProbs takes a list of production rules and checks whether, for every
rule with the same LHS, the probabilities sum to one (plus or minus some
epsilon, currently set to 0.001).

checkProbs :: $(Ord\ a, Eq\ a) \Rightarrow [(Rule\ a, Prob)] \to Bool$
checkProbs rs = *and* (*map checkSum* (*groupBy sameLHS* (*sort rs*)))
eps = 0.001

checkSum :: $[(Rule\ a, Prob)] \to Bool$
checkSum rules = **let** *mySum* = *sum* (*map snd rules*)
                       in *abs* $(1.0 - mySum) \leqslant eps$

sameLHS :: $Eq\ a \Rightarrow (Rule\ a, Prob) \to (Rule\ a, Prob) \to Bool$
sameLHS (*r1,f1*) (*r2,f2*) = *lhs r1* == *lhs r2*

generate takes a replacement function, a list of rules, a starting sentence,
and a source of random numbers and returns an infinite list of sentences.

generate :: $Eq\ a \Rightarrow$
                 $ReplFun\ a \to [(Rule\ a, Prob)] \to (a, [Rand]) \to [a]$
generate f rules xs =
  let *newRules*   = *map probDist* (*groupBy sameLHS rules*)
        probDist rrs = **let** (*rs, ps*) = *unzip rrs*
                           in *zip rs* (*tail* (*scanl* (+) 0 *ps*))
  in *map fst* (*iterate* (*f newRules*) *xs*)

A key aspect of the *generate* algorithm above is that it computes the
probability density of each successive rule, which is basically the sum of its
probability plus the probabilities of all rules that precede it.

13.3 An L-System Grammar for Music

The previous section gave a generative framework for a generic grammar. For
a musical L-system, we will define a specific grammar whose sentences are
defined as follows. A musical L-system sentence is either:

- A non-terminal symbol *N a*,
- A sequential composition *s1* :+ *s2*,

- A functional composition *s1* :. *s2*, or
- The symbol *Id*, which will eventually be interpreted as the identity function.

We capture this in the *LSys* data type:

data *LSys a* = *N a*
       | *LSys a* :+ *LSys a*
       | *LSys a* :. *LSys a*
       | *Id*
  deriving (*Eq*, *Ord*, *Show*)

The idea here is that sentences generated from this grammar are relative to a starting note, and thus the above constructions will be interpreted as functions that take that starting note as an argument. This will all become clear shortly, but first we need to define a replacement function for this grammar.

We will treat (:+) and (:.) as binary branches, and recursively traverse each of their arguments. We will treat *Id* as a constant that never gets replaced. Most importantly, each non-terminal of the form *N x* could each be the left-hand side of a rule, so we call the function *getNewRHS* to generate the replacement term for it.

replFun :: *Eq a* ⇒ *ReplFun* (*LSys a*)
replFun rules (*s*, *rands*) =
  case *s* **of**
    a :+ *b* → **let** (*a'*, *rands'*) = *replFun rules* (*a*, *rands*)
               (*b'*, *rands''*) = *replFun rules* (*b*, *rands'*)
          in (*a'* :+ *b'*, *rands''*)
    a :. *b* → **let** (*a'*, *rands'*) = *replFun rules* (*a*, *rands*)
               (*b'*, *rands''*) = *replFun rules* (*b*, *rands'*)
          in (*a'* :. *b'*, *rands''*)
    Id   → (*Id*, *rands*)
    N x → (*getNewRHS rules* (*N x*) (*head rands*), *tail rands*)

getNewRHS is defined as:

getNewRHS :: *Eq a* ⇒ [[(*Rule a*, *Prob*)]] → *a* → *Rand* → *a*
getNewRHS rrs ls rand =
  let *loop* ((*r*, *p*) : *rs*) = **if** *rand* ⩽ *p* **then** *rhs r* **else** *loop rs*
      loop [ ]   = *error* "getNewRHS anomaly"
  in case (*find* (λ((*r*, *p*): _) → *lhs r* == *ls*) *rrs*) **of**
    Just rs → *loop rs*
    Nothing → *error* "No rule match"

Details: *find* :: $(a \rightarrow Bool) \rightarrow [a] \rightarrow Maybe\ a$ is another *Data.List* function that returns the first element of a list that satisfies a predicate, or *Nothing* if there is no such element.

13.3.1 Examples

The final step is to interpret the resulting sentence (i.e., a value of type *LSys a*) as music. As mentioned earlier, the intent of the *LSys* design is that a value is interpreted as a *function* that is applied to a single note (or, more generally, a single *Music* value). The specific constructors are interpreted as follows:

type *IR a b* $= [\,(a, Music\ b \rightarrow Music\ b)\,]$ -- "interpretation rules"
interpret :: $(Eq\ a) \Rightarrow LSys\ a \rightarrow IR\ a\ b \rightarrow Music\ b \rightarrow Music\ b$
interpret $(a :. b)$ $r\ m = interpret\ a\ r\ (interpret\ b\ r\ m)$
interpret $(a :+ b)$ $r\ m = interpret\ a\ r\ m :+: interpret\ b\ r\ m$
interpret Id $r\ m = m$
interpret $(N\ x)$ $r\ m = $ **case** $(lookup\ x\ r)$ **of**
                 Just f $\rightarrow f\ m$
                 Nothing $\rightarrow error$ "No interpretation rule"

For example, we could define the following interpretation rules:

data *LFun* $= Inc\ |\ Dec\ |\ Same$
    deriving $(Eq, Ord, Show)$
ir :: *IR LFun Pitch*
ir $= [\,(Inc, transpose\ 1),$
    $(Dec, transpose\ (-1)),$
    $(Same, id)\,]$

inc, dec, same :: *LSys LFun*
inc $= N\ Inc$
dec $= N\ Dec$
same $= N\ Same$

In other words, *inc* transposes the music up by one semitone, *dec* transposes it down by a semitone, and *same* does nothing.

Now let's build an actual grammar. *sc* increments a note followed by its decrement – the two notes are one whole tone apart:

$sc = inc :+: dec$

Now let's define a bunch of rules:

r1a = Rule inc (sc :. sc)
r1b = Rule inc sc
r2a = Rule dec (sc :. sc)
r2b = Rule dec sc
r3a = Rule same inc
r3b = Rule same dec
r3c = Rule same same

and the corresponding grammar:

g1 = Grammar same (Uni [r1b, r1a, r2b, r2a, r3a, r3b])

Finally, we generate a sentence at some particular level and interpret it as music:

t1 n = instrument Vibraphone $
     interpret (gen replFun g1 42 !! n) ir (c 5 tn)

Try "*play (t1 3)*" or "*play (t1 4)*" to hear the result.

Exercise 13.3 Play with the L-system grammar defined in this chapter. Change the production rules. Add probabilities to the rules, i.e., change it into a *Sto* grammar. Change the random number seed. Change the depth of recursion. And also try changing the "musical seed" (i.e., the note *c 5 tn*).

Exercise 13.4 Define a new L-system structure. In particular, (a) define a new version of *LSys* (for example, add a parallel constructor) and its associated interpretation, and/or (b) define a new version of *LFun* (perhaps add something to control the volume) and its associated interpretation. Then define some grammars with the new design to generate interesting music.

14

Random Numbers, Probability Distributions, and Markov Chains

The use of randomness in composition can be justified by the somewhat random, exploratory nature of the creative mind, and indeed it has been used in computer music composition for many years. It is a powerful way to produce new and interesting musical structures that can be both inspirational and interesting in their own right. Randomness is also an important part of larger automated composition systems, since it can allow a single program to produce a vast array of unique and interesting results simply by running it more than once.

Randomness and probability distributions can be either used directly with sonification algorithms for sequences of numbers, or threaded through a larger framework to drive decision-making processes. Learning- or data-driven approaches are commonly combined with stochastic generative algorithms to create convincingly human-sounding music. EMI [20] and Kulitta [16] are examples of two large-scale systems for generating new, complete pieces of music emulating human styles. The details of these systems are beyond the scope of strategies covered within this book, although they still use the basic principles of randomness shown in the smaller-scale examples covered here and in later chapters.

In this chapter we will explore several sources of random numbers and how to use them in generating simple melodies. With this foundation, you will hopefully be able to use randomness in more sophisticated ways in your compositions. Music that relies at least to some degree on randomness is said to be *stochastic*, or *aleatoric*.

14.1 Random Numbers

This section describes the basic functionality of Haskell's *System.Random* module, which is a library for random numbers. The library presents a fairly

Figure 14.1 An example of a stochastically generated chorale phrase from Kulitta, which is a Haskell-based automated composition system. To create music, Kulitta uses a combination of probabilistic generative grammars similar to the L-systems from Chapter 13 and geometric models for harmony that employ stochastic path-finding algorithms. Kulitta also uses Euterpea to represent score-level musical structures.

abstract interface that is structured in two layers of type classes: one that captures the notion of a *random generator*, and one for using a random generator to create *random sequences*.

We can create a random number generator using the built-in *mkStdGen* function:

mkStdGen :: *Int* → *StdGen*

which takes an *Int* seed as argument, and returns a "standard generator" of type *StdGen*. For example, we can define:

sGen :: *StdGen*
sGen = *mkStdGen* 42

We will use this single random generator quite extensively in the remainder of this chapter.

StdGen is an instance of *Show*, and thus its values can be printed – but they appear in a rather strange way, basically as two integers. Try typing *sGen* into the GHCi prompt.

More importantly, *StdGen* is an instance of the *RandomGen* class:

class *RandomGen g* **where**
    genRange :: *g* → (*Int, Int*)
    next   :: *g* → (*Int, g*)
    split   :: *g* → (*g, g*)

The reason that *Int*s are used here is that essentially all pseudo-random number generator algorithms are based on a fixed-precision binary number, such as *Int*. We will see later how this can be coerced into other number types.

For now, try applying the operators in the above class to the *sGen* value above. The *next* function is particularly important, as it generates the next random number in a sequence as well as a new random number generator, which in turn can be used to generate the next number, and so on. It should be clear that we can then create an infinite list of random *Int*s like this:

$$randInts :: StdGen \rightarrow [Int]$$
$$randInts\ g = \textbf{let}\ (x, g') = next\ g$$
$$\textbf{in}\ x : randInts\ g'$$

Look at the value *take* 10 (*randInts sGen*) to see a sample output.

To support other number types, the *Random* library defines this type class:

class *Random a* **where**
   randomR   :: $RandomGen\ g \Rightarrow (a, a) \rightarrow g \rightarrow (a, g)$
   random   :: $RandomGen\ g \Rightarrow g \rightarrow (a, g)$

   randomRs :: $RandomGen\ g \Rightarrow (a, a) \rightarrow g \rightarrow [a]$
   randoms   :: $RandomGen\ g \Rightarrow g \rightarrow [a]$

   randomRIO :: $(a, a) \rightarrow IO\ a$
   randomIO :: $IO\ a$

Built-in instances of *Random* are provided for *Int*, *Integer*, *Float*, *Double*, *Bool*, and *Char*.

The set of operators in the *Random* class is rather daunting, so let's focus on just one of them for now, namely the third one, *RandomRs*, which is also perhaps the most useful one. This function takes a random number generator (such as *sGen*), along with a range of values, and generates an infinite list of random numbers within the given range (the pair representing the range is treated as a closed interval). Here are several examples of this idea:

$$randFloats :: [Float]$$
$$randFloats = randomRs\ (-1, 1)\ sGen$$

$$randIntegers :: [Integer]$$
$$randIntegers = randomRs\ (0, 100)\ sGen$$

$$randString :: String$$
$$randString = randomRs\ ('a', 'z')\ sGen$$

Recall that a string is a list of characters, so we choose here to use the name *randString* for our infinite list of characters. If you believe the story about a monkey typing a novel, then you might believe that *randString* contains something interesting to read.

So far we have used a seed to initialize our random number generators, and this is good in the sense that it allows us to generate repeatable, and therefore more easily testable, results. If instead you prefer a non-repeatable result, in which you can think of the seed as being the time of day when the program is executed, then you need to use a function that is in the IO monad. The last two operators in the *Random* class serve this purpose. For example, consider:

randIO :: *IO Float*
randIO = *randomRIO* (0, 1)

If you repeatedly type *randIO* at the GHCi prompt, it will return a different random number every time. This is clearly not purely "functional," and is why it is in the IO monad. As another example:

randIO′ :: *IO* ()
randIO′ = **do** *r1* ← *randomRIO* (0, 1) :: *IO Float*
        r2 ← *randomRIO* (0, 1) :: *IO Float*
        print (*r1* == *r2*)

will almost always return *False*, because the chance of two randomly generated floating-point numbers being the same is exceedingly small. (The type signature is needed to ensure that the value generated has an unambiguous type.)

Details: *print* :: *Show a* ⇒ *a* → *IO* () converts any showable value into a string and displays the result in the standard output area.

14.2 Probability Distributions

The random number generators described in the previous section are assumed to be *uniform*, meaning that the probability of generating a number within a given interval is the same everywhere in the range of the generator. For example, in the case of *Float* (which purportedly represents *continuous* real numbers), suppose we are generating numbers in the range 0–10. Then we would expect the probability of a number appearing in the range 2.3–2.4 to be the same as the probability of a number appearing in the range 7.6–7.7, namely 0.01, or 1% (i.e., 0.1/10). In the case of *Int* (a *discrete* or *integral* number type), we would expect the probability of generating a 5 to be the same as generating an 8. In both cases, we say that we have a *uniform distribution*.

But we don't always want a uniform distribution. When generating music, in fact, it's often the case that we want some kind of a non-uniform distribution. Mathematically, the best way to describe a distribution is by

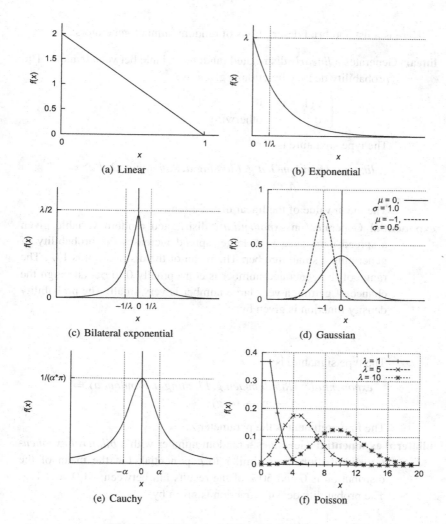

Figure 14.2 Various probability density functions.

plotting how the probability changes over the range of values that it produces. In the case of continuous numbers, this is called the *probability density function*, which has the property that its integral over the full range of values is equal to 1.

The *System.Random.Distributions* library provides a number of different probability distributions, which are described below. Figure 14.2 shows the probability density functions for each of them.

Here is a list and brief descriptions of random number generators:

linear Generates a *linearly* distributed random variable between 0 and 1. The probability density function is given by:

$$f(x) = \begin{cases} 2(1-x) & \text{if } 0 \leqslant x \leqslant 1 \\ 0 & \text{otherwise} \end{cases}$$

The type signature is:

$$linear :: (RandomGen\ g, Floating\ a, Random\ a, Ord\ a) \Rightarrow$$
$$g \rightarrow (a, g)$$

The mean value of the linear distribution is $1/3$.

exponential Generates an *exponentially* distributed random variable given a spread parameter λ. A larger spread increases the probability of generating a small number. The mean of the distribution is $1/\lambda$. The range of the generated number is conceptually 0 to ∞, although the chance of getting a very large number is very small. The probability density function is given by:

$$f(x) = \lambda e^{-\lambda x}$$

The type signature is:

$$exponential :: (RandomGen\ g, Floating\ a, Random\ a) \Rightarrow$$
$$a \rightarrow g \rightarrow (a, g)$$

The first argument is the parameter λ.

bilateral exponential Generates a random number with a *bilateral exponential* distribution. It is similar to exponential, but the mean of the distribution is 0 and 50% of the results fall between $-1/\lambda$ and $1/\lambda$. The probability density function is given by:

$$f(x) = \frac{1}{2}\lambda e^{-\lambda|x|}$$

The type signature is:

$$bilExp :: (Floating\ a, Ord\ a, Random\ a, RandomGen\ g) \Rightarrow$$
$$a \rightarrow g \rightarrow (a, g)$$

Gaussian Generates a random number with a *Gaussian*, also called *normal*, distribution, given mathematically by:

$$f(x) = \frac{1}{\sigma\sqrt{2\pi}}e^{-\frac{(x-\mu)^2}{2\sigma^2}}$$

where σ is the *standard deviation* and μ is the *mean*. The type signature is:

$gaussian :: (Floating\ a, Random\ a, RandomGen\ g) \Rightarrow$
$\qquad a \rightarrow a \rightarrow g \rightarrow (a, g)$

The first argument is the standard deviation σ and the second is the mean μ. Probabilistically, about 68.27% of the numbers in a Gaussian distribution fall within $\pm\sigma$ of the mean, about 95.45% are within $\pm 2\sigma$, and 99.73% are within $\pm 3\sigma$.

Cauchy Generates a *Cauchy*-distributed random variable. The distribution is symmetric, with a mean of 0. The density function is given by:

$$f(x) = \frac{\alpha}{\pi(\alpha^2 + x^2)}$$

As with the Gaussian distribution, it is unbounded both above and below the mean, but at its extremes it approaches 0 more slowly than the Gaussian. The type signature is:

$cauchy :: (Floating\ a, Random\ a, RandomGen\ g) \Rightarrow$
$\qquad a \rightarrow g \rightarrow (a, g)$

The first argument corresponds to α above and is called the *density*.

Poisson Generates a *Poisson*-distributed random variable. The Poisson distribution is discrete and generates only non-negative numbers. λ is the mean of the distribution. If λ is an integer, the probability that the result is $j = \lambda - 1$ is the same as that of $j = \lambda$. The probability of generating the number j is given by:

$$P\{X = j\} = \frac{\lambda^j}{j!}e^{-\lambda}$$

The type signature is:

$poisson :: (Num\ t, Ord\ a, Floating\ a, Random\ a$
$\qquad\qquad RandomGen\ g) \Rightarrow$
$\qquad a \rightarrow g \rightarrow (t, g)$

Custom Sometimes it is useful to define one's own discrete probability distribution function, and to generate random numbers based on it. The function *frequency* does this – given a list of weight-value pairs, it generates a value randomly picked from the list, weighting the probability of choosing each value by the given weight.

$frequency :: (Floating\ w, Ord\ w, Random\ w, RandomGen\ g) \Rightarrow$
$\qquad [(w, a)] \rightarrow g \rightarrow (a, g)$

14.2.1 Random Melodies and Random Walks

Note that each of the non-uniform distribution random number generators described in the last section takes zero or more parameters as arguments, along with a uniform random number generator, and returns a pair consisting of the next random number and a new generator. In other words, the tail end of each type signature has the form:

$$\ldots \rightarrow g \rightarrow (a, g)$$

where g is the type of the random number generator and a is the type of the next value generated.

Given such a function, we can generate an infinite sequence of random numbers with the given distribution in a way similar to what we did earlier for *randInts*. In fact, the following function is defined in the *Distributions* library to make this easy:

$$
\begin{aligned}
&rands \quad :: (RandomGen\ g, Random\ a) \Rightarrow \\
&\qquad\qquad (g \rightarrow (a, g)) \rightarrow g \rightarrow [a] \\
&rands\ f\ g = x : rands\ f\ g'\ \textbf{where}\ (x, g') = f\ g
\end{aligned}
$$

Let's work through a few musical examples. One thing we will need to do is convert a floating-point number to an absolute pitch:

$$
\begin{aligned}
&toAbsP1 \quad :: Float \rightarrow AbsPitch \\
&toAbsP1\ x = round\ (40 * x + 30)
\end{aligned}
$$

This function converts a number in the range 0–1 into an absolute pitch in the range 30–70.

And as we have often done, we will also need to convert an absolute pitch into a note, and a sequence of absolute pitches into a melody:

$$
\begin{aligned}
&mkNote1 :: AbsPitch \rightarrow Music\ Pitch \\
&mkNote1 = note\ tn \circ pitch \\
\\
&mkLine1 \quad\quad :: [AbsPitch] \rightarrow Music\ Pitch \\
&mkLine1\ rands = line\ (take\ 32\ (map\ mkNote1\ rands))
\end{aligned}
$$

With these functions in hand, we can now generate sequences of random numbers with a variety of distributions, and convert each of them into a melody. For example:

```
-- uniform distribution
m1 :: Music Pitch
m1 = mkLine1 (randomRs (30, 70) sGen)
    -- linear distribution
```

m2 :: *Music Pitch*
m2 = **let** *rs1* = *rands linear sGen*
     in *mkLine1* (*map toAbsP1 rs1*)

  -- exponential distribution
m3   :: *Float* → *Music Pitch*
m3 lam = **let** *rs1* = *rands* (*exponential lam*) *sGen*
       in *mkLine1* (*map toAbsP1 rs1*)

  -- Gaussian distribution
m4   :: *Float* → *Float* → *Music Pitch*
m4 sig mu = **let** *rs1* = *rands* (*gaussian sig mu*) *sGen*
        in *mkLine1* (*map toAbsP1 rs1*)

Exercise 14.1 Try playing each of the above melodies, and listen to the musical differences. For *lam*, try values of 0.1, 1, 5, and 10. For *mu*, a value of 0.5 will put the melody in the central part of the scale range. Then try values of 0.01, 0.05, and 0.1 for *sig*.

Exercise 14.2 Do the following:

• Try using some of the other probability distributions to generate a melody.
• Instead of using a chromatic scale, try using a diatonic or pentatonic scale.
• Try using randomness to control parameters other than pitch – in particular, duration and/or volume.

Another approach to generating a melody is sometimes called a *random walk*. The idea is to start on a particular note and treat the sequence of random numbers as *intervals*, rather than as pitches. To prevent the melody from wandering too far from the starting pitch, one should use a probability distribution whose mean is zero. This comes for free with something like the bilateral exponential, and is easily obtained with a distribution that takes the mean as a parameter (such as the Gaussian), but is also easily achieved for other distributions by simply subtracting the mean. To see these two situations, here are random melodic walks using first a Gaussian and then an exponential distribution:

  -- Gaussian distribution with mean set to 0
m5   :: *Float* → *Music Pitch*
m5 sig = **let** *rs1* = *rands* (*gaussian sig 0*) *sGen*
      in *mkLine2* 50 (*map toAbsP2 rs1*)

  -- exponential distribution with mean adjusted to 0
m6   :: *Float* → *Music Pitch*

$m6\ lam = $ **let** $rs1 = rands\ (exponential\ lam)\ sGen$
$\qquad\qquad$ **in** $mkLine2\ 50\ (map\ (toAbsP2 \circ subtract\ (1/lam))\ rs1)$

$toAbsP2\quad :: Float \rightarrow AbsPitch$
$toAbsP2\ x = round\ (5 * x)$

$mkLine2 :: AbsPitch \rightarrow [AbsPitch] \rightarrow Music\ Pitch$
$mkLine2\ start\ rands =$
$\quad line\ (take\ 64\ (map\ mkNote1\ (scanl\ (+)\ start\ rands)))$

Note that *toAbsP2* does something reasonable to interpret a floating-point number as an interval, and *mkLine2* uses *scanl* to generate a "running sum" that represents the melody line.

14.3 Markov Chains

Each number in the random number sequences that we have described thus far is *independent* of any previous values in the sequence. This is like flipping a coin – each flip has a 50% chance of being heads or tails, i.e., it is independent of any previous flips, even if the last 10 flips were all heads.

Sometimes, however, we would like the probability of a new choice to depend upon some number of previous choices. This is called a *conditional probability*. In a discrete system, if we look only at the previous value to help determine the next value, then these conditional probabilities can be conveniently represented in a matrix. For example, if we are choosing between the pitches *C*, *D*, *E*, and *F*, then Table 14.1 might represent the conditional probabilities of each possible outcome. The previous pitch is found in the left column – thus note that the sum of each row is 1.0. So, for example, the probability of choosing a *D* given that the previous pitch was an *E* is 0.6, and the probability of an *F* occurring twice in succession is 0.2. The resulting stochastic system is called a *Markov chain*.

Table 14.1. *First-order Markov chain.*

	C	D	E	F
C	0.4	0.2	0.2	0.2
D	0.3	0.2	0.0	0.5
E	0.1	0.6	0.1	0.2
F	0.2	0.3	0.3	0.2

This idea can, of course, be generalized to arbitrary numbers of previous events, and in general an $(n + 1)$-dimensional array can be used to store the various conditional probabilities. The number of previous values observed is called the *order* of the Markov chain.

14.3.1 Training Data

Instead of generating the conditional probability table ourselves, another approach is to use *training data* from which the conditional probabilities can be *inferred*. This is handy for music, because it means that we can feed in a bunch of melodies that we like, including melodies written by the masters, and use that as a stochastic basis for generating new melodies.

The *Data.MarkovChain* library provides this functionality through a function called *run*, whose type signature is:

```
run :: (Ord a, RandomGen g) ⇒
        Int         -- order of Markov chain
     → [a]          -- training sequence (treated as circular list)
     → Int          -- index to start within the training sequence
     → g            -- random number generator
     → [a]
```

The *runMulti* function is similar, except that it takes a list of training sequences as input and returns a list of lists as its result, each being an independent random walk whose probabilities are based on the training data. The following examples demonstrate how to use these functions.

```
-- some sample training sequences
ps0, ps1, ps2 :: [Pitch]
ps0 = [(C, 4), (D, 4), (E, 4)]
ps1 = [(C, 4), (D, 4), (E, 4), (F, 4), (G, 4), (A, 4), (B, 4)]
ps2 = [(C, 4), (E, 4), (G, 4), (E, 4), (F, 4), (A, 4), (G, 4), (E, 4),
       (C, 4), (E, 4), (G, 4), (E, 4), (F, 4), (D, 4), (C, 4)]

-- functions to package up run and runMulti
mc   ps  n = mkLine3 (M.run n ps 0 (mkStdGen 42))
mcm pss n = mkLine3 (concat (M.runMulti n pss 0
                                       (mkStdGen 42)))

-- music-making functions
mkNote3    :: Pitch → Music Pitch
mkNote3    = note tn

mkLine3    :: [Pitch] → Music Pitch
mkLine3 ps = line (take 64 (map mkNote3 ps))
```

Here are some things to try with the above definitions:

- *mc ps0* 0 will generate a completely random sequence, since it is a "zeroth-order" Markov chain that does not look at any previous output.
- *mc ps0* 1 looks back one value, which is enough in the case of this simple training sequence to generate an endless sequence of notes that sounds just like the training data. Using any order higher than 1 generates the same result.
- *mc ps1* 1 also generates a result that sounds just like its training data.
- *mc ps2* 1, on the other hand, has some (random) variety to it, because the training data has more than one occurrence of most of the notes. If we increase the order, however, the output will sound more and more like the training data.
- *mcm* [*ps0, ps2*] 1 and *mcm* [*ps1, ps2*] 1 generate perhaps the most interesting results yet, in which you can hear aspects of both the ascending melodic nature of *ps0* and *ps1* and the harmonic structure of *ps2*.
- *mcm* [*ps1, reverse ps1*] 1 has, not surprisingly, both ascending and descending lines in it, as reflected in the training data.

Exercise 14.3 Play with Markov chains. Use them to generate more melodies, or to control other aspects of the music, such as rhythm. Also consider other kinds of training data rather than simply sequences of pitches.

15

Basic Input/Output

So far the only input/output (IO) that we have seen in Euterpea is the use of the *play* function to generate the MIDI output corresponding to a *Music* value. But we have said very little about the *play* function itself. What is its type? How does it work? How does one do IO in a purely functional language such as Haskell? Our goal in this chapter is to answer these questions. Then, in Chapter 17, we will describe an elegant way to do IO involving a "musical user interface," or *MUI*.

15.1 IO in Haskell

The Haskell Report defines the result of a program to be the value of the variable *main* in the module *Main*. This is a mere technicality, however, only having relevance when you compile a program as a stand-alone executable (see the GHC documentation for a discussion of how to do that).

The way most people run Haskell programs, especially during program development, is through the GHCi command prompt. As you know, the GHCi implementation of Haskell allows you to type whatever expression you wish as the command prompt, and it will evaluate it for you.

In both cases, the Haskell system "executes a program" by evaluating an expression, which (for a well-behaved program) eventually yields a value. The system must then display that value on your computer screen in some way that makes sense to you. GHC does this by insisting that the type of the value be an instance of the *Show* class – in which case it "shows" the result by converting it to a string using the *show* function (recall the discussion in Section 7.1). So an integer is printed as an integer, a string as a string, a list as a list, and so on.

We will refer to the area of the computer screen where this result is printed as the *standard output area*, which may vary from one implementation to another.

But what if a program is intended to write to a file? Or print out a file on a printer? Or, the main topic of this book, to play some music through the computer's sound card or an external MIDI device? These are examples of *output*, and there are related questions about *input*: for example, how does a program receive input from the computer keyboard or mouse, or from a MIDI keyboard?

In general, how does Haskell's "expression-oriented" notion of "computation by calculation" accommodate these various kinds of input and output?

The answer is fairly simple: in Haskell there is a special kind of value called an *action*. When a Haskell system evaluates an expression that yields an action, it knows not to try to display the result in the standard output area, but rather to "take the appropriate action." There are primitive actions, such as writing a single character to a file or receiving a single character from a MIDI keyboard, as well as compound actions, such as printing an entire string to a file or playing an entire piece of music. Haskell expressions that evaluate to actions are commonly called *commands*.

Some commands return a value for subsequent use by the program: a character from the keyboard, for instance. A command that returns a value of type T has type $IO\ T$. If no useful value is returned, the command has type $IO\ ()$. The simplest example of a command is *return x*, which for a value $x :: T$ immediately returns x and has type $IO\ T$.

Details: The type () is called the *unit type*, and has exactly one value, which is also written (). Thus *return* () has type $IO\ ()$ and is often called a "no-op," because it is an operation that does nothing and returns no useful result. Despite the negative connotation, it is used quite often!

Remember that all expressions in Haskell must be well-typed before a program is run, so a Haskell implementation knows ahead of time, by looking at the type, that it is evaluating a command, and is thus ready to "take action."

15.2 do Syntax

To make these ideas clearer, let's consider a few examples. One useful IO command is *putStr*, which prints a string argument to the standard output area and has type *String* → *IO* (). The () simply indicates that there is no useful result returned from this action; its sole purpose is to print its argument to the standard output area. So the program:

module *Main* **where**
main = *putStr* "Hello World\n"

is the canonical "Hello World" program that is often the first program that people write in a new language.

Suppose now that we want to perform *two* actions, such as first writing to a file named "testFile.txt", then printing to the standard output area. Haskell has a special keyword, **do**, to denote the beginning of a sequence of commands such as this, and so we can write:

do *writeFile* "testFile.txt" "Hello File System"
    putStr "Hello World\n"

where the file-writing function *writeFile* has type:

writeFile   :: *FilePath* → *String* → *IO* ()
type *FilePath* = *String*

Details: A **do** expression allows one to sequence an arbitrary number of commands, each of type *IO* (), using layout to distinguish them (just as in a **let** or **where** expression). When used in this way, the result of a **do** expression also has type *IO* ().

So far we have only used actions having type *IO* (); i.e., output actions. But what about input? As above, we will consider input from both the user and the file system.

To receive a line of input from the user (which will be typed in the *standard input area* of the computer screen, usually the same as the standard output area), we can use the function:

getLine :: *IO String*

Suppose, for example, that we wish to read a line of input using this function, and then write that line (a string) to a file. To do this, we write the compound command:

do *s* ← *getLine*
    writeFile "testFile.txt" *s*

> **Details:** Note the syntax for binding *s* to the result of executing the *getLine* command – when doing this in your program, you will have to type < -. Since the type of *getLine* is *IO String*, the type of *s* is *String*. Its value is then used in the next line as an argument to the *writeFile* command.

Similarly, we can read the entire contents of a file using the command *readFile* :: *FilePath* → *IO String*, and then print the result to standard output:

```
do s ← readFile "testFile.txt"
   putStr s
```

> **Details:** Any type that is an instance of the *Monad* type class can be used with the **do** syntax to sequence actions. The *Monad* class is discussed in detail in Chapter 16. It suffices to say for now that the *IO* type is an instance of the *Monad* class.

15.3 Actions Are Just Values

There are many other commands available for file, system, and user IO, some in the Standard Prelude and some in various libraries (such as *IO*, *Directory*, *System*, and *Time*). We will not discuss many of these here, other than the MIDI IO commands described in Section 15.4.

Before that, however, we wish to emphasize that, despite the special **do** syntax, Haskell's IO commands are no different in status from any other Haskell function or value. For example, it is possible to create a *list* of actions, such as:

```
actionList = [putStr "Hello World\n",
              writeFile "testFile.txt" "Hello File System",
              putStr "File successfully written."]
```

However, a list of actions is just a list of values: they actually do not *do* anything until they are sequenced appropriately using a **do** expression, and then returned as the value of the overall program (either as the variable *main* in the module *Main*, or typed at the GHCi prompt). Still, it is often convenient to place actions into a list as above, and Haskell provides some useful functions for turning them into single commands. In particular, the function *sequence_* in the Standard Prelude, when used with IO, has type:

*sequence_* :: [*IO a*] → *IO* ()

and can thus be applied to the *actionList* above to yield the single command:

main :: *IO* ()
main = *sequence_ actionList*

For a more interesting example of this idea, we first note that Haskell's strings are really just *lists of characters*. Indeed, *String* is a type synonym for a list of characters:

type *String* = [*Char*]

Because strings are used so often, Haskell allows you to write "Hello" instead of ['H','e','l','l','o']. But keep in mind that this is just syntax – strings really are just lists of characters, and these two ways of writing them are identical from Haskell's perspective.

(Earlier, the type synonym *FilePath* was defined for *String*. This shows that type synonyms can be created using other type synonyms.)

Now back to the example. From the function *putChar* :: *Char* → *IO* (), which prints a single character to the standard output area, we can define the function *putStr* used earlier, which prints an entire string. To do this, let's first define a function that converts a list of characters (i.e., a string) into a list of IO actions:

putCharList :: *String* → [*IO* ()]
putCharList = *map putChar*

With this, *putStr* is easily defined:

putStr :: *String* → *IO* ()
putStr = *sequence_* ∘ *putCharList*

Or, more succinctly:

putStr :: *String* → *IO* ()
putStr = *sequence_* ∘ *map putStr*

Of course, *putStr* can also be defined directly as a recursive function, which we do here to emphasize that actions are just values, so we can use all of the functional programming skills that we normally use:

putStr   :: *String* → *IO* ()
putStr [ ]   = *return* ()
putStr (*c* : *cs*) = **do** *putChar c*
                      putStr cs

IO processing in Haskell is consistent with everything we have learned about programming with expressions and reasoning through calculation, although that may not be completely obvious yet. Indeed, it turns out that a **do** expression is just syntax for a more primitive way of combining actions using functions, namely a *monad*, to be revealed in full in Chapter 16.

15.4 Reading and Writing MIDI Files

Euterpea supports writing *Music* values to a MIDI file, given a file path to write to (which should end in ".mid"):

$writeMidi :: ToMusic1\ a \Rightarrow FilePath \rightarrow Music\ a \rightarrow IO\ ()$

There is also support for reading MIDI files and converting their contents to a *Music* value.

$importFile :: FilePath \rightarrow IO\ (Either\ String\ Midi)$

$fromMidi :: Midi \rightarrow Music1$

The *Either* data type is used to handle the possibility of file-reading errors.

data *Either a b = Left a | Right b*

In the event of a problem, *Left* is returned containing a *String* with the resulting error message. If the operation is successful, *Right* is returned with a *Midi*. What actions to take in the *Left* case is left to the user. Often it is simplest to use Haskell's *error* function, but in the context of an interactive program, it can be more useful to inform the user of the I/O problem in some other way without ending the program.

The *importFile* and *fromMidi* functions can also be easily be combined into a single operation to read a MIDI file to a *Music1* value:

$readMusic :: FilePath \rightarrow IO\ Music1$
$readMusic\ inFile = $ **do**
   $x \leftarrow importFile\ inFile$
  case x **of** $Left\ str \rightarrow error\ str$
                 $Right\ m \rightarrow return\ \$\ fromMidi\ m$

Note that the *Music*-to-MIDI conversion involves information loss: multiple tree structures can have the same linear event structure. This means that it is quite unlikely that a *Music* value can be recovered to its original state after being written to a MIDI file.

16

Higher-Order Types and Monads

All of the types that we have considered thus far in this text have been *first order*. For example, the type constructor *Music* has so far always been paired with an argument, as in *Music Pitch*. This is because *Music* by itself is a *type constructor*: something that takes a type as an argument and returns a type as a result. There are no *values* in Haskell that have this type, but such "higher-order types" can be used in type class declarations in useful ways, as we shall see in this chapter.

16.1 The *Functor* Class

To begin, consider the *Functor* class described previously in Section 7.4.3 and defined in the Standard Prelude:[1]

class *Functor f* **where**
  fmap :: $(a \rightarrow b) \rightarrow f\ a \rightarrow f\ b$

Details: Type applications are written in the same manner as function applications, and are also left associative: the type $T\ a\ b$ is equivalent to $((T\ a)\ b)$.

There is something new here: the type variable f is applied to other type variables, as in $f\ a$ and $f\ b$. Thus we would expect f to be a *type constructor*

---

[1] The term *functor* (as well as the term *monad*, to be introduced shortly) comes from a branch of abstract mathematics known as *category theory* [21]. This reflects the strong mathematical principles that underlie Haskell, but otherwise does not concern us here; i.e., you do not need to know anything about category theory to understand Haskell's functors and monads.

such as *Music* that can be applied to an argument. Indeed, a suitable instance of *Functor* for *Music* is:

> **instance** *Functor Music* **where**
>   *fmap f m* = *mMap f m*

Similarly for *Primitive*:

> **instance** *Functor Primitive* **where**
>   *fmap f p* = *pMap f p*

Indeed, in retrospect, back in Chapter 6, where we defined *mMap* and *pMap*, we could have declared *Music* and *Primitive* as instances of *Functor* directly and avoided defining the names *mMap* and *pMap* altogether:

> **instance** *Functor Music* **where**
>   *fmap f* (*Prim p*)   = *Prim* (*fmap f p*)
>   *fmap f* (*m1* :+: *m2*) = *fmap f m1* :+: *fmap f m2*
>   *fmap f* (*m1* :=: *m2*) = *fmap f m1* :=: *fmap f m2*
>   *fmap f* (*Modify c m*) = *Modify c* (*fmap f m*)

> **instance** *Functor Primitive* **where**
>   *pMap*   :: (*a* → *b*) → *Primitive a* → *Primitive b*
>   *pMap f* (*Note d x*) = *Note d* (*f x*)
>   *pMap f* (*Rest d*)   = *Rest d*

In Haskell we write *Music Pitch* for a *Music* value instantiated on *Pitch* values; *Music* is the type constructor. Similarly, we write [*Int*] for lists instantiated on integers. But what is the type constructor for lists? Because of Haskell's special syntax for the list data type, there is also a special syntax for its type constructor, namely [ ].

Details: Similarly, for tuples, the type constructors are (,), (, ,), (, , ,), and so on, and the type constructor for the function type is (→). This means that the following pairs of types are equivalent: [*a*] and [ ] *a*, *f* → *g* and (→) *f g*, (*a*, *b*) and (,) *a b*, and so on.

This allows us to create an instance of *Functor* for lists, as follows:

> **instance** *Functor* [ ] **where**
>   *fmap f* [ ]   = [ ]
>   *fmap f* (*x* : *xs*) = *f x* : *fmap f xs*

Note the use of [ ] here in two ways: as a value in the list data type, and as a type constructor as described above.

Of course, the above declaration is equivalent to:

instance *Functor* [ ] **where**
  fmap = *map*

where *map* is the familiar function that we have been using since Chapter 3. This instance is in fact predefined in the Standard Prelude.

One of the nice things about the *Functor* class, of course, is that we can now use the same name, *fmap*, for lists, *Music*, and *Primitive* values (and any other data type for which an instance of *Functor* is declared). This could not be done without higher-order type constructors, and here demonstrates the ability to handle generic "container" types, allowing functions such as *fmap* to work uniformly over them.

As mentioned in Section 7.7, type classes often imply a set of *laws* that govern the use of the operators in the class. In the case of the *Functor* class, the following laws are expected to hold:

$$fmap\ id \quad = id$$
$$fmap\ (f \circ g) = fmap\ f \circ fmap\ g$$

Details: *id* is the *identity function*, $\lambda x \rightarrow x$. Although *id* is polymorphic, note that if its type on the left-hand side of the equation above is $a \rightarrow a$, then its type on the right must be $t\ a \rightarrow t\ a$ for some type constructor t that is an instance of *Functor*.

These laws ensure that the shape of the "container type" is unchanged by *fmap*, and that the contents of the container are not rearranged by the mapping function.

Exercise 16.1 Verify that the instances of *Functor* for lists, *Primitive*, and *Music* are law-abiding.

16.2 The *Monad* Class

There are several classes in Haskell that are related to the notion of a monad, which can be viewed as a generalization of the principles that underlly IO. Because of this, although the names of the classes and methods may seem unusual, these "monadic" operations are rather intuitive and useful for general programming.[2]

---

[2] Moggi [22] was one of the first to point out the value of monads in describing the semantics of programming languages, and Wadler first popularized their use in functional programming [23, 24].

There are three classes associated with monads: *Functor* (which we have discussed already), *Monad* (also defined in the Standard Prelude), and *MonadPlus* (defined in *Control.Monad*).

The *Monad* class defines four basic operators: (⨝=) (often pronounced "bind"), (≫) (often pronounced "sequence"), *return*, and *fail*:

class *Monad m* **where**

$\quad$ (⨝=) $\;:: m\ a \rightarrow (a \rightarrow m\ b) \rightarrow m\ b$

$\quad$ (≫) $\;\;:: m\ a \rightarrow m\ b \rightarrow m\ b$

$\quad$ *return* $:: a \rightarrow m\ a$

$\quad$ *fail* $\quad:: String \rightarrow m\ a$

$\quad m \gg k = m \gg= \backslash\_ \rightarrow k$

$\quad$ *fail s* $\;= error\ s$

Details: The two infix operators above are typeset nicely here; using a text editor, you will have to type >>= and >> instead.

The default methods for (≫) and *fail* define behaviors that are almost always just what is needed. Therefore, most instances of *Monad* need to define only (⨝=) and *return*.

Before studying examples of particular instances of *Monad*, we will first reveal another secret in Haskell, namely that the **do** syntax is actually shorthand for use of the monadic operators! The rules for this are a bit more involved than those for other syntax we have seen, but are still straightforward. The first rule is this:

do $e \Rightarrow e$

So an expression such as **do** *putStr* `"Hello World"` is equivalent to *putStr* `"Hello World"`.

The next rule is:

do $e1; e2; ...; en$

$\Rightarrow e1 \gg$ **do** $e2; ...; en$

For example, combining this rule with the previous one means that:

do *writeFile* `"testFile.txt" "Hello File System"`

$\quad$ *putStr* `"Hello World"`

is equivalent to:

writeFile `"testFile.txt" "Hello File System"` $\gg$

putStr `"Hello World"`

Note now that the sequencing of two commands is just the application of the function ($\gg$) to two values of type *IO* (). There is no magic here – it is all just functional programming!

Details: What is the type of ($\gg$) above? From the type class declaration, we know that its most general type is:

$$(\gg) :: Monad\ m \Rightarrow m\ a \rightarrow m\ b \rightarrow m\ b$$

However, in the case above, its two arguments both have type *IO* (), so the type of ($\gg$) must be:

$$(\gg) :: IO\ () \rightarrow IO\ () \rightarrow IO\ ()$$

That is, $m = IO$, $a = ()$, and $b = ()$. Thus the type of the result is *IO* (), as expected.

The rule for pattern-matching is the most complex, because we must deal with the situation where the pattern match fails:

do *pat* ← *e1*; *e2*; ...; *en*
⇒ **let** *ok pat* = **do** *e2*; ...; *en*
    ok _ = *fail* " . . . "
  in *e1* $\ggeq$ *ok*

The right way to think of ($\ggeq$) above is simply this: it "executes" *e1* and then applies *ok* to the result. What happens after that is defined by *ok*: if the match succeeds, the rest of the commands are executed, otherwise the operation *fail* in the monad class is called, which in most cases (because of the default method) results in an *error*.

Details: The string argument to *error* is a compiler-generated error message, preferably giving some indication of the location of the pattern-match failure.

A special case of the above rule is the case where the pattern *pat* is just a name, in which case the match cannot fail, so the rule simplifies to:

do *x* ← *e1*; *e2*; ...; *en*
⇒ *e1* $\ggeq$ λ*x* → **do** *e2*; ...; *en*

The final rule deals with the **let** notation within a **do** expression:

> **do let** *decllist*; *e2*; ...; *en*
> ⇒ **let** *decllist* **in do** *e2*; ...; *en*

Details: Although we have not used this feature, note that a **let** inside of a **do** can take multiple definitions, as implied by the name *decllist*.

As mentioned earlier, because you already understand Haskell IO, you should have a fair amount of intuition about what the monadic operators do. Unfortunately, we cannot look very closely at the instance of *Monad* for the type *IO*, since it ultimately relies on the state of the underlying operating system, which we do not have direct access to other than through primitive operations that communicate with it. Even then, these operations vary from system to system.

Nevertheless, a proper implementation of IO in Haskell is obliged to obey the following *monad laws*:

$$
\begin{aligned}
return\ a \ggg k &= k\ a \\
m \ggg return &= m \\
m \ggg (\lambda x \rightarrow k\ x \ggg h) &= (m \ggg k) \ggg h
\end{aligned}
$$

The first of these laws expresses the fact that *return* simply "sends" its value to the next action. Likewise, the second law says that if we immediately return the result of an action, we might as well just let the action return the value itself. The third law is the most complex, and essentially expresses an *associativity* property for the bind operator ($\ggg$). A special case of this law applies to the sequence operator ($\gg$):

$$m1 \gg (m2 \gg m3) = (m1 \gg m2) \gg m3$$

in which case the associativity is more obvious.

There is one other monad law, whose purpose is to connect the *Monad* class to the *Functor* class, and therefore only applies to types that are instances of both:

$$fmap\ f\ xs = xs \ggg return \circ f$$

We will see an example of this shortly.

Of course, this law can also be expressed in **do** notation:

$$fmap\ f\ xs = \textbf{do}\ x \leftarrow xs;\ return\ (f\ x)$$

as can the previous ones for **do**:

$$
\begin{array}{ll}
\textbf{do } x \leftarrow return\ a; k\ x & = k\ a \\
\textbf{do } x \leftarrow m; return\ x & = m \\
\textbf{do } x \leftarrow m; y \leftarrow k\ x; h\ y & = \textbf{do } y \leftarrow (\textbf{do } x \leftarrow m; k\ x); h\ y \\
\textbf{do } m1; m2; m3 & = \textbf{do } (\textbf{do } m1; m2); m3
\end{array}
$$

So something like this:

> **do** $k \leftarrow getKey\ w$
>   *return k*

is equivalent to just *getKey w*, according to the second law above. As a final example, the third law above allows us to transform this:

> **do** $k \leftarrow getKey\ w$
> $n \leftarrow changeKey\ k$
>   *respond n*

into this:

> **let** $keyStuff = \textbf{do } k \leftarrow getKey\ w$
>   *changeKey k*
> **in do** $n \leftarrow keyStuff$
>   *respond n*

Exercise 16.2 Verify the associativity law for ($\gg$), starting with the associativity law for ($\ggg$).

16.2.1 Other Instances of *Monad*

Maybe In addition to *IO*, the Standard Prelude's *Maybe* data type is a predefined instance of *Monad*:

> **instance** *Monad Maybe* **where**
>   *Just x* $\ggg k = k\ x$
>   *Nothing* $\ggg k = Nothing$
>   *return* $\qquad = Just$
>   *fail s* $\qquad\ = Nothing$

Details: *Maybe* is also a predefined instance of *Functor*:

> **instance** *Functor Maybe* **where**
>   *fmap f Nothing = Nothing*
>   *fmap f (Just x) = Just (f x)*

When used with this instance, the types of the monad operators are:

$(\ggg)$ :: $Maybe\ a \rightarrow (a \rightarrow Maybe\ b) \rightarrow Maybe\ b$
$return$ :: $a \rightarrow Maybe\ a$

We leave as an exercise the task of proving that this instance is law-abiding.

To see how this might be used, consider a computation involving functions $f :: Int \rightarrow Int$, $g :: Int \rightarrow Int$, and $x :: Int$:

$g\ (f\ x)$

Now suppose that each of the calculations using f and g could, in fact, be erroneous, and thus the results are encoded using the *Maybe* data type. Unfortunately, this can become rather tedious to program, since each result that might be an error must be checked manually, as in:

case $(f\ x)$ **of**
    Nothing $\rightarrow$ *Nothing*
    Just y $\rightarrow$ **case** $(g\ y)$ **of**
            Nothing $\rightarrow$ *Nothing*
            Just z $\rightarrow z$

Alternatively, we could take advantage of *Maybe*'s membership in the *Monad* class and convert this into monadic form:

$f\ x \ggg \lambda y \rightarrow$
$g\ y \ggg \lambda z \rightarrow$
$return\ z$

Or, using the more familiar **do** notation:

do $y \leftarrow f\ x$
    $z \leftarrow g\ y$
    $return\ z$

Thus the tedium of the error check is "hidden" within the monad. In this sense, monads are a good example of the abstraction principle in action (pardon the pun)!

It is also worth noting the following simplification:

$f\ x \ggg \lambda y \rightarrow$
$g\ y \ggg \lambda z \rightarrow$
$return\ z$
    $\Rightarrow \{currying\ simplification\}$
$f\ x \ggg \lambda y \rightarrow$
$g\ y \ggg return$
    $\Rightarrow \{monad\ law\ for\ return\}$

$$f \; x \ggeq \lambda y \rightarrow$$
$$g \; y$$
$$\Rightarrow \{ \textit{currying simplification} \}$$
$$f \; x \ggeq g$$

So we started with $g \; (f \; x)$ and ended with $f \; x \ggeq g$; this is not too bad, considering the alternative that we started with!

For an even more pleasing result, we can define a monadic composition operator:

$$composeM :: Monad \; m \Rightarrow (b \rightarrow m \; c) \rightarrow (a \rightarrow m \; b) \rightarrow (a \rightarrow m \; c)$$
$$(g \; \text{`}composeM\text{`} \; f) \; x = f \; x \ggeq g$$

in which case we start with $(g \circ f) \; x$ and end with $(g \; \text{`}composeM\text{`} \; f) \; x$.

Details: Note the type of *composeM*. It demonstrates that higher-order type constructors are also useful in type signatures.

Lists The *list* data type in Haskell is also a predefined instance of class *Monad*:

instance *Monad* [ ] **where**
    $m \ggeq k = concat \; (map \; k \; m)$
    $return \; x = [x]$
    $fail \; x \quad = [\,]$

Details: Recall that *concat* takes a list of lists and concatenates them all together. It is defined in the Standard Prelude as:

$$concat :: [[a]] \rightarrow [a]$$
$$concat \; xss = foldr \; (+\!\!+) \; [\,] \; xss$$

The types of the monadic operators in this case are:

$$(\ggeq) :: [a] \rightarrow (b \rightarrow [b]) \rightarrow [b]$$
$$return :: a \rightarrow [a]$$

The monadic functions in this context can be thought of as dealing with "multiple values." Monadic binding takes a set (list) of values and applies a function to each of them, collecting all generated values together. The *return* function creates a singleton list, and *fail* an empty one. For example,

> **do** $x \leftarrow [1,2,3]$
> $y \leftarrow [4,5,6]$
> *return* (x,y)

returns the list:

> $[(1,4),(1,5),(1,6),(2,4),(2,5),(2,6),(3,4),(3,5),(3,6)]$

which happens to be the same list generated by:

> $[(x,y) \mid x \leftarrow [1,2,3], y \leftarrow [4,5,6]]$

So list comprehension syntax is, in essence, another kind of monad syntax; indeed, they are not very different! (However, list comprehensions can only be used with lists.)

Note that if:

> **do** $x \leftarrow xs$; *return* $(f\ x)$

is equivalent to:

> $[f\ x \mid x \leftarrow xs]$

(which is clearly just *map f xs*), then at least for the instance of lists in *Monad*, the last monad law makes perfect sense:

> *fmap f xs* $=$ **do** $x \leftarrow xs$; *return* $(f\ x)$

Also note that the *Maybe* data type in monadic form behaves as a sort of truncated list in monadic form: *Nothing* is the same as $[\ ]$ and *Just x* is the same as $[x]$.)

Exercise 16.3 Verify that all of the instance declarations in this section are law-abiding.

Exercise 16.4 Consider the *identity* data type defined by:

> **data** *Id a* = *Id a*

Create an instance of *Monad* for *Id*, and prove that it is law-abiding.

16.2.2 Other Monadic Operations

The Standard Prelude has several functions specifically designed for use with monads; they are shown in Figure 16.1. Indeed, one of these we have already used: *sequence_*. Any mystery about how it works should be gone now; it is a very simple fold of the sequencing operator ($\gg$), with *return* () at the end. Note also the definition of *sequence*, a generalization of *sequence_* that returns a list of values of the intermediate results.

$$sequence \quad :: Monad\ m \Rightarrow [m\ a] \rightarrow m\ [a]$$
$$sequence \quad = foldr\ mcons\ (return\ [\,])$$
$$\mathbf{where}\ mcons\ p\ q = \mathbf{do}\ x \leftarrow p$$
$$xs \leftarrow q$$
$$return\ (x : xs)$$
$$sequence\_ \quad :: Monad\ m \Rightarrow [m\ a] \rightarrow m\ (\,)$$
$$sequence\_ \quad = foldr\ (\ggg)\ (return\ (\,))$$
$$mapM \qquad :: Monad\ m \Rightarrow (a \rightarrow m\ b) \rightarrow [a] \rightarrow m\ [b]$$
$$mapM\ f\ as = sequence\ (map\ f\ as)$$
$$mapM\_ \qquad :: Monad\ m \Rightarrow (a \rightarrow m\ b) \rightarrow [a] \rightarrow m\ (\,)$$
$$mapM\_f\ as = sequence\_ (map\ f\ as)$$
$$(\lll) \qquad :: Monad\ m \Rightarrow (a \rightarrow m\ b) \rightarrow m\ a \rightarrow m\ b$$
$$f \lll x \qquad = x \ggg f$$

Figure 16.1 Monadic utility functions.

Finally, recall from Section 15.3 that *putStr* can be defined as:

$$putStr \quad :: String \rightarrow IO\ (\,)$$
$$putStr\ s = sequence\_ (map\ putChar\ s)$$

Using *mapM_* from Figure 16.1, this can be rewritten as:

$$putStr \quad :: String \rightarrow IO\ (\,)$$
$$putStr\ s = mapM\_\ putChar\ s$$

16.3 The *MonadPlus* Class

The class *MonadPlus*, defined in the Standard Library *Control.Monad*, is used
for monads that have a *zero element* and a *plus operator*:

class $Monad\ m \Rightarrow MonadPlus\ m$ **where**
    $mzero :: m\ a$
    $mplus :: m\ a \rightarrow m\ a \rightarrow m\ a$

The zero element should obey the following laws:

$$m \ggg (\lambda x \rightarrow mzero) = mzero$$
$$mzero \ggg m \qquad\qquad = mzero$$

and the plus operator should obey these:

$$m\ \text{`}mplus\text{`}\ mzero = m$$
$$mzero\ \text{`}mplus\text{`}\ m = m$$

By analogy to arithmetic, think of *mzero* as 0, *mplus* as addition, and $(\ggg)$ as
multiplication. The above laws should then make more sense.

For the *Maybe* data type, the zero and plus values are:

instance *MonadPlus Maybe* **where**
  mzero   = *Nothing*
  Nothing 'mplus' ys = ys
  xs   'mplus' ys = xs

and for lists they are:

  instance *MonadPlus* [ ] **where**
    mzero = [ ]
    mplus = (++)

So you can see now that the familiar concatenation operation (++) that we have been using all along for lists is just a special case of the *mplus* operator.

It is worth pointing out that the IO monad is not an instance of the *MonadPlus* class, since it has no zero element. If it did have a zero element, then the IO action *putStr* "Hello" $\gg$ *zero* should *not* print the string "Hello", according to the first zero law above. But this is counter-intuitive, or at least is certainly not what the designers of Haskell had in mind for IO.

The *Monad* module in the Standard Library also includes several other useful functions defined in terms of the monadic primitives. You are encouraged to read these for possible use in your own programs.

Exercise 16.5 Verify that the instances of *MonadPlus* for the *Maybe* and *list* data types are law-abiding.

16.4 State Monads

Monads are commonly used to simulate stateful, or imperative, computations, in which the details of updating and passing around the state are hidden within the mechanics of the monad. Generally speaking, a *state monad* has a type of the form:

  data *SM* s a = *SM* (s → (s, a))

where *s* is the state type and *a* is the value type. The instance of this type in *Monad* is given by:

  instance *Monad* (*SM* s) **where**
    return a
      = *SM* $ λs0 → (s0, a)
    SM sm0 $\gg=$ *fsm1*

$$= SM \ \$ \ \lambda s0 \rightarrow$$
$$\mathbf{let} \ (s1, a1) \ = sm0 \ s0$$
$$SM \ sm1 = fsm1 \ a1$$
$$(s2, a2) \ = sm1 \ s1$$
$$\mathbf{in} \ (s2, a2)$$

The last equation in the **let** expression could obviously be eliminated, but it is written this way to stress the symmetry in the treatment of the two commands.

Details: Note that *SM* is a type constructor that takes *two* type arguments. Applying it to one argument (as in *SM s* above) is a kind of type-level currying, yielding a new type constructor that takes one argument, as required by the *Monad* class.

A good example of a state monad, at least abstractly speaking, is Haskell's *IO* type, where the state *s* can be thought of as the "state of the world," such as the contents of the file system, the image on a display, or the output of a printer.

But what about creating our own state monad? As a simple example, consider this definition of a *Tree* data type:

data *Tree a = Leaf a | Branch (Tree a) (Tree a)*
    deriving *Show*

Suppose now we wish to define a function *label :: Tree a → Tree Int* such that, for example, the value *test*:

test = **let** *t = Branch (Leaf* ' a' *) (Leaf* 'b' *)*
    in *label (Branch t t)*

evaluates to:

Branch (Branch (Leaf 0) (Leaf 1))
    (Branch (Leaf 2) (Leaf 3))

Without knowing anything about monads, this job is relatively easy:

label   :: Tree a → Tree Int
label t = snd (lab t 0)
lab :: Tree a → Int → (Int, Tree Int)
lab (Leaf a) n
    $= (n + 1, Leaf \ n)$

lab (Branch t1 t2) n
  = **let** *(n1, t′1) = lab t1 n*
         (n2, t′2) = lab t2 n1
     in *(n2, Branch t′1 t′2)*

Although simple, there is an undeniable tedium in "threading" the value of n from one call to *lab* to the next. To solve this problem, note that *lab t* has type $Int \rightarrow (Int, Tree\ Int)$, which is in the right form for a state monad. Of course, we need a true data type, and so we write:

newtype *Label a = Label (Int → (Int, a))*

Details: A **newtype** declaration behaves just like a **data** declaration, except that only one constructor is allowed on the right-hand side. This allows the compiler to implement the data type more efficiently, since it "knows" that only one possibility exists. It is also more type-safe than a type synonym, since, like **data**, it generates a new type, rather than acting as a synonym for an existing type.

The *Monad* instance for *Label* is just like that for *SM* above:

instance *Monad Label* **where**
  return a
    = *Label $ λs → (s, a)*
  Label lt0 >>= *flt1*
    = *Label $ λs0 →*
        let *(s1, a1) = lt0 s0*
             Label lt1 = flt1 a1
        in *lt1 s1*

While the monad handles the threading of the state, we also need a way to extract information from the state, as needed in a particular application. In the case of labeling trees, we need to know what the current value of the state (an *Int*) is at each point where we encounter a leaf. So we define:

getLabel :: Label Int
getLabel = Label $ λn → (n + 1, n)

Now we can write the following monadic version of the labeling function:

mlabel :: Tree a → Tree Int
*mlabel t = **let** Label lt = mlab t*
             in *snd (lt 0)*

```
mlab :: Tree a ~ _abel (Tree Int)
mlab (Leaf getLabel
    = return (Leaf n)
    (Branch t1 t2)
    = do t'1 ← mlab t1
         t'2 ← mlab t2
         return (Branch t'1 t'2)
```

Note that the threading of the state has been completely eliminated from *mlab*, as has the incrementing of the state, which has been isolated in the function *getLabel*.

As an example, this test case:

mtest = **let** *t* = *Branch* (*Leaf* 'a') (*Leaf* 'b')
          in *mlabel* (*Branch t t*)

generates the same result as the non-monadic version above.

For this simple example, you may decide that eliminating the threading of the state is not worth it. Indeed, in reality it has just been moved from the definition of *lab* to the method declaration for (≫=), and the new version of the program is certainly longer than the old! But capturing repetitious code into one function is the whole point of the abstraction principle, and hopefully you can imagine a context where threading of the state happens often, perhaps hundreds of times, in which case the abstraction will surely pay off. IO is one example of this (imagine threading the state of the world on every IO command).

Exercise 16.6 Recall the definition of *replFun* in Chapter 13, Section 13.3. Note how it threads the random number source through the program. Rewrite this function using a state monad so that this threading is eliminated.

16.5 Type Class Type Errors

As you know, Haskell's type system detects ill-typed expressions. But what about errors due to malformed types? The value (+) 1 2 3 results in a type error, since (+) takes only two arguments. Similarly, the type *Tree Int Int* should result in some sort of an error, since the *Tree* type constructor takes only a single argument. So how does Haskell detect malformed types? By using a second type system that ensures the correctness of types! That is, each type is assigned its own type – which is called its *kind* – and kinds are used to ensure that types are used correctly. Kinds are indicated by the * symbol in type signature errors.

Kinds do not appear directly in Haskell programs; the Haskell system infers them without any need for "kind declarations." Kinds stay in the background of a Haskell program except when a kind error occurs, in which case error message may refer to the kind conflict. Fortunately, kinds are simple that your Haskell system should be able to provide descriptive error messages in most cases.

17

Musical User Interfaces
Daniel Winograd-Cort

This chapter describes how to create interactive musical applications called *musical user interfaces*, or MUIs, using the Euterpea and UISF libraries. MUIs allow the creation of graphical user interfaces (GUIs) as well as real-time processing of MIDI events and streams.

> **Details:** To use the *arrow syntax* described in this chapter, it is necessary to use the following compiler pragma in GHC:
>
> {-# LANGUAGE Arrows #-}

17.1 Introduction

Many music software packages have a graphical user interface (GUI) that provides varying degrees of functionality to the user. In the HSoM library, a basic set of widgets is provided that are collectively referred to as the *musical user interface*, or MUI. This interface is quite different from the GUI interfaces found in most conventional languages, and is built around the concepts of *signal functions* and *arrows* [25, 26].[1] Signal functions are an abstraction of the time-varying values inherent in an interactive system such as a GUI or HSoM's MUI. Signal functions are provided to create graphical sliders, push-buttons, and so on for input; textual displays, graphs, and graphic images for output; and textboxes, virtual keyboards, and more for combinations of input

---

[1] The HSoM's MUI framework is built using the arrow-based GUI library UISF, which is its own stand-alone package. UISF, in turn, borrows concepts from *Fruit* [27, 28].

and output. In addition to these graphical widgets, the MUI also provides an interface to standard MIDI input and output devices.

17.2 Basic Concepts

A *signal* is a time-varying quantity. Conceptually, at least, most things in our world, and many things that we program with, are time-varying. The position of a mouse is time-varying. So is the voltage used to control a motor in a robot arm. Even an animation can be thought of as a time-varying image.

A *signal function* is an abstract function that converts one signal into another. Using the examples above, a signal function can add an offset to a time-varying mouse position, filter out noise from the time-varying voltage for a robot motor, or speed up or slow down an animation.

Perhaps the simplest way to understand this approach to programming with signals is to think of it as a language for expressing *signal processing diagrams* (or, equivalently, electrical circuits). We can think of the lines in a typical signal processing diagram as signals, and the boxes that convert one signal into another as signal functions. For example, this very simple diagram has two signals, *x* and *y*, and one signal function, *sigfun*:

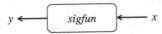

Using Haskell's *arrow syntax* [26, 29], this diagram can be expressed as a code fragment:

$$y \leftarrow sigfun \prec x$$

Details: The syntax $\leftarrow$ and $\prec$ is typeset here in an attractive way, but the user will have to type < - and - <, respectively, in his or her source file.

In summary, the arrow syntax provides a convenient way to compose signal functions together – i.e., to wire together the boxes that make up a signal processing diagram.

17.2.1 The Type of a Signal Function

Polymorphically speaking, a signal function has type *SF a b*, which should be read "the type of signal functions that convert signals of type *a* into signals of type *b*."

For example, suppose the signal function *sigfun* used earlier has type
SF T1 T2 for some types *T1* and *T2*. In that case, and using the example above,
x will have type *T1* and *y* will have type *T2*. Although signal functions act on
signals, the arrow notation allows us to manipulate the instantaneous values of
the signals, such as *x* and *y* above, directly.

A signal function whose type is of the form *SF* () *b* essentially takes no
input, but produces some output of type *b*. Because of this, we often refer to
such a signal function as a *signal source*. Similarly, a signal function of type
SF a () is called a *signal sink* – it takes input, but produces no output. Signal
sinks are essentially a form of output to the real world.

We can also create and use signal functions that operate on signals of tuples.
For example, a signal function *exp*::*SF* (*Double*, *Double*) *Double*, which raises
the first argument in a tuple to the power of its second at every point in time,
could be used as follows:

$$z \leftarrow exp \prec (x, y)$$

As mentioned earlier, a signal function is "abstract," in the sense that it
cannot be applied like an ordinary function. Indeed, *SF* is an instance of the
Arrow type class in Haskell, which only provides operations to *compose* one
signal function with another in several ways. Programming in this style can be
awkward, and Haskell provides the arrow syntax described above to make the
programming easier and more natural.

A MUI program expresses the composition of a possibly large number of
signal functions into a composite signal function that is then "run" at the top
level by a suitable interpreter. A good analogy for this idea is a state or IO
monad, where the state is hidden and a program consists of a linear sequencing
of actions that are eventually run by an interpreter or the operating system. But
in fact arrows are more general than monads, and in particular the composition
of signal functions does not have to be completely linear, as will be illustrated
shortly.

17.2.2 proc Declarations

Keep in mind that $\leftarrow$ and $\prec$ are part of the *syntax*, and are not simply binary
operators. Indeed, we cannot just write the earlier code fragments anywhere.
They have to be within an enclosing **proc** construct, whose result type is that
of a signal function. The **proc** construct begins with the keyword **proc** along
with a formal parameter, analogous to an anonymous function. For example, a
signal function that takes a signal of type *Double* and adds 1 to it at every point
in time, and then applies *sigfun* to the resulting signal, can be written:

```
proc y → do
    x ← sigfun ─< y + 1
    outA ─< x
```

outA is a special signal function that specifies the output of the signal function being defined.

> **Details:** The **do** keyword in arrow syntax introduces layout, just as it does in monad syntax.

Note that this code is analogous to the following snippet involving an ordinary anonymous function:

```
λy →
    let x = sigfun' (y + 1)
    in x
```

The important difference, however, is that *sigfun* works on a signal, i.e., a time-varying quantity. To make the analogy a little stronger, we could imagine a signal being implemented as a stream of discrete values. In which case, to achieve the effect of the arrow code given, we would have to write something like this:

```
λys →
    let xs = sigfun'' (map (+1) ys)
    in xs
```

The arrow syntax allows us to avoid worrying about the streams themselves.

17.2.3 Four Useful Functions

There are four useful auxiliary functions that will make writing signal functions a bit easier. The first two essentially "lift" constants and functions from the Haskell level to the arrow (signal function) level:

```
arr    :: (a → b) → SF a b
constA ::      b  → SF () b
```

For example, a signal function that adds one to every sample of its input can be written simply as *arr* (+1), and a signal function that returns the constant 440 as its result can be written *constA* 440 (and is a signal source, as defined earlier).

The other two functions allow us to *compose* signal functions:

```
(≫) :: SF a b → SF b c → SF a c
(≪) :: SF b c → SF a b → SF a c
```

($\lll$) is analogous to Haskell's standard composition operator ($\circ$), whereas ($\ggg$) is like "reverse composition."

As an example that combines both of the ideas above, recall the very first example given in this chapter:

proc $y \rightarrow$ **do**
   $x \leftarrow sigfun \prec y + 1$
   $outA \prec x$

which essentially applies *sigfun* to 1 plus the input. This signal function can be written more succinctly as either *arr* (+1) $\ggg$ *sigfun* or *sigfun* $\lll$ *arr* (+1).

The functions ($\ggg$), ($\lll$), and *arr* are actually generic operators on arrows, and thus to use them, one can import them from the *Arrow* library. However, UISF re-exports them automatically, so we need not do this.

17.2.4 Events

Although signals are a nice abstraction of time-varying entities, and the world is arguably full of such entities, there are some things that happen at discrete points in time, like a mouse click, a MIDI keyboard press, and so on. We call these *events*. To represent events and have them coexist with signals, recall the *Maybe* type defined in the Standard Prelude:

   data *Maybe a = Nothing | Just a*

Conceptually, we define an event simply as a value of type *Maybe a*, for some type *a*. We say that the value associated with an event is "attached to" or "carried by" that event.

However, to fit this into the signal function paradigm, we imagine *signals of events* – in other words, *event streams*. So a signal function that takes events of type *Maybe T1* as input and emits events of type *Maybe T2* would have type *SF* (*Maybe T1*) (*Maybe T2*). When there is no event, an event stream will have the instantaneous value *Nothing*, and when an event occurs, it will have the value *Just x* for some value *x*.

For convenience, the UISF library defines a type synonym for signal-level events:

   type *SEvent a = Maybe a*

SEvent can be read as "signal event."

17.2.5 Feedback

If we think about signal functions and arrows as signal processing diagrams, then so far we have only considered how to connect them so that the streams

all flow in the same direction. However, there may be times that we want to
feed an output of one signal function back in as one of its inputs, thus creating
a loop.

How can a signal function depend on its own output? At some point in the
loop, we need to introduce a *delay* function. Euterpea has a few different delay
functions that we will describe in more detail later in this chapter (Section
17.4.4), but for now we will casually introduce the simplest of these: *fcdelay*.

$$fcdelay :: b \rightarrow DeltaT \rightarrow SF\ b\ b$$

The name *fcdelay* stands for "fixed continuous delay," and it delays a continuous signal for a fixed amount of time. (Note that *DeltaT* is a type synonym
for *Double* and represents a change in time, or δt.) Thus, the signal function
fcdelay b t will delay its input signal for *t* seconds, emitting the constant signal
b for the first *t* seconds.

With a delay at the ready, we can create a loop in a signal function by using
the **rec** keyword in the arrow syntax. This keyword behaves much like it does
in monadic **do** syntax and allows us to use a signal before we have defined it.

For instance, we can create a signal function that will count how many
seconds have gone by since it started running:

```
secondCounter :: SF () Integer
secondCounter = proc () → do
    rec count ← fcdelay 0 1 —< count + 1
    outA —< count
```

Details: The **rec** keyword comes from an extension to arrows called
arrow loop. To use the same ability outside of the arrow syntax requires
the *loop* operator:

$$loop :: SF\ (b, d)\ (c, d) \rightarrow SF\ b\ c$$

17.2.6 [Advanced] Why Arrows?

It is possible, and fairly natural, to define signal functions directly, say as
an abstract type *Signal T*, and then define functions to add, multiply, take
the sine of, and perform other operations on, signals represented in this way.
For example, *Signal Float* would be the type of a time-varying floating-
point number, *Signal AbsPitch* would be the type of a time-varying absolute
pitch, and so on. Then, given *s1, s2 :: Signal Float*, we might simply write

s1 + *s2*, *s1* * *s2*, and *sin s1* as examples of applying the above operations. Haskell's numeric type class hierarchy makes this particularly easy to do. Indeed, several domain-specific languages based on this approach have been designed, beginning with the language *Fran* [30], designed for writing computer animation programs.

But years of experience and theoretical study have revealed that such an approach leads to a language with subtle time and space leaks,[2] for reasons that are beyond the scope of this textbook [31].

Perhaps surprisingly, these problems can be avoided by using arrows. Programming in this style gives the user access to signal functions and the individual values that comprise a signal, but not to the actual signal itself. By not giving the user direct access to signals and providing a disciplined way to compose signal functions (namely arrow syntax), time and space leaks are avoided.

17.3 The UISF Arrow

SF as used in this chapter so far is an instance of the *Arrow* class, but is not the actual type used for constructing MUIs. The core component of HSoM's MUI is the *user interface signal function*, captured by the type *UISF*, which is also an instance of the *Arrow* class. So instead of *SF*, in the remainder of this chapter we will use *UISF*, but the previous discussion about signal functions and arrows still applies.

Using *UISF*, we can create "graphical widgets" using a style very similar to the way we wired signal functions earlier. However, instead of having values of type *SF a b*, we will use values of type *UISF a b*. Just like *SF*, the *UISF* type is fully abstract (meaning its implementation is hidden) and, being an instance of the *Arrow* class, can be used with arrow syntax.

17.3.1 Graphical Input and Output Widgets

Euterpea's basic widgets are shown in Figure 17.1. Note that each of them is, ultimately, a value of type *UISF a b* for some input type *a* and output type *b*, and therefore may be used with the arrow syntax to help coordinate their

---

[2] A time leak in a real-time system occurs whenever a time-dependent computation falls behind the current time because its value or effect is not needed yet, but then requires "catching up" at a later point in time. This catching-up process can take an arbitrarily long time, and may consume additional space as well. It can destroy any hope for real-time behavior if not managed properly.

$$label \qquad\qquad :: String \rightarrow UISF\ a\ a$$
$$displayStr \qquad\quad :: UISF\ String\ ()$$
$$display \qquad\qquad\ :: Show\ a \Rightarrow UISF\ a\ ()$$
$$withDisplay \qquad\ :: Show\ b \Rightarrow UISF\ a\ b \rightarrow UISF\ a\ b$$
$$textbox \qquad\qquad :: String \rightarrow UISF\ (SEvent\ String)\ String$$
$$radio \qquad\qquad\ :: [String] \rightarrow Int \rightarrow UISF\ ()\ Int$$
$$button \qquad\qquad\ :: String \rightarrow UISF\ ()\ Bool$$
$$checkbox \qquad\qquad :: String \rightarrow Bool \rightarrow UISF\ ()\ Bool$$
$$checkGroup \qquad\ :: [(String, a)] \rightarrow UISF\ ()\ [a]$$
$$listbox \qquad\qquad :: (Eq\ a, Show\ a) \Rightarrow UISF\ ([a], Int)\ Int$$
$$hSlider, vSlider \ :: RealFrac\ a \Rightarrow (a,a) \rightarrow a \rightarrow UISF\ ()\ a$$
$$hiSlider, viSlider :: Integral\ a \Rightarrow a \rightarrow (a,a) \rightarrow a \rightarrow UISF\ ()\ a$$

Figure 17.1 Basic MUI input/output widgets.

functionality. The names and type signatures of these functions suggest their functionality, which we elaborate in more detail below:

- A simple (static) text string can be displayed using:

  $label :: String \rightarrow UISF\ a\ a$

- Alternatively, a time-varying string can be displayed using:

  $displayStr :: UISF\ String\ ()$

  For convenience, Euterpea defines the following useful variations of *displayStr*:

  $display :: Show\ a \Rightarrow UISF\ a\ ()$
  $display = arr\ show \ggg displayStr$

  $withDisplay \qquad :: Show\ b \Rightarrow UISF\ a\ b \rightarrow UISF\ a\ b$
  $withDisplay\ sf = \textbf{proc}\ a \rightarrow \textbf{do}$
  $\qquad b \leftarrow sf \prec a$
  $\qquad display \prec b$
  $\qquad outA \quad \prec b$

display allows us to display anything that is "*Show*-able." *withDisplay* is an example of a *signal function transformer*: it takes a signal function and attaches a display widget to it that displays the value of its time-varying output.

- A textbox that functions for both input and output can be created using:

  $textbox :: String \rightarrow UISF\ (SEvent\ String)\ String$

The static argument here is the initial string for the text box. The *textbox* is notable because it is "bidirectional." That is, the time-varying input is displayed, and the user can interact with it by typing or deleting, the result

being the time-varying output. If there is no input (no event is given), then
the current value that is being displayed is retained.

- *radio*, *button*, and *checkbox* are three kinds of "push-buttons." A *button* (or
  checkbox) is pressed and unpressed (or checked and unchecked)
  independently from others. In contrast, a *radio* button is dependent upon
  other radio buttons – specifically, only one can be "on" at a time, so
  pressing one will turn off the others. The string argument to these functions
  is the label attached to the button. *radio* takes a list of strings, each being
  the label of one of the buttons in the mutually exclusive group; indeed, the
  length of the list determines how many buttons are in the group.

  The *checkGroup* widget creates a group of *checkbox*es. As its static
  argument, it takes a list of pairs of strings and values. For each pair, one
  checkbox is created with the associated string as its label. Rather than
  simply returning *True* or *False* for each checked box, it returns a list of the
  values associated with each label as its output stream.

- The *listbox* widget creates a pane with selectable text entries. The input
  stream is the list of entries along with which entry is currently selected, and
  the output stream is the index of the newly selected entry. In many ways, this
  widget functions much like the *radio* widget, except that it is stylistically
  different, it is dynamic, and, like the *textbox* widget, it is bidirectional.

- *hSlider*, *vSlider*, *hiSlider*, and *viSlider* are four kinds of "slider" – a
  graphical widget that looks like a slider control as found on a hardware
  device. The first two yield floating-point numbers in a given range and
  are oriented horizontally and vertically, respectively, whereas the latter
  two return integral numbers. For the integral sliders, the first argument is
  the size of the step taken when the slider is clicked at any point on either
  side of the slider "handle." In each of the four cases, the other two
  arguments are the range and initial setting of the slider, respectively.

As a simple example, here is a MUI that has a single slider representing
absolute pitch, and a display widget that displays the pitch corresponding to
the current setting of the slider:

```
ui0 :: UISF () ()
ui0 = proc _ → do
    ap ← hiSlider 1 (0, 100) 0 —≺ ()
    display —≺ pitch ap
```

Note how the use of signal functions makes this dynamic MUI trivial to write.
But using the functions defined in Section 17.2.3, it can be defined even more
succinctly as:

$ui0 = hiSlider\ 1\ (0, 100)\ 0 \ggg arr\ pitch \ggg display$

We can execute this example using the function:

$runMUI' :: UI\ ()\ () \rightarrow IO\ ()$

So our first running example of a MUI is:

$mui0 = runMUI'\ ui0$

The resulting MUI, once the slider has been moved a bit, is shown in Figure 17.2a.

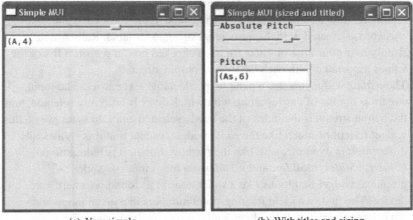

(a) Very simple   (b) With titles and sizing

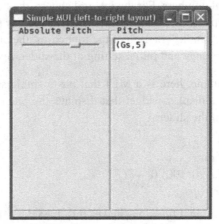

(c) With alternate (left-to-right) layout

Figure 17.2 Several simple MUIs.

> **Details:** Any MUI widgets have the capacity to be *focusable*, which is particularly relevant for graphical widgets. When a focusable widget is "in focus," not only can it update its appearance, but any key presses from the computer keyboard become visible to it as input events. This means that keyboard controls are possible with MUI widgets. Obviously, typing will affect the value of a textbox widget, but also, for instance, the arrow keys as well as the "Home" and "End" keys will affect the value of a slider widget. Focus can be shifted between widgets by clicking on them with the mouse as well as by using "Tab" and "Shift+Tab" to cycle focus through focusable widgets.

17.3.2 Widget Transformers

Figure 17.3 shows a set of "widget transformers," functions that take UISF values as input and return modified UISF values as output.

- *title* simply attaches a title (a string) to a UISF, and *setLayout* establishes a new layout for a UISF. The general way to make a new layout is to use *makeLayout*, which takes layout information for first the horizontal dimension and then the vertical. A dimension can be either stretchy (with a minimum size in pixels that will expand to fill the space it is given) or fixed (measured in pixels).

  The *setSize* function is convenient for setting the layout of a widget when both dimensions need to be fixed. It is defined as:

  $$setSize\ (w, h) = setLayout\ (makeLayout\ (Fixed\ w)\ (Fixed\ h))$$

  For example, we can modify the previous example to both set a fixed layout for the overall widget and attach titles to the slider and the display:

```
title          :: String           → UISF a b → UISF a b
setLayout      :: Layout            → UISF a b → UISF a b
setSize        :: (Int, Int)        → UISF a b → UISF a b
pad            :: (Int, Int, Int, Int) → UISF a b → UISF a b
topDown, bottomUp, leftRight, rightLeft :: UISF a b → UISF a b

makeLayout :: LayoutType → LayoutType → Layout
data LayoutType = Stretchy {minSize  :: Int}
                | Fixed    {fixedSize :: Int}
```

Figure 17.3 MUI layout widget transformers.

ui1 :: *UISF* () ()
ui1 = *setSize* (150, 150) $
  proc _ → **do**
    ap ← *title* "Absolute Pitch" (*hiSlider* 1 (0, 100) 0) —< ()
    title "Pitch" *display* —< *pitch ap*
  mui1 = *runMUI′ ui1*

This MUI is shown in Figure 17.2b.

- *pad* (*w, n, e, s*) *ui* adds *w* pixels of space to the "west" of the UISF *ui*, and *n*, *e*, and *s* pixels of space to the north, east, and south, respectively.
- The remaining four functions are used to control the relative layout of the widgets within a UISF. By default, widgets are arranged from top to bottom, but, for example, we could modify the previous UISF program to arrange the two widgets from left to right:

ui2 :: *UISF* () ()
ui2 = *leftRight* $
  proc _ → **do**
    ap ← *title* "Absolute Pitch" (*hiSlider* 1 (0, 100) 0) —< ()
    title "Pitch" *display* —< *pitch ap*
  mui2 = *runMUI′ ui2*

This MUI is shown in Figure 17.2c.

  Widget transformers can be nested (as demonstrated in some later examples), so a fair amount of flexibility is available.

17.3.3 MIDI Input and Output

An important application of signal-level events is real-time, interactive MIDI. There are two main UISF signal functions that handle MIDI, one for input and the other for output, but neither of them displays anything graphically:

midiIn   :: *UISF* (*Maybe InputDeviceID*)
                 (*SEvent* [*MidiMessage*])
midiOut :: *UISF* (*Maybe OutputDeviceID*,
                 SEvent [*MidiMessage*]) ()

Except for the input and output deviceIDs (about which more will be said shortly), these signal functions are fairly straightforward: *midiOut* takes a stream of *MidiMessage* events and sends them to the MIDI output device (thus a signal sink), whereas *midiIn* generates a stream of *MidiMessage* events corresponding to the messages sent by the MIDI input device (thus a signal source).[3] In both cases, note that the events carry *lists* of MIDI messages, accounting for the possibility of simultaneous events.

The *MidiMessage* data type is defined as:

data *MidiMessage* = *ANote* {*channel* :: *Channel*, *key* :: *Key*,
$\qquad\qquad\qquad\qquad$ *velocity* :: *Velocity*, *duration* :: *Time*}
$\qquad\qquad$| *Std Message*
$\quad$ **deriving** *Show*

A *MidiMessage* is either an *ANote*, which allows us to specify a note with duration, or a standard MIDI *Message*. MIDI does not have a notion of duration, but rather has separate *NoteOn* and *NoteOff* messages. With *ANote*, the design above is a bit more convenient, although what happens "behind the scenes" is that each *ANote* is transformed into a *NoteOn* and *NoteOff* event.

The *Message* data type is described in Chapter 8 and is defined in the *Codec.Midi* module. Its most important functionality is summarized here:

data *Message* =
$\quad$ -- Channel Messages
$\quad$ *NoteOff* $\qquad$ {*channel* :: *Channel*, *key* :: *Key*, *velocity* :: *Velocity*}
$\quad$| *NoteOn* $\qquad$ {*channel* :: *Channel*, *key* :: *Key*, *velocity* :: *Velocity*}
$\quad$| *ProgramChange* {*channel* :: *Channel*, *preset* :: *Preset*}
$\quad$| ...
$\quad$ -- Meta Messages
$\quad$| *TempoChange Tempo* |
$\quad$| ...
$\quad$ **deriving** (*Show*, *Eq*)

MIDI's notion of a "key" is the key pressed on a MIDI instrument, not to be confused with the "key" in "key signature." Also, MIDI's notion of "velocity" is the rate at which the key is pressed, and is roughly equivalent to what we have been calling "volume." So, for example, a MIDI message *NoteOn c k v* plays MIDI key *k* on MIDI channel *c* with velocity *v*.

17.3.4 MIDI Device IDs

Before we can create an example using *midiIn* or *midiOut*, we first must consider their other arguments: *InputDeviceID* and *OutputDeviceID*. The MIDI device ID is a system-dependent concept that provides an operating

---

[3] Technically, this is not a proper signal source, because it accepts an input stream of *Maybe InputDeviceID*, but the way it generates MIDI messages makes it feel very much like a source.

system with a simple way to uniquely identify various MIDI devices that may be attached to a computer. Indeed, as devices are dynamically connected and disconnected from a computer, the mapping of these IDs to particular devices may change. Thus, the only way to get an input or output device ID is by selecting with one of the following widgets:

> *selectInput*   :: *UISF* () (*Maybe InputDeviceID*)
> *selectOutput* :: *UISF* () (*Maybe OutputDeviceID*)

Each of these widgets automatically queries the operating system to obtain a list of connected MIDI devices, and then displays the list as a set of radio buttons, allowing the user to select one of them. In the event that there are no available devices, the widget can return *Nothing*.

With these functions, we can now create an example using MIDI output. Let's modify our previous MUI program to output an *ANote* message every time the absolute pitch changes:

> *ui3* :: *UISF* () ()
> *ui3* = **proc** _ → **do**
>   *devid* ← *selectOutput* —≺ ()
>   *ap* ← *title* "Absolute Pitch" (*hiSlider* 1 (0, 100) 0) —≺ ()
>   *title* "Pitch" *display* —≺ *pitch ap*
>   *uap* ← *unique* —≺ *ap*
>   *midiOut* —≺ (*devid*,*fmap* (λ*k* → [*ANote* 0 *k* 100 0.1]) *uap*)
> *mui3* = *runMUI'* *ui3*

The *unique* signal function used here is an example of a *mediator*, or a signal function that mediates between continuous and discrete signals. We will explore more mediators in Section 17.4.1, but in this case, note that *unique* will generate an event whenever its input, the continuous absolute pitch stream, changes. Each of those events, named *uap* above, carries the new absolute pitch, and that pitch is used directly as the MIDI key field in *ANote*.

To understand how that last part is done on the *midiOut* line, recall that *fmap* is the primary method in the *Functor* class as described in Section 7.4.3, and the *Maybe* type is an instance of *Functor*. Therefore, since *SEvent* is a type synonym for *Maybe*, the use of *fmap* above is valid – and all it does is apply the functional argument to the value "attached to" the event, which in this case is an absolute pitch.

For an example using MIDI input as well, here is a simple program that copies each MIDI message verbatim from the selected input device to the selected output device:

```
ui4 :: UISF () ()
ui4 = proc _ → do
    mi  ← selectInput   ─< ()
    mo  ← selectOutput  ─< ()
    m   ← midiIn        ─< mi
    midiOut ─< (mo, m)
mui4 = runMUI' ui4
```

Since determining device IDs for both input and output is common, we define a simple signal function to do both:

```
getDeviceIDs = topDown $
    proc () → do
        mi  ← selectInput   ─< ()
        mo  ← selectOutput  ─< ()
        outA ─< (mi, mo)
```

17.3.5 Putting It All Together

Recall that a Haskell program must eventually be a value of type *IO* (), and thus we need a function to turn a *UISF* value into an *IO* value – i.e. the UISF needs to be "run." We can do this using one of the following two functions, the first of which we have already been using:

```
runMUI' ::            UISF () () → IO ()
runMUI :: UIParams → UISF () () → IO ()
```

Executing *runMUI' ui* or *runMUI params ui* will create a single MUI window whose behavior is governed by the argument *ui* :: *UISF* () (). The additional *UIParams* argument of *runMUI* contains parameters that can affect the appearance and performance of the MUI window that is created. There is a default value of *UIParams* that is typical for regular MUI usage, and *runMUI'* is defined using it:

```
defaultMUIParams :: UIParams
runMUI' = runMUI defaultMUIParams
```

When using *runMUI*, it is advisable to simply modify the default value rather than build a whole new *UIParams* value. The easiest way to do this is with Haskell's *record syntax*.

There are many fields of data in a value of type *UIParams*, but we will focus only on the *uiTitle* and *uiSize*, which will control the value displayed in the title bar of the graphical window and the initial size of the window, respectively. Thus, the title is a *String* value and the size is a *Dimension* value (where *Dimension* is a type synonym for (*Int*, *Int*), which in turn represents a width and height measured in pixels). By default, the size is (300, 300) and the title is `"MUI"`, but we can change these like so:

$$mui'4 = runMUI\ (defaultMUIParams$$
$$\{uiTitle = \texttt{"MIDI Input / Output UI"},$$
$$uiSize = (200, 200)\})$$
$$ui4$$

This version of *mui4* (from the previous subsection) will run identically to the original, except that its title will read "MIDI Input / Output UI" and its initial size will be smaller.

17.4 Non-Widget Signal Functions

All of the signal functions we have seen so far are effectful widgets. That is, they all do something graphical or audible when they are used. For regular computation, we have been using pure functions (which we can insert arbitrarily in arrow syntax or lift with *arr* otherwise). However, there are signal functions that are important and useful that have no visible effects. We will look at a few different types of these signal functions in this section.

Details: Note that the mediators and folds in the next two subsections are generic signal functions and are not restricted to use only in MUIs. To highlight this, we present them with the *SF* type rather than the *UISF* type. However, they can be (and often are) used as *UISF*s in MUIs.

The timers and delay functions in Sections 17.4.3 and 17.4.4 require the MUI's internal notion of time, and so we present those directly with the *UISF* type.

17.4.1 Mediators

In order to use event streams in the context of continuous signals, the UISF library defines a set of functions that mediate between the continuous and the discrete. These "mediators," as well as some functions that deal exclusively with events, are shown in Figure 17.4, along with their type signatures and brief descriptions. Their use will be better understood through some examples that follow in Section 17.5.

unique :: *Eq a* ⟹ *SF a* (*SEvent a*)
   -- Generates an event whenever the input changes
edge :: *SF Bool* (*SEvent* ())
   -- Generates an event whenever the input changes from *False* to *True*
hold :: *a* → *SF* (*SEvent a*) *a*
   -- *hold x* begins as value *x*, but changes to the subsequent values
   -- attached to each of its input events
accum :: *a* → *SF* (*SEvent* (*a* → *a*)) *a*
   -- *accum x* starts with the value *x*, but then applies the function
   -- attached to the first event to *x* to get the next value, and so on
now :: *SF* () (*SEvent* ())
   -- Creates a single event "now" and forever after does nothing
evMap :: *SF a b* → *SF* (*SEvent a*) (*SEvent b*)
   -- Lifts a continuous signal function into one that handles events

Figure 17.4 Mediators between the continuous and the discrete.

17.4.2 Folds

In traditional functional programming, a folding, or reducing, operation is one that joins together a set of data. The typical case would be an operation that operates over a list of data, such as a function that sums all elements of a list of numbers.

There are a few different ways, given the UISF library, to fold together signal functions to create new ones:

maybeA :: *SF* () *c* → *SF b c* → *SF* (*Maybe b*) *c*
concatA :: [*SF b c*] → *SF* [*b*] [*c*]
runDynamic :: *SF b c* → *SF* [*b*] [*c*]

- *maybeA* is a fold over the *Maybe* (or *SEvent*) data type. The signal function *maybeA n j* accepts as input a stream of *Maybe b* values; at any given moment, if those values are *Nothing*, then the signal function behaves like *n*, and if they are *Just b*, then it behaves like *j*.
- The *concatA* fold takes a list of signal functions and converts them to a single signal function whose streaming values are themselves lists. For example, perhaps we want to display a bunch of buttons to a user in a MUI window. Rather than coding them in one at a time, we can use *concatA* to fold them into one operation that will return their results all together in a list. In essence, we are *concat*enating the signal functions together.
- The *runDynamic* signal function is similar to *concatA*, except that it takes a single signal function as an argument rather than a list. What, then, does it

fold over? Instead of folding over the static signal function list, it folds over the [*b*] list that it accepts as its input streaming argument.

The *concatA* and *runDynamic* signal functions are definitely similar, but they are also subtly different. With *concatA*, there can be many different signal functions that are grouped together, but with *runDynamic*, there is only one. However, *runDynamic* may have a variable number of internally running signal functions at runtime, because that number depends on a streaming argument. *concatA* is fixed once it is created.

17.4.3 Timers

HSoM's MUIs have an implicit notion of elapsed time, but it can be made explicit by the following signal source:

  getTime :: *UISF* () *Time*

where *Time* is a type synonym for *Double*.

Although the explicit time may be desired, some MUI widgets depend on the time implicitly. For example, the following signal function creates a *timer*:

  timer :: *UISF DeltaT* (*SEvent* ())

In practice, *timer* ─< *i* takes a signal *i* that represents the timer interval (in seconds) and generates an event stream, where each pair of consecutive events is separated by the timer interval. Note that the timer interval is itself a signal, so the timer output can have varying frequency.

To see how a timer might be used, let's modify our MUI working example from earlier so that, instead of playing a note every time the absolute pitch changes, we will output a note continuously, at a rate controlled by a second slider:

  ui5 :: *UISF* () ()
  ui5 = **proc** _ → **do**
    devid ← *selectOutput* ─< ()
    ap   ← *title* "Absolute Pitch" (*hiSlider* 1 (0, 100) 0) ─< ()
    title "Pitch" *display* ─< *pitch ap*
    f   ← *title* "Tempo" (*hSlider* (1, 10) 1) ─< ()
    tick ← *timer* ─< 1/*f*
    midiOut ─< (*devid*, *fmap* (*const* [*ANote* 0 *ap* 100 0.1]) *tick*)

    -- Pitch Player with Timer
  mui5 = *runMUI'* *ui5*

Note that the rate of *tick*s is controlled by the second slider – a larger slider value causes a smaller time between ticks, and thus a higher frequency, or tempo.

In some cases, the simple unit events of the *timer* are not enough. Rather, we would like each event to be different while we progress through a predetermined sequence. To do this, we can use the *genEvents* signal function:

$genEvents :: [b] \rightarrow UISF\ DeltaT\ (SEvent\ b)$

Just like *timer*, this signal function will output events at a variable frequency, but each successive event will contain the next value in the given list. When every value of the list *lst* has been emitted, *genEvents lst* will never again produce an event.

17.4.4 Delays

Another way in which a widget can use time implicitly is in a *delay*. The UISF library comes with five different delaying widgets, each serving a specific role depending on whether the streams are continuous or event-based and the delay is of fixed length or can be variable:

$delay\ \ \ :: b \rightarrow UISF\ b\ b$
$fcdelay :: b \rightarrow DeltaT \rightarrow UISF\ b\ b$
$fdelay\ \ :: DeltaT \rightarrow UISF\ (SEvent\ b)\ (SEvent\ b)$
$vdelay\ \ :: UISF\ (DeltaT, SEvent\ b)\ (SEvent\ b)$
$vcdelay :: DeltaT \rightarrow b \rightarrow UISF\ (DeltaT, b)\ b$

To start, we will examine the most straightforward one. The *delay* function creates what is called a "unit delay," which can be thought of as a delay by the shortest amount of time possible. This delay should be treated in the same way that we may treat δt in calculus; that is, although we can assume that a delay takes place, the amount of time delayed approaches zero. Thus, in practice, this should be used only in continuous cases and only as a means to initialize arrow feedback.

The rest of the delay operators delay by some amount of actual time, and we will look at each in turn. *fcdelay b t* will emit the constant value *b* for the first *t* seconds of the output stream and from then on emit its input stream delayed by *t* seconds. The name comes from "fixed continuous delay."

One potential problem with *fcdelay* is that it makes no guarantees that every instantaneous value on the input stream will be seen in the output stream. This should not be a problem for continuous signals, but for an event stream it could mean that entire events are accidentally skipped over. Therefore, there is a specialized delay for event streams: *fdelay t* guarantees that every input event will be emitted, but in order to achieve this, it is not as strict about timing – that is, some events may end up being over-delayed. Due to the nature of events, we no longer need an initial value for output: for the first *t* second, there will simply be no events emitted.

We can make both of the above delay widgets a little more complicated by introducing the idea of a variable delay. For instance, we can expand the capabilities of *fdelay* into *vdelay*. Now, the delay time is part of the signal and can change dynamically. Regardless, this event-based version will still guarantee that every input event will be emitted. *vdelay* can be read "variable delay."

For the variable continuous version, we must add one extra input parameter to prevent a possible space leak. Thus, the first argument to *vcdelay* is the maximum amount that the widget can delay. Due to the variable nature of *vcdelay*, some portions of the input signal may be omitted entirely from the output signal, while others may be outputted more than once. Thus, once again, it is highly advisable to use *vdelay* rather than *vcdelay* when dealing with event-based signals.

17.5 Musical Examples

In this section we work through three larger musical examples that use HSoM's MUIs in interesting ways.

17.5.1 Chord Builder

This MUI will display a collection of chord types (Maj, Maj7, Maj9, min, min7, min9, and so on), one of which is selectable via a radio button. Then, when a key is pressed on a MIDI keyboard, the selected chord is built and played using that key as the root.

To begin, we define a "database" that associates chord types with their intervals starting with the root note:

$chordIntervals :: [(String, [Int])]$
$chordIntervals = [("Maj", \quad [4,3,5]), \quad ("Maj7", \quad [4,3,4,1]),$
$\qquad\qquad\qquad ("Maj9", [4,3,4,3]), ("Maj6", \quad [4,3,2,3]),$
$\qquad\qquad\qquad ("min", \quad [3,4,5]), \quad ("min7", \quad [3,4,3,2]),$
$\qquad\qquad\qquad ("min9", [3,4,3,4]), ("min7b5", [3,3,4,2]),$
$\qquad\qquad\qquad ("mMaj7", [3,4,4,1]), ("dim", \quad [3,3,3]),$

$$("dim7", [3, 3, 3, 3]), ("Dom7", \quad [4, 3, 3, 2]),$$
$$("Dom9", [4, 3, 3, 4]), ("Dom7b9", [4, 3, 3, 3])]$$

We will display the list of chords on the screen as radio buttons for the user to click on.

The *toChord* function takes an input MIDI message as the root note and the index of the selected chord, and outputs the notes of the selected chord.

toChord :: *Int* → *MidiMessage* → [*MidiMessage*]
toChord i m =
   case *m* **of**
      Std (*NoteOn c k v*)   → *f NoteOn c k v*
      Std (*NoteOff c k v*) → *f NoteOff c k v*
      _ → [ ]
   where *f g c k v* = *map* (λ*k'* → *Std* (*g c k' v*))
                                  (*scanl* (+) *k* (*snd* (*chordIntervals* !! *i*)))

Details: *scanl* :: (*a* → *b* → *a*) → *a* → [*b*] → [*a*] is a standard Haskell function that is like *foldl* :: (*a* → *b* → *a*) → *a* → [*b*] → *a*, except that every intermediate result is returned, collected together in a list.

The overall MUI is laid out in the following way: On the left side, the list of input and output devices is displayed from the top down. On the right is the list of chord types. We take the name of each chord type from the *chordIntervals* list to create the radio buttons.

When a MIDI input event occurs, the input message and the currently selected index to the list of chords is sent to the *toChord* function, and the resulting chord is then sent to the MIDI output device.

buildChord :: *UISF* () ()
buildChord = *leftRight* $
   proc _ → **do**
     (*mi, mo*) ← *getDeviceIDs* −≺ ()
     m   ← *midiIn* −≺ *mi*
     i   ← *topDown* $ *title* "Chord Type" $
              radio (*fst* (*unzip chordIntervals*)) 0 −≺ ()
   midiOut −≺ (*mo, fmap* (*concatMap* $ *toChord i*) *m*)
chordBuilder = *runMUI* (*defaultMUIParams*
                 {*uiTitle* = "Chord Builder",
               uiSize = (600, 400)})
           buildChord

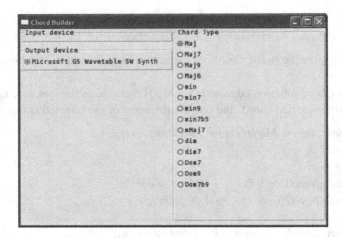

Figure 17.5 A chord-builder MUI.

Details: *unzip* :: $[(a, b)] \rightarrow ([a], [b])$ is a standard Haskell function that does the opposite of *zip* :: $[a] \rightarrow [b] \rightarrow [(a, b)]$.

concatMap :: $(a \rightarrow [b]) \rightarrow [a] \rightarrow [b]$ is another standard Haskell function that acts as a combination of *map* and *concat*. It maps the given function over the given list and then concatenates all of the outputs into a single output list.

Figure 17.5 shows this MUI in action.

17.5.2 Chaotic Composition

In this section we describe a UISF that borrows some ideas from Gary Lee Nelson's composition "Bifurcate Me, Baby!".

The basic idea is to evaluate a formula called the *logistic growth function*, from a branch of mathematics called chaos theory, at different points and convert the values to musical notes. The growth function is given by the recurrence equation:

$$x_{n+1} = rx_n(1 - x_n)$$

Mathematically, we start with an initial population x_0 and iteratively apply the growth function to it, where r is the growth rate. For certain values of r, the population stabilizes to a certain value, but as r increases, the period doubles, quadruples, and eventually leads to chaos. It is one of the classic examples of chaotic behavior.

We can capture the growth rate equation above in Haskell by defining a function that, given rate r and current population x, generates the next population:

$grow :: Double \rightarrow Double \rightarrow Double$
$grow\ r\ x = r * x * (1 - x)$

To generate a time-varying population, the *accum* signal function comes in handy. *accum* is one of the mediators mentioned in Section 17.4.1: it takes an initial value and an event signal carrying a modifying function and updates the current value by applying the function to it.

```
...
r   ← title "Growth rate" $ withDisplay (hSlider (2.4, 4.0) 2.4) —≺ ()
pop ← accum 0.1 —≺ fmap (const (grow r)) tick
...
```

The *tick* above is the "clock tick" that drives the simulation. We wish to define a signal *tick* that pulsates at a given frequency specified by a slider.

```
...
f    ← title "Frequency" $ withDisplay (hSlider (1, 10) 1) —≺ ()
tick ← timer —≺ 1/f
...
```

We also need a simple function that maps a population value to a musical note. As usual, this can be done in a variety of ways – here is one way:

$popToNote :: Double \rightarrow [MidiMessage]$
$popToNote\ x = [ANote\ 0\ n\ 64\ 0.05]$
$\qquad\qquad$ **where** $n = truncate\ (x * 127)$

Finally, to play the note at every tick, we simply apply *popToNote* to every value in the time-varying population *pop*. *fmap* makes this straightforward. Putting it all together, we arrive at:

```
bifurcateUI :: UISF () ()
bifurcateUI = proc _ → do
  mo   ← selectOutput —≺ ()
  f    ← title "Frequency" $ withDisplay (hSlider (1, 10) 1) —≺ ()
  tick ← timer —≺ 1/f
  r    ← title "Growth rate" $ withDisplay (hSlider (2.4, 4.0) 2.4) —≺ ()
  pop  ← accum 0.1 —≺ fmap (const (grow r)) tick
  _    ← title "Population" $ display —≺ pop
  midiOut —≺ (mo, fmap (const (popToNote pop)) tick)
```

$bifurcate = runMUI\ (defaultMUIParams$
$\{uiTitle = \texttt{"Bifurcate!"},$
$uiSize = (300, 500)\})$
$bifurcateUI$

17.5.3 MIDI Echo Effect

As a final example, we present a program that receives a MIDI event stream and, in addition to playing each note received from the input device, also echoes the note at a given rate, while playing each successive note more softly until the velocity reduces to 0.

The key component we need for this problem is a delay function that can delay a given event signal for a certain amount of time. Recall that the function *vdelay* takes a time signal, the amount of time to delay, and an input signal and returns a delayed version of the input signal.

There are two signals we want to attenuate, or "decay." One is the signal coming from the input device, and the other is the delayed and decayed signal containing the echoes. In the code shown below, they are denoted as *m* and *s*, respectively. First we merge the two event streams into one, then remove events with empty MIDI messages by replacing them with *Nothing*. The resulting signal m' is then processed further as follows.

The MIDI messages and the current decay rate are processed with *decay*, which softens each note in the list of messages. Specifically, *decay* works by reducing the velocity of each note by the given rate and removing the note if the velocity drops to 0. The resulting signal is then delayed by the amount of time determined by another slider, f, producing signal *s*. Signal *s* is then merged with *m* in order to define m' (note that *mappend* is a function that merges event lists), thus closing the loop of the recursive signal. Finally, m' is sent to the output device. Note that *mapMaybe* is found within *Data.Maybe*, and therefore must be imported.

```
echoUI :: UISF () ()
echoUI = proc _ → do
  (mi, mo) ← getDeviceIDs ─< ()
  m ← midiIn ─< mi
  r ← title "Decay rate" $ withDisplay (hSlider (0, 0.9) 0.5) ─< ()
  f ← title "Echoing frequency" $ withDisplay (hSlider (1, 10) 10) ─< ()
  rec s ← vdelay ─< (1/f, fmap (mapMaybe (decay 0.1 r)) m')
      let m' = mappend m s
  midiOut ─< (mo, m')
```

$echo = runMUI'\ echoUI$

$decay :: Time \rightarrow Double \rightarrow MidiMessage \rightarrow Maybe\ MidiMessage$

$decay\ dur\ r\ m =$
  let $f\ c\ k\ v\ d =$ **if** $v > 0$
                 then let $v' = truncate\ (fromIntegral\ v * r)$
                    in $Just\ (ANote\ c\ k\ v'\ d)$
                 else $Nothing$
  in case m **of**
    $ANote\ c\ k\ v\ d \qquad \rightarrow f\ c\ k\ v\ d$
    $Std\ (NoteOn\ c\ k\ v) \rightarrow f\ c\ k\ v\ dur$
    $- \qquad\qquad\qquad \rightarrow Nothing$

17.6 Special Purpose and Custom Widgets

Although the widgets and signal functions described so far enable the creation of many basic MUIs, there are times when something more specific is required. Thus, in this section, we will look at some special purpose widgets as well as some functions that aid in the creation of custom widgets.

Some of the functions described in this section are included in Euterpea by default, but others require extra imports of specific Euterpea or UISF modules. We will note this where applicable.

17.6.1 *realtimeGraphs, histograms*

So far, the only way to display the value of a stream in the MUI is to use the *display* widget. Although this is usually enough, there may be times when another view is more enlightening. For instance, if the stream represents a sound wave, then rather than displaying the instantaneous values of the wave as numbers, we may wish to see them graphed.

Euterpea provides support for a few different widgets that will graph streaming data visually.

$realtimeGraph \qquad :: RealFrac\ a \Rightarrow Layout$
                         $\rightarrow Time \rightarrow Color \rightarrow UISF\ [(a, Time)]\ ()$
$histogram \qquad\quad :: RealFrac\ a \Rightarrow Layout$
                         $\rightarrow UISF\ (SEvent\ [a])\ ()$
$histogramWithScale :: RealFrac\ a \Rightarrow Layout$
                         $\rightarrow UISF\ (SEvent\ [(a, String)])\ ()$

Note that each of these three functions requires a *Layout* argument (recall the *Layout* data type from Section 17.3.2); this is because the layout of a graph is not as easily inferred as that for, say, a button.

We will walk through the descriptions of these widgets:

- *realtimeGraph l t c* will produce a graph widget with layout *l*. This graph will accept as input a stream of events of pairs of values and time.[4] The values are plotted vertically in color *c* and the horizontal axis represents time, where the width of the graph represents an amount of time *t*.
- The histogram widgets' inputs are events that each contain a complete set of data. The data are plotted as a histogram within the given layout. For the histogram with the scale, each value must be paired with a *String* representing its label, and the labels are printed under the plot.

These widgets will prove useful when we are dealing with sound signals directly in future chapters.

17.6.2 More MIDI Widgets

In Sections 17.3.3 and 17.3.4, we presented simple widgets for selecting devices and polling and playing MIDI messages. However, these widgets allow for only one input device and one output device at a time. For a more complex scenario where multiple devices are to be used simultaneously, we have the following four widgets:

> *midiInM*   :: *UISF* [*InputDeviceID*] (*SEvent* [*MidiMessage*])
> *midiOutM*   :: *UISF* [(*OutputDeviceID*, *SEvent* [*MidiMessage*])] ()
> *selectInputM* :: *UISF* () [*InputDeviceID*]
> *selectOutputM* :: *UISF* () [*OutputDeviceID*]

The M on the end can be read as "Multiple." These widgets can be used just like their singular counterparts to handle MIDI, except that they allow for simultaneous use of multiple devices.

We can add even more behavior into the MIDI output widgets by considering a *buffered* output. When using *midiOut* (or *midiOutM*), all of the MIDI messages sent to the device are immediately played, but sometimes we might prefer to queue up messages for playback later. We can do this with the following two midi output widgets:

---

[4] These events are represented as a list rather than using the *SEvent* type, because there may be more than one event at the same time. The absence of any events would be indicated by an empty list.

$$midiOutB \quad :: UISF \ (Maybe \ OutputDeviceID,$$
$$BufferOperation \ MidiMessage) \quad Bool$$
$$midiOutMB :: UISF \ [(OutputDeviceID,$$
$$BufferOperation \ MidiMessage)] \ Bool$$

Notice that these two widgets have a *Bool* output stream; this stream is *True* when the buffer is empty and there is nothing queued up to play and *False* otherwise. The *BufferOperation* data type gives information along with the MIDI messages about when or how to play the messages. It is defined as follows:

data *BufferOperation b* =
  NoBOp
  | *ClearBuffer*
  | *SkipAheadInBuffer DeltaT*
  | *MergeInBuffer* [(DeltaT, b)]
  | *AppendToBuffer* [(DeltaT, b)]
  | *SetBufferPlayStatus Bool* (*BufferOperation b*)
  | *SetBufferTempo Tempo* \quad (*BufferOperation b*)

where

- *NoBOp* indicates that there is no new information for the buffer.
- *ClearBuffer* erases the current buffer.
- *SkipAheadInBuffer t* skips ahead in the buffer by *t* seconds.
- *MergeInBuffer ms* merges messages *ms* into the buffer to play concurrently with what is currently playing.
- *AppendToBuffer ms* adds messages *ms* to the end of the buffer to play immediately following whatever is playing.
- *SetBufferPlayStatus p b* indicates whether the buffer should be playing (*True*) or paused (*False*).
- *SetBufferTempo t b* sets the play speed of the buffer to *t* (the default is 1, indicating real time).

Note that the final two options recursively take a buffer operation, meaning that they can be attached to any other buffer operation as additional modifications.

Details: The *midiOutB* and *midiOutMB* widgets are essentially the regular *midiOut* widgets connected to an *eventBuffer*. The *eventBuffer* signal function can also be used directly to buffer any kind of data that fits into the *BufferOperation* format. It can be brought into scope by importing FRP.UISF.AuxFunctions.

17.6.3 A Graphical Canvas

In addition to the standard musical widgets, the musical user interface provides support for arbitrary graphical output. It does this via the *canvas* widget, which allows the user to "paint" graphics right into the MUI:

> *canvas* :: *Dimension* → *UISF* (*Event Graphic*) ()
> *canvas'* :: *Layout* → (*a* → *Dimension* → *Graphic*) → *UISF* (*Event a*) ()

The main *canvas* widget takes a fixed size and displays in the MUI the most recent *Graphic* it received. The *canvas'* function is a little more complex, as it can handle a changing size: rather than a fixed dimension, it accepts a layout and a function that, when given the dimension (which is generated at runtime based on the window size), can produce the appropriate graphic.

In either case, the user is responsible for generating the graphic that should be shown by generating a value of type *Graphic*. However, Euterpea does not export *Graphic* constructors by default, so we will need to add the following imports to our file:

> **import** *FRP.UISF.Graphics.Graphic*
> **import** *FRP.UISF.Graphics.Color*

Rather than go into detail about the various types of graphics one can create with these imports, we will leave it to the reader to read the documentation directly. Instead, we will only point out three functions, as we will use them in our upcoming example:

> *rectangleFilled* :: *Rect* → *Graphic*
> *rgbE*   :: *Int* → *Int* → *Int* → *RGB*
> *withColor'*   :: *RGB* → *Graphic* → *Graphic*

The *rectangleFilled* function takes a *Rect*, which is a pair consisting of a point representing the bottom left corner and a width and height, and constructs a rectangle bounded by the *Rect*. The *rgbE* function produces an *RGB* color from red, green, and blue values, and *withColor'* applies the given *RGB* color to the given *Graphic*.

In the following example, we will create three sliders to control the red, green, and blue values, and then use these to create a simple color swatch out of the *canvas* widget.

> *colorSwatchUI* :: *UISF* () ()
> *colorSwatchUI* = *setSize* (300, 220) $ *pad* (4, 0, 4, 0) $ *leftRight* $
>   **proc** _ → **do**
>   *r* ← *newColorSlider* "R" —< ()
>   *g* ← *newColorSlider* "G" —< ()

$b \leftarrow newColorSlider$ "B" $\prec ()$

$e \leftarrow unique \prec (r, g, b)$

let $rect = withColor'\ (rgbE\ r\ g\ b)\ (rectangleFilled\ ((0,0), d))$

$pad\ (4, 8, 0, 0)\ \$\ canvas\ d \prec fmap\ (const\ rect)\ e$

where

$d = (170, 170)$

$newColorSlider\ l = title\ l\ \$\ withDisplay\ \$\ viSlider\ 16\ (0, 255)\ 0$

$colorSwatch = runMUI'\ colorSwatchUI$

We use the *rectangleFilled* function to create a simple box, and then color it with the data from the sliders. Whenever the color changes, we redraw the box by sending a new *Graphic* event to the *canvas* widget.

17.6.4 [Advanced] mkWidget

In some cases, even the *canvas* widget is not powerful enough, and we would want to create our own custom widget. For this, there is the *mkWidget* function. To bring this into scope, we must import UISF's widget module directly:

import *FRP.UISF.Widget.Construction* (*mkWidget*)

The type of *mkWidget* is as follows:

$mkWidget\ ::\ s$

$\rightarrow Layout$

$\rightarrow (a \rightarrow s \rightarrow Rect \rightarrow UIEvent \rightarrow (b, s, DirtyBit))$

$\rightarrow (Rect \rightarrow Bool \rightarrow s \rightarrow Graphic)$

$\rightarrow UISF\ a\ b$

This widget building function takes arguments particularly designed to make a real-time interactive widget. The arguments work like so:

- The first argument is an initial state for the widget. The widget will be able to internally keep track of state, and the value that it should start with is given here.
- The second argument is the layout of the widget.
- The third argument is the computation that this layout performs. Given an instantaneous value of the streaming input, the current state, the rectangle describing the current allotted dimensions, and the current *UIEvent*,[5] it should produce an output value, a new state, and a *DirtyBit*, which is a

---

[5] The *UIEvent* can contain information like mouse clicks or key presses. For complete documentation on *UIEvent*, look to the UISF documentation.

boolean value indicating whether the visual representation of the widget
will change.

- The final argument is the drawing routine. Given the rectangle describing
  the current allotted dimensions for the widget (the same as that given to the
  computation function), a boolean indicating whether this widget is in focus,
  and the state, it produces the graphic that this widget will appear as.

The specifics of *mkWidget* are beyond the scope of this text, and readers
interested in making their own widgets are encouraged to look at the documentation of the UISF package. However, as a demonstration of its use, here
we will show the definition of *canvas* using *mkWidget*.

$$canvas\ (w, h) = mkWidget\ nullGraphic\ layout\ process\ draw$$
where
$$layout = makeLayout\ (Fixed\ w)\ (Fixed\ h)$$
$$draw\ ((x, y), (w, h))\ \_ = translateGraphic\ (x, y)$$
$$process\ (Just\ g)\ \_\ \_\ \_ = ((), g, True)$$
$$process\ Nothing\ g\ \_\ \_ = ((), g, False)$$

17.7 Advanced Topics

In the final section of this chapter, we will explore some advanced topics
related to the MUI.

17.7.1 Banana Brackets

When dealing with layout, we have so far shown two ways to apply the various
layout transformers (e.g., *topDown*, *leftRight*, etc.) to signal functions. One
way involves using the transformer on the whole signal function by applying
it on the first line, like so:

$$\ldots = leftRight\ \$\ \mathbf{proc}\ \_ \rightarrow \mathbf{do}\ \ldots$$

The other option is to apply the transformation in-line for the signal function
it should act upon:

$$\ldots$$
$$x \leftarrow topDown\ mySF \prec y$$
$$\ldots$$

However, the situation is not so clear-cut, and at times, we may want a sub-
portion of our signal function to have a different layout flow than the rest.

For example, assume we have a signal function that should have four buttons. The second and third buttons should be left-right aligned, but vertically,

together they should be between the first and second. One way we can try to write this is:

$ui6 = topDown$ $ proc $ _ \to$ **do**
   $b1 \leftarrow button$ "Button 1" $\prec ()$
   $(b2, b3) \leftarrow leftRight$ (**proc** $\_ \to$ **do**
      $b2 \leftarrow button$ "Button 2" $\prec ()$
      $b3 \leftarrow button$ "Button 3" $\prec ()$
      $returnA \prec (b2, b3)) \prec ()$
   $b4 \leftarrow button$ "Button 4" $\prec ()$
   $display \prec b1 \lor b2 \lor b3 \lor b4$

This looks a little funny, especially because we have an extra arrow tail (the $\prec$) after the inner $returnA$ on the sixth line, but it gets the job done.

However, what if we wanted to do something with the value $b1$ within the inner **proc** part? In its current state, $b1$ is not in scope in there. We can add it to the scope, but we would have to explicitly accept that value from the outer scope. It would look like this:

$ui'6 = topDown$ $ proc $ _ \to$ **do**
   $b1 \leftarrow button$ "Button 1" $\prec ()$
   $(b2, b3) \leftarrow leftRight$ (**proc** $b1 \to$ **do**
      $b2 \leftarrow button$ "Button 2" $\prec ()$
      $display \prec b1$
      $b3 \leftarrow button$ "Button 3" $\prec ()$
      $returnA \prec (b2, b3)) \prec b1$
   $b4 \leftarrow button$ "Button 4" $\prec ()$
   $display \prec b1 \lor b2 \lor b3 \lor b4$

This is getting hard to deal with! Fortunately, there is an arrow syntax feature to help us with this known as *banana brackets*.

Banana brackets are a component of arrow syntax that allow us to apply a function to one or more arrow commands without losing the scope of the arrow syntax. To use, we write in the form:

$(| f \ cmd1 \ cmd2... |)$

where f is a function on arrow commands and $cmd1$, $cmd2$, etc., are arrow commands.

> **Details:** An *arrow command* is a portion of arrow syntax that contains the arrow and the input but not the binding to output. Generally, this looks like $sf \prec x$, but if it starts with **do**, then it can be an entire arrow in itself (albeit one that does not start with **proc** $\_ \to$).

Banana brackets preserve the original arrow scope, so we can rewrite our example as:

$ui''6 = $ **proc** $() \rightarrow$ **do**
$\quad b1 \leftarrow button$ "Button 1" $\prec ()$
$\quad (b2, b3) \leftarrow (|\ leftRight\ (\textbf{do}$
$\quad\quad b2 \leftarrow button$ "Button 2" $\prec ()$
$\quad\quad display \prec b1$
$\quad\quad b3 \leftarrow button$ "Button 3" $\prec ()$
$\quad\quad returnA \prec (b2, b3))\ |)$
$\quad b4 \leftarrow button$ "Button 4" $\prec ()$
$\quad display \prec b1 \vee b2 \vee b3 \vee b4$

Note that we no longer need the **proc** $\_ \rightarrow$ in the third line, nor do we have an arrow tail on the seventh line. That said, banana brackets do have a limitation, in that the variables used internally are not exposed outside; that is, we still need the seventh line to explicitly return $b2$ and $b3$ in order to bind them to the outer scope in the third line so that they are visible when displayed on the last line.

17.7.2 General I/O from within a MUI

So far, through specific widgets, we have shown how to perform specific effects through the MUI: one can poll MIDI devices, send MIDI output, display graphics on the screen, and so on. However, the MUI is capable of arbitrary *IO* actions. In general, arbitrary *IO* actions can be dangerous, so the functions that allow them are relegated to Euterpea.Experimental, and they should be used with care.

The first arbitrary *IO* arrow to consider is:

$initialAIO :: IO\ d \rightarrow (d \rightarrow UISF\ b\ c) \rightarrow UISF\ b\ c$

This function allows an *IO* action to be performed upon MUI initialization, the result of which is used to finish constructing the widget. Thus, its name can be read as "initial Arrow IO."

In practice, one might use *initialAIO* to do something like read the contents of a file to be used at runtime. For instance, if we had a file called "songData" that contained data we would like to use in the MUI, we could use the following function:

$initialAIO\ (readFile$ "songData")
$\quad\quad (\lambda x \rightarrow now \ggg arr\ (fmap\ \$\ const\ x))$
$\quad :: UISF\ ()\ (SEvent\ String)$

This function will read the file and then produce a single event containing the contents of the file when the MUI first starts.

Performing an initial action is simple and useful, but at times we might like the freedom to perform actions mid-execution as well, and for that we have the following six functions:

$$
\begin{array}{ll}
uisfSource & :: IO\ c \qquad\qquad \rightarrow UISF\ ()\ c \\
uisfSink & :: (b \rightarrow IO\ ()) \rightarrow UISF\ b\ () \\
uisfPipe & :: (b \rightarrow IO\ c) \ \rightarrow UISF\ b\ c \\
uisfSourceE & :: IO\ c \qquad\qquad \rightarrow UISF\ (SEvent\ ())\ (SEvent\ c) \\
uisfSinkE & :: (b \rightarrow IO\ ()) \rightarrow UISF\ (SEvent\ b)\ (SEvent\ ()) \\
uisfPipeE & :: (b \rightarrow IO\ c) \ \rightarrow UISF\ (SEvent\ b)\ (SEvent\ c)
\end{array}
$$

The first three of these are for continuous-type actions and the last three are for event-based actions. As an example of a continuous action, one could consider a stream of random numbers:

$$uisfSource\ randomIO :: Random\ r \Rightarrow UISF\ ()\ r$$

Most *IO* actions are better handled by the event-based functions. For instance, we could update our file-reading widget from earlier so that it is capable of reading a dynamically named file and can perform more than one read at runtime:

$$uisfPipeE\ readFile :: UISF\ (SEvent\ FilePath)\ (SEvent\ String)$$

Whenever this signal function is given an event containing a file, it reads the file and returns an event containing the contents.

Details: This sort of arbitrary *IO* access that the functions from this subsection allow can have negative effects on a program, ranging from unusual behavior to performance problems to crashing. Research has been done to handle these problems, and a promising solution using what are called *resource types* has been proposed [32, 33]. However, the UISF library does not implement resource types, so it is left to the programmer to be exceptionally careful to use these appropriately.

17.7.3 Asynchrony

Although we have discussed the MUI as being able to act both continuously and discretely (event-based) depending on the required circumstances, in actual fact, the system is entirely built in a discrete way. When run, the MUI does many calculations per second to create the illusion of continuity, and as long as this sample rate is high enough, the illusion persists without any problem.

However, there are two primary ways in which the illusion of continuity fails:

- Computations can be sensitive to the sampling rate itself, such that a low enough rate will cause poor behavior.
- Computations can be sensitive to the variability of the sampling rate, such that drastic differences in the rate can cause poor behavior.

These are two subtly different problems, and we will address them with subtly different forms of *asynchrony*.

The idea of using asynchrony is to allow these sensitive computations to run separately from the MUI process so that they are unaffected by the MUI's sampling rate and are allowed to set and use their own arbitrary rate. We achieve this with the following functions:

$$asyncUISFE \circ toAutomaton :: NFData\ b \Rightarrow$$
$$SF\ a\ b \rightarrow UISF\ (SEvent\ a)\ (SEvent\ b)$$
$$clockedSFToUISF \qquad :: (NFData\ b, Clock\ c) \Rightarrow$$
$$DeltaT \rightarrow SigFun\ c\ a\ b \rightarrow UISF\ a\ [(b, Time)]$$

The *SF* and *SigFun* types will be discussed further in Chapter 19, but they are both arrows, and thus we can lift pure functions of type $a \rightarrow b$ to them with the *arr* function. These two functions are designed to address the two different sampling rate pitfalls we raised above.

- *asyncUISFE* ∘ *toAutomaton* is technically a composition of two functions, but in Euterpea, it would be rare to use them apart. Together, they are used to deal with the scenario where a computation takes a long time to compute (or perhaps blocks internally, delaying its completion). This slow computation may have deleterious effects on the MUI, causing it to become unresponsive and slow, so we allow it to run asynchronously. The computation is lifted into the discrete event realm, and for each input event given to it, a corresponding output event will be created eventually. Of course, the output event will likely not be generated immediately, but it will be generated eventually, and the ordering of output events will match the ordering of input events.
- The *clockedSFToUISF* function can convert a signal function with a fixed, virtual clock rate to a real-time UISF. The first input parameter is a buffer size, in seconds, that indicates how far ahead of real time the signal

function is allowed to get, but the goal is to allow it to run at a fixed clock rate as close to real time as possible. Thus, the output stream is a list of pairs providing the output values along with the timestamp for when they were generated. This should contain the right number of samples to approach real time, but on slow computers or when the virtual clock rate is exceptionally high, it will lag behind. This can be checked and monitored by checking the length of the output list and the time associated with the final element of the list at each time step.

Rather than show an example here, we will wait until Chapter 20, once the *SigFun* type has been introduced. An example that uses *clockedSFToUISF* can be found at the end of the chapter in Figure 20.5.

Exercise 17.1 Define a MUI that has a textbox in which the user can type a pitch using the normal syntax $(C, 4)$, $(D, 5)$, etc., and a push-button labeled "Play" that, when pushed, will play the pitch appearing in the textbox.

Hint: Use the Haskell function *reads* :: *Read a* $\Rightarrow$ *String* $\rightarrow$ [(a, String)] to parse the input.

Exercise 17.2 Modify the previous example so that it has *two* textboxes and plays both notes simultaneously when the push-button is pressed.

Exercise 17.3 Modify the previous example so that, in place of the push-button, the pitches are played at a rate specified by a horizontal slider.

Exercise 17.4 Define a MUI for a pseudo-keyboard that has radio buttons to choose one of the 12 pitches in the conventional chromatic scale. Every time a new pitch is selected, that note is played.

Exercise 17.5 Modify the previous example so that an integral slider is used to specify the octave in which the pitch is played.

18

Sound and Signals

In this chapter we study the fundamental nature of sound and its basic mathematical representation as a signal. We also discuss discrete digital representations of a signal, which form the basis of modern sound synthesis and audio processing.

18.1 The Nature of Sound

Before studying digital audio, it's important that we first know what *sound* is. In essence, sound is the rapid compression and relaxation of air traveling as a *wave* from the physical source of the sound ultimately to our ears. The source could be the vibration of our vocal cords (resulting in speech or singing), the vibration of a speaker cone, the vibration of a car engine, the vibration of a string in a piano or violin, the vibration of the reed in a saxophone or someone's lips when playing a trumpet, or even the (brief and chaotic) vibrations that result when our hands come together as we clap. The "compression and relaxation" of the air (or of a coiled spring) is called a *longitudinal* wave, in which the vibrations occur parallel to the direction of travel of the wave. In contrast, a rope that is fixed at one end and being shaken at the other and a wave in the ocean are examples of a *transverse* wave, in which the rope's or water's movement is perpendicular to the direction the wave is traveling.

If the rate and amplitude of the sound are within a suitable range, we can *hear* it – i.e., it is *audible sound*. "Hearing" results when the vibrating air waves cause our eardrum to vibrate, in turn stimulating nerves that enter our brain. Sound above our hearing range (i.e., vibration that is too quick to induce any nerve impulses) is called *ultrasonic sound*, and sound below our hearing range is said to be *infrasonic*.

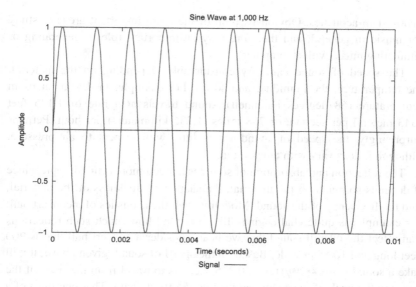

Figure 18.1 A sine wave.

Staying within the analog world, sound can also be turned into an *electrical* signal using a *microphone* (or "mic" for short). Several common kinds of microphones are:

1. Carbon microphone, based on the resistance of a pocket of carbon particles that are compressed and relaxed by sound waves hitting a diaphram
2. Condenser microphone, based on the capacitance between two diaphrams, one being vibrated by the sound
3. Dynamic microphone, based on the inductance of a coil of wire suspended in a magnetic field (the inverse of a speaker)
4. Piezoelectric microphone, based on the property of certain crystals to induce current when they are bent

Perhaps the most common and natural way to represent a wave diagrammatically, either a sound wave or electrical wave, longitudinal or transverse, is as a *graph* of its amplitude versus time. For example, Figure 18.1 shows a *sinusoidal wave* of 1,000 cycles per second with an amplitude that varies between +1 and −1. A sinusoidal wave follows precisely the definition of the mathematical sine function, but also relates strongly, as we shall soon see, to the vibration of sound produced by most musical instruments. In the remainder of this text, we will refer to a sinusoidal wave simply as a sine wave.

Acoustics is the study of the properties, in particular the propagation and reflection, of sound. *Psychoacoustics* is the study of the mind's interpretation of sound, which is not always as tidy as the physical properties that are manifest in acoustics. Obviously, both of these are important areas of study for music in general, and therefore play an important role in generating or simulating music with a computer.

The speed of sound can vary considerably, depending on the material, the temperature, the humidity, and so on. For example, in dry air at room temperature (68 degrees Farenheit), sound travels at a rate of 1,125 feet (343 meters) per second, or 768 miles (1,236 kilometers) per hour. Perhaps surprisingly, the speed of sound varies little with respect to air pressure, although it does vary with temperature.

The reflection and absorption of sound is a much more difficult topic, since it depends so much on the material, the shape and thickness of the material, and the frequency of the sound. Modeling well the acoustics of a concert hall, for example, is quite challenging. To understand how much such reflections can affect the overall sound that we hear, consider a concert hall that is 200 feet long and 100 feet wide. Based on the speed of sound, given above, it will take a sound wave $2 \times 200/1125 = 0.355$ seconds to travel from the front of the room to the back of the room and back to the front again. That one-third of a second, if loud enough, would result in a significant distortion of the music, and corresponds to about one beat on a metronome set at 168.

With respect to our interpretation of music, sound has (at least) three key properties:

1. *Frequency* (perceived as *pitch*)
2. *Amplitude* (perceived as *loudness*)
3. *Spectrum* (perceived as *timbre*)

We discuss each of these in the sections that follow.

18.1.1 Frequency and Period

The *frequency f* is simply the rate of the vibrations (or repetitions, or cycles) of the sound, and is the inverse of the *period p* (or duration, or wavelength) of each of the vibrations:

$$f = \frac{1}{p}$$

Frequency is measured in *Hertz* (abbreviated Hz), where 1 Hz is defined as one cycle per second. For example, the sound wave in Figure 18.1 has a frequency of 1,000 Hz (i.e. 1 kHz) and a period of $1/1000$ second (1 ms).

In trigonometry, functions like sine and cosine are typically applied to angles that range from 0 to 360 degrees. In audio processing (and signal processing in general), angles are usually measured in *radians*, where 2π radians is equal to $360°$. Since the sine function has a period of 2π and a frequency of $1/2\pi$, it repeats itself every 2π radians:

$$\sin(2\pi k + \theta) = \sin\theta$$

for any integer k.

But for our purposes, it is better to parameterize these functions over frequency as follows. Since $\sin(2\pi t)$ covers one full cycle in one second, i.e., has a frequency of 1 Hz, it makes sense that $\sin(2\pi f t)$ covers f cycles in one second, i.e., has a frequency of f. Indeed, in signal processing the quantity ω is defined as:

$$\omega = 2\pi f$$

That is, a pure sine wave as a function of time behaves as $\sin(\omega t)$.

Finally, it is convenient to add a *phase* (or *phase angle*) to our formula, which effectively shifts the sine wave in time. The phase is usually represented by ϕ. Adding a multiplicative factor A for amplitude (see next section), we arrive at our final formula for a sine wave as a function of time:

$$s(t) = A\sin(\omega t + \phi)$$

A negative value for ϕ has the effect of "delaying" the sine wave, whereas a positive value has the effect of "starting early." Note also that this equation holds for negative values of t.

All of the above can be related to cosine by recalling the following identity:

$$\sin\left(\omega t + \frac{\pi}{2}\right) = \cos(\omega t)$$

More generally:

$$A\sin(\omega t + \phi) = a\cos(\omega t) + b\sin(\omega t)$$

Given a and b, we can solve for A and ϕ:

$$A = \sqrt{a^2 + b^2}$$

$$\phi = \tan^{-1}\frac{b}{a}$$

Given A and ϕ, we can also solve for a and b:

$$a = A\cos(\phi)$$
$$b = A\sin(\phi)$$

18.1.2 Amplitude and Loudness

Amplitude can be measured in several ways. The *peak amplitude* of a signal is its maximum deviation from zero; for example, our sine wave in Figure 18.1 has a peak amplitude of 1. But different signals with the same peak amplitude have more or less "energy," depending on their "shape." For example, Figure 18.2 shows four kinds of signals: a sine wave, a square wave, a sawtooth wave, and a triangular wave (whose names are suitably descriptive). Each has a peak amplitude of 1. But intuitively, one would expect the square wave, for example, to have more "energy," or "power," than a sine wave, because it is "fatter." In fact, its value is everywhere either $+1$ or -1.

To measure this characteristic of a signal, scientists and engineers often refer to the *root-mean-square* amplitude, or RMS. Mathematically, the root-mean-square is the square root of the mean of the squared values of a given quantity. If x is a discrete quantity given by the values $x_1, x_2, \ldots, x_n$, the formula for RMS is:

$$x_{RMS} = \sqrt{\frac{x_1^2 + x_2^2 + \cdots + x_n^2}{n}}$$

And if f is a continuous function, its RMS value over the interval $T_1 \leqslant t \leqslant T_2$ is given by:

$$\sqrt{\frac{1}{T_2 - T_1} \int_{-T_1}^{T_2} f(t)^2 dt}$$

For a sine wave, it can be shown that the RMS value is approximately 0.707 of the peak value. For a square wave, it is 1.0. And for both a sawtooth wave and a triangular wave, it is approximately 0.577. Figure 18.2 shows these RMS values superimposed on each of the four signals.

Another way to measure amplitude is to use a relative logarithmic scale that more aptly reflects how we hear sound. This is usually done by measuring the sound level (usually in RMS) with respect to some reference level. The number of *decibels* (dB) of sound is given by:

$$S_{dB} = 10 \log_{10} \frac{S}{R}$$

where S is the RMS sound level and R is the RMS reference level. The accepted reference level for the human ear is 10^{-12} watts per square meter, which is roughly the threshold of hearing.

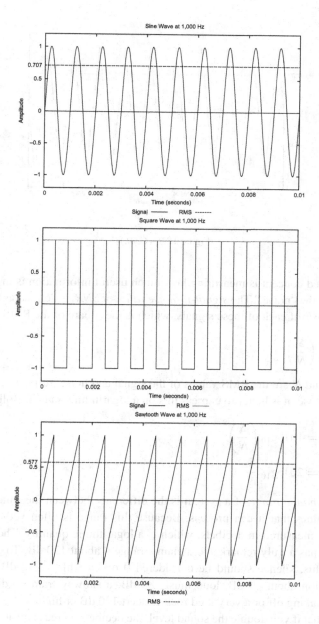

Figure 18.2 RMS amplitude for different signals.

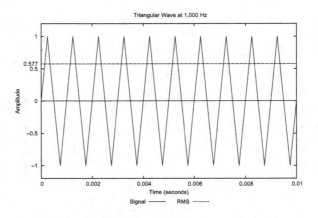

Figure 18.2 (*Cont.*)

A related concept is measuring how much useful information is in a signal relative to the "noise." The *signal-to-noise ratio*, or *SNR*, is defined as the ratio of the *power* of each of these signals, which is the square of the RMS value:

$$SNR = \left(\frac{S}{N}\right)^2$$

where S and N are the RMS values of the signal and noise, respectively. As is often the case, it is better to express this on a logarithmic scale, as follows:

$$SNR_{dB} = 10\log_{10}\left(\frac{S}{N}\right)^2$$
$$= 20\log_{10}\frac{S}{N}$$

The *dynamic range* of a system is the difference between the smallest and largest values that it can process. Because this range is often very large, it is usually measured in decibels, which is a logarithmic quantity. The ear, for example, has a truly remarkable dynamic range – about 130 dB. To get some feel for this, silence should be considered 0 dB, a whisper 30 dB, normal conversation about 60 dB, loud music 80 dB, a subway train 90 dB, and a jet plane taking off or a very loud rock concert 120 dB or higher.

Note that if you double the sound level, the decibels increase by about 3 dB, whereas a million-fold increase corresponds to 60 dB:

$$10\log_{10} 2 \quad = 10 \times 0.301029996 \cong 3$$
$$10\log_{10} 10^6 = 10 \times 6 \qquad\qquad = 60$$

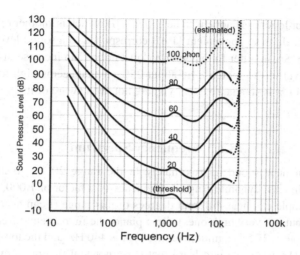

Figure 18.3 Equal-loudness contours.

So the ear is truly adaptive! (The eye also has a large dynamic range with respect to light intensity, but not quite as much as the ear, and its response time is much slower.)

Loudness is the perceived measure of amplitude, or volume, of sound, and is thus subjective. It is most closely aligned with RMS amplitude, with one important exception: loudness depends somewhat on frequency! Of course that's obvious for really high and really low frequencies (since at some point we can't hear them at all), but in between, things aren't constant either. Furthermore, no two humans are the same. Figure 18.3 shows equal loudness contours, which reflect the perceived equality of sound intensity by the average human ear with respect to frequency. Note from this figure that:

- The human ear is less sensitive to low frequencies.
- The maximum sensitivity is around 3–4 kHz, which roughly corresponds to the resonance of the auditory canal.

Another important psychoacoustical property is captured in the *Weber-Fechner Law*, which states that the *just noticeable difference* (jnd) in a quantity – i.e., the minimal change necessary for humans to notice something in a cognitive sense – is a relative constant, independent of the absolute level. That is, the ratio of the change to the absolute measure of that quantity is constant:

$$\frac{\Delta q}{q} = k$$

The jnd for loudness happens to be about 1 dB, which is another reason why the decibel scale is so convenient (1 dB corresponds to a sound level ratio of 1.25892541). So, in order for a person to "just notice" an increase in loudness, the sound level has to increase by about 25%. If that seems high to you, it's because your ear is so adaptive that you are not even aware of it.

18.1.3 Frequency Spectrum

Humans can hear sound approximately in the range 20 Hz to 20,000 Hz (20 kHz). This is a dynamic range in frequency of a factor of 1,000, or 30 dB. Different people can hear different degrees of this range (I can hear very low tones well, but not very high ones). On a piano, the fundamental frequency of the lowest note is 27.5 Hz, middle (concert) A is 440 Hz, and the top-most note is about 4 kHz. Later we will learn that these notes also contain *overtones* – multiples of the fundamental frequency – that contribute to the *timbre*, or sound quality, that distinguishes one instrument from another. (Overtones are also called *harmonics* or *partials*.)

The *phase*, or time delay, of a signal is important too, and comes into play when we start mixing signals together, which can happen naturally, deliberately, from reverberations (room acoustics), and so on. Recall that a pure sine wave can be expressed as $\sin(\omega t + \phi)$, where ϕ is the *phase angle*. Manipulating the phase angle is common in additive synthesis and amplitude modulation, topics to be covered in later chapters.

A key point is that most sounds do not consist of a single, pure sine wave – rather, they are a combination of many frequencies, and at varying phases relative to one another. Thus it is helpful to talk of a signal's *frequency spectrum*, or spectral content. If we have a regular repetitive sound (called a *periodic signal*), we can plot its spectral content instead of its time-varying graph. For a pure sine wave, this looks like an impulse function, as shown in Figure 18.4a.

But for a richer sound, it gets more complicated. First, the distribution of the energy is not typically a pure impulse, meaning that the signal might vary slightly above and below a particular frequency, and thus its frequency spectrum typically looks more like Figure 18.4b.

In addition, a typical sound has many different frequencies associated with it, not just one. Even for an instrument playing a single note, this will include not just the perceived pitch, which is called the *fundamental frequency*, but also many *overtones* (or harmonics), which are multiples of the fundamental, as shown in Figure 18.4c. The *natural harmonic series* is one that is approximated often in nature, and has a harmonically decaying series of overtones.

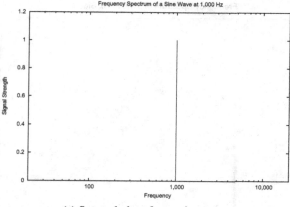

(a) Spectral plot of pure sine wave

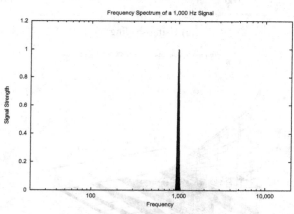

(b) Spectral plot of a noisy sine wave

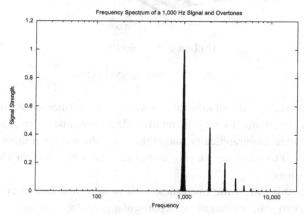

(c) Spectral plot of a musical tone

Figure 18.4 Spectral plots of different signals.

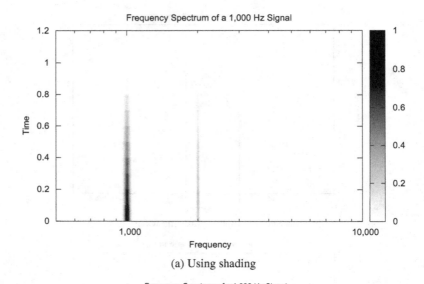

(a) Using shading

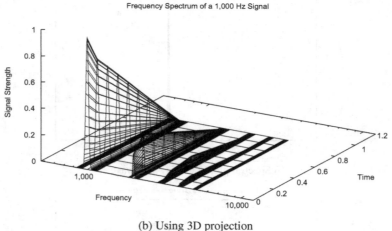

(b) Using 3D projection

Figure 18.5 Time-varying spectral plots.

What's more, the articulation of a note by a performer on an instrument causes these overtones to vary in relative size over time. There are several ways to visualize this graphically, and Figure 18.5 shows two of them. In 18.5a, shading is used to show the varying amplitude over time. And in 18.5b, a 3D projection is used.

The precise blend of the overtones, their phases, and how they vary over time is primarily what distinguishes a particular note, say concert A, on a piano from the same note on a guitar, a violin, a saxophone, and so on. We will have much more to say about these issues in later chapters.

18.2 Digital Audio

The preceding discussion has assumed that sound is a continuous quantity, which of course it is, and thus we represent it using continuous mathematical functions. If we were using an analog computer, we could continue with this representation and create electronic music accordingly. Indeed, the earliest electronic synthesizers, such as the *Moog synthesizer* of the 1960s, were completely analog.

However, most computers today are *digital*, which require representing sound (or signals in general) using digital values. The simplest way to do this is to represent a continuous signal as a *sequence of discrete samples* of the signal of interest. An *analog-to-digital converter*, or ADC, is a device that converts an instantaneous sample of a continuous signal into a binary value. The microphone input on a computer, for example, connects to an ADC.

Normally, the discrete samples are taken at a fixed *sampling rate*. Choosing a proper sampling rate is quite important. If it is too low, we will not acquire sufficient samples to adequately represent the signal of interest. And if the rate is too high, it may be overkill, thus wasting precious computing resources (both time and memory consumption). Intuitively, it seems that the highest frequency signal that we could represent using a sampling rate r would have a frequency of $r/2$, in which case the result would have the appearance of a square wave, as shown in Figure 18.6a. Indeed, it is easy to see that problems could arise if we sampled at a rate significantly lower than the frequency of the signal, as shown in Figure 18.6b and c for sampling rates equal to and half of the frequency of the signal of interest – in both cases the result is a sampled signal of 0 Hz!

Indeed, this observation is captured in what is known as the *Nyquist-Shannon sampling theorem* which, stated informally, says that the accurate reproduction of an analog signal (no matter how complicated) requires a sampling rate that is at least twice the highest frequency of the signal of interest.

For example, for audio signals, if the highest frequency humans can hear is 20 kHz, then we need to sample at a rate of at least 40 kHz for a faithful reproduction of sound. In fact, CDs are recorded at 44.1 kHz. But many people feel that this rate is too low, as some people can hear beyond 20 kHz. Another recording studio standard is 48 kHz. Interestingly, a good analog tape recorder from generations ago was able to record signals with frequency content even higher than this – perhaps digital is not always better!

18.2.1 From Continuous to Discrete

Recall the definition of a sine wave from Section 18.1.1:

$$s(t) = A \sin(\omega t + \phi)$$

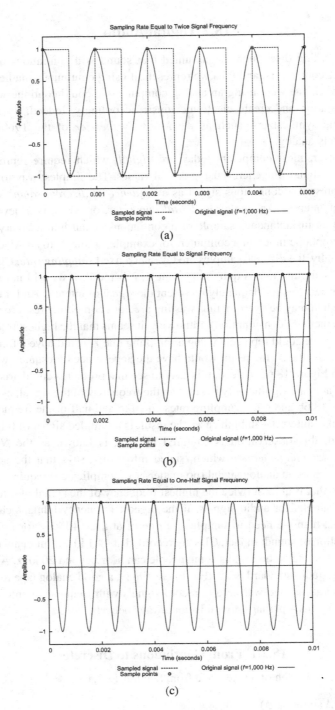

Figure 18.6 Choice of sampling rate.

We can easily and intuitively convert this to the discrete domain by replacing time t with the quantity n/r, where n is the integer index into the sequence of discrete samples and r is the sampling rate discussed above. If we use $s[n]$ to denote the $(n + 1)$th sample of the signal, we have:

$$s[n] = A \sin\left(\frac{\omega n}{r} + \phi\right), \qquad n = 0, 1, \ldots, \infty$$

Thus $s[n]$ corresponds to the signal's value at time n/r.

18.2.2 Fixed-Waveform Table-Lookup Synthesis

One of the most fundamental questions in digital audio is how to generate a sine wave as efficiently as possible, or, in general, how to generate a fixed periodic signal of any form (sine wave, square wave, sawtooth wave, even a sampled sound bite). A common and efficient way to generate a periodic signal is through *fixed-waveform table-lookup synthesis*. The idea is very simple: store in a table the samples of a desired periodic signal, and then index through the table at a suitable rate to reproduce that signal at some desired frequency. The table is often called a *wavetable*.

In general, if we let:

L = table length
f = resulting frequency
i = indexing increment
r = sample rate

then we have:

$$f = \frac{ir}{L}$$

For example, suppose the table contains 8,196 samples. If the sample rate is 44.1 kHz, how do we generate a tone of, say, 440 Hz? Plugging in the numbers and solving the above equation for i, we get:

$$440 = \frac{i \times 44.1 \text{ kHz}}{8196}$$
$$i = \frac{440 \times 8196}{44.1 \text{ kHz}}$$
$$= 81.77$$

So, if we were to sample approximately every 81.77th value in the table, we would generate a signal of 440 Hz.

Now suppose the table T is a vector and $T[n]$ is the nth element. Let's call the exact index increment i into a continuous signal the *phase* and the actual index into the corresponding table the *phase index p*. The computation of successive values of the phase index and output signal s is then captured by these equations:

$$p_o = \lfloor \phi_0 + 0.5 \rfloor$$
$$p_{n+1} = (p_n + i) \bmod L$$
$$s_n = T[\ \lfloor p_n + 0.5 \rfloor\ ]$$

$\lfloor a + 0.5 \rfloor$ denotes the floor of $a + 0.5$, which effectively rounds a to the nearest integer. ϕ_0 is the initial phase angle (recall earlier discussion), so p_0 is the initial index into the table that specifies where the fixed waveform should begin.

Instead of rounding the index, one could do better by *interpolating* between values in the table, at the expense of efficiency. In practice, rounding the index is often good enough. Another way to increase accuracy is to simply increase the size of the table.

18.2.3 Aliasing

Earlier, we saw examples of problems that can arise if the sampling rate is not high enough. We saw that if we sample a sine wave at twice its frequency, we can suitably capture that frequency. If we sample at exactly its frequency, we get 0 Hz. But what happens in between? Consider a sampling rate ever so slightly higher or lower than the sine wave's fundamental frequency – in both cases, this will result in a frequency much lower than the original signal, as shown in Figures 18.7 and 18.8. This is analogous to the effect of seeing spinning objects under fluorescent or LED light, or the spokes in the wheels of horse-drawn carriages in old motion pictures.

These figures suggest the following. Suppose that m is one-half the sampling rate. Then:

Original signal	Reproduced signal
0 – m	0 – m
m – 2m	m – 0
2m – 3m	0 – m
3m – 4m	m – 0
. . .	. . .

This phenomenon is called *aliasing*, or *foldover* of the signal onto itself.

This is not good! In particular, it means that audio signals in the ultrasonic range will get "folded" into the audible range. To solve this problem, we can add an analog *low-pass filter* in front of the ADC, usually called an *anti-aliasing* filter, to eliminate all but the audible sound before it is digitized. In practice, however, this can be tricky. For example, a steep analog filter introduces *phase distortion* (i.e., frequency-dependent time delays), and early

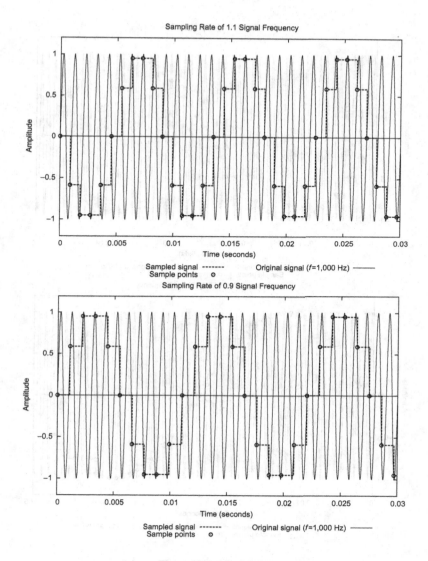

Figure 18.7 Aliasing 1.

digital recordings were notorious in the "harsh" sound that resulted. This can be fixed by using a filter with less steepness (but results in more aliasing), or using a time correlation filter to compensate, or using a technique called *oversampling*, which is beyond the scope of this text.

A similar problem occurs at the other end of the digital audio process – i.e., when we reconstruct an analog signal from a digital signal using a

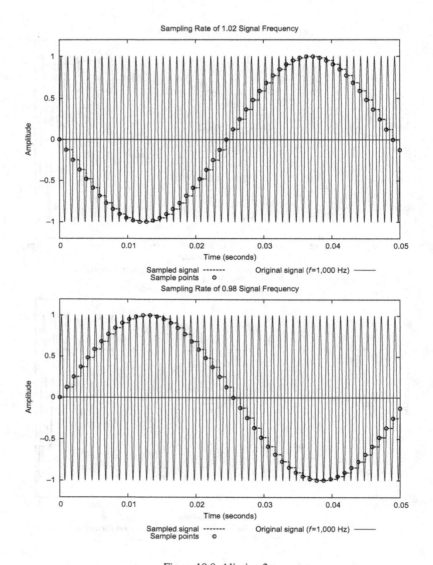

Figure 18.8 Aliasing 2.

digital-to-analog converter, or DAC. The digital representation of a signal can be viewed mathematically as a stepwise approximation to the real signal, as shown in Figure 18.9, where the sampling rate is 10 times the frequency of interest. As discussed earlier, at the highest frequency (i.e., one-half the sampling rate), we get a square wave. As we will see in Chapter 20, a square

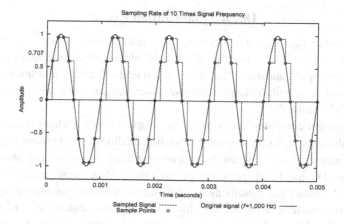

Figure 18.9 A properly sampled signal.

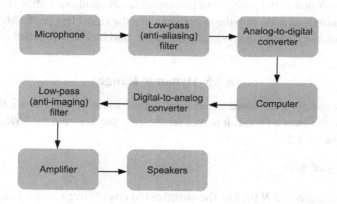

Figure 18.10 Block diagram of typical digital audio system.

wave can be represented mathematically as the sum of an infinite sequence of sine waves, consisting of the fundamental frequency and all of its odd harmonics. These harmonics can enter the ultrasonic region, causing potential havoc in the analog circuitry or in a dog's ear (dogs can hear frequencies much higher than humans). The solution is to add yet another low-pass filter, called an *anti-imaging* or *smoothing* filter, to the output of the DAC. In effect, this filter "connects the dots," or interpolates, between successive values of the stepwise approximation.

In any case, a basic block diagram of a typical digital audio system, from sound input to sound output, is shown in Figure 18.10.

18.2.4 Quantization Error

In terms of amplitude, remember that we are using digital numbers to represent an analog signal. For conventional CDs, 16 bits of precision are used. If we were to compute and then "listen to" the round-off errors that are induced, we would hear subtle imperfections, called *quantization error*, or more commonly "noise."

One might compare this to "hiss" on a tape recorder (which is due to the molecular disarray of the magnetic recording medium), but there are important differences. First of all, when there is no sound, there is no quantization error in a digital signal, but there is still hiss on a tape. Also, when the signal is very low and regular, the quantization error becomes somewhat regular as well, and is thus audible as something different from hiss. Indeed, it's only when the signal is loud and complex that quantization error compares favorably to tape hiss.

One solution to the problem of low signal levels mentioned above is to purposely introduce noise into the system to make the signal less predictable. This fortuitous use of noise deserves a better name, and indeed it is called *dither*.

18.2.5 Dynamic Range

What is the dynamic range of an n-bit digital audio system? If we think of quantization error as noise, it makes sense to use the equation for SNR_{dB} given in Section 18.1.2:

$$SNR_{dB} = 20 \log_{10} \frac{S}{N}$$

But what should N be, i.e., the quantization error? Given a signal amplitude range of $\pm a$, with n bits of resolution it is divided into $2a/2^n$ points. Therefore the dynamic range is:

$$20 \log_{10} \left(\frac{2a}{2a/2^n} \right) = 20 \times \log_{10}(2^n)$$
$$= 20 \times n \times \log_{10}(2)$$
$$\approx 20 \times n \times (0.3)$$
$$= 6n$$

For example, a 16-bit digital audio system results in a dynamic range of 96 dB, which is pretty good, although a 20-bit system yields 120 dB, corresponding to the dynamic range of the human ear.

Exercise 18.1 For each of the following, say whether it is a longitudinal wave or a transverse wave:

- A vibrating violin string
- Stop-and-go traffic on a highway
- The "wave" in a crowd at a stadium
- "Water hammer" in the plumbing of your house
- A "water caused by a stone falling in a pond
- A radio wave

Exercise 18.2 You see a lightning strike, and five seconds later you hear the thunder. How far away is the lightning?

Exercise 18.3 You clap your hands in a canyon, and two seconds later you hear an echo. How far away is the canyon wall?

Exercise 18.4 By what factor must one increase the RMS level of a signal to yield a 10 dB increase in sound level?

Exercise 18.5 A dog can hear in the range 60–45,000 Hz, and a bat 2,000–110,000 Hz. In terms of the frequency response, what are the corresponding dynamic ranges for these two animals, and how do they compare to that of humans?

Exercise 18.6 What is the maximum number of audible overtones in a note whose fundamental frequency is 100 Hz? 500 Hz? 1500 Hz? 5 kHz?

Exercise 18.7 Consider a continuous input signal whose frequency is f. Devise a formula for the frequency r of the reproduced signal given a sample rate s.

Exercise 18.8 How much memory is needed to record three minutes of stereo sound using 16-bit samples taken at a rate of 44.1 kHz?

Exercise 18.9 If we want the best possible sound, how large should the table be using fixed-waveform table-lookup synthesis in order to cover the audible frequency range?

Exercise 18.10 The Doppler effect occurs when a sound source is in motion. For example, as a police car moves toward you, its siren sounds higher than it really is, and as it goes past you, it sounds lower. How fast would a police car have to go to change a siren whose frequency is the same as concert A to a pitch an octave higher (i.e., twice the frequency)? At that speed, what frequency would you hear after the police car passes you?

19

Euterpea's Signal Functions

In this chapter we show how the theoretical concepts involving sound and signals studied in the last chapter are manifested in Euterpea. The techniques learned will lay the groundwork for doing two broad kinds of activities: *sound synthesis* and *audio processing*. Sound synthesis might include creating the sound of a footstep on dry leaves, simulating a conventional musical instrument, creating an entirely new instrument sound, or composing a single "soundscape" that stands alone as a musical composition. Audio processing includes such things as equalization, filtering, reverb, special effects, and so on.

Euterpea's framework for sound synthesis uses the same arrow syntax discussed in Chapter 17, although the types of the signal functions are somewhat different. As with MUIs, this means that programs using Euterpea's sound synthesis functions must start with the following:

{-# LANGUAGE Arrows #-}

19.1 The Type of Audio Signals

When working in the audio domain, the rate at which a signal is processed becomes very important. This means a signal function has a type somewhat different from that of the MUIs described in Chapter 17. Instead, we have the following:

Clock c $\Rightarrow$ *SigFun c a b*

which should be read "for some clock type (i.e., sampling rate) c, this is the type of signal functions that convert signals of type a into signals of type b."

The type variable c indicates what clock rate is being used, and for our purposes will always be one of two types: *AudRate* or *CtrRate* (for *audio rate* and *control rate*, respectively). Being able to express the sampling rate of a signal function is what we call *clock polymorphism*. Although we like to think of signals as continuous, time-varying quantities, in practice we know that they are sampled representations of continuous quantities, as discussed in the last chapter. However, some signals need to be sampled at a very high rate, say an audio signal, whereas other signals need not be sampled at such a high rate, say a signal representing the setting of a slider. The problem is, we often want to mix signals sampled at different rates; for example, the slider might control the volume of the audio signal.

One solution to this problem would be to simply sample everything at the very highest rate, but this is computationally inefficient. A better approach is to sample signals at their most appropriate rate, and to perform coercions to "up sample" or "down sample" a signal when it needs to be combined with a signal sampled at a different rate. This is the approach used in Euterpea.

More specifically, the base type of each signal into and out of a signal function must satisfy the type class constraint *Clock c*, where *c* is a *clock type*. The *Clocked* class is defined as:

class *Clock c* **where**
   rate :: *c* → *Double*

The single method *rate* allows the user to extract the sampling rate from the type. In Euterpea, the *AudRate* is predefined to be 44.1 kHz and the *CtrRate* is set at 4.41 kHz. Here are the definitions of *AudRate* and *CtrRate*, along with their instance declarations in the *Clock* class, to achieve this:

data *AudRate*
data *CtrRate*

instance *Clock AudRate* **where**
   rate _ = 44100

instance *Clock CtrRate* **where**
   rate _ = 4410

Because these two clock types are so often used, it is helpful to define a couple of type synonyms:

type *AudSF a b* = *SigFun AudRate a b*
type *CtrSF a b* = *SigFun CtrRate a b*

From these definitions it should be clear how to define your own clock type.

Details: Note that *AudRate* and *CtrRate* have no constructors – they are called *empty* data types. More precisely, they are each inhabited by exactly one value, namely ⊥.

The sampling rate can be determined from a given clock type. In this way, a coercion function can be written to change a signal sampled at one rate to a signal sampled at some other rate. In Euterpea, there are two such functions that are predefined:

$$coerce, upsample :: (Clock\ c1, Clock\ c2) \Rightarrow$$
$$SigFun\ c1\ a\ b \rightarrow SigFun\ c2\ a\ b$$

The function *coerce* looks up the sampling rates of the input and output signals from the type variables $c1$ and $c2$. It then either stretches the input stream by duplicating the same element or contracts it by skipping elements. (It is also possible to define a more accurate coercion function that performs interpolation, at the expense of performance.)

For simpler programs, the overhead of calling *coerce* might not be worth the time saved by generating signals with lower resolution. (Haskell's fractional number implementation is relatively slow.) The specialized coercion function *upsample* avoids this overhead, but only works properly when the output rate is an integral multiple of the input rate (which is true in the case of *AudRate* and *CtrRate*).

Keep in mind that one does not have to commit a signal function to a particular clock rate – it can be left *polymorphic*. Then that signal function will adapt its sampling rate to whatever is needed in the context in which it is used.

Also keep in mind that a signal function is an abstract function. You cannot just apply it to an argument like an ordinary function – that is the purpose of the arrow syntax. There are no values that directly represent *signals* in Euterpea, there are only signal *functions*.

The arrow syntax provides a convenient way to compose signal functions together – i.e., to wire together the boxes that make up a signal processing diagram. By not giving the user direct access to signals and providing a disciplined way to compose signal functions (namely arrow syntax), time and space leaks are avoided. In fact, the resulting framework is highly amenable to optimization.

A signal function whose type is of the form $Clock\ c \Rightarrow SigFun\ c\ ()\ b$ essentially takes no input, but produces some output of type b. Because of this, we often refer to such a signal function as a *signal source*.

19.1.1 Some Simple Examples

Let's now work through a few examples that focus on the behavior of signal functions, so that we can get a feel for how they are used in practice. Euterpea has many predefined signal functions, including ones for sine waves,

osc, oscI :: *Clock c* $\Rightarrow$
     Table $\rightarrow$ *Double* $\rightarrow$ *SigFun c Double Double*

osc tab ph is a signal function whose input is a frequency and output is a signal having that frequency. The output is generated using fixed-waveform table-lookup, using the table *tab*, starting with initial offset *ph* (phase angle) expressed as a fraction of a cycle (0–1). *oscI* is the same, but uses linear interpolation between points.

oscFixed :: *Clock c* $\Rightarrow$
     Double $\rightarrow$ *SigFun c* () *Double*

oscFixed freq is a signal source whose sinusoidal output frequency is *freq*. It uses a recurrence relation that requires only one multiply and two add operations for each sample of output.

oscDur, oscDurI :: *Clock c* $\Rightarrow$
     Table $\rightarrow$ *Double* $\rightarrow$ *Double* $\rightarrow$ *SigFun* () *Double*

oscDur tab del dur samples just once through the table *tab* at a rate determined by *dur*. For the first *del* seconds, the point of scan will reside at the first location of the table; it will then move through the table at a constant rate, reaching the end in another *dur* seconds; from that time on (i.e., after *del* + *dur* seconds) it will remain pointing at the last location. *oscDurI* is similar but uses linear interpolation between points.

oscPartials :: *Clock c* $\Rightarrow$
     Table $\rightarrow$ *Double* $\rightarrow$ *SigFun c* (*Double, Int*) *Double*

oscPartials tab ph is a signal function whose pair of inputs determines the frequency (as with *osc*), as well as the number of harmonics of that frequency, of the output. *tab* is the table that is cycled through, and *ph* is the phase angle (as with *osc*).

Figure 19.1 Euterpea's oscillators.

numeric computations, transcendental functions, delay lines, filtering, noise generation, integration, and so on. Many of these signal functions are inspired by csound [34], where they are called *unit generators*. Some of them are not signal functions *per se*, but take a few fixed arguments to yield a signal function, and it is important to understand this distinction.

For example, there are several predefined functions for generating sine waves and periodic waveforms in Euterpea. Collectively, these are called *oscillators*, a name taken from electronic circuit design. They are summarized in Figure 19.1.

The two most common oscillators in Euterpea are:

osc   :: *Clock c* $\Rightarrow$
     Table $\rightarrow$ *Double* $\rightarrow$ *SigFun c Double Double*
oscFixed :: *Clock c* $\Rightarrow$
     Double $\rightarrow$ *SigFun c* () *Double*

osc uses fixed-waveform table-lookup synthesis as described in Section 18.2.2. The first argument is the fixed wavetable; we will see shortly how such a table can be generated. The second argument is the initial phase angle, represented as a fraction between 0 and 1. The resulting signal function then converts a signal representing the desired output frequency to a signal that has that output frequency.

oscFixed uses an efficient recurrence relation to compute a pure sinusoidal wave. In contrast with *osc*, its single argument is the desired output frequency. The resulting signal function is therefore a signal source (i.e., its input type is ()).

The key point here is that the frequency that is output by *osc* is an *input to the signal function* and therefore can vary with time, whereas the frequency output by *oscFixed* is a *fixed argument* and cannot vary with time. To see this concretely, let's define a signal source that generates a pure sine wave using *oscFixed* at a fixed frequency, say 440 Hz:

$s1 :: Clock\ c \Rightarrow SigFun\ c\ ()\ Double$
$s1 = \textbf{proc}\ () \rightarrow \textbf{do}$
$\quad s \leftarrow oscFixed\ 440 \prec ()$
$\quad outA \prec s$

Since the resulting signal *s* is directly returned through *outA*, this example can also be written:

$s1 = \textbf{proc}\ () \rightarrow \textbf{do}$
$\quad oscFixed\ 440 \prec ()$

Alternatively, we could simply write *oscFixed* 440.

Details: As has been the case with the typesetting of $\rightarrow$ and $\leftarrow$ in type signatures, list comprehensions, and monadic contexts, the arrow-based syntax of $y \leftarrow f \prec x$ must be coded as `y <- f -< x`.

To use *osc* instead, we first need to generate a wavetable that represents one full cycle of a sine wave. We can do this using one of Eutperpea's table-generating functions, which are summarized in Figure 19.2. For example, using Euterpea's *tableSinesN* function, we can define:

$tab1 :: Table$
$tab1 = tableSinesN\ 4096\ [1]$

```
type TableSize       = Int
type PartialNum      = Double
type PartialStrength = Double
type PhaseOffset     = Double
type StartPt         = Double
type SegLength       = Double
type EndPt           = Double
```

tableLinear, tableLinearN ::
    TableSize → *StartPt* → [(*SegLength, EndPt*)] → *Table*

tableLinear size sp pts is a table of size *size* that has a starting point at (0, *sp*) and uses straight lines to move from that point to, successively, each of the points in *pts*, which are segment-length/endpoint pairs (segment lengths are projections along the x-axis). *tableLinearN* is a normalized version of the result.

tableExpon, tableExponN ::
    TableSize → *StartPt* → [(*SegLength, EndPt*)] → *Table*

This is just like *tableLinear* and *tableLinearN*, respectively, except that exponential curves are used to connect the points.

tableSines3, tableSines3N ::
    TableSize → [(*PartialNum, PartialStrength, PhaseOffset*)] → *Table*

tableSines3 size triples is a table of size *size* that represents a sinusoidal wave and an arbitrary number of partials, whose relationship to the fundamental frequency, amplitude, and phase are determined by each of the triples in *triples*. *tableSines3N* is a normalized version of the result.

tableSines, tableSinesN ::
    TableSize → [*PartialStrength*] → *Table*

This is like *tableSines3* and *tableSines3N*, respectively, except that the second argument is an ordered list of the strengths of each partial, starting with the fundamental.

tableBesselN ::
    TableSize → *Double* → *Table*

tableBesselN size x is a table representing the log of a modified Bessel function of the second kind, order 0, suitable for use in amplitude-modulated FM. x is the x-interval (0 to x) over which the function is defined.

Figure 19.2 Table-generating functions.

This will generate a table of 4,096 elements, consisting of one sine wave whose peak amplitude is 1.0. Then we can define the following signal source:

s2 :: *Clock c* ⇒ *SigFun c* () *Double*
s2 = **proc** () → **do**
    osc tab1 0 ⤙ 440

Alternatively, we could use the *const* and composition operators to write either *constA* 440 ⋙ *osc tab1* 0 or *osc tab2* 0 ⋘ *constA* 440. *s1* and *s2* should be compared closely.

Keep in mind that *oscFixed* only generates a sine wave, whereas *osc* generates whatever is stored in the wavetable. Indeed, *tableSinesN* actually creates a table that is the sum of a series of overtones, i.e., multiples of the fundamental frequency (recall the discussion in Section 18.1.3). For example:

$tab2 = tableSinesN\ 4096\ [1.0, 0.5, 0.33]$

generates a waveform consisting of a fundamental frequency with amplitude 1.0, a first overtone at amplitude 0.5, and a second overtone at amplitude 0.33. So a more complex sound can be synthesized just by changing the wavetable:

$s3 :: Clock\ c \Rightarrow SigFun\ c\ ()\ Double$
$s3 = \textbf{proc}\ ()\ \rightarrow \textbf{do}$
  $osc\ tab2\ 0 \prec 440$

To get the same effect using *oscFixed*, we would have to write:

$s4 :: Clock\ c \Rightarrow SigFun\ c\ ()\ Double$
$s4 = \textbf{proc}\ ()\ \rightarrow \textbf{do}$
  $f0 \leftarrow oscFixed\ 440\ \prec ()$
  $f1 \leftarrow oscFixed\ 880\ \prec ()$
  $f2 \leftarrow oscFixed\ 1320\ \prec ()$
  $outA \prec (f0 + 0.5 * f1 + 0.33 * f2)/1.83$

Not only is this more complex, it is less efficient. (The division by 1.83 is to normalize the result – if the peaks of the three signals $f0$, $f1$, and $f2$ align properly, the peak amplitude will be 1.83 (or -1.83), which is outside the range ± 1.0 and may cause clipping (see discussion in Section 19.3).

So far in these examples we have generated a signal whose fundamental frequency is 440 Hz. But as mentioned, in the case of *osc*, the input to the oscillator is a signal and can therefore itself be time-varying. As an example of this idea, let's implement *vibrato*, the performance effect whereby a musician slightly varies the frequency of a note in a pulsating rhythm. On a string instrument this is typically achieved by wiggling the finger on the fingerboard, on a reed instrument by adjusting the breath and emboucher to compress and relax the reed in a suitable way, and so on.

Specifically, let's define a function:

$vibrato :: Clock\ c \Rightarrow$
    $Double \rightarrow Double \rightarrow SigFun\ c\ Double\ Double$

such that *vibrato f d* is a signal function that takes a frequency argument (this is not a signal of a given frequency, it is the frequency itself) and generates a signal at that frequency, but with vibrato added, where *f* is the vibrato frequency and *d* is the vibrato depth. We will consider "depth" to be a measure of how many Hertz the input frequency is modulated.

Intuitively, it seems as if we need *two* oscillators, one to generate the fundamental frequency of interest and the other to generate the vibrato (much lower in frequency). Here is a solution:

```
vibrato :: Clock c ⇒
           Double → Double → SigFun c Double Double
vibrato vfrq dep = proc afrq → do
  vib ← osc tab1 0 —< vfrq
  aud ← osc tab2 0 —< afrq + vib * dep
  outA —< aud
```

Note that a pure sine wave is used for the vibrato signal, whereas *tab2*, a sum of three sine waves, is chosen for the signal itself.

For example, to play a 1,000 Hz tone with a vibrato frequency of 5 Hz and a depth of 20 Hz, we could write:

```
s5 :: AudSF () Double
s5 = constA 1000 ⋙ vibrato 5 20
```

Vibrato is actually an example of a more general sound synthesis technique called *frequency modulation* (since one signal is being used to vary, or modulate, the frequency of another signal) and will be explained in more detail in Chapter 22. Other chapters include synthesis techniques such as additive and subtractive synthesis, plucked instruments using waveguides, physical modeling, granular synthesis, as well as audio processing techniques such as filter design, reverb, and other effects. Now that we have a basic understanding of signal functions, these techniques will be straightforward to express in Euterpea.

19.2 Generating Sound

Euterpea can execute some programs in real time, but sufficiently complex programs require writing the result to a file. The function for achieving this is:

```
outFile :: (AudioSample a, Clock c) ⇒
           String → Double → SigFun c () a → IO ()
```

The first argument is the name of the WAV file to which the result is written. The second argument is the duration of the result, in seconds (remember that signals are conceptually infinite). The third argument is a signal function that takes no input and generates a signal of type *a* as output (i.e., a signal source), where *a* is required to be an instance of the *AudioSample* type class, which allows one to choose between mono, stereo, etc.

For convenience, Euterpea defines these type synonyms:

type *Mono p* $=$ *SigFun p* () *Double*
type *Stereo p* $=$ *SigFun p* () (*Double, Double*)

For example, the IO command *outfile* "test.wav" 5 *sf* generates five seconds of output from the signal function *sf* and writes the result to the file "test.wav". If *sf* has type *Mono AudRate* (i.e., *SigFun AudRate* () *Double*), then the result will be monophonic; if the type is *Stereo AudRate* (i.e., *SigFun AudRate* () *Double, Double*), the result will be stereophonic.

One might think that *outFile* should be restricted to *AudRate*. However, by allowing a signal of any clock rate to be written to a file, one can use external tools to analyze the result of control signals or other signals of interest as well.

19.3 Clipping

An important detail in writing WAV files with *outFile* is that care must be taken to ensure that each sample falls in the range ± 1.0. If this range is exceeded, the output sound will be distorted, a phenomenon known as *clipping*. The reason for this is that signals exceeding ± 1.0 result in a flat line until they fall back within the acceptable range of values. This has the effect of "shaving off" any parts of a signal that fall outside the range of ± 1.0. Figure 19.3 illustrates the effect of clipping on a sine wave.

Avoiding clipping involves ensuring that the final signal is scaled appropriately. This is especially important when adding two or more signals together. For example, consider the sum of two in-phase sine waves at the same frequency. If the amplitude of each is 1.0, the maximum possible amplitude of their sum is 2.0, which is well beyond the acceptable range for a WAV file. If the frequencies are different, say f and $2f$, the maximum possible amplitude is less than 2.0, but still greater than 1.0.

A couple of simple strategies for avoiding clipping when summing signals are:

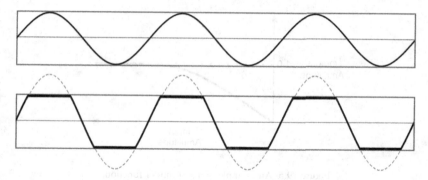

Figure 19.3 A regular sine wave (top) and a clipped sine wave (bottom). Notice that the clipped sine wave appears more like a square wave.

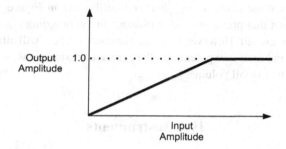

Figure 19.4 An example of a hard limiter function.

- For a summation of n signals, simply divide by n in the *returnA* statement. Note that this can result in a very small final amplitude if the maximum amplitudes of many of the signals is <1.0.
- For a summation of n signals where the ith partial has a known maximum amplitude of k_i, divide by $\sum_{i=1}^{n} k_i$. This avoids the overly cautious scaling of the previous approach, although it is not always possible to know the maximum value of a signal in advance.

Euterpea also provides *outFileNorm* as a method to automatically search for the largest value in a signal before writing it to a WAV file, scaling the output accordingly to fit within ±1.0 if it would otherwise clip. Signals that do not exceed ±1.0 will remain unchanged by *outFileNorm*.

Another strategy for avoiding clipping is to implement a *limiter*, which is a function that scales its input according to either a straight line or a curve to reduce the chance of hitting ±1.0. A *hard limiter*, such as the function shown in

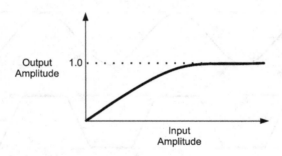

Figure 19.5 An example of a soft limiter function.

Figure 19.4, will scale back the amplitude as it approaches 1.0 but still causes clipping in extreme cases. A *soft limiter* like the one in Figure 19.5 uses a curved function that prevents sudden plateaus in the outgoing signal, giving a much smoother result. However, both hard and soft limiters will alter the shape of the input (and therefore potentially the perceived texture as well) in addition to changing the overall volume.

19.4 Instruments

So far we have only considered signal functions as stand-alone values whose output we can write to a WAV file. But how do we connect the ideas in previous chapters about *Music* values, *Performances*, and so on to the ideas presented in this chapter? This section presents a bridge between the two worlds.

19.4.1 Turning a Signal Function into an Instrument

Suppose that we have a *Music* value that previously we would have played using a MIDI instrument, and now we want to play using an instrument that we have designed using signal functions. To do this, first recall from Chapter 2 that the *InstrumentName* data type has a special constructor called *CustomInstrument*:

```
data InstrumentName =
    AcousticGrandPiano
  | BrightAcousticPiano
  | ...
  | CustomInstrument String
  deriving (Show, Eq, Ord)
```

With this constructor, names (represented as strings) can be given to instruments that we have designed using signal functions. For example:

simpleInstr :: *InstrumentName*
simpleInstr = *CustomInstrument* `"Simple Instrument"`

Now we need to define the instrument itself. Euterpea defines the following type synonym:

type *Instr a* = *Dur* → *AbsPitch* → *Volume* → [*Double*] → *a*

Although *Instr* is polymorphic, by far its most common instantiation is the type *Instr (AufSF () Double)*. An instrument of this type is a function that takes a duration, an absolute pitch, a volume, and a list of parameters and returns a signal source that generates the resulting sound.

The list of parameters (similar to the "pfields" in csound) are not used by MIDI instruments, and thus have not been discussed until now. They afford us unlimited expressiveness in controlling the sound of our signal function–based instruments. Recall from Chapter 9 the types:

type *Music1* = *Music Note1*
type *Note1* = (*Pitch*, [*NoteAttribute*])

data *NoteAttribute* =
    Volume Int
  | *Fingering Integer*
  | *Dynamics String*
  | *Params* [*Double*]
    deriving (*Eq*, *Show*)

Using the *Params* constructor, each individual note in a *Music1* value can be given a different list of parameters. It is up to the instrument designer to decide how these parameters are used.

There are three steps to playing a *Music* value using a user-defined instrument. First, we must coerce our signal function into an instrument that has the proper type *Instr* as described above. For example, let's turn the *vibrato* function from the last section into a (rather primitive) instrument:

myInstr :: *Instr (AudSF () Double)*
    -- *Dur* → *AbsPitch* → *Volume* → [*Double*] → (*AudSF () Double*)
myInstr dur ap vol [*vfrq, dep*] =
    proc () → **do**
      vib ← *osc tab1 0* ─≺ *vfrq*
      aud ← *osc tab2 0* ─≺ *apToHz ap* + *vib* ∗ *dep*
      outA ─≺ *aud*

Aside from the reshuffling of arguments, note the use of the function *apToHz*, which converts an absolute pitch into its corresponding frequency:

apToHz :: *Floating a* $\Rightarrow$ *AbsPitch* $\rightarrow$ *a*

Next, we must connect our instrument name (used in the *Music* value) to the instrument itself (such as defined above). This is achieved using a simple association list, or *instrument map*:

type *InstrMap a* = [(*InstrumentName*, *Instr a*)]

Continuing the example started above:

myInstrMap :: *InstrMap* (*AudSF* () *Double*)
myInstrMap = [(*simpleInstr*, *myInstr*)]

Finally, we need a function that is analogous to *hsomPerform* from Chapter 9, except that instead of generating a *Performance*, it creates a single signal function that will "play" our *Music* value for us. In Euterpea that function is called *renderSF*:

renderSF :: (*ToMusic1 a*, *AudioSample b*, *Clock c*) $\Rightarrow$
            Music a $\rightarrow$
            InstrMap (*SigFun p* () *b*) $\rightarrow$
            (*Double*, *SigFun p* () *b*)

The first element of the pair that is returned is the duration of the *Music* value, just as is returned by *hsomPerform*. That way we know how much of the signal function to render in order to hear the entire composition.

Using the simple melody *mel* in Figure 19.6 and the simple vibrato instrument defined above, we can generate our result and write it to a file, as follows:

(*dr*, *sf*) = *renderSF mel myInstrMap*
main   = *outFile* `"simple.wav"` *dr sf*

Euterpea also contains a built-in function called *writeWav* that is a wrapper for this functionality:

writeWav fname iMap m =
  let (*d*, *s*) = *renderSF m iMap*
  in *outFile fname d s*

There is also a similar function, *writeWavNorm*, that utilizes *outFileNorm* to prevent clipping.

For clarity, we show in Figure 19.7 all of the pieces of this running example as one program.

mel :: *Music1*
mel =
  let *m* = *Euterpea.line* [*na1* (*c* 4 *en*), *na1* (*ef* 4 *en*), *na1* (*f* 4 *en*),
           na2 (*af* 4 *qn*), *na1* (*f* 4 *en*), *na1* (*af* 4 *en*),
           na2 (*bf* 4 *qn*), *na1* (*af* 4 *en*), *na1* (*bf* 4 *en*),
           na1 (*c* 5 *en*), *na1* (*ef* 5 *en*), *na1* (*f* 5 *en*),
           na3 (*af* 5 *wn*)]
        na1 (*Prim* (*Note* *d* *p*)) = *Prim* (*Note* *d* (*p*, [*Params* [0, 0]]))
        na2 (*Prim* (*Note* *d* *p*)) = *Prim* (*Note* *d* (*p*, [*Params* [5, 10]]))
        na3 (*Prim* (*Note* *d* *p*)) = *Prim* (*Note* *d* (*p*, [*Params* [5, 20]]))
  in *instrument simpleInstr m*

Figure 19.6 A simple melody.

simpleInstr :: *InstrumentName*
simpleInstr = *CustomInstrument* "Simple Instrument"

myInstr :: *Instr* (*AudSF* () *Double*)
myInstr dur ap vol [*vfrq*, *dep*] =
  proc () → **do**
     vib ← *osc tab1* 0 —≺ *vfrq*
     aud ← *osc tab2* 0 —≺ *apToHz ap* + *vib* ∗ *dep*
     outA —≺ *aud*

myInstrMap :: *InstrMap* (*AudSF* () *Double*)
myInstrMap = [(*simpleInstr*, *myInstr*)]

main = *writeWav* "simple.wav" *myInstrMap mel*

Figure 19.7 A complete example of a signal function–based instrument.

19.4.2 Envelopes

Most instruments played by humans have a distinctive sound that is partially dependent on how the performer plays a particular note. For example, when a wind instrument is played (whether a flute, a saxophone, or a trumpet), the note does not begin instantaneously – it depends on how quickly and forcibly the performer blows into the instrument. This is called the "attack." Indeed, it is not uncommon for the initial pulse of energy to generate a sound that is louder than the "sustained" portion of the sound. And when the note ends, the airflow does not stop instantaneously, so there is variability in the "release" of the note.

The overall variability in the loudness of a note can be simulated by multiplying the output of a signal function by an *envelope*, which is a time-varying signal that captures the desired behavior. Indeed, the *ADSR envelope* (attack, decay, sustain, release) introduced above is one of the most common envelopes used in practice. It is shown pictorially in Figure 19.8.

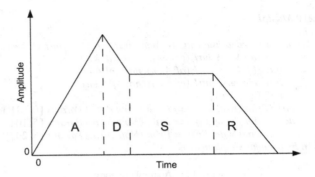

Figure 19.8 ADSR envelope: A = attack, D = decay, S = sustain, R = release.

Before defining it in Euterpea, however, we first describe a collection of simpler envelopes.

Figure 19.9 shows six predefined envelope-generating functions. Read the code comments carefully to understand what they do.

Here are some additional comments regarding *envCSEnvplx*, easily the most sophisticated of the envelope generators:

1. The fifth argument to *envCSEnvplx*: A value greater than 1 causes exponential growth; a value less than 1 causes exponential decay; a value = 1 will maintain a true steady state at the last rise value. The attenuation is not by a fixed rate (as in a piano), but is sensitive to a note's duration. However, if this argument is less than 0 (or if steady state is less than four k-periods), a fixed attenuation rate of *abs atss* per second is used. A value of 0 is illegal.
2. The sixth arg to *envCSEnvplx*: It must be positive and is normally of the order of 0.01. A large or excessively small value is apt to produce a cutoff that is not audible. Values less than or equal to 0 are disallowed.

Exercise 19.1 Using the Euterpea function *osc*, create a simple sinusoidal wave, but using different table sizes and different frequencies, and see if you can hear the differences (report on what you hear). Use *outFile* to write your results to a file, and be sure to use a decent set of speakers or headphones.

Exercise 19.2 The *vibrato* function varies a signal's frequency at a given rate and depth. Define an analogous function *tremolo* that varies the volume at a given rate and depth. However, in a sense, *tremolo* is a kind of envelope (infinite in duration), so define it as a signal source with which you can then shape whatever signal you wish. Consider the "depth" to be the fractional

-- a linear envelope
envLine   :: *Clock p* ⇒
  Double   →   -- starting value
  Double   →   -- duration in seconds
  Double   →   -- value after dur seconds
  SigFun p () *Double*

-- an exponential envelope
envExpon   :: *Clock p* ⇒
  Double   →   -- starting value; zero is illegal for exponentials
  Double   →   -- duration in seconds
  Double   →   -- value after dur seconds (must be non-zero
                   -- and agree in sign with first argument)
  SigFun p () *Double*

-- a series of linear envelopes
envLineSeg   :: *Clock p* ⇒
  [*Double*] →   -- list of points to trace through
  [*Double*] →   -- list of durations for each line segment
                  -- (one element fewer than previous argument)
  SigFun p () *Double*

-- a series of exponential envelopes
envExponSeg :: *Clock p* ⇒
  [*Double*] →   -- list of points to trace through
  [*Double*] →   -- list of durations for each line segment
                  -- (one element fewer than previous argument)
  SigFun p () *Double*

-- an "attack/decay/release" envelope; each segment is linear
envASR   :: *Clock p* ⇒
  Double   →   -- rise time in seconds
  Double   →   -- overall duration in seconds
  Double   →   -- decay time in seconds
  SigFun p () *Double*

-- a more sophisticated ASR
envCSEnvlpx :: *Clock p* ⇒
  Double   →   -- rise time in seconds
  Double   →   -- overall duration in seconds
  Double   →   -- decay time in seconds
  Table   →   -- table representing rise shape
  Double   →   -- attenuation factor, by which the last value
                   -- of the envlpx rise is modified during the
                   -- note's pseudo steady state
  Double   →   -- attenuation factor by which the closing
                   -- steady state value is reduced exponentially
                   -- over the decay period
  SigFun p () *Double*

Figure 19.9 Envelopes.

change to the volume; that is, a value of 0 would result in no tremolo, a value of 0.1 would vary the amplitude from 0.9 to 1.1, and so on. Test your result.

Exercise 19.3 Define an ADSR ("attack/decay/sustain/release") envelope generator (i.e., a signal source) called *envADSR*, with type:

> **type** *DPair* = (*Double, Double*)   -- pair of duration and amplitude
> *envADSR*   :: *DPair* → *DPair* → *DPair* → *Double* → *AudSF* () *Double*

The three *DPair* arguments are the duration and amplitude of the attack, decay, and release "phases," respectively, of the envelope. The sustain phase should hold the last value of the decay phase. The fourth argument is the duration of the entire envelope, and thus the duration of the sustain phase should be that value minus the sum of the durations of the other three phases. (Hint: Use Euterpeas *envLineSeg* function.) Test your result.

Generate a signal that causes significant clipping and listen to the result. Then, implement a limiter and apply it to the signal. Can you hear the difference? Does it sound different than simply scaling the output with *outFileNorm*?

Exercise 19.4 Define two instruments, each of type *Instr (AudSF () Double)*. These can be as simple as you like, but each must take at least two *Params*. Define an *InstrMap* that uses these, and then use *renderSF* to "drive" your instruments from a *Music1* value. Test your result.

20

Spectrum Analysis

There are many situations where it is desirable to take an existing sound signal – in particular one that is recorded by a microphone – and analyze it for its spectral content. If one can do this effectively, it is then possible (at least in theory) to recreate the original sound, or to create novel variations of it. The theory behind this approach is based on *Fourier's theorem*, which states that any periodic signal can be decomposed into a weighted sum of (a potentially infinite number of) sine waves. In this chapter, we discuss the theory as well as the pragmatics for doing spectrum analysis.

20.1 Fourier's Theorem

A *periodic signal* is a signal that repeats itself infinitely often. Mathematically, a signal x is periodic if there exists a real number T such that for all integers n:

$$x(t) = x(t + nT)$$

T is called the *period*, which can be just a few microseconds, a few seconds, or perhaps days – the only thing that matters is that the signal repeats itself. Usually we want to find the smallest value of T that satisfies the above property. For example, a sine wave is surely periodic; indeed, recall from Section 18.1.1 that:

$$\sin(2\pi k + \theta) = \sin\theta$$

for any integer k. In this case, $T = 2\pi$, and it is the smallest value that satisfies this property.

But in what sense is, for example, a single musical note periodic? Indeed it is not, unless it is repeated infinitely often, which would not be very interesting musically. Yet something we would like to know is the spectral content of

299

that single note, or even of a small portion of that note, within an entire composition. This is one of the practical problems that we will address later in the chapter.

Recall from Section 18.1.1 that a sine wave can be represented by $x(t) = A\sin(\omega t + \phi)$, where A is the amplitude, ω is the radian frequency, and ϕ is the phase angle. Joseph Fourier, a french mathematician and physicist, showed the following result. Any periodic signal $x(t)$ with period T can be represented as:

$$x(t) = C_0 + \sum_{n=1}^{\infty} C_n \cos(\omega_0 n t + \phi_n) \tag{20.1}$$

This is called *Fourier's theorem*. $\omega_0 = 2\pi/T$ is called the *fundamental frequency*. Note that the frequency of each cosine wave in the series is an integer multiple of the fundamental frequency. The above equation is also called the *Fourier series* or *harmonic series* (related to, but not to be confused with, the mathematical definition of harmonic series, which has the precise form $1 + 1/2 + 1/3 + 1/4 + \cdots$).

The trick, of course, is determining what the coefficients $C_0, ..., C_n$ and phase angles $\phi_1, ..., \phi_n$ are. Determining the above equation for a particular periodic signal is called *Fourier analysis*, and synthesizing a sound based on the above equation is called *Fourier synthesis*. Theoretically, at least, we should be able to use Fourier analysis to decompose a sound of interest into its composite sine waves, and then regenerate it by artificially generating those composite sine waves and adding them together (i.e., additive synthesis, to be described in Chapter 21). Of course, we also have to deal with the fact that the representation may involve an *infinite* number of composite signals.

As discussed somewhat in Chapter 18, many naturally occurring vibrations in nature – including the resonances of most musical instruments – are characterized as having a fundamental frequency (the perceived pitch) and some combination of multiples of that frequency, which are often called *harmonics*, *overtones*, or *partials*. So Fourier's theorem seems to be a good match for this musical application.

20.1.1 The Fourier Transform

When studying Fourier analysis, it is more convenient, mathematically, to use *complex exponentials*. We can relate working with complex exponentials back to sines and cosines using *Euler's formula*:

$$e^{j\theta} = cos(\theta) + jsin(\theta)$$

$$cos(\theta) = \frac{1}{2}(e^{j\theta} + e^{-j\theta})$$

$$sin(\theta) = \frac{1}{2}(e^{j\theta} - e^{-j\theta})$$

For a periodic signal $x(t)$, which we consider to be a function of time, we denote its *Fourier transform* by $\hat{x}(f)$, which is a function of frequency. Each point in $\hat{x}$ is a complex number that represents the magnitude and phase of the frequency f's presence in $x(t)$. Using complex exponentials, the formula for $\hat{x}(f)$ in terms of $x(t)$ is:

$$\hat{x}(f) = \int_{-\infty}^{\infty} x(t)e^{-j\omega t}dt$$

where $\omega = 2\pi f$ and j is the same as the imaginary unit i used in mathematics.[1] Intuitively, the Fourier transform at a particular frequency f is the integral of the product of the original signal and a pure sinusoidal wave $e^{-j\omega t}$. This latter process is related to the *convolution* of the two signals, and intuitively will be non-zero only when the signal has some content of that pure signal in it.

The above equation describes $\hat{x}$ in terms of x. We can also go the other way around, defining x in terms of $\hat{x}$:

$$x(t) = \int_{-\infty}^{\infty} \hat{x}(f)e^{j\hat{\omega} f}df$$

where $\hat{\omega} = 2\pi t$. This is called the *inverse* Fourier transform.

If we expand the definitions of ω and $\hat{\omega}$, we can see how similar these two equations are:

$$\hat{x}(f) = \int_{-\infty}^{\infty} x(t)e^{-j2\pi ft}dt \tag{20.2}$$

$$x(t) = \int_{-\infty}^{\infty} \hat{x}(f)e^{j2\pi ft}df \tag{20.3}$$

These two equations, for the Fourier transform and its inverse, are remarkable in their simplicity and power. They are also remarkable in the following sense: *no information is lost when converting from one to the other.* In other words, a signal can be represented in terms of its time-varying behavior or its spectral content – they are equivalent!

---

[1] Historically, engineers have preferred to use the symbol j rather than i, because i is generally used to represent current in an electrical circuit.

A function that has the property $f(x) = f(-x)$ is called an *even* function; if $f(x) = -f(-x)$, it is said to be *odd*. It turns out that, perhaps surprisingly, *any* function can be expressed as the sum of a single even function and a single odd function. This may help provide some intuition about the equations for the Fourier transform, because the complex exponential $e^{j2\pi ft}$ separates the waveform by which it is being multiplied into its even and odd parts (recall Euler's formula). The real (cosine) part affects only the even part of the input, and the imaginary (sine) part affects only the odd part of the input.

20.1.2 Examples

Let's consider some examples, which are illustrated in Figure 20.1:

- Intuitively, the Fourier transform of a pure cosine wave should be an impulse function – that is, the spectral content of a cosine wave should be concentrated completely at the frequency of the cosine wave. The only catch is that when working in the complex domain, the Fourier transform also yields the mirror image of the spectral content, at a frequency that is the negation of the cosine wave's frequency, as shown in Figure 20.1a. In other words, in this case, $\hat{x}(f) = \hat{x}(-f)$, i.e., $\hat{x}$ is even. So the spectral content is the *real* part of the complex number returned from the Fourier transform (recall Euler's formula).
- In the case of a pure sine wave, we should expect a similar result. The only catch now is that the spectral content is contained in the *imaginary* part of the complex number returned from the Fourier transform (recall Euler's formula), and the mirror image is negated. That is, $\hat{x}(f) = -\hat{x}(-f)$, i.e., $\hat{x}$ is odd. This is illustrated in Figure 20.1b.
- Conversely, consider what the spectral content of an impulse function should be. Because an impulse function is infinitely "sharp," it would seem that its spectrum should contain energy at every point in the frequency domain. Indeed, the Fourier transform of an impulse function centered at zero is a constant, as shown in Figure 20.1c.
- Consider now the spectral content of a square wave. It can be shown that the Fourier series representation of a square wave is the sum of the square wave's fundamental frequency plus its harmonically decreasing (in magnitude) odd harmonics. Specifically:

$$sq(t) = \sum_{k=1}^{\infty} \frac{1}{k} \sin k\omega t, \quad \text{for odd } k \tag{20.4}$$

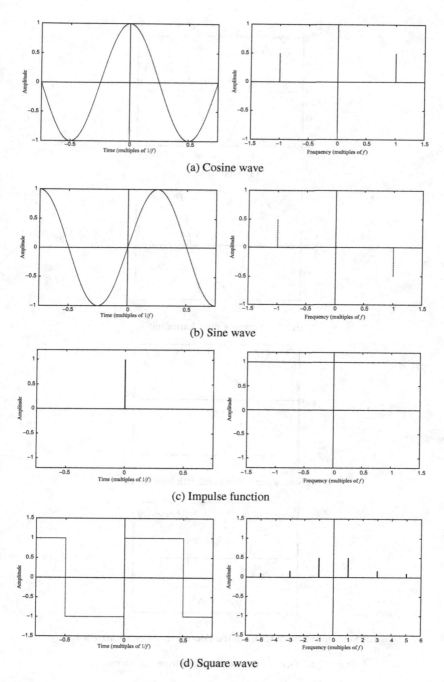

(a) Cosine wave

(b) Sine wave

(c) Impulse function

(d) Square wave

Figure 20.1 Examples of Fourier transforms.

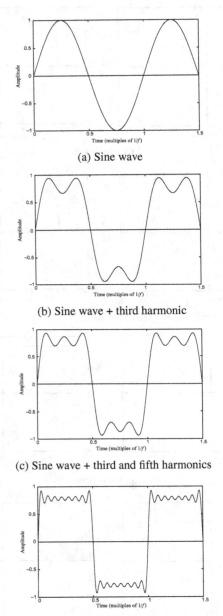

(a) Sine wave

(b) Sine wave + third harmonic

(c) Sine wave + third and fifth harmonics

(d) Sum of first eight terms of the Fourier series of a square wave

Figure 20.2 Generating a square wave from odd harmonics.

The spectral content of this signal in shown in Figure 20.1d. Figure 20.2 also shows partial reconstruction of the square wave from a finite number of its composite signals.

It is worth noting that the diagrams in Figure 20.1 make no assumptions about time or frequency. Therefore, because the Fourier transform and its inverse are true mathematical inverses, we can read the diagrams as time domain/frequency domain pairs, or the other way around, as frequency domain/time domain pairs. For example, interpreting the diagram on the left of Figure 20.1a in the frequency domain is to say that it is the Fourier transform of the signal on the right (interpreted in the time domain).

20.2 The Discrete Fourier Transform

Recall from Section 18.2.1 that we can move from the continuous signal domain to the discrete domain by replacing the time t with the quantity n/r, where n is the integer index into the sequence of discrete samples and r is the sampling rate. Let us assume that we have done this for x, and we will use square brackets to denote the difference. That is, $x[n]$ denotes the nth sample of the continuous signal $x(t)$, corresponding to the value $x(n/r)$.

We would now like to compute the *discrete Fourier transform* (DFT) of our discrete signal. But instead of being concerned about the sampling rate (which can introduce aliasing, for example), our concern turns to the *number of samples* that we use in computing the DFT – let's call this N. Intuitively, the integrals used in our equations for the Fourier transform and its inverse should become sums over the range $0 \ldots N - 1$. This leads to a reformulation of our two equations (20.2 and 20.3) as follows:[2]

$$\hat{x}[k] = \frac{1}{N} \sum_{n=0}^{N-1} x[n] e^{-j\frac{2\pi kn}{N}}, \quad k = 0, 1, \ldots, N - 1 \tag{20.5}$$

$$x[n] = \sum_{k=0}^{N-1} \hat{x}[k] e^{j\frac{2\pi kn}{N}}, \quad n = 0, 1, \ldots, N - 1 \tag{20.6}$$

---

[2] The purpose of the factor $1/N$ in Equation 20.5 is to ensure that the DFT and the inverse DFT are in fact inverses of each other. But it is just by convention that one equation has this factor and the other does not – it would be sufficient if it were done the other way around. In fact, all that matters is that the product of the two coefficients be $1/N$, and thus it would also be sufficient for each equation to have the same coefficient, namely $1/\sqrt{N}$. Similarly, the negative exponent in one equation and positive in the other is also by convention – it would be sufficient to do it the other way around.

Despite all of the mathematics up to this point, the reader may now realize that the discrete Fourier transform as expressed above is amenable to implementation – for example, it should not be difficult to write Haskell functions that realize each of the above equations. But before addressing implementation issues, let's discuss a bit more what the results actually *mean*.

20.2.1 Interpreting the Frequency Spectrum

Just as $x[n]$ represents a sampled version of the continuous input signal, $\hat{x}[k]$ represents a sampled version of the continuous frequency spectrum. Care must be taken when interpreting either of these results, keeping in mind the Nyquist-Shannon sampling theorem (recall Section 18.2) and aliasing (Section 18.2.3).

Also recall that the result of a Fourier transform of a periodic signal is a Fourier series (see Section 20.1), in which the signal being analyzed is expressed as multiples of a fundamental frequency. In Equation 20.5 above, that fundamental frequency is the inverse of the duration of the N samples, i.e., the inverse of N/r, or r/N. For example, if the sampling rate is 44.1 kHz (the CD standard), then:

• If we take $N = 441$ samples, the fundamental frequency will be
  $r/N = 100$ Hz.
• If we take $N = 4,410$ samples, the fundamental frequency will be
  $r/N = 10$ Hz.
• If we take $N = 44,100$ samples, the fundamental frequency will be
  $r/N = 1$ Hz.

Thus, as would be expected, taking more samples yields a *finer* resolution of the frequency spectrum. On the other hand, note that if we increase the sampling rate and keep the number of samples fixed, we get a *coarser* resolution of the spectrum – this also should be expected, because if we increase the sampling rate, we would expect to have to look at more samples to get the same accuracy.

Analogous to the Nyquist-Shannon sampling theorem, the representable points in the resulting frequency spectrum lie in the range $\pm r/2$, i.e., between plus and minus one-half of the sampling rate. For the above three cases, respectively, that means the points are:

• -22.0 kHz, -21.9 kHz, $\ldots$, -0.1 kHz, 0, 0.1 kHz, $\ldots$, 21.9 kHz, 22.0 kHz
• -22.05 kHz, -22.04 kHz, $\ldots$, -10 Hz, 0, 10 Hz, $\ldots$, 22.04 kHz, 22.05 kHz
• -22.05 kHz, -22.049 kHz, $\ldots$, -1 Hz, 0, 1 Hz, $\ldots$, 22.049 kHz, 22.05 kHz

For practical purposes, the first of these is usually too coarse, the third is too fine, and the middle one is useful for many applications.

Note that the first range of frequencies above does not quite cover the range $\pm r/2$. But remember that this is a discrete representation of the actual frequency spectrum, and the proper interpretation would include the frequencies $+r/2$ and $-r/2$.

Also note that there are $N + 1$ points in each of the above ranges, not N. Indeed, the more general question is, how do these points in the frequency spectrum correspond to the indices $i = 0, 1, \ldots, N - 1$ in $\hat{x}[i]$? If we denote each of these frequencies as f, the answer is that:

$$f = \frac{ir}{N}, \quad i = 0, 1, \ldots, N - 1 \tag{20.7}$$

But note that this range of frequencies extends from 0 to $(N - 1)(r/N)$, which exceeds the Nyquist-Shannon sampling limit of $r/2$. The way out of this dilemma is to realize that the DFT assumes that the input signal is periodic in time, and therefore the DFT is periodic in frequency. In other words, values of f for indices i greater than $N/2$ can be interpreted as frequencies that are the *negation* of the frequency given by the formula above. Assuming even N, we can revise Equation 20.7 as follows:

$$f = \begin{cases} i\dfrac{r}{N}, & i = 0, 1, \ldots, \dfrac{N}{2} \\ (i - N)\dfrac{r}{N} & i = \dfrac{N}{2}, \dfrac{N}{2} + 1, \ldots, N - 1 \end{cases} \tag{20.8}$$

Note that when $i = N/2$, both equations apply, yielding $f = r/2$ in the first case and $f = -r/2$ in the second. Indeed, the magnitude of the DFT for each of these frequencies is the same (see discussion in the next section), reflecting the periodicity of the DFT, and thus is simply a form of redundancy.

The above discussion has assumed a periodic signal whose fundamental frequency is known, thus allowing us to parameterize the DFT with the same fundamental frequency. In practice, this rarely happens. That is, the fundamental frequency of the DFT typically has no integral relationship to the period of the periodic signal. This raises the question, what happens to the frequencies that "fall in the gaps" between the frequencies discussed above? The answer is that the energy of that frequency component will be distributed among neighboring points in a way that makes sense mathematically, although the result may look a little funny compared to the ideal result (where every frequency component is an integer multiple of the fundamental). The important thing to remember is that these are digital representations of the exact spectra, just as a digitized signal is representative of an exact signal. Two digitized signals can look very different (depending on sample rate, phase angle, and so on), yet represent the same underlying signal – the same is true of a digitized spectrum.

In practice, for reasons of computational efficiency, N is usually chosen to be a power of two. We will return to this issue when we discuss implementing the DFT.

20.2.2 Amplitude and Power of Spectrum

We discussed above how each sample in the result of a DFT relates to a point in the frequency spectrum of the input signal. But how do we determine the amplitude and phase angle of each of those frequency components? In general, each sample in the result of a DFT is a complex number, having both a real and imaginary part, of the form $a + jb$. We can visualize this number as a point in the complex Cartesian plane, where the abscissa (x-axis) represents the real part and the ordinate (y-axis) represents the imaginary part, as shown in Figure 20.3. It is easy to see that the line from the origin to the point of interest is a vector A, whose length is the *amplitude* of the frequency component in the spectrum:

$$A = \sqrt{a^2 + b^2} \tag{20.9}$$

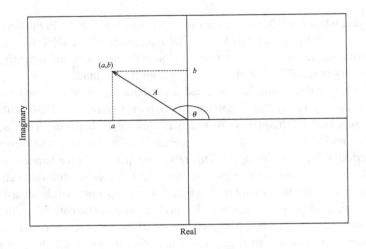

Figure 20.3 Complex and polar coordinates.

The angle θ is the *phase*, and it is easily defined from the figure as:

$$\theta = tan^{-1}\frac{b}{a} \tag{20.10}$$

(This amplitude/phase pair is often called the *polar* representation of a complex number.)

Recall from Section 18.1.2 that power is proportional to the square of the amplitude. Since taking a square root adds computational expense, the square root is often omitted from Equation 20.9, thus yielding a *power spectrum* instead of an *amplitude spectrum*.

One subtle aspect of the resulting DFT is how to interpret *negative* frequencies. In the case of having an input whose samples are all real numbers (i.e., there are no imaginary components), which is true for audio applications, the negative spectrum is a mirror image of the positive spectrum, and the amplitude/power is distributed evenly between the two.

20.2.3 A Haskell Implementation of the DFT

From Equation 20.5, which defines the DFT mathematically, we can write a Haskell program that implements the DFT.

The first thing we need to do is understand how complex numbers are handled in Haskell. They are captured in the *Complex* library, which must be imported into any program that uses them. The type *Complex T* is the type of complex numbers whose underlying numeric type is *T*. We will use, for example, *Complex Double* to test our DFT. A complex number $a + jb$ is represented in Haskell as $a :+ b$, and since $(:+)$ is a constructor, such values can be pattern-matched.

Details: Complex numbers in Haskell are captured in the *Complex* library, in which complex numbers are defined as a polymorphic data type:

infix 6 :+
data (*RealFloat a*) $\Rightarrow$ *Complex a* = !a :+ !a

The "!" in front of the type variables declares that the constructor $(:+)$ is strict in its arguments. For example, the complex number $a + jb$ is represented by $a :+ b$ in Haskell. One can pattern-match on complex number values to extract the real and imaginary parts, or use one of the predefined selectors defined in the *Complex* library:

realPart, imagPart :: *RealFloat a* $\Rightarrow$ *Complex a* $\rightarrow$ *a*

The *Complex* library also defines the following functions:

conjugate	:: *RealFloat a* ⇒ *Complex a* → *Complex a*
mkPolar	:: *RealFloat a* ⇒ *a* → *a* → *Complex a*
cis	:: *RealFloat a* ⇒ *a* → *Complex a*
polar	:: *RealFloat a* ⇒ *Complex a* → (*a, a*)
magnitude, phase	:: *RealFloat a* ⇒ *Complex a* → *a*

The library also declares instances of *Complex* for the type classes *Num*, *Fractional*, and *Floating*.

Although not as efficient as arrays, for simplicity we choose to use lists to represent the vectors that are the input and output of the DFT. Thus if *xs* is the list that represents the signal x, then *xs* !! *n* is the $n + 1$th sample of that signal and is equivalent to $x[n]$. Furthermore, using list comprehensions, we can make the Haskell code look very much like the mathematical definition captured in Equation 20.5. Finally, we adopt the convention that the length of the input signal is the number of samples that we will use for the DFT.

Probably the trickiest part of writing a Haskell program for the DFT is dealing with the types! In particular, if you look closely at Equation 20.5, you will see that N is used in three different ways – as an integer (for indexing), as a real number (in the exponent of e), and as a complex number (in the expression $1/N$).

Here is a Haskell program that implements the DFT:

```
dft :: RealFloat a ⇒ [Complex a] → [Complex a]
dft xs =
  let lenI = length xs
      lenR = fromIntegral lenI
      lenC = lenR :+ 0
  in [let i = −2 * pi * fromIntegral k / lenR
      in (1 / lenC) * sum [ (xs !! n) * exp (0 :+ i * fromIntegral n)
                          | n ← [0, 1 .. lenI − 1]]
     | k ← [0, 1 .. lenI − 1]]
```

Note that *lenI*, *lenR*, and *lenC* are the integer, real, and complex versions, respectively, of N. Otherwise the code is fairly straightforward – note in particular how list comprehensions are used to implement the ranges of n and k in Equation 20.5.

To test our program, let's first create a couple of waveforms. For example, recall that Equation 20.4 defines the Fourier series for a square wave. We can

```
printComplexL :: [Complex Double] → IO ()
printComplexL xs =
    let f (i, rl :+ im) =
            do putStr (spaces (3 − length (show i)))
               putStr (show i ++ " :    (" )
               putStr (niceNum rl ++ ",  " )
               putStr (niceNum im ++ ")\n" )
    in mapM_ f (zip [0 .. length xs − 1] xs)
niceNum :: Double → String
niceNum d =
    let d' = fromIntegral (round (1e10 ∗ d))/1e10
        (dec, fra) = break (== '.') (show d')
        (fra', exp) = break (== 'e') fra
    in spaces (3 − length dec) ++ dec ++ take 11 fra'
       ++ exp ++ spaces (12 − length fra' − length exp)
spaces :: Int → String
spaces n = take n (repeat ' ')
```

Figure 20.4 Helper code for pretty-printing DFT results.

implement the first, first two, and first three terms of this series, corresponding respectively to Figure 20.2a, b, and c, by the following Haskell code:

```
mkTerm :: Int → Double → [Complex Double]
mkTerm num n = let f = 2 ∗ pi/fromIntegral num
    in [sin (n ∗ f ∗ fromIntegral i)/n :+ 0
       | i ← [0, 1 .. num − 1]]

mkxa, mkxb, mkxc :: Int → [Complex Double]
mkxa num = mkTerm num 1
mkxb num = zipWith (+) (mkxa num) (mkTerm num 3)
mkxc num = zipWith (+) (mkxb num) (mkTerm num 5)
```

Thus *mkTerm num n* is the *n*th term in the series, using *num* samples.

Using the helper function *printComplexL* defined in Figure 20.4, which "pretty prints" a list of complex numbers, we can look at the result of our DFT in a more readable form.[3]

---

[3] "Pretty-printing" real numbers is a subtle task. The code in Figure 20.4 rounds the number to 10 decimal places of accuracy, and inserts spaces before and after to line up the decimal points and give a consistent string length. The fractional part is not padded with zeros, since that would give a false impression of its accuracy. (It is not necessary to understand this code in order to understand the concepts in this chapter.)

For example, suppose we want to take the DFT of a 16-sample representation of the first three terms of the square wave series. Typing the following at the GHCi prompt:

printComplexL (*dft* (*mkxc* 16))

will yield the result of the DFT, pretty-printing each number as a pair, along with its index:

```
 0 :  (   0.0          ,     0.0          )
 1 :  (   0.0          ,    -0.5          )
 2 :  (   0.0          ,     0.0          )
 3 :  (   0.0          ,    -0.1666666667 )
 4 :  (   0.0          ,     0.0          )
 5 :  (   0.0          ,    -0.1          )
 6 :  (   0.0          ,     0.0          )
 7 :  (   0.0          ,     0.0          )
 8 :  (   0.0          ,     0.0          )
 9 :  (   0.0          ,     0.0          )
10 :  (   0.0          ,     0.0          )
11 :  (   0.0          ,     0.1          )
12 :  (   0.0          ,     0.0          )
13 :  (   0.0          ,     0.1666666667 )
14 :  (   0.0          ,     0.0          )
15 :  (   0.0          ,     0.5          )
```

Let's study this result more closely. For the sake of argument, assume a sample rate of 1.6 kHz. Then by construction using *mkxc*, our square-wave input's fundamental frequency is 100 Hz. Similarly, recall that the resolution of the DFT is r/N, which is also 100 Hz.

Now compare the overall result to Figure 20.1b. Recalling also Equation 20.8, we note that the above DFT results are non-zero precisely at 100, 300, 500, −500, −300, and −100 Hz. This is just what we would expect. Furthermore, the amplitudes are one-half of the corresponding harmonically decreasing weights dictated by Equation 20.4, namely the values 1, 1/6, and 1/10 (recall the discussion in Section 20.2.2).

Let's do another example. We can create an impulse function as follows:

mkPulse :: *Int* → [*Complex Double*]
mkPulse n = 100 : *take* (n − 1) (*repeat* 0)

and print its DFT with the command:

printComplexL (*dft* (*mkPulse* 16))

whose effect is:

```
 0 :  (   6.25         ,     0.0          )
 1 :  (   6.25         ,     0.0          )
```

```
 2 :   (    6.25         ,     0.0              )
 3 :   (    6.25         ,     0.0              )
 4 :   (    6.25         ,     0.0              )
 5 :   (    6.25         ,     0.0              )
 6 :   (    6.25         ,     0.0              )
 7 :   (    6.25         ,     0.0              )
 8 :   (    6.25         ,     0.0              )
 9 :   (    6.25         ,     0.0              )
10 :   (    6.25         ,     0.0              )
11 :   (    6.25         ,     0.0              )
12 :   (    6.25         ,     0.0              )
13 :   (    6.25         ,     0.0              )
14 :   (    6.25         ,     0.0              )
15 :   (    6.25         ,     0.0              )
```

Compare this to Figure 20.1c, and note how the original magnitude of
the impulse (100) is distributed evenly among the 16 points in the DFT
(100/16 = 6.25).

So far we have considered only input signals whose frequency components
are integral multiples of the DFT's resolution. This rarely happens in practice,
however, because music is simply too complex, and noisy. As mentioned in
Section 20.2.1, the energy of the signals that "fall in the gaps" is distributed
among neighboring points, although not in as simple a way as you might
think. To get some perspective on this, let's do one other example. We define
a function to generate a signal whose frequency is π times the fundamental
frequency:

$x1\ num = \textbf{let}\ f = pi * 2 * pi / fromIntegral\ num$
   $\textbf{in}\ map\ (:+0)\ [sin\ (f * fromIntegral\ i)$
                  $|\ i \leftarrow [0, 1 .. num - 1]]$

π is an irrational number, but any number that "falls in the gaps" between
indices would do. We can see the result by typing the command:

$printComplexL\ (dft\ x1)$

which yields:

```
 0 :   ( -7.9582433e-3 ,      0.0              )
 1 :   ( -5.8639942e-3 ,   -1.56630897e-2)
 2 :   (  4.7412105e-3 ,   -4.56112124e-2)
 3 :   (  0.1860052232 ,   -0.4318552865 )
 4 :   ( -5.72962095e-2,    7.33993364e-2)
 5 :   ( -3.95845728e-2,    3.14378088e-2)
 6 :   ( -3.47994673e-2,    1.65400768e-2)
 7 :   ( -3.29813518e-2,    7.4048103e-3 )
 8 :   ( -3.24834325e-2,    0.0              )
 9 :   ( -3.29813518e-2,   -7.4048103e-3 )
10 :   ( -3.47994673e-2,   -1.65400768e-2)
```

```
11:   ( -3.95845728e-2,   -3.14378088e-2)
12:   ( -5.72962095e-2,   -7.33993364e-2)
13:   (  0.1860052232 ,    0.4318552865 )
14:   (  4.7412105e-3 ,    4.56112124e-2)
15:   ( -5.8639942e-3 ,    1.56630897e-2)
```

This is much more complicated than the previous examples! Not only do the points in the spectrum seem to have varying amounts of energy, they also have both non-zero real and non-zero imaginary components, meaning that the magnitude and phase vary at each point. We can define a function that converts a list of complex numbers into a list of their polar representations as follows:

$mkPolars :: [\,Complex\ Double\,] \to [\,Complex\ Double\,]$

$mkPolars = map\ ((\lambda(m,p) \to m \mathbin{:+} p) \circ polar)$

which we can then use to reprint our result:

$printComplexL\ (mkPolars\ (dft\ x1))$

```
 0:   (   7.9582433e-3 ,     3.1415926536 )
 1:   (   1.67247961e-2,    -1.9290259418 )
 2:   (   4.58569709e-2,    -1.4672199604 )
 3:   (   0.470209455 ,     -1.1640975898 )
 4:   (   9.31145435e-2,     2.2336013741 )
 5:   (   5.05497204e-2,     2.4704023271 )
 6:   (   3.85302097e-2,     2.6979021519 )
 7:   (   3.38023784e-2,     2.9207398294 )
 8:   (   3.24834325e-2,    -3.1415926536 )
 9:   (   3.38023784e-2,    -2.9207398294 )
10:   (   3.85302097e-2,    -2.6979021519 )
11:   (   5.05497204e-2,    -2.4704023271 )
12:   (   9.31145435e-2,    -2.2336013741 )
13:   (   0.470209455 ,      1.1640975898 )
14:   (   4.58569709e-2,     1.4672199604 )
15:   (   1.67247961e-2,     1.9290259418 )
```

If we focus on the magnitude (the first column), we can see that there is a peak near index 3 (corresponding roughly to the frequency π), with small amounts of energy elsewhere.

Exercise 20.1 Write a Haskell function *idft* that implements the *inverse* DFT as captured in Equation 20.3. Test your code by applying *idft* to one of the signals used earlier in this section. In other words, show empirically that, up to round-off errors, *idft (dft xs)* == *xs*.

Exercise 20.2 Use *dft* to analyze some of the signals generated using signal functions defined in Chapter 19.

Exercise 20.3 Define a function $mkSqWave :: Int \rightarrow Int \rightarrow [Complex\ Double]$ such that $mkSqWave\ num\ n$ is the sum of the first n terms of the Fourier series of a square wave, having num samples in the result.

Exercise 20.4 Prove mathematically that x and $\hat{x}$ are inverses. Also prove, using equational reasoning, that dft and $idft$ are inverses. (For the latter, you may assume that Haskell numeric types obey the standard axioms of real arithmetic.)   .

20.3 The Fast Fourier Transform

In the last section, a DFT program was developed in Haskell that was easy to understand, being a faithful translation of Equation 20.5. For pedagogical purposes, this effort served us well. However, for practical purposes, the program is inherently inefficient.

To see why, think of $x[n]$ and $\hat{x}[k]$ as vectors. Thus, for example, each element of $\hat{x}$ is the sum of N multiplications of a vector by a complex exponential (which can be represented as a pair, the real and imaginary parts). And this overall process must be repeated for each value of k, also N times. Therefore the overall time complexity of the implied algorithm is $O(N^2)$. For even moderate values of N, this can be computationally intractable. (Our choice of lists for the implementation of vectors makes the complexity even worse because of the linear-time complexity of indexing, but the discussion below makes this a moot point.)

Fortunately, there exists a much faster algorithm, called the *fast Fourier transform*, or FFT, that reduces the complexity to $O(N \log N)$. This difference is quite significant for large values of N and is the standard algorithm used in most signal processing applications. We will not go into the details of the FFT algorithm, other than to note that it is a divide-and-conquer algorithm that depends on the vector size being a power of two.[4]

Rather than developing our own program for the FFT, we will instead use the Haskell library *Numeric.FFT* to import a function that will do the job for us. Specifically:

fft :: ...

With this function, we can explore the use of the FFT on specific iinput vectors, as we did earlier with *dft*.

---

[4] The basic FFT algorithm was invented by James Cooley and John Tukey in 1965.

```
fftEx :: UISF () ()
fftEx = proc _ → do
    f ← hSlider (1, 2000) 440 —< ()
    (d, _) ← clockedSFToUISF 100 simpleSig —< f
    let (s, fft) = unzip d
    _ ← histogram (500, 150) 20 —< listToMaybe (catMaybes fft)
    _ ← realtimeGraph' (500, 150) 200 20 Black —< s
    outA —< ()
  where
    simpleSig :: SigFun CtrRate Double (Double, Event [Double])
    simpleSig = proc f → do
        s ← osc (tableSinesN 4096 [1]) 0 —< f
        fftData ← fftA 100 256 —< s
        outA —< (s, fftData)
t0 = runMUI (500, 600) "fft Test" fftEx
```

Figure 20.5 A real-time display of FFT results.

However, our ultimate goal is to have a version of the FFT that works on *signals*. We would like to be able to specify the number of samples as a power of two (which we can think of as the "window size"), the clock rate, and how often we would like to take a snapshot of the current window (and thus successive windows may or may not overlap). The resulting signal function takes a signal as input, and outputs *events* at the specified rate. Events are discussed in more detail in Chapter 17.

The HSoM library provides this functionality for us in a function called *fftA*:

$fftA :: Int → Double → Int → SF\ Double\ (Event\ FFTData)$
type $FFTData = Map\ Double\ Double$

SF is a signal function type similar to *SigFun*, except that it is targeted for use in the Musical User Interface (MUI) discussed in detail in Chapter 17, and thus, for example, does not have a clock rate. *Map T1 T2* is an abstract type that maps values of type *T1* to values of type *T2* and is imported from *Data.Map*.

fftA winInt rate size is a signal function that, for every *winInt* sample of the input, creates a window of size 2^{size} and computes the FFT of that window. For every such result, it issues an *Event* that maps from frequency to magnitude (using the clock rate *rate* to determine the proper mapping).

Combining *fftA* with the MUI widgets discussed in Chapter 17, we can write a simple program that generates a sine wave whose frequency is controlled by a slider, and whose real-time graph and FFT are displayed. The program to do this is shown in Figure 20.5.

20.4 Further Pragmatics

Exercise 20.5 Modify the program in Figure 20.5 in the following ways:

1. Add a second slider, and use it to control the frequency of a second oscillator.
2. Let *s1* and *s2* be the names of the signals whose frequencies are controlled by the first and second sliders, respectively. Instead of displaying the FFT of just *s1*, try a variety of combinations of *s1* and *s2*, such as *s1* + *s2*, *s1* − *s2*, *s1* ∗ *s2*, 1/*s1* + 1/*s2*, and *s1*/*s2*. Comment on the results.
3. Use *s2* to control the frequency of *s1* (as was done with *vibrato* in Chapter 19). Plot the fft of *s1* and comment on the result.
4. Instead of using *osc* to generate a pure sine wave, try using other oscillators and/or table generators to create more complex tones, and plot their FFTs. Comment on the results.

21

Additive and Subtractive Synthesis

There are many techniques for synthesizing sound. In this chapter we will discuss two of them: *additive synthesis* and *subtractive synthesis*. In practice it is rare for either of these, or any of the ones discussed in future chapters, to be utilized alone – a typical application may in fact employ all of them. But it is helpful to *study* them in isolation, so that the sound designer has a suitably rich toolbox of techniques at his or her disposal.

Additive synthesis is, conceptually at least, the simplest of the many sound synthesis techniques. Simply put, the idea is to add signals (usually sine waves of differing amplitudes, frequencies, and phases) together to form a sound of interest. It is based on Fourier's theorem, as discussed in the previous chapter, and indeed is sometimes called *Fourier synthesis*.

Subtractive synthesis is the dual of additive synthesis. The basic idea is to start with a signal rich in harmonic content, and selectively "remove" signals to create a desired effect.

In understanding the difference between the two, it is helpful to consider the following analogy to art:

- Additive synthesis is like painting a picture – each stroke of the brush, each color, each shape, each texture, and so on adds to the artist's conception of the final artistic artifact.
- In contract, subtractive synthesis is like creating a sculpture from stone – each stroke of the chisel takes away material that is unwanted, eventually revealing the artist's conception of what the artistic artifact should be.

Additive synthesis in the context of Euterpea will be discussed in Section 21.1, and subtractive synthesis in Section 21.2.

> **Details:** To use the *arrow syntax* described in this chapter, it is necessary to use the following compiler pragma in GHC:
>
> {-# LANGUAGE Arrows #-}

21.1 Additive Synthesis

When doing pure additive synthesis, it is often convenient to work with a *list of signal sources* whose elements are eventually summed together to form a result. To facilitate this, we define a few auxiliary functions, shown in Figure 21.1.

constSF s sf simply lifts the value *s* to the signal function level and composes that with *sf*, thus yielding a signal source.

foldSF f b sfs is analogous to *foldr* for lists: it returns the signal source *constA b* if the list is empty, and otherwise uses *f* to combine the results, pointwise, from the right. In other words, if *sfs* has the form:

[*sf1, sf2, ..., sfn*]

then the result will be:

proc () → **do**
    s1 ← *sf1* ─≺ ()
    s2 ← *sf2* ─≺ ()
    ...
    sn ← *sfn* ─≺ ()
    outA ─≺ *f s1* (*f s2* (...(*f sn b*)))

$constSF :: Clock\ c \Rightarrow a \to SigFun\ c\ a\ b \to SigFun\ c\ ()\ b$
$constSF\ s\ sf = constA\ s \ggg sf$
$foldSF :: Clock\ c \Rightarrow$
    $(a \to b \to b) \to b \to [SigFun\ c\ ()\ a] \to SigFun\ c\ ()\ b$
$foldSF\ f\ b\ sfs =$
    $foldr\ g\ (constA\ b)\ sfs$ **where**
        $g\ sfa\ sfb =$
            proc () → **do**
                s1 ← *sfa* ─≺ ()
                s2 ← *sfb* ─≺ ()
                outA ─≺ *f s1 s2*

Figure 21.1 Working with lists of signal sources.

21.1.1 Overtone Synthesis

Perhaps the simplest form of additive synthesis is combining a sine wave with some of its overtones to create a rich sound that is closer in harmonic content to that of a real instrument, as discussed in Chapter 18. Indeed, in Chapter 19 we saw several ways to do this using built-in Euterpea signal functions. For example, recall the function:

$oscPartials :: Clock\ c \Rightarrow$
$$Table \rightarrow Double \rightarrow SigFun\ c\ (Double, Int)\ Double$$

$oscPartials\ tab\ ph$ is a signal function whose pair of dynamic inputs determines the frequency of the output, as well as the number of harmonics of that frequency. So this is a "built-in" notion of additive synthesis. A problem with this approach in modeling a conventional instrument is that the partials all have the same strength, which does not reflect the harmonic content of most physical instruments.

A more sophisticated approach, also described in Chapter 19, is based on various ways to build look-up tables. In particular, this function was defined:

$tableSines3 ::$
$$TableSize \rightarrow [(PartialNum, PartialStrength, PhaseOffset)] \rightarrow Table$$

Recall that $tableSines3\ size\ triples$ is a table of size $size$ that represents a sinusoidal wave and an arbitrary number of partials, whose relationship to the fundamental frequency, amplitude, and phase are determined by each of the triples in $triples$.

21.1.2 Resonance and Standing Waves

As we know from Fourier's theorem, any periodic signal can be represented as a sum of a fundamental frequency and multiples of that fundamental frequency. We also know that a musical instrument's sound consists primarily of the sum of a fundamental frequency (the perceived pitch) and some of the multiples of that pitch (called harmonics, partials, or overtones). But what is it that makes a musical instrument behave this way in the first place? Answering this question can help us to understand how to use additive synthesis to generate an instrument sound, but becomes even more important in Chapter 23, where we attempt to model the physical attributes of a particular instrument.

String Instruments

To answer this question, let's start with a simple string, fixed at both ends. Now imagine that energy is inserted at some point along the string – perhaps by a finger pluck, a guitar pick, a violin bow, or a piano hammer. This energy will cause the string to vibrate in some way. The energy will flow along the string as a wave, just like ripples in water radiating from a dropped pebble, except that the energy only flows in one dimension, i.e., only along the orientation of the string. How fast the wave travels will depend on the string material and how taut it is. For example, the tauter the string, the faster the wave travels.

Because the ends of the string are fixed, however, the string can only vibrate in certain ways, which are called *modes*, or *resonances*. The most obvious mode for a string is shown in Figure 21.2a, where the center of the string is moving up and down, say, and the endpoints do not move at all. Energy that is not directly contributing to a particular mode is quickly absorbed by the fixed endpoints. A mode is sometimes called a "standin wave," since it appears to be standing still – it does not seem to be moving up or down the string. But another way to think of it is that the energy in the string is being *reflected back* at each endpoint of the string, and those reflections reinforce one another to form the standing wave.

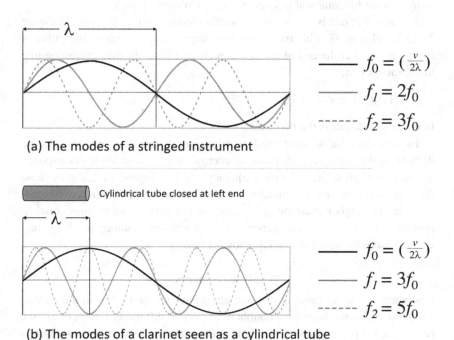

$$f_0 = \left(\frac{v}{2\lambda}\right)$$
$$f_1 = 2f_0$$
$$f_2 = 3f_0$$

(a) The modes of a stringed instrument

Cylindrical tube closed at left end

$$f_0 = \left(\frac{v}{2\lambda}\right)$$
$$f_1 = 3f_0$$
$$f_2 = 5f_0$$

(b) The modes of a clarinet seen as a cylindrical tube

Figure 21.2 Modes of a string and a wind instrument.

Eventually, of course, even the energy in a mode will dissipate, for three reasons: (1) since the ends of the string are never perfectly fixed, the reflections are not perfect either, and thus some energy is absorbed; (2) the movement of the string creates friction in the string material, generating heat and also absorbing energy; and (3) the transverse vibration of the string induces a longitudinal vibration in the air – i.e., the sound we hear – and that also absorbs some energy.

To better understand the nature of modes, suppose a pulse of energy is introduced at one end of the string. If v is the velocity of the resulting wave traveling along the string and λ is the string length, then it takes λ/v seconds for a wave to travel the length of the string and $p = 2\lambda/v$ for it to travel up and back. So if the pulse is repeated every p seconds, it will reinforce the previous pulse. If we think of p as the period of a periodic signal, its frequency in Hertz is the *reciprocal* of the period p:

$$f_0 = v/(2\lambda)$$

Indeed, this is the frequency of the mode shown in Figure 21.2a and corresponds to the fundamental frequency, i.e., the observed pitch.

But note that this is not the only possible mode – another is shown in Figure 21.2a, labeled as f_1. This mode can be interpreted as repeating the pulse of energy inserted at the end of the string every $p/2$ seconds, thus corresponding to a frequency of:

$$f_1 = 1/(p/2) = v/\lambda = 2f_0$$

In other words, this is the first overtone.

Indeed, each subsequent mode corresponds to an overtone and can be derived in the same way. A pulse of energy every p/n seconds corresponds to the $(n-1)$th overtone with frequency nf_0 Hz. Figure 21.2 shows these derivations for the first four modes; i.e., the fundamental plus three overtones.

Note: The higher overtones generally, but not always, decay more quickly, primarily because they are generated by a quicker bending of the string, causing more friction and a quicker loss of energy.

Wind Instruments

Resonances in other musical instruments behave similarly. But in the case of a wind instrument, there are a couple of important differences. First of all, the resonance happens within the air itelf, rather than on a string. For example, a clarinet can be thought of as a *cylindrical tube* closed at one end. The closed end is the mouthpiece, and the open end is called the "bell." The closed end, like the fixed end of a string, reflects energy directly back in the opposite direction. But because the open end is open, it behaves differently. In particular, as energy (a wave) escapes the open end, its pressure is dissipated into the air. This causes a pressure drop that induces a negative pressure – i.e., a vacuum – in the opposite direction, causing the wave to reflect back, *but inverted!*

Unfortunately, we cannot easily visualize the standing wave in a clarinet, partly because the air is invisible, but also because (1) the wave is *longitudinal*, whereas for a string it is transverse, and (2) as just discussed, the open end inverts the signal upon reflection. The best we can do is create a transverse representation. For example, Figure 21.2a represents the fundamental mode, or fundamental frequency. Note that the left, closed end looks the same as for a fixed string – i.e., it is at the zero crossing of the sine wave. But the right end is different – it is intended to depict the inversion at the open end of the clarinet as the maximum absolute value of the sine wave. If the signal comes in at $+1$, it is inverted to the value -1, and so on.

Analogous to our detailed analysis of a string, we can analyze a clarinet's acoustic behavior as follows: Suppose a pulse of energy is introduced at the mouthpiece (i.e., closed end). If v is the velocity of sound in the air and λ is the length of the clarinet, that wave appears at the open end in λ/v seconds. Its *inverted* reflection then appears back at the mouthpiece in $2 * \lambda/v$ seconds. But because it is inverted, *it will cancel out another pulse emitted $2 * \lambda/v$ seconds after the first!* On the other hand, suppose we let that reflection bounce off the closed end, travel back to the open end to be inverted a second time, and then return to the closed end. Two inversions are like no inversion at all, and so if we were to insert another pulse of energy at that moment, the two signals will be "in sync." In other words, if we repeat the pulse every $4\lambda/v$ seconds, the peaks and troughs of the signals line up and will reinforce one another. This corresponds to a frequency of:

$$f_0 = v/(4\lambda)$$

and is in fact the fundamental mode, or fundamental frequency, of the clarinet. This situation corresponds precisely to Figure 21.2a.

Now here is the interesting part: If we were to double the pulse rate in hopes of generating the first overtone, we would arrive precisely at the situation we were in above: the signals cancel out. Thus, *a clarinet has no first overtone!* On the other hand, if we triple the pulse rate, the signals line up again, corresponding to a frequency of:

$$f_1 = v/((4/3)\lambda) = (3v)/(4\lambda) = 3f_0$$

This is the clarinet's second mode, and corresponds to Figure 21.2.

By a similar argument, it can be shown that all the even overtones of a clarinet don't exist (or, equivalently, have zero amplitude), whereas all of the odd overtones do exist. Figure 21.2b shows the first three modes of a clarinet, corresponding to the fundamental frequency and third and fifth overtones. (Note, by the way, the similarity of this to the spectral content of a square wave.)

Exercise 21.1 If $\omega = 2\pi f$ is the fundamental radial frequency, the sound of a sustained note for a typical clarinet can be approximated by:

$$s(t) = \sin(\omega t) + 0.75 \sin(3\omega t) + 0.5 \sin(5\omega t) + 0.14 \sin(7\omega t)$$
$$+ 0.5 \sin(9\omega t) + 0.12 \sin(11\omega t) + 0.17 \sin(13\omega t)$$

Define an instrument *clarinet* :: *Instr* (*Mono AudRate*) that simulates this sound. Add an envelope to it to make it more realistic. Then test it with a simple melody.

21.1.3 Deviating from Pure Overtones

Sometimes, however, these built-in functions don't achieve exactly what we want. In that case, we can define our own customized notion of additive synthesis, in whatever way we desire. For a simple example, traditional harmony is the simultaneous playing of more than one note at a time, and thus an instance of additive synthesis. More interestingly, richer sounds can be created by using slightly "out-of-tune" overtones; that is, overtones that are not an exact multiple of the fundamental frequency. This creates a kind of "chorusing" effect, very "electronic" in nature. Some real instruments in fact exhibit this kind of behavior, and sometimes the degree of being "out of tune" is not quite fixed.

21.1.4 A Bell Sound

Synthesizing a bell or gong sound is a good example of "brute force" additive synthesis. Physically, a bell or gong can be thought of as a bunch of concentric rings, each having a different resonant frequency, because they differ in diameter depending on the shape of the bell. Some of the rings will be more dominant than others, but the important thing to note is that these resonant frequencies often do not have an integral relationship with one another, and sometimes the higher frequencies can be quite strong, rather than roll off significantly, as with many other instruments. Indeed, it is sometime difficult to say exactly what the pitch of a particular bell is (especially a large bell),

```
bell1 :: Instr (Mono AudRate)
    -- Dur → AbsPitch → Volume → AudSF () Double
bell1 dur ap vol [] =
  let f  = apToHz ap
      v  = fromIntegral vol / 100
      d  = fromRational dur
      sfs = map (λp → constA (f * p) ⋙ osc tab1 0)
              [4.07, 3.76, 3, 2.74, 2, 1.71, 1.19, 0.92, 0.56]
  in proc () → do
      aenv ← envExponSeg [0, 1, 0.001] [0.003, d − 0.003] ⤙ ()
      a1   ← foldSF (+) 0 sfs ⤙ ()
      outA ⤙ a1 * aenv * v / 9
tab1 = tableSinesN 4096 [1]
bellTest1 = outFile "bell1.wav" 6 (bell1 6 (absPitch (C, 5)) 100 [])
```

Figure 21.3 A bell instrument.

so complex is its sound. Of course, the pitch of a bell can be controlled by minimizing the taper of its shape (especially for a small bell), thus giving it more of a pitched sound.

In any case, a pitched instrument representing a bell sound can be designed using additive synthesis by using the instrument's absolute pitch to create a series of partials that are conspicuously non-integral multiples of the fundamental. If this sound is then shaped by an envelope with a sharp rise time and a relatively slow, exponentially decreasing decay, we get a decent result. A Euterpea program to achieve this is shown in Figure 21.3. Note the use of *map* to create the list of partials and *foldSF* to add them together. Also note that some of the partials are expressed as *fractions* of the fundamental – i.e., their frequencies are less than that of the fundamental!

The reader might wonder why we don't just use one of Euterpea's table-generating functions, such as *tableSines3* discussed above, to generate a table with all the desired partials. The problem is, even though the *PartialNum* argument to *tableSines3* is a *Double*, the normal intent is that the partial numbers should all be integral. To see why, suppose 1.5 were one of the partial numbers; then 1.5 cycles of a sine wave would be written into the table. But the whole point of wavetable look-up synthesis is to repeatedly cycle through the table, which means that this 1.5 cycle would get repeated, since the wavetable is a periodic representation of the desired sound. The situation gets worse with partials such as 4.07, 3.75, 2.74, 0.56, and so on.

In any case, we can do even better than *bell1*. An important aspect of a bell sound that is not captured by the program in Figure 21.3 is that the higher-frequency partials tend to decay more quickly than the lower ones. We can

```
bell2 :: Instr (Mono AudRate)
       -- Dur → AbsPitch → Volume → AudSF () Double
bell2 dur ap vol [] =
  let f  = apToHz ap
      v  = fromIntegral vol / 100
      d  = fromRational dur
      sfs = map (mySF f d)
              [4.07, 3.76, 3, 2.74, 2, 1.71, 1.19, 0.92, 0.56]
  in proc () → do
      a1  ← foldSF (+) 0 sfs ―≺ ()
      outA ―≺ a1 * v/9
mySF f d p = proc () → do
      s    ← osc tab1 0 ≪ constA (f * p) ―≺ ()
      aenv ← envExponSeg [0, 1, 0.001] [0.003, d/p − 0.003] ―≺ ()
      outA ―≺ s * aenv
bellTest2 = outFile "bell2.wav" 6 (bell2 6 (absPitch (C, 5)) 100 [])
```

Figure 21.4 A more sophisticated bell instrument.

remedy this by giving each partial its own envelope (recall Section 19.4.2) and making the duration of the envelope inversely proportional to the partial number. Such a more sophisticated instrument is shown in Figure 21.4. This results in a much more pleasing and realistic sound.

Exercise 21.2 A problem with the more sophisticated bell sound in Figure 21.4 is that the duration of the resulting sound exceeds the specified duration of the note, because some of the partial numbers are less than one. Fix this.

Exercise 21.3 Neither of the bell sounds shown in Figures 21.3 and 21.4 actually contains the fundamental frequency – i.e., a partial number of 1.0. Yet they contain the partials at the integer multiples 2 and 3. How does this affect the result? What happens if you add in the fundamental?

Exercise 21.4 Use the idea of the "more sophisticated bell" to synthesize sounds other than a bell. In particular, try using only integral multiples of the fundamental frequency.

21.2 Subtractive Synthesis

As mentioned in the introduction to this chapter, subtractive synthesis involves starting with a harmonically rich sound source and selectively taking away sounds to create a desired effect. In signal processing terms, we "take away" sounds using *filters*.

21.2.1 Filters

Filters can be arbitrarily complex, but are characterized by a *transfer function* that captures, in the frequency domain, how much of each frequency component of the input is transferred to the output. Figure 21.5 shows the general transfer function for the four most common forms of filters:

1. A *low-pass* filter passes low frequencies and rejects (i.e., attenuates) high frequencies.
2. A *high-pass* filter passes high frequencies and rejects (i.e., attenuates) low frequencies.
3. A *band-pass* filter passes a particular band of frequencies while rejecting others.
4. A *band-reject* (or *band-stop*, or *notch*) filter rejects a particular band of frequencies while passing others.

It should be clear that filters can be combined in sequence or in parallel to achieve more complex transfer functions. For example, a low-pass and a high-pass filter can be combined in sequence to create a band-pass filter, and can be combined in parallel to create a band-reject filter.

In the case of a low-pass or high-pass filter, the *cut-off frequency* is usually defined as the point at which the signal is attenuated by 6 dB. A similar strategy is used to define the upper and lower bounds of the band that is passed by a band-pass filter or rejected by a band-reject filter, except that the band is usually specified using a *center frequency* (the midpoint of the band) and a *bandwidth* (the width of the band).

It is important to realize that not all filters of a particular type are alike. Two low-pass filters, for example, may, of course, have different cutoff frequencies, but even if the cutoff frequencies are the same, the "steepness" of the cutoff curves may be different (a filter with an ideal step curve for its transfer function does not exist), and the other parts of the curve might not be the same – they are never completely flat or even linear, and might not even be monotonically increasing or decreasing. (Although the diagrams in Figure 21.5 at least do not show a step curve, they are stll oversimplified in the smoothness and flatness of the curves.) Furthermore, all filters have some degree of *phase distortion*, which is to say that the transferred phase angle can vary with frequency.

In the digital domain, filters are often described using *recurrence equations* of varying degrees, and there is an elegant theory of filter design that can help predict and therefore control the various characteristics mentioned above. However, this theory is beyond the scope of this textbook. A good book on digital signal processing will elaborate on these issues in detail.

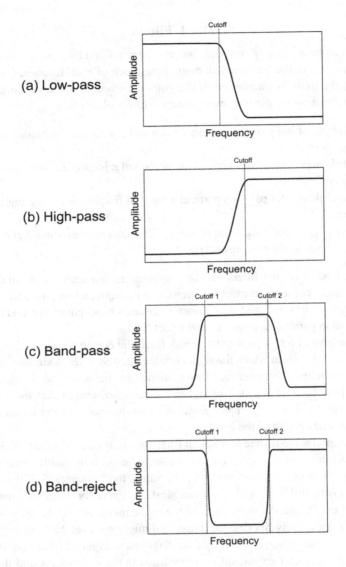

Figure 21.5 Transfer functions for the four most common types of filters.

21.2.2 Euterpea's Filters

Instead of designing our own filters, we will use a set of predefined filters in Euterpea that are adequate for most sound synthesis applications. Their type signatures are shown in Figure 21.6. As you can see, each of the filter types discussed previously is included, but their use requires a bit more explanation.

filterLowPass, filterHighPass, filterLowPassBW, filterHighPassBW ::
  Clock p ⇒ *SigFun p* (*Double, Double*) *Double*
filterBandPass, filterBandStop ::
  Clock p ⇒ *Int* → *SigFun p* (*Double, Double, Double*) *Double*
filterBandPassBW, filterBandStopBW ::
  Clock p ⇒ *SigFun p* (*Double, Double, Double*) *Double*

Figure 21.6 Euterpea's filters.

First of all, all of the filters ending in "*BW*" are what are called *Butterworth filters*, which are based on a second-order filter design that represents a good balance of filter characteristics: a good cutoff steepness, little phase distortion, and a reasonably flat response in both the pass and reject regions. Those filters without the *BW* suffix are first-order filters whose characteristics are not quite as good as the Butterworth filters, but are computationally more efficient.

In addition, the following points help explain the details of specific Euterpea filters:

- *filterLowPass* is a signal function whose input is a pair consisting of the signal being filtered and the cutoff frequency (in that order). Note that this means the cutoff frequency can vary dynamically. *filterHighPass*, *filterLowPassBW*, and *filterHighPassBW* behave analogously.
- *filterBandPassBW* is a signal function that takes a triple as input: the signal being filtered, the center frequency of the band, and the width of the band, in that order. For example:

  ...

  filterBandPassBW —≺ (*s*, 2000, 100)

  ...

  will pass the frequencies in *s* that are in the range 1,950–2,050 Hz, and reject the others. *filterBandStop* behaves analogously.
- *filterBandPass* and *filterBandStop* also behave analogously, except that they take a static *Int* argument, let's call it *m*, that has the following effect on the magnitude of the output:

  - $m = 0$ signifies no scaling of the output signal.
  - $m = 1$ signifies a peak response factor of 1; i.e., all frequencies other than the center frequency are attenuated in accordance with a normalized response curve.
  - $m = 2$ raises the response factor so that the output signal's overall RMS value equals 1.

21.2.3 Sources of Noise

Returning to the art metaphor at the beginning of this chapter, filters are like the chisels and other tools that a sculptor might use to fashion his or her work. But what about the block of stone that the sculptor begins with? What is the sound synthesis analogy to that?

The answer is some kind of a "noisy signal." It does not have to be pure noise in a signal processing sense, but in general its frequency spectrum will be rather broad and dense. Indeed, we have already seen (but not discussed) one way to do this in Euterpea: Recall the table generators *tableSines*, *tableSinesN*, *tableSines3*, and *tableSines3N*. When used with *osc*, these can generate very dense series of partials, which in the limit sound like pure noise.

In addition, Euterpea provides three sources of pure noise, that is, noise derived from a random number generator: *noiseWhite*, *noiseBLI*, and *noiseBLH*. More specifically:

1. *noiseWhite* :: *Clock p* $\Rightarrow$ *Int* $\rightarrow$ *SigFun p* () *Double*
   noiseWhite n is a signal source that generates uniform white noise with an RMS value of $1/\sqrt{2}$, where n is the "seed" of the underlying random number generator.
2. *noiseBLI* :: *Clock p* $\Rightarrow$ *Int* $\rightarrow$ *SigFun p Double Double*
   noiseBLI n is like *noiseWhite n*, except that the signal samples are generated at a rate controlled by the (dynamic) input signal (presumably less than 44.1kHz), with interpolation performed between samples. Such a signal is called "band-limited" because the slower rate prevents spectral content higher than half the rate.
3. *noiseBLH* :: *Clock p* $\Rightarrow$ *Int* $\rightarrow$ *SigFun p Double Double*
   noiseBLH is like *noiseBLI*, but does not interpolate between samples; rather, it "holds" the value fo the last sample.

22
Amplitude and Frequency Modulation

To *modulate* something is to change it in some way. In signal processing, *amplitude modulation* is the process of modifying a signal's amplitude *by another signal*. Similarly, *frequency modulation* is the process of modifying a signal's frequency *by another signal*. These are both powerful sound synthesis techniques that will be discussed in this chapter.

22.1 Amplitude Modulation

Technically speaking, whenever the amplitude of a signal is dynamically changed, it is a form of *amplitude modulation,* or *AM* for short; that is, we are modulating the amplitude of a signal. So, for example, shaping a signal with an envelope and adding tremolo are both forms of AM. In this section more interesting forms of AM are explored, including their mathematical basis. To help distinguish these forms of AM from others, we define a few terms:

- The dynamically changing signal that is doing the modulation is called the *modulating signal.*
- The signal being modulated is sometimes called the *carrier.*
- A *unipolar signal* is one that is always either positive or negative (usually positive).
- A *bipolar signal* is one that takes on both positive and negative values (that are often symmetric and thus average out to zero over time).

So, shaping a signal using an envelope is an example of amplitude modulation using a unipolar modulating signal whose frequency is very low (to be precise, $1/dur$, where *dur* is the length of the note), and in fact only one cycle of that signal is used. Likewise, tremolo is an example of amplitude

331

modulation with a unipolar modulating signal whose frequency is a bit higher than with envelope shaping, but still quite low (typically 2–10 Hz). In both cases, the modulating signal is infrasonic.

Note that a bipolar signal can be made unipolar, or the other way around, by adding or subtracting an offset (sometimes called a DC offset, where DC is short for "direct current"). This is readily seen if we try to mathematically formalize the notion of tremolo. Specifically, tremolo can be defined as adding an offset of 1 to an infrasonic sine wave whose frequency is f_t (typically 2–10 Hz), multiplying that by a "depth" argument d (in the range 0–1), and using the result as the modulating signal; the carrier frequency is f:

$$(1 + d \times \sin(2\pi f_t t)) \times \sin(2\pi f t)$$

Based on this equation, here is a simple tremolo envelope generator written in Euterpea and defined as a signal source (see Exercise 19.2):

```
tremolo :: Clock c ⇒
           Double → Double → SigFun c () Double
tremolo tfrq dep = proc () → do
    trem ← osc tab1 0 ─≺ tfrq
    outA ─≺ 1 + dep * trem
```

22.1.1 AM Sound Synthesis

But what happens when the modulating signal is audible, just like the carrier signal? This is where things get interesting from a sound synthesis point of view, and can result in a rich blend of sounds. To understand this mathematically, recall this trigonometric identity:

$$\sin(C) \times \sin(M) = \frac{1}{2}(\cos(C - M) - \cos(C + M))$$

or, sticking entirely with cosines:

$$\cos(C) \times \cos(M) = \frac{1}{2}(\cos(C - M) + \cos(C + M))$$

These equations demonstrate that AM in a sense is just a form of additive synthesis. Indeed, the equations imply two ways to implement AM in Euterpea: We could directly multiply the two outputs, as specified by the left-hand sides of the equations above, or we could add two signals, as specified by the right-hand sides of the equations.

Note the following:

1. When the modulating frequency is the same as the carrier frequency, the right-hand sides above reduce to $1/2 \cos(2C)$. That is, we essentially double the frequency.
2. Since multiplication is commutative, the following is also true:

$$\cos(C) \times \cos(M) = \frac{1}{2}(\cos(M - C) + \cos(M + C))$$

which is valid because $\cos(t) = \cos(-t)$.
3. Scaling the modulating signal or carrier just scales the entire signal, since multiplication is associative.

Also note that adding a third modulating frequency yields the following:

$$
\begin{aligned}
&\cos(C) \times \cos(M1) \times \cos(M2) \\
&= (0.5 \times (\cos(C - M1) \times \cos(C + M1))) \times \cos(M2) \\
&= 0.5 \times (\cos(C - M1) \times \cos(M2) + \cos(C + M1) \times \cos(M2)) \\
&= 0.25 \times (\cos(C - M1 - M2) + \cos(C - M1 + M2) \\
&\quad + \cos(C + M1 - M2) + \cos(C + M1 + M2))
\end{aligned}
$$

In general, combining n signals using amplitude modulation results in 2^{n-1} signals. AM used in this way for sound synthesis is sometimes called *ring modulation*, because the analog circuit (of diodes) originally used to implement this technique took the shape of a ring. Some nice "bell-like" tones can be generated with this technique.

22.1.2 What Do Tremolo and AM Radio Have in Common?

Combining the previous two ideas, we can use a bipolar carrier in the *electromagnetic spectrum* (i.e., the radio spectrum) and a unipolar modulating frequency in the *audible* range, which we can represent mathematically as:

$$\cos(C) \times (1 + \cos(M)) = \cos(C) + 0.5 \times (\cos(C - M) + \cos(C + M))$$

Indeed, this is how AM radio works. The above equation says that AM radio results in a carrier signal plus two sidebands. To completely cover the audible frequency range, the modulating frequency would need to be as much as 20 kHz, thus yielding sidebands of ±20 kHz, thus requiring station separation of at least 40 kHz. Yet, note that AM radio stations are separated by only 10 kHz! (540 kHz, 550 kHz, ..., 1,600 kHz). This is because at the time commercial AM radio was developed, a fidelity of 5 kHz was considered "good enough."

Also note that the amplitude of the modulating frequency does matter:

$$\cos(C) \times (1 + A \times \cos(M)) = \cos(C) + 0.5 \times A \times (\cos(C - M) + \cos(C + M))$$

A, called the *modulation index*, controls the size of the sidebands. Note the similarity of this equation to that for tremolo.

22.2 Frequency Modulation

Frequency modulation, or *FM*, modulates the frequency of a signal. In music, vibrato is an example of this: the frequency of a signal varies sinusoidally at a particular frequency, usually less than 10 Hz. Vibrato is typically used for melodic emphasis. Similarly to AM modulation, it is also used to send signals over radio waves.

22.3 Examples

Here is an example of an instrument that combines AM and FM synthesis by taking the frequency and amplitude for both tremolo and vibrato from *PField*s in the *Music* value:

```
amfmInst :: Instr (Mono AudRate)
amfmInst dur ap vol ps =
  let f = apToHz ap
      v = fromIntegral vol / 100
      d = fromRational dur
      (tremAmt, tremFreq, vibAmt, vibFreq) =
          if length ps < 4 then (0, 1, 0, 1)
          else (ps !! 0, ps !! 1, ps !! 2, ps !! 3)
  in proc () → do
      asr     ← envLineSeg [0, 1, 1, 0] [d ∗ 0.01, d ∗ 0.98, d ∗ 0.01] ─≺ ()
      vibSig  ← osc tab1 0 ─≺ vibFreq
      sineSig ← osc tab1 0 ─≺ f + f ∗ vibSig ∗ vibAmt
      tremEnv ← tremolo tremFreq tremAmt ─≺ ()
      outA ─≺ (1 − tremAmt) ∗ asr ∗ tremEnv ∗ sineSig
```

We can now observe the output from different combinations of parameters. Note that tremolo and vibrato can sometimes sound quite similar, even though the effect on the waveform is quite different!

iMap :: *InstrMap* (*Mono AudRate*)

iMap = [(*CustomInstrument* "AMFM", *amfmInst*)]

mkAMFM :: *FilePath* → [*Double*] → *IO* ()

mkAMFM str p = *writeWav str iMap* $
  instrument (*CustomInstrument* "AMFM") $
  note 2 ((*C*, 4 :: *Octave*), [*Params p*])

amfm1 = *mkAMFM* "amfm1.wav" []   -- neither trem nor vib
amfm2 = *mkAMFM* "amfm2.wav" [0.2, 1.5, 0.0, 1.0]   -- trem only
amfm3 = *mkAMFM* "amfm3.wav" [0.0, 1.0, 0.02, 4.0]   -- vib only
amfm4 = *mkAMFM* "amfm4.wav" [0.2, 1.5, 0.02, 4.0]   -- both

When the frequencies for tremolo and vibrato are taken into the audible range (typically over 20 Hz), the effects can be interesting, introducing overtones or distortion into the sound.

amfm5 = *mkAMFM* "amfm5.wav" [0.2, 50.0, 0.0, 1.0]   -- trem only
amfm6 = *mkAMFM* "amfm6.wav" [0.0, 1.0, 0.05, 100.0]   -- vib only
amfm7 = *mkAMFM* "amfm7.wav" [0.2, 50.0, 0.05, 100.0]   -- both

23

Physical Modeling

23.1 Introduction

So far we have focused on sound synthesis techniques that are isolated from any notion of a physical object. Physical modeling is a technique that involves emulating actual parts of something, such as simulating the effect of air flowing through a tube or the motion of a plucked string on a guitar.

23.2 Delay Lines

An important tool for physical modeling is the *delay line*. In this section we will discuss the basic concepts of a delay line and the delay line signal functions in Eutperpea, and give a couple of fun examples that do not yet involve physical modeling.

Conceptually, a delay line is fairly simple: it delays a signal by a certain number of seconds (or, equivalently, by a certain number of samples at some given sample rate). If s is the number of samples in the delay line and r is the clock rate, then the delay d is given by:

$$d = s/r$$

In the case of audio, of course, r will be 44.1 kHz. So to achieve a one-second delay, s would be chosen to be 44,100. In essence, a delay line is a *queue* or *FIFO* data structure.

In Euterpea there is a family of delay lines whose type signatures are given in Figure 23.1. Their behaviors can be described as follows:

- *delay x* is a delay line with one element, which is initialized to *x*.
- *delayLineT s tab* is a delay line whose length is *s* and whose contents are initialized to the values in the table *tab* (presumably of length *s*).

Fixed-length delay line, initialized with a table:

$delayLineT :: Clock\ c \Rightarrow$
$\qquad Int \rightarrow Table \rightarrow SigFun\ c\ Double\ Double$

Fixed-length delay line, initialized with zeros:

$delayLine :: Clock\ c \Rightarrow$
$\qquad Double \rightarrow SigFun\ c\ Double\ Double$

Delay line with variable tap:

$delayLine1 :: Clock\ c \Rightarrow$
$\qquad Double \rightarrow SigFun\ c\ (Double, Double)\ Double$

Figure 23.1 Euterpea's delay lines.

- *delayLine d* is a delay line whose length achieves a delay of d seconds.
- *delayLine1 d* is a "tapped delay line" whose length achieves a maximum delay of d seconds, but whose actual output is a "tap" that results in a delay of somewhere between 0 and d seconds. The tap is controlled dynamically. For example, in:

$\qquad \ldots$
$\qquad out \leftarrow delayLine1\ d \prec (s, t)$
$\qquad \ldots$

s is the input signal and t is the tap delay, which can vary between 0 and d.

Before using delay lines for physical modeling, we will explore a few simple applications that should give the reader a good sense of how they work.

23.2.1 Simulating an Oscillator

Let's contrast a delay line to the oscillators introduced in Chapter 19 that are initialized with a table (like *osc*). These oscillators cycle repetitively through a given table at a variable rate. Using *delayLineT*, a delay line can also be initialized as a table, but it is processed at a fixed rate (i.e., the clock rate) – at each step, one value goes in and one goes out.

Nevertheless, we can simulate an oscillator by initializing the delay line with one cycle of a sine wave and "feeding back" the output to the input, as shown in Figure 23.2a. At the standard audio sample rate, if the table size is s, then it takes $s/44,100$ seconds to output one cycle, and therefore the resulting frequency is the reciprocal of that:

$$f = 44,100/s$$

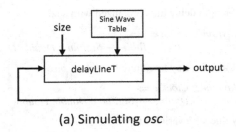

(a) Simulating *osc*

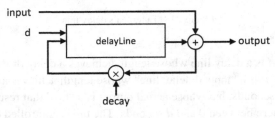

(b) Echo effect

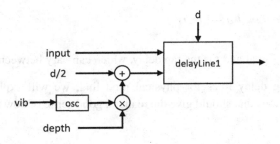

(c) Modular vibrato

Figure 23.2 Delay line examples.

There is one problem, however: when coding this idea in Haskell, we'd like to write something like:

```
...
x ← delayLineT s table ≺ x
...
```

However, arrow syntax in its standard form does not allow recursion! Fortunately, arrow syntax supports a keyword **rec** that allows us to specify where recursion takes place. For example to generate a tone of 441 Hz we need a table size of 44,100/441 = 100, leading to:

sineTable441 :: *Table*
sineTable441 = *tableSinesN* 100 [1]
s441 :: *AudSF* () *Double*
s441 = **proc** () → **do**
   rec *s* ← *delayLineT* 100 *sineTable441* ⤙ *s*
   outA ⤙ *s*
ts441 = *outFile* "s441.wav" 5 *s441*

23.2.2 Echo Effect

Perhaps a more obvious use of a delay line is to simply delay a signal! But to make this more exciting, let's go one step further and *echo* the signal, using feedback. To prevent the signal from echoing forever, let's decay it a bit each time it is fed back. A diagram showing this strategy is shown in Figure 23.2b, and the resulting code is:

echo :: *AudSF Double Double*
echo = **proc** *s* → **do**
   rec *fb* ← *delayLine* 0.5 ⤙ *s* + 0.7 ∗ *fb*
   outA ⤙ *fb* / 3

Here the delay time is 0.5 seconds and the decay rate is 0.7.

23.2.3 Modular Vibrato

Recall that we previously defined a tremolo signal function that could take an arbitrary signal and add tremolo. This is because tremolo simply modulates the amplitude of a signal, which could be anything – music, speech, whatever – and can be done after that sound is generated. So we could define a function:

tremolo :: *Rate* → *Depth* → *AudSF Double Double*

to achieve the result we want.

Can we do the same for vibrato? In the version of vibrato we defined in Chapter 22, we used frequency modulation – but that involved modulating the actual frequency of a specific oscillator, *not* the output of the oscillator that generated a sine wave of that frequency. So using that technique, at least, it doesn't seem possible to define a function such as:

vibrato :: *Rate* → *Depth* → *AudSF Double Double*

that would achieve our needs. Indeed, if we were using additive synthesis, we might imagine having to add vibrato to every sine wave that makes up the result. Not only is this a daunting task, but in effect we would lose modularity!

But in fact we can define a "modular" vibrato using a delay line with a variable tap. The idea is this: Send a signal into a tapped delay line, adjust the initial tap to the center of that delay line, then move it back and forth sinusoidally at a certain rate to control the frequency of the vibrato, and move it a certain distance (with a maximum of one-half the delay line's maximum delay) to achieve the depth. This idea is shown pictorially in Figure 23.2c, and the code is as follows:

```
modVib :: Double → Double → AudSF Double Double
modVib rate depth =
    proc sin → do
        vib  ← osc sineTable 0 −≺ rate
        sout ← delayLine1 0.2 −≺ (sin, 0.1 + 0.005 * vib)
        outA −≺ sout
tModVib = outFile "modvib.wav" 6 $
    constA 440 ⋙ osc sineTable 0 ⋙ modVib 5 0.005
```

23.3 Karplus-Strong Algorithm

Now that we know how delay lines work, let's look at their use in physical modeling. The *Karplus-Strong algorithm* [35] was one of the first algorithms classified as "physical modeling." It's a good model for synthesizing plucked strings and drum-like sounds. The basic idea is to use a recursive delay line to feed back a signal onto itself, thus simulating the standing wave modes discussed in Section 21.1.2. The result is affected by the initial values in the delay line, the length of the delay line, and any processing in the feedback loop. A diagram that depicts this algorithm is shown in Figure 23.3a.

23.3.1 Physical Model of a Flute

Figure 23.4 shows a physical model of a flute, based on the model of a "slide flute" proposed by Perry Cook in [36]. Although described as a slide flute, it sounds remarkably similar to a regular flute. Note that the lower-right part of the diagram looks just like the feedback loop in the Karplus-Strong algorithm. The rest of the diagram is intended to model the breath, including vibrato, which drives a "pitched" embouchure that in turn drives the flute bore.

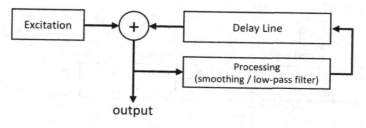

(a) Karplus-strong

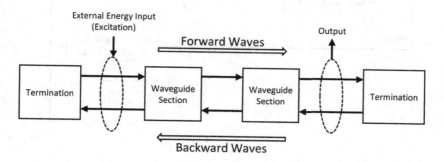

(b) Waveguide synthesis

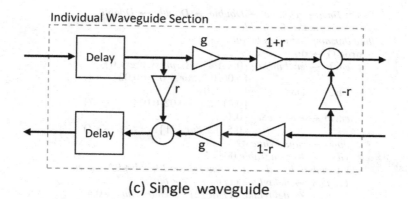

(c) Single waveguide

Figure 23.3 Karplus-strong and waveguides.

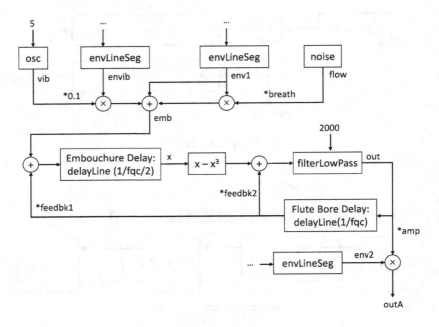

Figure 23.4 A physical model of a flute.

$flute :: Time \rightarrow Double \rightarrow Double \rightarrow Double \rightarrow Double$
$\qquad \rightarrow AudSF\ ()\ Double$
$flute\ dur\ amp\ fqc\ press\ breath =$
$\quad \textbf{proc}\ () \rightarrow \textbf{do}$
$\quad\quad env1\ \leftarrow envLineSeg\ [0, 1.1 * press, press, press, 0]$
$\quad\quad\quad\quad\quad\quad\quad\quad\quad [0.06, 0.2, dur - 0.16, 0.02] \prec ()$
$\quad\quad env2\ \leftarrow envLineSeg\ [0, 1, 1, 0]$
$\quad\quad\quad\quad\quad\quad\quad\quad\quad [0.01, dur - 0.02, 0.01] \quad\quad \prec ()$
$\quad\quad envib \leftarrow envLineSeg\ [0, 0, 1, 1]$
$\quad\quad\quad\quad\quad\quad\quad\quad\quad [0.5, 0.5, dur - 1] \quad\quad\quad \prec ()$
$\quad\quad flow\ \ \leftarrow noiseWhite\ 42\ \prec ()$
$\quad\quad vib\ \ \ \ \leftarrow osc\ sineTable\ 0 \prec 5$
$\quad\quad \textbf{let}\ emb = breath * flow * env1 + env1 + vib * 0.1 * envib$
$\quad\quad \textbf{rec}\ flute\ \leftarrow delayLine\ (1/fqc)\ \ \ \ \ \prec out$
$\quad\quad\quad x\ \ \ \ \leftarrow delayLine\ (1/fqc/2) \prec emb + flute * 0.4$
$\quad\quad\quad out\ \ \leftarrow filterLowPassBW \prec (x - x * x * x + flute * 0.4, 2000)$
$\quad\quad outA \prec out * amp * env2$
$sineTable :: Table$
$sineTable = tableSinesN\ 4096\ [1]$
$tFlute = outFile\ \texttt{"tFlute.wav"}\ 5\ \$\ flute\ 5\ 0.7\ 440\ 0.99\ 0.2$

Figure 23.5 Euterpea program for flute model.

The Euterpea code for this model is essentially a direct translation of the diagram, with details of the envelopes added in, and is shown in Figure 23.5. Some useful test cases are:

$f0 = flute$ 3 0.35 440 0.93 0.02 -- average breath
$f1 = flute$ 3 0.35 440 0.83 0.05 -- weak breath, soft note
$f2 = flute$ 3 0.35 440 0.53 0.04 -- very weak breath, no note

23.4 Waveguide Synthesis

The Karplus-Strong algorithm can be generalized to a more accurate model of the transmission of sound up and down a medium, whether it is a string, the air in a chamber, the surface of a drum, the metal plate of a xylophone, and so on. This more accurate model is called a *waveguide*, and mathematically can be seen as a discrete model of d'Alembert's solution to the *one-dimensional wave equation*, which captures the superposition of a right-going wave and a left-going wave, as discussed in Section 21.1.2. In its simplest form, we can express the value of a wave at position m and time n as:

$$y(m, n) = y^+(m - n) + y^-(m + n)$$

where y^+ is the right-going wave and y^- is the left-going wave. Intuitively, the value of y at point m and time n is the sum of two delayed copies of its traveling waves. As discussed before, these traveling waves will reflect at boundaries such as the fixed ends of a string or the open and closed ends of a tube.

What distinguishes this model from the simpler Karplus-Strong model is that it captures waves traveling in *both* directions – and to realize that, we need a closed loop of delay lines. But even with that generalization, the equation above assumes a *lossless* system and does not account for interactions *between* the left- and right-traveling waves. The former quantity is often called the *gain*, and the latter the *reflection coefficient*. We have discussed previously the notion that waves are reflected at the ends of a string, a tube, etc., but in general some interaction/reflection between the left- and right-traveling waves can happen anywhere. This more general model is shown diagramatically in Figure 23.3c, where g is the gain and r is the reflection coefficient.

Figure 23.3b shows a sequence of waveguides "wired together" to allow for the possibility that the gain and reflection characteristics are different at different points along the medium. The "termination" boxes can be thought of as special waveguides that capture the effect of reflection at the end of a string, tube, etc.

$$dcBlock :: Double \rightarrow AudSF\ Double\ Double$$
$$dcBlock\ a = \mathbf{proc}\ xn \rightarrow \mathbf{do}$$
$$\mathbf{rec\ let}\ yn = xn - xn\_1 + a * yn\_1$$
$$xn\_1 \leftarrow delay\ 0 \prec xn$$
$$yn\_1 \leftarrow delay\ 0 \prec yn$$
$$outA \prec yn$$

Figure 23.6 DC blocking filter in Euterpea.

23.4.1 Waveguides in Euterpea

A simple waveguide that has looping delay lines and gain factors but ignores reflection is as follows:

$$waveguide :: Double \rightarrow Double \rightarrow Double \rightarrow$$
$$AudSF\ (Double, Double)\ (Double, Double)$$
$$waveguide\ del\ ga\ gb = \mathbf{proc}\ (ain, bin) \rightarrow \mathbf{do}$$
$$\mathbf{rec}\ bout \leftarrow delayLine\ del \prec bin - ga * aout$$
$$aout \leftarrow delayLine\ del \prec ain - gb * bout$$
$$outA \prec (aout, bout)$$

Here ga and gb are the gains and del is the delay time of one delay line.

This waveguide is good enough for the examples studied in this book, in that we assume no reflections occur along the waveguide, and that reflections at the endpoints can be expressed manually with suitable feedback. Similarly, any filtering or output processing can be expressed manually.

23.4.2 A Pragmatic Issue

In a circuit with feedback, DC (direct current) offsets can accumulate, resulting in clipping. The DC offset can be "blocked" using a special high-pass filter whose cutoff frequency is infrasonic. This filter can be captured by the difference equation:

$$y[n] = x[n] - x[n - 1] + a * y[n - 1]$$

Where $x[n]$ and $y[n]$ are the input and output, respectively, at the current time n, and a is called the gain factor. If we think of the indexing of n versus $n - 1$ as a one-unit delay, we can view the equation above as the diagram shown in Figure 23.7, where z^{-1} is the mathematical notation for a one-unit delay.[1]

---

[1] This representation is called the Z *transform* of a signal.

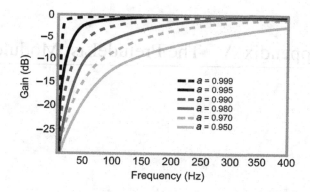

Figure 23.7 Transfer function for DC blocker.

If you recall from Section 21.2.2, the one-unit delay operator in Euterpea is called *delay*. With that in mind, it is easy to write a Euterpea program for a DC blocking filter, as shown in Figure 23.6. The transfer function corresponding to this filter for different values of *a* is shown in Figure 23.7. In practice, a value of 0.99 for *a* works well.

Appendix A   The PreludeList Module

The use of lists is particularly common when programming in Haskell, and thus, not surprisingly, there are many predefined polymorphic functions for lists. The list data type itself, plus some of the most useful functions on it, are contained in the Standard Prelude's *PreludeList* module, which we will look at in detail in this chapter. There is also a Standard Library module called *List* that has additional useful functions. It is a good idea to become familiar with both modules.

Although this chapter may feel like a long list of "Haskell features," the functions described here capture many common patterns of list usage that have been discovered by functional programmers over many years of trials and tribulations. In many ways higher-order declarative programming with lists takes the place of lower-level imperative control structures in more conventional languages. By becoming familiar with these list functions you will be able to more quickly and confidently develop your own applications using lists. Furthermore, if all of us do this, we will have a common vocabulary with which to understand each others' programs. Finally, by reading through the code in this module you will develop a good feel for how to write proper function definitions in Haskell.

It is not necessary for you to understand the details of every function, but you should try to get a sense for what is available so that you can return later when your programming needs demand it. In the long run, you are well-advised to read the rest of the Standard Prelude as well as the various Standard Libraries, to discover a host of other functions and data types that you might someday find useful in your own work.

A.1   The PreludeList Module

To get a feel for the *PreludeList* module, let's first look at its module declaration:

```
module PreludeList (
    map, (++), filter, concat,
    head, last, tail, init, null, length, (!!),
    foldl, foldl1, scanl, scanl1, foldr, foldr1, scanr, scanr1,
```

346

    iterate, repeat, replicate, cycle,
    take, drop, splitAt, takeWhile, dropWhile, span, break,
    lines, words, unlines, unwords, reverse, and, or,
    any, all, elem, notElem, lookup,
    sum, product, maximum, minimum, concatMap,
    zip, zip3, zipWith, zipWith3, unzip, unzip3)
    where

import *qualified Char (isSpace)*

infixl 9 !!
infixr 5 ++
infix 4 $\in, \notin$

We will not discuss all of the functions listed above, but will cover most of them (and some were discussed in previous chapters).

A.2 Simple List Selector Functions

head and *tail* extract the first element and remaining elements, respectively, from a list, which must be non-empty. *last* and *init* are the dual functions that work from the end of a list, rather than from the beginning.

```
head       :: [a] → a
head (x:_) = x
head []    = error "PreludeList.head: empty list"
last       :: [a] → a
last [x]   = x
last (_:xs) = last xs
last []    = error "PreludeList.last: empty list"
tail       :: [a] → [a]
tail (_:xs) = xs
tail []    = error "PreludeList.tail: empty list"
init       :: [a] → [a]
init [x]   = []
init (x:xs) = x : init xs
init []    = error "PreludeList.init: empty list"
```

Although *head* and *tail* were previously discussed in Section 3.1, the definitions here include an equation describing their behaviors under erroneous situations – such as selecting the head of an empty list – in which case the *error* function is called. It is a good idea to include such an equation for any definition in which you have not covered every possible case in pattern-matching; i.e., if it is possible that the pattern-matching could "run off the end" of the set of equations. The string argument that you supply to the *error* function should be detailed enough that you can easily track down the precise location of the error in your program.

> **Details:** If such an error equation is omitted, and then during pattern-matching all equations fail, most Haskell systems will invoke the *error* function anyway, but most likely with a string that will be less informative than one you can supply on your own.

The *null* function tests to see if a list is empty.

$$null \qquad :: [a] \to Bool$$
$$null\ [\,] \qquad = True$$
$$null\ (\_:\_) = False$$

A.3 Index-Based Selector Functions

To select the *n*th element from a list, with the first element being the 0th element, we can use the indexing function (!!):

$$(!!) \qquad :: [a] \to Int \to a$$
$$(x:\_)\ !!\ 0 = \qquad x$$
$$(\_:xs)\ !!\ n\ |\ n > 0 = xs\ !!\ (n-1)$$
$$(\_:\_)\ !!\ \_ = \qquad error\ \texttt{"PreludeList.!!: negative index"}$$
$$[\,] \quad\ !!\ \_ = \qquad error\ \texttt{"PreludeList.!!: index too large"}$$

> **Details:** Note the definition of two error conditions; be sure that you understand under what conditions these two equations would succeed. In particular, recall that equations are matched in top-down order: the first to match is the one that is chosen.

take n xs returns the prefix of *xs* of length *n*, or *xs* itself if $n > length\ xs$. Similarly, *drop n xs* returns the suffix of *xs* after the first *n* elements, or [] if $n > length\ xs$. Finally, *splitAt n xs* is equivalent to $(take\ n\ xs, drop\ n\ xs)$.

$$take \qquad\qquad :: Int \to [a] \to [a]$$
$$take\ 0\ \_ \qquad\qquad = [\,]$$
$$take\ \_\ [\,] \qquad\qquad = [\,]$$
$$take\ n\ (x:xs)\ |\ n > 0 = x:take\ (n-1)\ xs$$
$$take\ \_\ \_ \qquad\qquad =$$
$$\qquad error\ \texttt{"PreludeList.take: negative argument"}$$
$$drop \qquad\qquad :: Int \to [a] \to [a]$$
$$drop\ 0\ xs \qquad\qquad = xs$$
$$drop\ \_\ [\,] \qquad\qquad = [\,]$$
$$drop\ n\ (\_:xs)\ |\ n > 0 = drop\ (n-1)\ xs$$
$$drop\ \_\ \_ \qquad\qquad =$$

error `"PreludeList.drop: negative argument"`

$$splitAt \qquad :: Int \to [a] \to ([a],[a])$$
$$splitAt\ 0\ xs \qquad = ([\,],xs)$$
$$splitAt\ \_\ [\,] \qquad = ([\,],[\,])$$
$$splitAt\ n\ (x:xs)\mid n > 0 = (x:xs',xs'')$$
$$\textbf{where }(xs',xs'') = splitAt\ (n-1)\ xs$$
$$splitAt\ \_\ \_ =$$

   error `"PreludeList.splitAt: negative argument"`

$$length \qquad :: [a] \to Int$$
$$length\ [\,] \qquad = 0$$
$$length\ (\_:l) = 1 + length\ l$$

For example:

$$take\ 3\ [0,1..5] \Rightarrow [0,1,2]$$
$$drop\ 3\ [0,1..5] \Rightarrow [3,4,5]$$
$$splitAt\ 3\ [0,1..5] \Rightarrow ([0,1,2],[3,4,5])$$

A.4 Predicate-Based Selector Functions

takeWhile p xs returns the longest (possibly empty) prefix of *xs*, all of whose elements satisfy the predicate *p*. *dropWhile p xs* returns the remaining suffix. Finally, *span p xs* is equivalent to (*takeWhile p xs*, *dropWhile p xs*), while *break p* uses the negation of *p*.

$$takeWhile \qquad :: (a \to Bool) \to [a] \to [a]$$
$$takeWhile\ p\ [\,] = [\,]$$
$$takeWhile\ p\ (x:xs)$$
$$\mid p\ x \qquad = x:takeWhile\ p\ xs$$
$$\mid otherwise = [\,]$$

$$dropWhile \qquad :: (a \to Bool) \to [a] \to [a]$$
$$dropWhile\ p\ [\,] = [\,]$$
$$dropWhile\ p\ xs@(x:xs')$$
$$\mid p\ x \qquad = dropWhile\ p\ xs'$$
$$\mid otherwise = xs$$

$$span, break \qquad :: (a \to Bool) \to [a] \to ([a],[a])$$
$$span\ p\ [\,] \qquad = ([\,],[\,])$$
$$span\ p\ xs@(x:xs')$$
$$\mid p\ x \qquad = (x:xs',xs'')\ \textbf{where}\ (xs',xs'') = span\ p\ xs$$
$$\mid otherwise = (xs,[\,])$$

$$break\ p \qquad = span\ (\neg \circ p)$$

filter removes all elements not satisfying a predicate:

$$filter :: (a \to Bool) \to [a] \to [a]$$
$$filter\ p\ [\,] = [\,]$$
$$filter\ p\ (x:xs)\mid p\ x = x:filter\ p\ xs$$
$$\mid otherwise = filter\ p\ xs$$

A.5 Fold-Like Functions

foldl1 and *foldr1* are variants of *foldl* and *foldr* that have no starting value argument, and thus must be applied to non-empty lists.

$$foldl \qquad\qquad :: (a \to b \to a) \to a \to [b] \to a$$
$$foldl\ f\ z\ [\ ] \qquad = z$$
$$foldl\ f\ z\ (x:xs) = foldl\ f\ (f\ z\ x)\ xs$$

$$foldl1 \qquad\qquad :: (a \to a \to a) \to [a] \to a$$
$$foldl1\ f\ (x:xs) = foldl\ f\ x\ xs$$
$$foldl1\ \_\ [\ ] \qquad = error\ \texttt{"PreludeList.foldl1: empty list"}$$

$$foldr \qquad\qquad :: (a \to b \to b) \to b \to [a] \to b$$
$$foldr\ f\ z\ [\ ] \qquad = z$$
$$foldr\ f\ z\ (x:xs) = f\ x\ (foldr\ f\ z\ xs)$$

$$foldr1 \qquad\qquad :: (a \to a \to a) \to [a] \to a$$
$$foldr1\ f\ [x] \qquad = x$$
$$foldr1\ f\ (x:xs) = f\ x\ (foldr1\ f\ xs)$$
$$foldr1\ \_\ [\ ] \qquad = error\ \texttt{"PreludeList.foldr1: empty list"}$$

foldl1 and *foldr1* are best used in cases where an empty list makes no sense for the application. For example, computing the maximum or minimum element of a list does not make sense if the list is empty. Thus *foldl1 max* is a proper function to compute the maximum element of a list.

scanl is similar to *foldl*, but returns a list of successive reduced values from the left:

$$scanl\ f\ z\ [x1, x2, ...] == [z, z\ `f`\ x1, (z\ `f`\ x1)\ `f`\ x2, ...]$$

For example:

$$scanl\ (+)\ 0\ [1, 2, 3] \Rightarrow [0, 1, 3, 6]$$

Note that *last* (*scanl f z xs*) = *foldl f z xs*. *scanl1* is similar, but without the starting element:

$$scanl1\ f\ [x1, x2, ...] == [x1, x1\ `f`\ x2, ...]$$

Here are the full definitions:

$$scanl \qquad\qquad :: (a \to b \to a) \to a \to [b] \to [a]$$
$$scanl\ f\ q\ xs \quad = q : (\textbf{case}\ xs\ \textbf{of}$$
$$\qquad\qquad\qquad\qquad [\ ] \to [\ ]$$
$$\qquad\qquad\qquad\qquad x:xs \to scanl\ f\ (f\ q\ x)\ xs)$$

$$scanl1 \qquad\qquad :: (a \to a \to a) \to [a] \to [a]$$
$$scanl1\ f\ (x:xs) = scanl\ f\ x\ xs$$
$$scanl1\ \_\ [\ ] \qquad = error\ \texttt{"PreludeList.scanl1: empty list"}$$

$$scanr \qquad\qquad :: (a \to b \to b) \to b \to [a] \to [b]$$
$$scanr\ f\ q0\ [\ ] = \qquad [q0]$$
$$scanr\ f\ q0\ (x:xs) = f\ x\ q : qs$$
$$\qquad\qquad\qquad \textbf{where}\ qs@(q:\_) = scanr\ f\ q0\ xs$$

$$scanr1 \qquad\qquad :: (a \to a \to a) \to [a] \to [a]$$
$$scanr1\ f\ [x] \qquad = [x]$$
$$scanr1\ f\ (x:xs) = f\ x\ q : qs$$
$$\qquad\qquad\qquad \textbf{where}\ qs@(q:\_) = scanr1\ f\ xs$$
$$scanr1\ \_\ [\ ] \qquad = error\ \texttt{"PreludeList.scanr1: empty list"}$$

A.6 List Generators

There are some functions that are very useful for generating lists from scratch in interesting ways. To start, *iterate f x* returns an *infinite list* of repeated applications of *f* to *x*. That is:

$$iterate\ f\ x \Rightarrow [x, f\ x, f\ (f\ x), ...]$$

The "infinite" nature of this list may at first seem alarming, but in fact is one of the more powerful and useful features of Haskell.

[say more]

$$iterate \quad :: (a \rightarrow a) \rightarrow a \rightarrow [a]$$
$$iterate\ f\ x = x : iterate\ f\ (f\ x)$$

repeat x is an infinite list, with *x* the value of every element. *replicate n x* is a list of length *n* with *x* the value of every element. And *cycle* ties a finite list into a circular one, or equivalently the infinite repetition of the original list.

$$repeat \qquad :: a \rightarrow [a]$$
$$repeat\ x \qquad = xs\ \textbf{where}\ xs = x : xs$$

$$replicate \quad :: Int \rightarrow a \rightarrow [a]$$
$$replicate\ n\ x = take\ n\ (repeat\ x)$$

$$cycle \qquad :: [a] \rightarrow [a]$$
$$cycle\ [\,] \qquad = error\ \texttt{"Prelude.cycle: empty list"}$$
$$cycle\ xs \qquad = xs'\ \textbf{where}\ xs' = xs \mathbin{+\!\!+} xs'$$

A.7 String-Based Functions

Recall that strings in Haskell are just lists of characters. Manipulating strings (i.e., text) is a very common practice, so it makes sense that Haskell would have a few predefined functions to make this easier for you.

lines breaks a string at every newline character (written as `'\n'` in Haskell), thus yielding a *list* of strings, each of which contains no newline characters. Similarly, *words* breaks a string up into a list of words, which were delimited by white space. Finally, *unlines* and *unwords* are the inverse operations: *unlines* joins lines with terminating newline characters, and *unwords* joins words with separating spaces. (Because of the potential presence of multiple spaces and newline characters, however, these pairs of functions are not true inverses of each other.)

$$lines \qquad :: String \rightarrow [String]$$
$$lines\ \texttt{""} = [\,]$$
$$lines\ s \quad = \textbf{let}\ (l, s') = break\ (== \texttt{'\textbackslash n'})\ s$$
$$\qquad \qquad \textbf{in}\ l : \textbf{case}\ s'\ \textbf{of}$$
$$\qquad \qquad \qquad [\,] \rightarrow [\,]$$
$$\qquad \qquad \qquad (\_ : s'') \rightarrow lines\ s''$$

$$words \quad :: String \rightarrow [String]$$
$$words\ s \ = \textbf{case}\ dropWhile\ Char.isSpace\ s\ \textbf{of}$$
$$\qquad \qquad \texttt{""} \rightarrow [\,]$$
$$\qquad \qquad s' \rightarrow w : words\ s''$$
$$\qquad \qquad \textbf{where}\ (w, s'') = break\ Char.isSpace\ s'$$

$unlines$ $:: [String] \rightarrow String$
$unlines$ $= concatMap\ (+\!\!+ "\backslash n")$

$unwords$ $:: [String] \rightarrow String$
$unwords\ [\,] = ""$
$unwords\ ws = foldr1\ (\lambda w\ s \rightarrow w +\!\!+ '\ \ ' : s)\ ws$

reverse reverses the elements in a finite list.

$reverse :: [a] - [a]$
$reverse = foldl\ (flip\ (:))\ [\,]$

A.8 Boolean List Functions

and and *or* compute the logical "and" and "or," respectively, of all of the elements in a list of Boolean values.

$and, or :: [Bool] \rightarrow Bool$
$and\quad = foldr\ (\wedge)\ True$
$or\quad\ \ = foldr\ (\vee)\ False$

Applied to a predicate and a list, *any* determines if any element of the list satisfies the predicate. An analogous behavior holds for *all*.

$any, all :: (a \rightarrow Bool) \rightarrow [a] \rightarrow Bool$
$any\ p\quad = or \circ map\ p$
$all\ p\quad = and \circ map\ p$

A.9 List Membership Functions

elem is the list membership predicate, usually written in infix form, e.g., $x \in xs$ (which is why it was given a fixity declaration at the beginning of the module). *notElem* is the negation of this function.

$elem, notElem :: (Eq\ a) \Rightarrow a \rightarrow [a] \rightarrow Bool$
$elem\ x\quad\quad = any\ (== x)$
$notElem\ x\quad\ = all\ (\neq x)$

It is common to store "key/value" pairs in a list, and to access the list by finding the value associated with a given key (for this reason the list is often called an *association list*). The function *lookup* looks up a key in an association list, returning *Nothing* if it is not found, or *Just y* if *y* is the value associated with the key.

$lookup\quad\quad :: (Eq\ a) \Rightarrow a \rightarrow [(a, b)] \rightarrow Maybe\ b$
$lookup\ key\ [\,] = Nothing$
$lookup\ key\ ((x, y) : xys)$
$\quad |\ key == x = Just\ y$
$\quad |\ otherwise = lookup\ key\ xys$

A.10 Arithmetic on Lists

sum and *product* compute the sum and product, respectively, of a finite list of numbers.

$$sum, product :: (Num\ a) \Rightarrow [a] \rightarrow a$$
$$sum \qquad = foldl\ (+)\ 0$$
$$product \qquad = foldl\ (*)\ 1$$

maximum and *minimum* return the maximum and minimum value, respectively from a non-empty, finite list whose element type is ordered.

$$maximum, minimum :: (Ord\ a) \Rightarrow [a] \rightarrow a$$
$$maximum\ [\,] = error\ \texttt{"Prelude.maximum: empty list"}$$
$$maximum\ xs = foldl1\ max\ xs$$

$$minimum\ [\,] = error\ \texttt{"Prelude.minimum: empty list"}$$
$$minimum\ xs\ = foldl1\ min\ xs$$

Note that even though *foldl1* is used in the definition, a test is made for the empty list to give an error message that more accurately reflects the source of the problem.

A.11 List Combining Functions

map and (++) were defined in previous chapters, but are repeated here for completeness:

$$map :: (a \rightarrow b) \rightarrow [a] \rightarrow [a]$$
$$map\ f\ [\,] = [\,]$$
$$map\ f\ (x : xs) = f\ x : map\ f\ xs$$

$$(++) :: [a] \rightarrow [a] \rightarrow [a]$$
$$[\,] ++ ys = ys$$
$$(x : xs) ++ ys = x : (xs ++ ys)$$

concat appends together a list of lists:

$$concat :: [[a]] \rightarrow [a]$$
$$concat\ xss = foldr\ (++)\ [\,]\ xss$$

concatMap does what it says: it concatenates the result of mapping a function down a list.

$$concatMap \quad :: (a \rightarrow [b]) \rightarrow [a] \rightarrow [b]$$
$$concatMap\ f = concat \circ map\ f$$

zip takes two lists and returns a list of corresponding pairs. If one input list is short, excess elements of the longer list are discarded. *zip3* takes three lists and returns a list of triples. ("Zips" for larger tuples are contained in the List Library.)

$$zip \ :: [a] \rightarrow [b] \rightarrow [(a, b)]$$
$$zip \ = zipWith\ (,)$$

$$zip3 :: [a] \rightarrow [b] \rightarrow [c] \rightarrow [(a, b, c)]$$
$$zip3 = zipWith3\ (,,)$$

Details: The functions *(,)* and *(,,)* are the pairing and tripling functions, respectively:

$(,) \Rightarrow \lambda x\, y \rightarrow (x, y)$
$(,,) \Rightarrow \lambda x\, y\, z \rightarrow (x, y, z)$

The *zipWith* family generalizes the *zip* and *map* families (or, in a sense, combines them) by applying a function (given as the first argument) to each pair (or triple, etc.) of values. For example, *zipWith* (+) is applied to two lists to produce the list of corresponding sums.

zipWith $:: (a \rightarrow b \rightarrow c) \rightarrow [a] \rightarrow [b] \rightarrow [c]$
zipWith z $(a : as)$ $(b : bs)$
           $=$ $z\ a\ b : zipWith\ z\ as\ bs$
zipWith _ _ _ $=$ [ ]
zipWith3 $:: (a \rightarrow b \rightarrow c \rightarrow d) \rightarrow [a] \rightarrow [b] \rightarrow [c] \rightarrow [d]$
zipWith3 z $(a : as)$ $(b : bs)$ $(c : cs)$
           $=$ $z\ a\ b\ c : zipWith3\ z\ as\ bs\ cs$
zipWith3 _ _ _ _ $= [\ ]$

The following two functions perform the inverse operations of *zip* and *zip3*, respectively.

unzip $:: [(a, b)] \rightarrow ([a], [b])$
unzip $= foldr\ (\lambda(a, b) \sim (as, bs) \rightarrow (a : as, b : bs))\ ([\ ], [\ ])$

unzip3 $:: [(a, b, c)] \rightarrow ([a], [b], [c])$
unzip3 $= foldr\ (\lambda(a, b, c) \sim (as, bs, cs) \rightarrow (a : as, b : bs, c : cs))$
           $([\ ], [\ ], [\ ])$

Appendix B   Haskell's Standard Type Classes

This provides a "tour" through the predefined standard type classes in Haskell, as was done for lists in Appendix A. We have simplified these classes somewhat by omitting some of the less interesting methods; the Haskell Report and Standard Library Report contain more complete descriptions.

B.1   The Ordered Class

The equality class Eq was defined precisely in Chapter 7, along with a simplified version of the class Ord. Here is its full specification of class Ord; note the many default methods.

```
class (Eq a) ⇒ Ord a where
    compare :: a → a → Ordering
    (<), (⩽), (⩾), (>) :: a → a → Bool
    max, min :: a → a → a
    compare x y
        | x == y    =  EQ
        | x ⩽ y     =  LT
        | otherwise =  GT
    x ⩽ y           =  compare x y ≠ GT
    x < y           =  compare x y == LT
    x ⩾ y           =  compare x y ≠ LT
    x > y           =  compare x y == GT
    max x y
        | x ⩾ y     =  x
        | otherwise =  y
    min x y
        | x <  y    =  x
        | otherwise =  y
data Ordering = LT | EQ | GT
        deriving (Eq, Ord, Enum, Read, Show, Bounded)
```

Note that the default method for *compare* is defined in terms of (≤), and that the default method for (≤) is defined in terms of *compare*. This means that an instance of *Ord* should contain a method for at least one of these for everything to be well defined. (Using *compare* can be more efficient for complex types.) This is a common idea in designing a type class.

B.2 The Enumeration Class

Class *Enum* has a set of operations that underlie the syntactic sugar of *arithmetic sequences*; for example, the arithmetic sequence [1, 3 . . .] is actually shorthand for *enumFromThen* 1 3. If this is true, then we should be able to generate arithmetic sequences for any type that is an instance of *Enum*. This includes not only most numeric types but also *Char*, so that, for instance, ['a' .. 'z'] denotes the list of lowercase letters in alphabetical order. Furthermore, a user-defined enumerated type such as *Color*:

data *Color* = *Red* | *Orange* | *Yellow* | *Green* | *Blue* | *Indigo* | *Violet*

can easily be given an *Enum* instance declaration, after which we can calculate the following results:

$$[Red . . Violet] \implies \quad [\quad Red, Orange, Yellow, Green,$$
$$Blue, Indigo, Violet]$$
$$[Red, Yellow . .] \implies \quad [\quad Red, Yellow, Blue, Violet]$$
$$fromEnum\ Green \implies \quad 3$$
$$toEnum\ 5 :: Color \implies Indigo$$

Indeed, the derived instance will give this result. Note that the sequences are still *arithmetic* in the sense that the increment between values is constant, even though the values are not numbers.

The complete definition of the *Enum* class is given below:

```
class Enum a where
    succ, pred        :: a → a
    toEnum            :: Int → a
    fromEnum          :: a → Int
    enumFrom          :: a → [a]              -- [n..]
    enumFromThen      :: a → a → [a]          -- [n,n'..]
    enumFromTo        :: a → a → [a]          -- [n..m]
    enumFromThenTo    :: a → a → a → [a]      -- [n,n'..m]

    -- Minimal complete definition: toEnum, fromEnum
    succ              = toEnum ∘ (+1) ∘ fromEnum
    pred              = toEnum ∘ (subtract 1) ∘ fromEnum
    enumFrom x        = map toEnum [fromEnum x..]
    enumFromThen x y  = map toEnum [fromEnum x, fromEnum y..]
    enumFromTo x y    = map toEnum [fromEnum x..fromEnum y]
    enumFromThenTo x y z =
        map toEnum [fromEnum x, fromEnum y..fromEnum z]
```

The six default methods are sufficient for most applications, so when writing your own instance declaration, it is usually sufficient to only provide methods for the remaining two operations: *toEnum* and *fromEnum*.

In terms of arithmetic sequences, the expressions on the left below are equivalent to those on the right:

$$
\begin{array}{ll}
enumFrom\ n & [n\,..] \\
enumFromThen\ n\ n' & [n,n'\,..] \\
enumFromTo\ n\ m & [n\,..\,m] \\
enumFromThenTo\ n\ n'\ m & [n,n'\,..\,m]
\end{array}
$$

B.3 The Bounded Class

The class *Bounded* captures data types that are linearly bounded in some way; i.e., they have both a minimum value and a maximum value.

```
class Bounded a where
  minBound :: a
  maxBound :: a
```

B.4 The Show Class

Instances of the class *Show* are those types that can be converted to character strings. This is useful, for example, when writing a representation of a value to the standard output area or to a file. The class *Read* works in the other direction: it provides operations for parsing character strings to obtain the values that they represent. In this section we will look at the *Show* class; in the next we will look at *Read*.

For efficiency reasons the primitive operations in these classes are somewhat esoteric, but they provide good lessons in both algorithm and software design, so we will look at them in some detail.

First, let's look at one of the higher-level functions that is defined in terms of the lower-level primitives:

$$show :: (Show\ a) \Rightarrow a \rightarrow String$$

Naturally enough, *show* takes a value of any type that is a member of *Show*, and returns its representation as a string. For example, *show* $(2 + 2)$ yields the string `"4"`, as does *show* $(6 - 2)$ and *show* applied to any other expression whose value is 4.

Furthermore, we can construct strings such as

```
"The sum of  " ++ show x ++ "  and  " ++ show y ++ "  is  "
  ++ show (x + y) ++ "."
```

with no difficulty. In particular, because (++) is right associative, the number of steps to construct this string is directly proportional to its total length, and we can't expect to do any better than that. (Since (++) needs to reconstruct its left argument, if it were left associative, the above expression would repeatedly reconstruct the same sub-string on each application of ($+\!\!\!+$). If the total string length were n, then in the worst case the number of steps needed to do this would be proportional to n^2, instead of proportional to n in the case where ($+\!\!\!+$) is right associative.)

Unfortunately, this strategy breaks down when construction of the list is nested. A particularly nasty version of this problem arises for tree-shaped data structures. Consider a function *showTree* that converts a value of type *Tree* into a string, as in:

> *showTree* (*Branch* (*Branch* (*Leaf* 2) (*Leaf* 3)) (*Leaf* 4))
> $\implies$ "< <2|3>|4>"

We can define this behavior straightforwardly as follows:

> *showTree* :: (*Show a*) $\Rightarrow$ *Tree a* $\rightarrow$ *String*
> *showTree* (*Leaf x*)
>   = *show x*
> *showTree* (*Branch l r*)
>   = "<" $+\!\!\!+$ *showTree l* $+\!\!\!+$ "|" $+\!\!\!+$ *showTree r* $+\!\!\!+$ ">"

Each of the recursive calls to *showTree* introduces more applications of ($+\!\!\!+$), but since they are nested, a large amount of list reconstruction takes place (similar to the problem that would arise if ($+\!\!\!+$) were left associative). If the tree being converted has size n, then in the worst case the number of steps needed to perform this conversion is proportional to n^2. This is no good!

To restore linear complexity, suppose we had a function *shows*:

> *shows* :: (*Show a*) $\Rightarrow$ *a* $\rightarrow$ *String* $\rightarrow$ *String*

which takes a showable value and a string and returns that string with the value's representation concatenated at the front. For example, we would expect *shows* $(2 + 2)$ "hello" to return the string "4hello". The string argument should be thought of as an "accumulator" for the final result.

Using *shows* we can define a more efficient version of *showTree* which, like *shows*, has a string accumulator argument. Let's call this function *showsTree*:

> *showsTree* :: (*Show a*) $\Rightarrow$ *Tree a* $\rightarrow$ *String* $\rightarrow$ *String*
> *showsTree* (*Leaf x*) *s*
>   = *shows x s*
> *showsTree* (*Branch l r*) *s*
>   = "<" $+\!\!\!+$ *showsTree l* ("|" $+\!\!\!+$ *showsTree r* (">" $+\!\!\!+$ *s*))

This function requires a number of steps directly proportional to the size of the tree, thus solving our efficiency problem. To see why this is so, note that the accumulator argument *s* is never reconstructed. It is simply passed as an argument in one recursive call to *shows* or *showsTree*, and is incrementally extended to its left using ($+\!\!\!+$).

showTree can now be re-defined in terms of *showsTree* using an empty accumulator:

> *showTree t* = *showsTree t* " "

Exercise B.1 Prove that this version of *showTree* is equivalent to the old.

Although this solves our efficiency problem, the presentation of this function (and others like it) can be improved somewhat. First, let's create a type synonym (part of the Standard Prelude):

> **type** *ShowS* = *String* $\rightarrow$ *String*

Second, we can avoid carrying accumulators around, and also avoid amassing parentheses at the right end of long sequences of concatenations, by using functional composition:

$$showsTree :: (Show\ a) \Rightarrow Tree\ a \rightarrow ShowS$$
$$showsTree\ (Leaf\ x)$$
$$= shows\ x$$
$$showsTree\ (Branch\ l\ r)$$
$$= ("<"{+\!\!+}) \circ showsTree\ l \circ ("\,|\,"{+\!\!+}) \circ showsTree\ r \circ (">"{+\!\!+})$$

Details: This can be simplified slightly more by noting that $("c"{+\!\!+})$ is equivalent to $('c':)$ for any character c.

Something more important than just tidying up the code has come about by this transformation: We have raised the presentation from an *object level* (in this case, strings) to a *function level*. You can read the type signature of *showsTree* as saying that *showsTree* maps a tree into a *showing function*. Functions like $("<"{+\!\!+})$ and $("a\ string"{+\!\!+})$ are primitive showing functions, and we build up more complex ones by function composition.

The actual *Show* class in Haskell has two additional levels of complexity (and functionality): (1) the ability to specify the *precedence* of a string being generated, which is important when *show*ing a data type that has infix constructors, since it determines when parentheses are needed; and (2) a function for *show*ing a *list* of values of the type under consideration, since lists have special syntax in Haskell and are so commonly used that they deserve special treatment. The full definition of the *Show* class is given by:

class *Show a* **where**
  $showsPrec :: Int \rightarrow a \rightarrow ShowS$
  $showList\ :: [a] \rightarrow ShowS$
  $showList\ [\,]\qquad = showString\ "\,[\,]\,"$
  $showList\ (x:xs) = showChar\ '\,[\,' \circ shows\ x \circ showl\ xs$
    where $showl\ [\,]\qquad = showChar\ '\,]\,'$
      $showl\ (x:xs) = showString\ ",\ \ " \circ shows\ x \circ showl\ xs$

Note the default method for *showList*, and its "function level" style of definition.

In addition to this class declaration, the Standard Prelude defines the following functions, which return us to where we started our journey in this section:

$$shows :: (Show\ a) \Rightarrow a \rightarrow ShowS$$
$$shows = showsPrec\ 0$$

$$show\ :: (Show\ a) \Rightarrow a \rightarrow String$$
$$show\ x = shows\ x\ "\,"$$

Some details about *showsPrec* can be found in the Haskell Report, but if you are not displaying constructors in infix notation, the precedence can be ignored. Furthermore, the default method for *showList* is perfectly good for most uses of lists that you will encounter. Thus, for example, we can finish our *Tree* example by declaring it to be an instance of the class *Show* very simply as:

> **instance** (*Show a*) ⇒ *Show* (*Tree a*) **where**
> *showsPrec n* = *showsTree*

B.5 The Read Class

Now that we can convert trees into strings, let's turn to the inverse problem: converting strings into trees. The basic idea is to define a *parser* for a type *a*, which at first glance seems as if it should be a function of type *String* → *a*. This simple approach has two problems, however: (1) it's possible that the string is ambiguous, leading to more than one way to interpret it as a value of type *a*; and (2) it's possible that only a prefix of the string will parse correctly. Thus we choose instead to return a list of (*a*, *String*) pairs as the result of a parse. If all goes well, we will always get a singleton list such as [(*v*, " ")] as the result of a parse, but we cannot count on it (in fact, when recursively parsing sub-strings, we will expect a singleton list with a *non-empty* trailing string).

The Standard Prelude provides a type synonym for parsers of the kind just described:

> **type** *ReadS a* = *String* → [(*a*, *String*)]

and also defines a function *reads* that by analogy is similar to *shows*:

> *reads* :: (*Read a*) ⇒ *ReadS a*

We will return later to the precise definition of this function, but for now let's use it to define a parser for the *Tree* data type, whose string representation is as described in the previous section. List comprehensions give us a convenient idiom for constructing such parsers:[1]

> *readsTree* :: (*Read a*) ⇒ *ReadS* (*Tree a*)
> *readsTree* (' < ' : *s*) = [(*Branch l r, u*) | (*l*, ' | ' : *t*) ← *readsTree s*,
> 　　　　　　　　　　　　　(*r*, ' > ' : *u*) ← *readsTree t*]
> *readsTree s* = 　　　[(*Leaf x, t*) | (*x, t*) ← *reads s*]

Let's take a moment to examine this function definition in detail. There are two main cases to consider: If the string has the form ' < ' : *s*, we should have the representation of a branch, in which case parsing *s* as a tree should yield a left branch *l* followed by a string of the form ' | ' : *t*; parsing *t* as a tree should then yield the right branch *r* followed by a string of the form ' > ' : *u*. The resulting tree *Branch l r* is then returned, along with the trailing string *u*. Note the expressive power we get from the combination of pattern matching and list comprehension.

If the initial string is not of the form ' < ' : *s*, then we must have a leaf, in which case the string is parsed using the generic *reads* function, and the result is directly returned.

If we accept on faith for the moment that there is a *Read* instance for *Int* that behaves as one would expect, e.g.,

> (*reads* "5 golden rings") :: [(*Int, String*)]
> ⟹ [(5, " golden rings")]

---

[1] An even more elegant approach to parsing uses monads and parser combinators. These are part of a standard parsing library distributed with most Haskell systems.

then you should be able to verify the following calculations:

$readsTree$ "< <1|2>|3>"
$\implies$

There are a couple of shortcomings, however, in our definition of *readsTree*. One is that the parser is quite rigid in that it allows no "white space" (such as extra spaces, tabs, or line feeds) before or between the elements of the tree representation. The other is that the way we parse our punctuation symbols (' < ', ' | ', and ' > ') is quite different from the way we parse leaf values and sub-trees. This lack of uniformity makes the function definition harder to read.

We can address both of these problems by using a *lexical analyzer*, which parses a string into primitive "lexemes" defined by some rules about the string construction. The Standard Prelude defines a lexical analyzer:

$lex :: ReadS\ String$

whose lexical rules are those of the Haskell language, which can be found in the Haskell Report. For our purposes, an informal explanation is sufficient:

lex normally returns a singleton list containing a pair of strings: the first string is the first lexeme in the input string, and the second string is the remainder of the input. White space – including Haskell comments – is completely ignored. If the input string is empty or contains only white-space and comments, *lex* returns [("","")]; if the input is not empty in this sense, but also does not begin with a valid lexeme after any leading white-space, *lex* returns [].

Using this lexical analyzer, our tree parser can be rewritten as:

$readsTree :: (Read\ a) \Rightarrow ReadS\ (Tree\ a)$
$readsTree\ s = [\,(Branch\ l\ r, x)\ |\ ("<", t) \leftarrow lex\ s,$
$\qquad\qquad\qquad\ (l, \qquad\qquad u) \leftarrow readsTree\ t,$
$\qquad\qquad\qquad\ ("\,|\,", v) \leftarrow lex\ u,$
$\qquad\qquad\qquad\ (r, \qquad\qquad w) \leftarrow readsTree\ v,$
$\qquad\qquad\qquad\ (">", x) \leftarrow lex\ w \qquad]$
$\qquad +\!\!+$
$\qquad [\,(Leaf\ x, t)\ |\ (x, t) \leftarrow reads\ s\,]$

This definition solves both problems mentioned earlier: white-space is suitably ignored, and parsing of sub-strings has a more uniform structure.

To tie all of this together, let's first look at the definition of the class *Read* in the Standard Prelude:

class *Read a* **where**
$\quad readsPrec :: Int \rightarrow ReadS\ a$
$\quad readList\ \ :: ReadS\ [a]$

$\quad readList\ \ = readParen\ False\ (\lambda r \rightarrow [pr\ |\ ("[", s) \leftarrow lex\ r,$
$\qquad\qquad\qquad\qquad\qquad\qquad\qquad\quad pr \qquad\qquad \leftarrow readl\ s])$
$\qquad\quad$ **where** $readl\ s = [([\,], t)\ |\ ("]", t) \leftarrow lex\ s] +\!\!+$
$\qquad\qquad\qquad\qquad\quad [(x : xs, u)\ |\ (x, t)\ \ \leftarrow reads\ s,$
$\qquad\qquad\qquad\qquad\qquad\qquad\qquad (xs, u)\ \ \leftarrow readl'\ t]$
$\qquad\qquad\quad readl'\ s = [([\,], t)\ |\ ("]", t) \leftarrow lex\ s] +\!\!+$
$\qquad\qquad\qquad\qquad\quad\ [(x : xs, v)\ |\ (",", t) \leftarrow lex\ s,$
$\qquad\qquad\qquad\qquad\qquad\qquad\qquad (x, u)\ \ \ \leftarrow reads\ t,$
$\qquad\qquad\qquad\qquad\qquad\qquad\qquad (xs, v)\ \ \leftarrow readl'\ u]$

$$readParen \quad :: Bool \to ReadS\ a \to ReadS\ a$$
$$readParen\ b\ g = \textbf{if}\ b\ \textbf{then}\ mandatory\ \textbf{else}\ optional$$
$$\textbf{where}\ optional\ r = g\ r \mathbin{+\!\!+} mandatory\ r$$
$$mandatory\ r = [(x,u)\mid (" (",s) \leftarrow lex\ r,$$
$$sc \qquad\qquad (x,t) \leftarrow optional\ s,$$
$$(")",u) \leftarrow lex\ t]$$

The default method for *readList* is rather tedious, but otherwise straightforward.

reads can now be defined, along with an even higher-level function, *read*:

$$reads :: (Read\ a) \Rightarrow ReadS\ a$$
$$reads = readsPrec\ 0$$

$$read \quad :: (Read\ a) \Rightarrow String \to a$$
$$read\ s = \textbf{case}\ [x \mid (x,t) \leftarrow reads\ s, ("","") \leftarrow lex\ t]\ \textbf{of}$$
$$[x] \to x$$
$$[] \to error\ \texttt{"PreludeText.read: no parse"}$$
$$\_ \to error\ \texttt{"PreludeText.read: ambiguous parse"}$$

The definition of *reads* (like *shows*) should not be surprising. The definition of *read* assumes that exactly one parse is expected, and thus causes a run-time error if there is no unique parse or if the input contains anything more than a representation of exactly one value of type *a* (and possibly comments and white-space).

You can test that the *Read* and *Show* instances for a particular type are working correctly by applying (*read* ∘ *show*) to a value in that type, which in most situations should be the identity function.

B.6 The Index Class

The Standard Prelude defines a type class of array indices:

$$\textbf{class}\ (Ord\ a) \Rightarrow Ix\ a\ \textbf{where}$$
$$range \quad :: (a,a) \to [a]$$
$$index \quad :: (a,a) \to a \to Int$$
$$inRange :: (a,a) \to a \to Bool$$

Arrays are defined elsewhere, but the index class is useful for other things besides arrays, so I will describe it here.

Instance declarations are provided for *Int*, *Integer*, *Char*, *Bool*, and tuples of *Ix* types; in addition, instances may be automatically derived for enumerated and tuple types. You should think of the primitive types as vector indices, and tuple types as indices of multidimensional rectangular arrays. Note that the first argument of each of the operations of class *Ix* is a pair of indices; these are typically the *bounds* (first and last indices) of an array. For example, the bounds of a 10-element, zero-origin vector with *Int* indices would be $(0, 9)$, while a 100 by 100 1-origin matrix might have the bounds $((1, 1), (100, 100))$. (In many other languages, such bounds would be written in a form like $1 : 100, 1 : 100$, but the present form fits the type system better, since each bound is of the same type as a general index.)

The *range* operation takes a bounds pair and produces the list of indices lying between those bounds, in index order. For example,

range $(0, 4) \Longrightarrow [0, 1, 2, 3, 4]$

range $((0, 0), (1, 2)) \Longrightarrow [(0, 0), (0, 1), (0, 2), (1, 0), (1, 1), (1, 2)]$

The *inRange* predicate determines whether an index lies between a given pair of bounds. (For a tuple type, this test is performed componentwise, and then combined with ($\wedge$).)

```
class (Eq a, Show a) ⇒ Num a where
    (+), (−), (∗) :: a → a → a
    negate :: a → a
    abs, signum :: a → a
    fromInteger :: Integer → a

class (Num a, Ord a) ⇒ Real a where
    toRational :: a → Rational

class (Real a, Enum a) ⇒ Integral a where
    quot, rem, div, mod :: a → a → a
    quotRem, divMod :: a → a → (a, a)
    toInteger :: a → Integer

class (Num a) ⇒ Fractional a where
    (/) :: a → a → a
    recip :: a → a
    fromRational :: Rational → a

class (Fractional a) ⇒ Floating a where
    pi :: a
    exp, log, sqrt :: a → a
    (∗∗), logBase :: a → a → a
    sin, cos, tan :: a → a
    asin, acos, atan :: a → a
    sinh, cosh, tanh :: a → a
    asinh, acosh, atanh :: a → a

class (Real a, Fractional a) ⇒ RealFrac a where
    properFraction :: (Integral b) ⇒ a → (b, a)
    truncate, round :: (Integral b) ⇒ a → b
    ceiling, floor :: (Integral b) ⇒ a → b

class (RealFrac a, Floating a) ⇒ RealFloat a where
    floatRadix :: a → Integer
    floatDigits :: a → Int
    floatRange :: a → (Int, Int)
    decodeFloat :: a → (Integer, Int)
    encodeFloat :: Integer → Int → a
    exponent :: a → Int
    significand :: a → a
    scaleFloat :: Int → a → a
    isNaN, isInfinite, isDenormalized, isNegativeZero, isIEEE
        :: a → Bool
```

Figure B.1 Standard numeric classes.

Finally, the *index* operation determines the (zero-based) position of an index within a bounded range; for example:

$index\ (1,9)\ 2 \Longrightarrow 1$

$index\ ((0,0),(1,2))\ (1,1) \Longrightarrow 4$

B.7 The Numeric Classes

The *Num* class and the numeric class hierarchy were briefly described in Section 7.4. Figure B.1 gives the full class declarations.

Appendix C   Built-In Types Are Not Special

Throughout this text we have introduced many "built-in" types such as lists, tuples, integers, and characters. We have also shown how new user-defined types can be defined. Aside from special syntax, you might be wondering if the built-in types are in any way more special than the user-defined ones. The answer is *no*. The special syntax is for convenience and for consistency with historical convention, but has no semantic consequence.

We can emphasize this point by considering what the type declarations would look like for these built-in types if in fact we were allowed to use the special syntax in defining them. For example, the *Char* type might be written as:

data *Char* = 'a' | 'b' | 'c' | ...   -- This is not valid
       | 'A' | 'B' | 'C' | ...   -- Haskell code!
       | '1' | '2' | '3' | ...

These constructor names are not syntactically valid; to fix them we would have to write something like:

data *Char* = *Ca* | *Cb* | *Cc* | ...
       | *CA* | *CB* | *CC* | ...
       | *C1* | *C2* | *C3* | ...

Even though these constructors are actually more concise, they are quite unconventional for representing characters, and thus the special syntax is used instead.

In any case, writing "pseudo-Haskell" code in this way helps us see through the special syntax. We see now that *Char* is just a data type consisting of a large number of nullary (meaning they take no arguments) constructors. Thinking of *Char* in this way makes it clear why, for example, we can pattern-match against characters; i.e., we would expect to be able to do so for any of a data type's constructors.

Similarly, using pseudo-Haskell, we could define *Int* and *Integer* by:

-- more pseudo-code:
data *Int* = $(-2\char`^29)$ | ... | $-1$ | $0$ | $1$ | ... | $(2\char`^29 - 1)$
data *Integer* = ... -2 | -1 | 0 | 1 | 2 ...

(Recall that -2^{29} to 2^{29-1} is the minimum range for the *Int* data type.) *Int* is clearly a much larger enumeration than *Char*, but it's still finite! In contrast, the pseudo-code

365

for *Integer* (the type of arbitrary precision integers) is intended to convey an *infinite* enumeration (and in that sense only, the *Integer* data type *is* somewhat special).

Haskell has a data type called *unit* which has exactly one value: (). The name of this data type is also written (). This is trivially expressed in Haskell pseudo-code:

data () = ()   -- more pseudo-code

Tuples are also easy to define playing this game:

data (a, b) = (a, b) -- more pseudo-code
data (a, b, c) = (a, b, c)
data (a, b, c, d) = (a, b, c, d)

and so on. Each declaration above defines a tuple type of a particular length, with parentheses playing a role in both the expression syntax (as data constructor) and type-expression syntax (as type constructor). By "and so on" we mean that there are an infinite number of such declarations, reflecting the fact that tuples of all finite lengths are allowed in Haskell.

The list data type is also easily handled in pseudo-Haskell, and more interestingly, it is recursive:

data $[a]$ = [] | $a : [a]$ -- more pseudo-code
infixr 5 :

We can now see clearly what we described about lists earlier: [ ] is the empty list, and (:) is the infix list constructor; thus $[1, 2, 3]$ must be equivalent to the list $1 : 2 : 3 : [\,]$. (Note that (:) is right associative.) The type of [ ] is $[a]$, and the type of (:) is $a \to [a] \to [a]$.

Details: The way (:) is defined here is actually legal syntax – infix constructors are permitted in **data** declarations, and are distinguished from infix operators (for pattern-matching purposes) by the fact that they must begin with a colon (a property trivially satisfied by ":").

At this point the reader should note carefully the differences between tuples and lists, which the above definitions make abundantly clear. In particular, note the recursive nature of the list type whose elements are homogeneous and of arbitrary length, and the non-recursive nature of a (particular) tuple type whose elements are heterogeneous and of fixed length. The typing rules for tuples and lists should now also be clear:

For $(e1, e2, ..., en)$, $n \geqslant 2$, if Ti is the type of ei, then the type of the tuple is $(T1, T2, ..., Tn)$.

For $[e1, e2, ..., en]$, $n \geqslant 0$, each ei must have the same type T, and the type of the list is $[T]$.

Appendix D   Pattern-Matching Details

In this appendix we will look at Haskell's pattern-matching process in greater detail.

Haskell defines a fixed set of patterns for use in case expressions and function definitions. Pattern matching is permitted using the constructors of any type, whether user-defined or predefined in Haskell. This includes tuples, strings, numbers, characters, etc. For example, here's a contrived function that matches against a tuple of "constants:"

> $contrived :: ([a], Char, (Int, Float), String, Bool) \rightarrow Bool$
> $contrived ([], 'b', (1, 2.0), "hi", True) = False$

This example also demonstrates that *nesting* of patterns is permitted (to arbitrary depth).

Technically speaking, *formal parameters* to functions are also patterns – it's just that they *never fail to match a value*. As a "side effect" of a successful match, the formal parameter is bound to the value it is being matched against. For this reason patterns in any one equation are not allowed to have more than one occurrence of the same formal parameter.

A pattern that may fail to match is said to be *refutable*; for example, the empty list [ ] is refutable. Patterns such as formal parameters that never fail to match are said to be *irrefutable*. There are three other kinds of irrefutable patterns, which are summarized below.

As-Patterns Sometimes it is convenient to name a pattern for use on the right-hand side of an equation. For example, a function that duplicates the first element in a list might be written as:

> $f (x : xs) = x : x : xs$

Note that $x : xs$ appears both as a pattern on the left-hand side, and as an expression on the right-hand side. To improve readability, we might prefer to write $x : xs$ just once, which we can achieve using an *as-pattern* as follows:[1]

> $f s@(x : xs) = x : s$

Technically speaking, as-patterns always result in a successful match, although the sub-pattern (in this case $x : xs$) could, of course, fail.

---

[1] Another advantage to doing this is that a naive implementation might otherwise completely reconstruct $x : xs$ rather than reuse the value being matched against.

Wildcards Another common situation is matching against a value we really care nothing about. For example, the functions *head* and *tail* can be written as:

$$head\ (x: \_) = x$$
$$tail\ (\_ : xs) = xs$$

in which we have "advertised" the fact that we don't care what a certain part of the input is. Each wildcard will independently match anything, but in contrast to a formal parameter, each will bind nothing; for this reason more than one are allowed in an equation.

Lazy Patterns There is one other kind of pattern allowed in Haskell. It is called a *lazy pattern*, and has the form ~*pat*. Lazy patterns are *irrefutable*: matching a value v against ~*pat* always succeeds, regardless of *pat*. Operationally speaking, if an identifier in *pat* is later "used" on the right-hand side, it will be bound to that portion of the value that would result if v were to successfully match *pat*, and $\perp$ otherwise.

Lazy patterns are useful in contexts where infinite data structures are being defined recursively. For example, infinite lists are an excellent vehicle for writing *simulation* programs, and in this context the infinite lists are often called *streams*.

Pattern-Matching Semantics

So far we have discussed how individual patterns are matched, how some are refutable, some are irrefutable, etc. But what drives the overall process? In what order are the matches attempted? What if none succeed? This section addresses these questions.

Pattern matching can either *fail*, *succeed*, or *diverge*. A successful match binds the formal parameters in the pattern. Divergence occurs when a value needed by the pattern diverges (i.e., is non-terminating) or results in an error ($\perp$). The matching process itself occurs "top-down, left-to-right." Failure of a pattern anywhere in one equation results in failure of the whole equation, and the next equation is then tried. If all equations fail, the value of the function application is $\perp$, and results in a run-time error.

For example, if *bot* is a divergent or erroneous computation, and if $[1, 2]$ is matched against $[0, bot]$, then 1 fails to match 0, so the result is a failed match. But if $[1, 2]$ is matched against $[bot, 0]$, then matching 1 against *bot* causes divergence (i.e. $\perp$).

The only other twist to this set of rules is that top-level patterns may also have a boolean *guard*, as in this definition of a function that forms an abstract version of a number's sign:

$$sign\ x\ |\ x > 0\quad = 1$$
$$|\quad x == 0 = 0$$
$$|\quad x < 0\quad = -1$$

Note here that a sequence of guards is given for a single pattern; as with patterns, these guards are evaluated top-down, and the first that evaluates to *True* results in a successful match.

An Example The pattern-matching rules can have subtle effects on the meaning of functions. For example, consider this definition of *take*:

$$take\ 0\ \_\quad\ = [\,]$$
$$take\ \_\ [\,]\quad = [\,]$$
$$take\ n\ (x : xs) = x : take\ (n - 1)\ xs$$

and this slightly different version (the first two equations have been reversed):

$take1 \_ [] = []$
$take1 \ 0 \_ = []$
$take1 \ n \ (x : xs) = x : take1 \ (n - 1) \ xs$

Now note the following:

$take \ 0 \ bot \implies []$
$take1 \ 0 \ bot \implies \bot$

$take \ bot \ [] \implies \bot$
$take1 \ bot \ [] \implies []$

We see that *take* is "more defined" with respect to its second argument, whereas *take1* is more defined with respect to its first. It is difficult to say in this case which definition is better. Just remember that in certain applications, it may make a difference. (The Standard Prelude includes a definition corresponding to *take*.)

Case Expressions

Pattern matching provides a way to "dispatch control" based on structural properties of a value. However, in many circumstances, we don't wish to define a *function* every time we need to do this. Haskell's *case expression* provides a way to solve this problem. Indeed, the meaning of pattern matching in function definitions is specified in the Haskell Report in terms of case expressions, which are considered more primitive. In particular, a function definition of the form:

$f p_{11} \cdots p_{1k} = e_1$
...
$f p_{n1} \cdots p_{nk} = e_n$

where each p_{ij} is a pattern, is semantically equivalent to:

$f \ x1 \ x2 \ldots xk = \mathbf{case} \ (x1, \ldots, xk) \ \mathbf{of} \ (p_{11}, \ldots, p_{1k}) \rightarrow e_1$
...
$\qquad\qquad\qquad\qquad\qquad\qquad (p_{n1}, \ldots, p_{nk}) \rightarrow e_n$

where the xi are new identifiers. For example, the definition of *take* given earlier is equivalent to:

$take \ m \ ys = \mathbf{case} \ (m, ys) \ \mathbf{of}$
$\quad (0, \_) \quad \rightarrow []$
$\quad (\_, []) \quad \rightarrow []$
$\quad (n, x : xs) \rightarrow x : take \ (n - 1) \ xs$

For type correctness, the types of the right-hand sides of a case expression or set of equations comprising a function definition must all be the same; more precisely, they must all share a common principal type.

The pattern-matching rules for case expressions are the same as we have given for function definitions.

Appendix E   Haskell Quick Reference

GHCi Interpreter Commands

Load a module	*:load Foo.lhs* or *:l Foo*
Reload the current module	*:reload* or *:r*
Quit GHCi	*:quit* or *:q*
Information on a name	*:info name* or *:i name* (e.g. *:i map*)

Exiting an infinite loop / terminating computation early: Ctrl+C

Working with Numbers

Types: *Int, Integer, Double, Rational*
Type classes: *Integral, Fractional, RealFrac*
Conversions: *fromIntegral, toRational, fromRational, round, ceiling, floor*

Mathematical Operations:

Addition:	$x + y$	Subtraction:	$x - y$
Multiplication:	$x * y$	Negation:	$(-x)$
Fractional division:	x/y	Ingetral division:	x '*div*' y
Fractional power:	$x ** y$	Integral power:	$x\text{^}y$
Modulus:	x '*mod*' y	Div. with remainder:	x '*divmod*' y

Lists

(Constructor) empty list: [ ]
(Constructor) value x followed by list xs: $(x : xs)$
A list of three things: $[x, y, z]$

List Tricks with Numbers:

$[0 . . 2] \Rightarrow [0, 1, 2]$
$[1 . .] \Rightarrow [1, 2, 3, ...]$ (infinite)
$[0, 2 . .] \Rightarrow [0, 2, 4, 6, ...]$ (infinite)

Commonly Used Functions on Lists:

Keep only the first n values:	*take n someList*
Remove the first n values:	*drop n someList*
Repeat a single value infinitely:	*repeat* $x \Rightarrow [x, x, x, x, ...]$ (infinite)
Get the value at index i	*aList* ! ! *i*, where $i :: Int$
Length of a list:	*length aList*, e.g. length $[3, 4, 5] \Rightarrow 3$
Combine (concatenate) two lists:	*aList* ++ *anotherList*
Combine two lists:	*zip* $:: [a] \rightarrow [b] \rightarrow [(a, b)]$
See also:	*zipWith, zip3, zipWith3*

List Comprehensions:

```
[x | x <- someList, f x]
```

Read as: "the set of all x such that x is in someList and f(x) is true:"

Pattern Matching against Lists:

$f :: [SomeType] \rightarrow ...$

$f [] = ...$	matches against empty lists
$f [x] = ...$	matches a list of exactly one element
$f [x, y] = ...$	matches a list of exactly two elements
$f (x : y) = ...$	matches a list with *at least* one element

Tuples

A tuple of four things, each having a different type:

$(1, 3.0, 'a', "foo") :: (Int, Double, Char, String)$

Access the first and second items in a pair (2-tuple):

$fst :: (a, b) \rightarrow a \quad snd :: (a, b) \rightarrow b$

Check membership within a list: *elem anItem aList* $:: a \rightarrow [a] \rightarrow Bool$

Pattern matching against tuples:

$f :: (a, b) \rightarrow ...$
$f (x, y) = ...$

Types and Type Classes

```
type MyType = (Int, String)
class MyClass where
  someFun :: ...
data Foo = Constructor1 | Constructor2 Arg1 Arg2
  deriving (Eq, Show)
instance MyClass Foo where
  someFun Constructor1 = ...
  someFun (Constructor2 x y) = ...
```

Other commonly derived type classes: *Ord*, *Read*, *Enum*

Useful language pragmas for working with type classes: *TypeSynonymInstances*, *FlexibleInstances*, *OverlappingInstances*. Language pragma format:

```
{-# LANGUAGE  Pragma1, Pragma2, ... #-}
```

Randomness

Using random numbers requires the *System.Random* library.

Creating a generator:	$g = mkStdGen\ seed :: StdGen$
Get a number and new generator:	$(n, g') = next\ g$
Split a generator:	$(g1, g2) = split\ g$
Random within a range:	$(n, g') = randomR\ (lower, upper)\ g$
Infinite random numbers:	$randoms\ g$
Infinite random numbers in a range:	$randomRs\ (lower, upper)\ g$

Appendix F   Euterpea Quick Reference

Use *:i* in GHCi to get more information on any of the names appearing here.

Note-/Score-Level Features

This section is a reference for Euterpea's note- or signal-level features, which can be exported to MIDI or using custom instruments as described in the next section.

Musical Types and Data Structures

type *AbsPitch = Int*	MIDI pitch numbers.
type *Dur = Rational*	1.0 = a whole note in 4/4
data *PitchClass = C | Cs | Df | D | Ds | ... |*	f = flat, s = sharp
type *Octave = Int*	Octave numbers.
type *Pitch = (PitchClass, Octave)*	Tuple representation for pitches

Pitch standard: C4 = (*C*, 4) = pitch number 60
General MIDI pitch range: 0–127, or (*C*, −1) to (*G*, 9)

data *Primitive a = Note Dur a | Rest Dur*	Notes and rests
data *Music a = Prim (Primitive a)*	Musical leaf node
| *(Music a)* :+: *(Music a)*	Sequential composition
| *(Music a)* :=: *(Music a)*	Parallel composition
| *Modify Control (Music a)*	Modifier node
data *Control = Tempo Rational*	Interpret w/tempo multiplier
| *Transpose AbsPitch*	Interpret transposed
| *Instrument InstrumentName*	Interpret as specified instrument

Note: *Instrument x* (*Instrument y m*) results in instrument *y* being used.

type *Music1 = Music (Pitch, [NoteAttribute])*
class *ToMusic1 a* **where** *toMusic1 :: Music a → Music1*

Note: An *NFData* and *ToMusic1* instance are required to export a given *Music a* to MIDI (via playback or file I/O). Instances exist for *Pitch*, *AbsPitch*, (*Pitch*, *Volume*), and *Note1*.

Musical Constants and Functions

Building Musical Structures:

Duration values:	*wn, hn, qn, en, sn, tn, ...*
Create notes:	*note* :: *Dur* → *a* → *Music a*
Create notes by pitch class:	*c* :: *Octave* → *Dur* → *Music Pitch*
	cs, df, d, ds, ...
Combine a list sequentially:	*line* :: [*Music a*] → *Music a*
Combine a list in parallel:	*chord* :: [*Music a*] → *Music a*
Create percussion sounds:	*perc* :: *PercussionSound* → *Dur* → *Music Pitch*
Modifier shorthands:	*instrument, tempo, transpose*
Functions that don't use *Modify*:	*shiftPitches, shiftPitches1,*
	scaleDurations, changeInstrument,
	removeInstrumets

Manipulating Music:

Retrograde (reverse):	*retro* :: *Music a* → *Music a*
Inversion (flip upside-down):	*invert* :: *Music Pitch* → *Music Pitch,*
	invertAt
Delay by some amount of time:	*offset* :: *Dur* → *Music a* → *Music a*
Repeat a finite number of times:	*times*
Repeat indefinitely:	*forever*
Preserve/remove the first *n* measures:	*cut/remove*
Apply a function to all notes:	*mMap*
Apply functions to all nodes:	*mFold*

MIDI Playback and File I/O:

List all MIDI devices:	*devices*
Play to the default device:	*play*
Play to a custom device:	*playDev*
Timing-strict playback:	*playS/playDevS* (finite values only!)
Write a MIDI file:	*writeMidi*
Read a MIDI file:	*importFile*
Convert *Midi* to *Music*:	*fromMidi*
Event-style representation:	**type** *Performance* = [*MEvent*]
Convert *Music* to *Performance*:	*perform*
Convert *Performance* to *Midi*:	*toMidi*

Signal-Level Features

The features in this section are part of Euterpea's virtual instrument and audio generation framework. When using these features, the top of your file will need to begin with the following:

```
{-# LANGUAGE Arrows}
```

Wave Tables and Oscillators

$t = tableSinesN\ numSamples\ partialList$ ex: $tableSinesN$ 4096 [1]
$t = tableLinear\ y0\ syPairs$
$y \leftarrow osc\ tableName\ phaseOffset \multimap freq$ Basic oscillator usage

Note: *syPairs* represents pairs of *segment lengths* (not absolute *x*-coordinates) and *y*-values (amplitudes). For example: *tableLinear* 0 [(0.5, 1.0), [(0.5, −1.0)].

See also: *tableExponN* and *tablesSines3N* (takes triples of partials, strengths, and phase offsets).

Basic Signal Construction

General Format

$sigName :: AudSF\ InType\ OutType$
$sigName = \textbf{proc}\ inSig \rightarrow \textbf{do}$
  $outSig \leftarrow anotherSigFun \multimap inSig$
  $returnA \multimap outSig$

Example: Two Seconds of 440Hz Sine Wave

$sine440 :: AudSF\ ()\ Double$
$sine440 = \textbf{proc}\ \_ \rightarrow \textbf{do}$
  $y \leftarrow osc\ sineTable\ 0 \multimap 440$
  $returnA \multimap y$
$main = outFile\ \texttt{"x.wav"}\ 2.0\ sine440$

Signal Functions

Delay line:	$y \leftarrow delayLine\ sec \multimap x$
Variable delay:	$y \leftarrow delayLineT\ maxDel \multimap (x, delAmt)$
White noise:	$x \leftarrow noiseWhite\ seed \multimap ()$
Low-pass filter:	$y \leftarrow filterLowPass \multimap (x, cutoff)$
High-pass filter:	$y \leftarrow filterHighPass \multimap (x, cutoff)$
Butterworth low-pass:	$y \leftarrow filterLowPassBW \multimap (x, cutoff)$
Butterworth high-pass:	$y \leftarrow filterHighPassBW \multimap (x, cutoff)$
Butterworth band-pass:	$y \leftarrow filterBandPassBW \multimap (x, cutoff1, bandWidth)$
Butterworth band-stop:	$y \leftarrow filterBandStopBW \multimap (x, cutoff1, bandWidth)$

Linear envelope: $e \leftarrow envLineSeg\ [y0, y1, ..., yn]\ [d1, ..., dn] \prec ()$
where $yi :: Double$ is an amplitude and
$di :: Double$ is duration in seconds.

Note: For *envLineSeg*, the list of amplitudes should always have *one more* element than the list of durations.

Virtual Instrument Creation and Usage

Mono Instrument Format

instr1 :: Instr (Mono AudRate)
instr1 dur pch vol params =
   let *freq = apToHz pch*
   in proc _ $\rightarrow$ **do**
      ...
      returnA $\prec$ *outSignal*

Stereo Instrument Format

instr1 :: Instr (Stereo AudRate)
instr1 dur pch vol params =
   let *freq = apToHz pch*
   in proc _ $\rightarrow$ **do**
      ...
      returnA $\prec$ *(leftSig, rightSig)*

Using Virtual Instruments

myName = CustomInstrument "MyInstrName"
instrMap :: InstrMap (Mono AudRate)   -- or Stereo AudRate
instrMap = [(myName, instr1), ...]
myMel = instrument myName musicVal
writeIt = writeWav "m.wav" *instrMap myMel*   -- or writeWavNorm

See also: *writeWavNorm* (normalizes amplitudes to -1.0 to 1.0)

Appendix G   HSoM Quick Reference

Use *:i* in GHCi to get more information on any of the names appearing here.

Performance

hsomPerform	Player-based conversion from *Music* to *Performance*
Performable	Type class with one function, *perfDur*
playA	Like Euterpea's *play*, but for use with *Players*
Player	Record type for controlling performance
writeMidiA	Like Euterpea's *writeMidi*, but for use with *Players*

Musical User Interfaces

MIDI Widgets

midiIn	Receive from a single MIDI device
midiInM	Receive from multiple MIDI inputs
midiOut	Send to a single MIDI device
midiOutB	Buffered output for playback over time (one device)
midiOutM	Send to multiple MIDI outputs
midiOutMB	Buffered output to multiple devices
selectInput	Choose a single MIDI input device
selectInputM	Choose multiple MIDI inputs
selectOutput	Choose a single MIDI output device
selectOutputM	Choose multiple MIDI outputs

Other UISF Widgets

button	Button widget
checkbox	Checkbox widget
checkGroup	Group of checkbox widgets
defaultMUIParams	Default window settings

display	Display a value that has a *Show* instance
displayStr	Display a *String* without quotes showing
getTime	Time since program start in milliseconds
hSlider/hiSlider	Horizontal floating-point/integral sliders
label	Text label
leftRight/rightLeft	Horizontal widget layouts
listbox	List box widget
radio	Group of radio buttons
runMUI	Run a moo-ee specifying window parameters
runMUI'	Run a moo-ee with default parameters
setLayout	Set window layout
stickyButton	Button that must be clicked again to release
textbox	Interactive textbox
title	Set the title of a widget or group of widgets
topDown/bottomUp	Vertical widget layouts
vSlider/viSlider	Vertical floating-point/integral sliders
withDisplay	Automatically display anther widget's value

Bibliography

[1] (2016) The Glasgow Haskell Compiler. [Online]. Available: www.haskell.org/ghc/

[2] (2016) Haskell platform. [Online]. Available: www.haskell.org/platform/

[3] MIDI Association, "Complete MIDI 1.0 detailed specification," La Habre, CA, 1995–2013. [Online]. Available: www.midi.org/techspecs/

[4] MIDI Association, "General MIDI 1, 2 and lite specifications," La Habre, CA, 1995–2013. [Online]. Available: www.midi.org/techspecs/

[5] R. Hindley, "The principal type scheme of an object in combinatory logic," *Transactions of the American Mathematical Society*, vol. 146, pp. 29–60, 1969.

[6] R. Milner, "A theory of type polymorphism in programming," *Journal of Computer and System Sciences*, vol. 17, no. 3, pp. 348–375, 1978.

[7] R. Milner, M. Tofte, and R. Harper, *The Definition of Standard ML*. Cambridge, MA: MIT Press, 1990.

[8] P. Hudak, "Conception, evolution, and application of functional programming languages," *ACM Computing Surveys*, vol. 21, no. 3, pp. 359–411, 1989.

[9] M. Schönfinkel, "Uber die bausteine der mathematischen logik," *Mathematische Annalen*, vol. 92, p. 305, 1924.

[10] C. Corea, *Children's Songs – 20 Pieces for Keyboard (ED 7254)*. Mainz: Schott, 1994.

[11] A. Church, *The Calculi of Lambda Conversion*. Princeton, NJ: Princeton University Press, 1941.

[12] R. N. Shepard, "Circularity in judgements of relative pitch," *Journal of the Acoustical Society of America*, vol. 36, no. 12, pp. 2346–2353, 1964.

[13] W. Quine, *The Ways of Paradox, and Other Essays*. New York: Random House, 1966.

[14] D. Hofstadter, *Gödel, Escher, Bach: An Eternal Golden Braid*. New York: Vintage, 1979.

[15] J. Cage, *Silence: Lectures and Writings*. Middletown, CT: Wesleyan University Press, 1986.

[16] D. Quick, "Kulitta: A framework for automated music composition," Ph.D. dissertation, Yale University, 2014.

[17] R. Bird and P. Wadler, *Introduction to Functional Programming*. New York: Prentice Hall, 1988.

[18] R. Bird, *Introduction to Functional Programming Using Haskell* (second edition). London: Prentice Hall, 1998.

[19] P. Hudak, "An algebraic theory of polymorphic temporal media," in *Proceedings of PADL'04: 6th International Workshop on Practical Aspects of Declarative Languages*. Springer Verlag LNCS 3057, June 2004, pp. 1–15.

[20] D. Cope, "Computer modeling of musical intelligence in EMI," *Computer Music Journal*, vol. 16, no. 2, pp. 69–83, 1992.

[21] B. Pierce, *Basic Category Theory for Computer Scientists*. Cambridge, MA: MIT Press, 1991.

[22] E. Moggi, "Computational lambda-calculus and monads," in *Proceedings of Symposium on Logic in Computer Science*. IEEE, June 1989, pp. 14–23.

[23] P. Wadler, "The essence of functional programming," in *Proceedings of the 19th Symposium on Principles of Programming Languages*. ACM, January 1992, pp. 1–14.

[24] S. Peyton Jones and P. Wadler, "Imperative functional programming," in *Proceedings of the 20th Symposium on Principles of Programming Languages*. ACM, January 1993, pp. 71–84.

[25] P. Hudak, A. Courtney, H. Nilsson, and J. Peterson, "Arrows, robots, and functional reactive programming," in *Summer School on Advanced Functional Programming, Oxford University*. Springer Verlag LNCS 2638, 2003, pp. 159–187.

[26] J. Hughes, "Generalising monads to arrows," *Science of Computer Programming*, vol. 37, pp. 67–111, 2000.

[27] A. Courtney and C. Elliott, "Genuinely functional user interfaces," in *Proceedings of the 2001 Haskell Workshop*, September 2001, pp. 41–69.

[28] A. Courtney, "Modelling user interfaces in a functional language," Ph.D. dissertation, Yale University, 2004.

[29] R. Paterson, "A new notation for arrows," in *ICFP'01: International Conference on Functional Programming*, Firenze, Italy, September 2001, pp. 229–240.

[30] C. Elliott and P. Hudak, "Functional reactive animation," in *International Conference on Functional Programming*, Amsterdam, June 1997, pp. 163–173.

[31] P. Liu and P. Hudak, "Plugging a space leak with an arrow," *Electronic Notes in Theoretical Computer Science*, vol. 193, pp. 29–45, 2007.

[32] D. Winograd-Cort, H. Liu, and P. Hudak, "Virtualizing real-world objects in FRP," Yale University, Technical Report YALEU/DCS/RR-1446, July 2011.

[33] D. Winograd-Cort and P. Hudak, "Wormholes: Introducing effects to FRP," in *Haskell Symposium*. ACM, September 2012, pp. 91–103.

[34] B. Vercoe, "Csound: A manual for the audio processing system and supporting programs," MIT Media Lab, Technical Report, 1986.

[35] K. Karplus and A. Strong, "Digital synthesis of plucked string and drum timbres," *Computer Music Journal*, vol. 7, no. 2, pp. 43–55, 1983.

[36] P. Cook, *Real Sound Synthesis for Interactive Applications*. Natick MA: A. K. Peters Press, 2002.

Index

(), 206
(++), 47, 353
(,), 354
(,,), 354
(-) (negation), 114
(.), 80
(/=), 111
(¡), 355
(¡=), 355
(=¡¡), 220
(==), 106
(¿), 355
(¿=), 355
(&&), 164
::, 10
(^), 170

abs, 114
abstraction, 12–21
    data, 18–21
    functional, 16
    naming, 13–15
    principle, 13
accumulator, 55, 358
action (IO), 205
algebraic properties, 175
all, 352
and, 352
any, 352
arithmetic sequence, 79
associativity, 18

binding, 15
bottom, 9, 60, 163
Bounded, 118, 357
break, 349

case, 369
case sensitivity, 10
Char, 9, 106, 365
chord, 51
class, 104, 105
    class, 108
    deriving, 118
    declaration, 108
    default method, 111
    derived instance, 118
    inheritance, 112
    instance, 108
    laws, 122
    method, 108
    multiple inheritance, 112
    operation, 108
    subclass, 112
    superclass, 112
comments, 14
compare, 355
composeM, 219
computation by calculation, 4
concat, 53, 353
concatMap, 353
conditional expression, 50
Curry, Haskell B., 57
cycle, 351

deriving, 118
do, 207
Double, 24
drop, 348
dropWhile, 349

efficiency, 5, 49, 53, 171
elem, 352

Enum, 118, 356
enumFrom, 356
enumFromThen, 356
enumFromThenTo, 356
enumFromTo, 356
Eq, 106, 111
equality, 106
error, 60, 348
errors, 60
expressions, 8

field labels, 131
FilePath, 207
filter, 349
fix, 77
flip, 59
Float, 24
fmap, 211
fold, 49
fold (in a calculation), 7
foldl, 52, 350
foldl1, 350
foldr, 52, 157, 350
foldr1, 350
fractal music, 148
fromEnum, 356
fromInteger, 115
function
  anonymous, 75
  application, 11, 56
  composition, 80–83
  currying, 56–60
  strict, 163
  type, 11–12

generalization, 161
generator, 78
getLine, 207
GHC, xiii

head, 43, 347
Hindley-Milner type system, 46

if then else, 50
ill-typed, 11, 106
import, 66
index, 362
induction, 156
infix, 12
infix constructors, 31, 366
init, 347

inRange, 362
InstrumentName, 33
Int, 25, 365
Integer, 9, 24, 106, 365
IO, 206
iterate, 351
Ix, 118, 362

kinds, 225

last, 347
layout rule, 37
length, 43, 158, 348
let, 15, 36, 216
lex, 361
lexicographic ordering, 123
line, 51
lines, 351
List (library), 346
list, 8, 18
  indexing, 40, 348
list comprehension, 220
lookup, 352

Main, 205
main, 205
map, 45, 353
mapM, 220
*mapM_*, 220
max, 355
maxBound, 357
maximum, 353
maxPitch, 51
Maybe, 217
MIDI, 125
min, 355
minBound, 357
minimum, 353
modularity, 23
module
  import, 66
  interface, 66
module, 65
Monad (library), 214
Monad (type class), 214
monad laws, 216
mplus, 221
mzero, 221

negate, 114
notElem, 352

null, 348
Num, 105, 113, 364
number systems, 23–26
numerical analysis, 24

operators, 12
or, 352
Ord, 112, 355

pair, 8
parser, 360
pattern, 20
   as-pattern, 367
   guard, 368
   irrefutable, 367
   lazy, 368
   matching, 20, 164, 367–369
   refutable, 367
   wildcard, 367
polymorphism, 42–44
precedence, 12, 170
PreludeList, 346
product, 353
putCharList, 209
putStr, 206, 209, 221

quot, 172

range, 362
Rational, 24
Read, 118, 357, 360
read, 362
readList, 361
readParen, 361
ReadS, 360
reads, 360, 362
readsPrec, 361
recursion, 20, 156
repeat, 351
replicate, 351
return, 206
reverse, 54, 59, 160, 352

scanl, 350
scanl1, 350
scanr, 350
scanr1, 350
section, 74
self-similar music, 148
selfSim, 149

sequence, 220
*sequence_*, 208, 220
Show, 118, 357
show, 357, 359
showList, 359
ShowS, 358
shows, 358, 359
showsPrec, 359
signum, 114
simple, 5
sort, 112
span, 349
splitAt, 348
state monad, 222
sum, 353

tail, 43, 347
take, 348
takeWhile, 349
toEnum, 356
tuples, 366
type, 9, 11, 365
   constructor, 211
   higher-order, 211
   inference, 11
   polymorphic, 42–44
   principal, 46
   qualified, 104, 122
   recursive, 32
   signature, 11
   variable, 43

unfold (in a calculation), 6
unit type, 206, 366
unlines, 351
unwords, 351
unzip, 354
unzip3, 354

values, 8

well-typed, 11
words, 351
writeFile, 207

zip, 353
zip3, 353
zipWith, 354
zipWith3, 354

Printed in the United States
By Bookmasters